Once Upon a Time of Transition:
Fourteen Exercises in Political Thought

Martin Palouš

Once Upon a Time of Transition:
Fourteen Exercises in Political Thought

Martin Palouš

Academica Press
Washington – London

Library of Congress Cataloging-in-Publication Data

Names: Palouš, Martin, author.
Title: Once upon a time of transition : fourteen exercises in political thought
Description: Washington : Academica Press, 2021. | Includes references.
Identifiers: LCCN 2020951311 | ISBN 9781680539264 (hardcover) | ISBN 9781680539271 (paperback) | ISBN 9781680532265 (ebook)

Copyright 2021 Martin Palouš

Contents

Acknowledgements

I would like to express my deep gratitude to all of my friends who have participated in one way or another in an on-going philosophical dialogue with me over the past five decades – during which the ideas presented here have been debated and tested against changing political realities. I especially have in mind members of Kampademia – a group of people who have helped me to find my personal way to think through and reflect upon the perplexities of our times. Needless to say, any mistakes, biases, or flawed interpretations of the past and present that may be wrong or misleading are my own. Special thanks go to Glenn Hughes, Ivan Chvatík, Jay Kimball, William Dansie, and Gerald Turner for their kind help with the final edition of this book. And last, but not least, I would also like to thank Paul du Quenoy and his team at Academica Press for going forward with this book.

Laying My Cards on the Table

I am now a retired Czech diplomat, and in the past decade I have been operating in the academic environment in the United States. This book contains the texts I wrote in the course of the past four decades in efforts to understand and reflect on my own political experience of transition from the 20th to the 21st century.[1] In fact, the beginning of this project goes back to the late 1960s, when I was taking my first steps, both in the realm of Western philosophy and in the realm of public affairs – trying to learn how to resist all the deformations of political reality in Central Europe, until the revolutions of 1989 under totalitarian domination.

A word of warning for potential academic readers. The fourteen Arendtian "exercises in political thought" presented here – sometime overlapping, repeating the same arguments and using the same quotations – certainly do not offer a rigorous and systematic contribution to any field of social or political science, at least in the form in which these disciplines are conceived and studied at American universities. Their aim is much more modest: to contribute meaningfully to on-going public debates and to a better understanding of our current political situation. They are written in a personal way, by someone who is not a specialist in many of the topics under discussion, but who is trying, as he always was – often lost in all the perplexities of the realities he was confronted with in his adult life – to bridge that "gap" in which we all seem to be living between our past and our future.

By exploring the uncertain territory between philosophy and politics, I want to offer my modest contribution to the revival of an almost forgotten, but at the same time classical, tradition of political thought in our contemporary environment. Directly or indirectly, all the texts gathered here

---

[1] Eight texts in this volume were already published in various edited volumes. Some of them have been slightly re-edited for this publication.

have been inspired by three great Central European thinkers of the 20th century, Hannah Arendt, Jan Patočka[2] and Erich Voegelin. What is at stake is the classical Socratic question concerning "common good," which they all raised and departed from in their investigations of the human situation; according to Aristotle this question directs all our actions, no matter whether we still adhere to some form of metaphysics or theology rooted in the past, or subscribe to post-modern nihilism so fashionable these days. [3]

In the beginning of European history, Socrates – because of his emphasis on the need for the "care for the soul" as the most important prerequisite of all "good" politics - ran into conflict with his fellow-citizens of Athens, the cradle of democracy and at the peak of its glory the greatest city-state of the Mediterranean region. Who could be seen today, in the beginning of the third decade of the 21st century as a discussion partner, or an opponent, of a contemporary Socratic philosopher? Who does belong to his/her "substantive public" in the post-European age of globalization we are living in? Could this plurality be characterized as a "cosmopolis?"

Throughout my life this call for a greater self-understanding, and the desire to promote more openness and a higher mobility of our spirit, have been the sole motives of my political actions and philosophical reflection. And it is this attitude which can now be offered as the only meaningful justification (or maybe excuse) for the publication of this book.

---

[2] Jan Patočka (1907-1977) was the most influential Czech philosopher of the 20th century. He became the Associate Professor at Charles University in 1936. He was allowed to lecture only in the years 1945-1950, then forced to leave Charles University and returned, thanks to the Prague Spring, in 1968, and forced to leave finally in 1972. In the meantime he worked in various academic institutions as a researcher, being under the surveillance of the Communist regime, and always regarded as its ideological enemy. In the fall of 1976 he was actively involved in the process of the formation of Charter 77, the most important Czechoslovak human rights movement, and, together with Jiří Hájek and Václav Havel, he became one of its first spokespersons. In spite of his limited opportunities of teaching publicly, he raised at least two generations of students, lecturing and having seminars in all sorts of private and semiprivate places and venues, laying the foundations of what was in the years of Charter 77 nicknamed as Patočka's "flying university."

[3] *"Every art and every investigation, and similarly every action and pursuit, is considered to aim at some good. Hence the Good has been rightly defined as that at which all things aim."* Aristotle, *Nicomachean Ethics,* book I, 1094, a 1-4, translated by J.A.K. Thompson, rev. version by Hugh Tredennick, Penguin Books, 1955, rev. ed. 1976

The works of Arendt, Patočka and Voegelin used and quoted in this volume:

Hannah Arendt

The Origins of Totalitarianism, Harcourt Brace Jovanovich, 5th edition, 1973,

The Human Condition, The University of Chicago Press, Chicago, London, 1958

Eichmann in Jerusalem. A Report on the Banality of Evil. First Published by the Viking Press, 1963, the quotations in this volume are from the Penguin Books Edition, 2006

On Revolution, first published by The Viking Press, 1963, the quotations in this volume are from the Penguin Books Edition, 1990

On Violence, Hartcourt, Brace and World, Inc. New York, 1970

Between Past and Future: Eight Exercises in Political Thought, New York: first published by The Viking Press, 1961, the quotations in this volume are from the Penguin Books Edition, 1993

Life of the Mind, One-volume Edition, Harcourt Brace Jovanovich Publishers, 1978

Essays in Understanding 1930-1954. Edited by Jerome Kohn. Hartcourt, Brace & Company, 1994

Men in Dark Times, A Harvest Book, 1983

Jan Patočka

(where it is possible, quotations are from the existing English translations. All other quotations are translated from Czech, German or French by the author)

Péče od duši I [The Care for the Soul] (Sebrané spisy Svazek 1). Edited by Ivan Chvatík and Pavel Kouba, OIKOUMENÉ, Praha 1996

Péče o duši II (Sebrané spisy, Svazek 2). Edited by Ivan Chvatík and Pavel Kouba, OIKOUMENE, Praha 1999

Péče o duši III (Sebrané spisy, Svazek 3). Edited by Ivan Chvatík and Pavel Kouba, OIKOUMENÉ, Praha, 2002

Umění a čas [Art and Time] (Sebrané spisy Svazek 4). Edited by Daniel Vojtěch and Ivan Chvatík, OIKOUMENÉ, Praha, 2004

Fenomenologické spisy I [Phenomenological Writings] (Sebrané spisy Svazek 6).Edited by Ivan Chvatík and Jan Frei, OIKOUMENÉ, Praha 2008

Češi I [Czechs] (Sebrané spisy Jana Patočky Svazek 12). Edited by Karel Palek and Ivan Chvatík, OIKOYMENÉ, Praha, 2006

Češi II (Sebrané spisy Jana Patočky Svazek 13). Edited by Karel Palek and Ivan Chvatík, OIKOYMENÉ, Praha, 2008

Platónova péče o duši a spravedlivý stát [Plato's Care of the Soul and Just State] (Sebrané spisy Svazek 14/4). Edited by Jiří Polívka, OIKOUMENÉ, Praha, 2012

Erazim Kohák: *Jan Patočka. Philosophy and Selected Writings*. The University of Chicago Press, Chicago & London, 1989

Heretical Essays in the Philosophy of History. Translated by Erazim Kohák. Edited by James Dodd, Open Court, Chicago and La Salle, Illinois, 1996

An Introduction to Husserl's Phenomenology. Translated by Erazim Kohák. Edited with an Introduction by James Dodd, Open Court, Chicago and La Salle, Illinois, 1996

Body, Community, Language, World. Translated by Erazim Kohák. Edited with an introduction by James Dodd, Open Court, Chicago and La Salle, Illinois, 1998

Plato and Europe. Translated by Petr Lom, Stanford University Press, Stanford, California, 2002

Living in Problematicity. Translated and Edited by Eric Manton, OIKOUMENÉ, Praha, 2007

The Natural World as a Philosophical Problem. Edited by Ivan Chvatík and Lubica Učník. Translated by Erica Abrams. Foreword by Ludwig Landgrebe. Northwestern University Press, Evanston, Illinois, 2016

Eric Voegelin

Anamnesis. On the Theory of History and Politics (Collected Works of Eric Voegelin, Vol. 6). Translated from German by M.J. Hanak, edited with an introduction by David Walsh, University of Missouri Press, Columbia and London, 2002

Published Essays 1922-1928 (Collected Works, Vol. 7). Translated by M.J. Hanak, edited with an introduction by Thomas W. Heilke and John von Heyking, University of Missouri Press, Columbia and London, 2003

Published Essays 1953-1965 (Collected Works, vol. 11). Edited by Ellis Sandoz, Louisiana State University Press Baton Rouge and London, 2000

Published Essays 1966-1985 (Collected Works, vol. 12). Edited by Ellis Sandoz, Louisiana State University Press Baton Rouge and London, 1990

Order and History Volume II. The World of the Polis (Collected Works, Vol. 15,). Edited by A. Moulakis, Columbia and London: University of Missouri Press, Columbia and London, 2000

The Nature of the Law and Related Legal Writings (Collected Works, Vol. 27). Edited by Robert Anthony Pascal, James Lee Babin and John William Corrington, Louisiana State University Press Baton Rouge and London, 1991

Autobiographical Reflections. Revised Edition with a Voegelin Glossary and Cumulative Index (Collected Works of Eric Voegelin, Vol. 34). Edited with introductions by Ellis Sandoz, University of Missouri Press, Columbia and London, 2006

Exercise 1

Revolutions and Revolutionaries, Lessons of the Years of Crisis (Three Czech Encounters with Freedom)[4]

More than four decades have already passed since 1968 and there is no doubt that what happened during this year of promises and hopes turned into illusions and utopias, leaving behind a significant trace – both locally and globally – in our recent history. The legacies of 1968 are worth being explored and discussed today, not only from the historical point of view, but also in the light of our current political experience. The declared aim of this project is *"to put forth a discussion of 1968 as both a global event and a local moment of crisis."* The global versus local connections become, indeed, especially manifest in moments of crisis. Seen from my own locus – from the Czech point of view – any meaningful discussion of 1968 must address, in one way or another, the following questions: What actually was the place and significance of the Prague Spring and all other events that occurred during the subsequent seasons of this year, in the broader context of modem Czech political experience? What are the lessons we should have learned from them? What is the legacy of 1968 – freedom rediscovered and lost again – as far as all future Czech encounters with freedom in the second half of the twentieth century are concerned?

In 2007 we commemorated the thirtieth anniversary of the foundation of Charter 77, a Czechoslovak human-rights movement initiated by a small group of people who decided to make a stand against the post-1968

---

[4] This text originated at the conference on 1968 in Washington in 2005 and was published in: *Promises of 1968. Crisis, Illusion, Utopia*, edited by Vladimir Tismaneanu, Central University Press, Budapest-New York, 2011, p. 21-42

"normalization" process. In 2009, we celebrated the twentieth anniversary of the revolutionary events of 1989 that brough our Babylonian captivity to its end; that reversed, abruptly and unexpectedly, what looked in 1968 as our inescapable fate – to remain forever a satellite vegetating on the periphery of the Soviet "evil empire." Is it possible at all to understand the significance and meaning of 1968 without also taking into account the other two recent Czech anniversaries?

It needs to be said that all three years just mentioned – 1968, 1977, and 1989 – were also turning points in my own biography. Is it something that makes me unfit to perceive and analyze them now as their unbiased observer? I frankly do not know. Being aware of this dilemma, I have decided not to aspire to an observer's detachment and instead to hold onto my experience. Instead of attempting an impartial analysis of these three Czech encounters with freedom in the second half of the twentieth century, I will offer three short sketches of 1968, 1977, and 1989, based primarily on my personal memories, three "anamnetic experiments" (to borrow the term from Eric Voegelin),[5] in the hope that they may be capable of revealing something of general relevance.

1968

In 1968 I was a teenager just entering the world of grown-ups. I certainly was not shocked nor too surprised when the "process of renewal," announced by the "progressive" reformist leadership of the Communist Party, which replaced its "conservative" wing, got into full swing in early 1968. On the contrary, I perceived the sudden irruption of freedom into our closed society as a logical, one would say almost natural, outcome of the "thaw" which had been taking place during the 1960s, when I myself, born in 1950, was progressing through my teens. Growing up in the environment of an intellectual, non-Communist family, I became during this decade (later symptomatically nicknamed "golden") an avid consumer of everything – books, essays, and articles published in "progressive" journals and periodicals, films, theater plays, music – that was bringing a fresh breeze into our socialist everydayness. I hoped to

---

[5] Eric Voegelin: *On the Theory of Consciousness*. In: *Anamnesis. On the Theory of History and Politics*, p.62-84

learn more about the world beyond our borders, which was becoming more accessible thanks to the gradual removal of ideological barriers. I desired to travel to the West and to establish new lines of communication. I had the same basic feelings as all other youngsters anywhere else in the world, believing, because of their age, that the future is a kind of reservoir of opportunities; that what one should expect realistically as an essential part of the human condition is the arrival of the unexpected; that tomorrow may always be different from today, because the very essence of human life is the human capacity for new beginnings.

As Czechoslovak society was awakening in the 1960s from the Stalinist nightmare, I was following this trend in my own way, discovering the world out there, seeking guidance and inspiration from the ever-growing group of thinkers and public intellectuals, both Marxists and non-Marxists, who were influencing Czechoslovak public discourse at this time. I never believed in socialism of any kind; it was not a matter of creed for me, but just a reality experienced. I did not feel at all to have been "brainwashed" or indoctrinated by the Communist education and certainly did not need to sober up from the previous temporary intoxication by Marxist-Leninist ideology. My political convictions were, indeed, products of *"the mind of the young man"* in Plato's sense;[6] fuzzy, regrettably uninformed, and certainly not clearly articulated. In this receptive, open, but rather messy and eclectic state of mind, I did not hesitate for a second to agree that the project to "endow socialism with a human face" – if it meant to free our society from worn-out and debilitating ideology, to introduce at least some rational economic reforms, to start respecting freedom of speech and other fundamental human rights, to allow civic associations to arise freely with their initiatives, to let people travel abroad – was a very good idea, indeed.

The Soviet-led invasion of August 21 was a shock for me as it was for the whole nation, although many informed political realists were apparently not surprised at all by this act of imperialist aggression. After

---

[6] Plato: Theaitetus, 150a, quoted from *Plato in Twelve Volumes*, Vol. 12 translated by Harold N. Fowler,
Cambridge, MA, Harvard University Press; London, William Heinemann Ltd. 1921,
https://www.perseus.tufts.edu/hopper

it happened, I was as amazed as anybody else by the spontaneous collective reaction of Czechs and Slovaks to this situation. The national response to the invasion of the Warsaw Pact armies was, indeed, unforgettable. The days which followed the military occupation of Czechoslovakia turned, contrary to the designs of those who planned this act of "fraternal international assistance," into a genuine, although short-lived revolution.

Without any official appeal or order, people immediately started to struggle both collectively and individually against the official Soviet propaganda. They launched their own public campaigns, not only protesting loudly against the unlawful occupation, but also debating with the occupiers, jumping on their tanks, trying to explain to them that there was no "counter-revolution," no civil war, no enemies of socialism in Czechoslovakia, but just peaceful freedom-loving people who wanted to live their lives in their own way. It was absolutely fascinating to observe the whole nation standing united behind its Communist – but at this moment genuinely popular – government, ready to act in defense of its rights, committed to its values and principles, well-organized, disciplined, and unfrightened.

This revolution quickly invented its own language, with its specific messaging and semantics, its specific means of free, unhindered communication. Looking at it retrospectively forty years later, I would say it was the language of our "Golden Sixties" at its best: starting with improvised posters and leaflets displayed in practically every shop win-dow on the streets, through the regular newspapers and journals produced in clandestine printing works and regularly distributed by a network of volunteers, and resulting within a couple of days in a functioning system of independent radio and TV broadcasting. The leading members of the progressive wing of the Communist Party who managed to escape arrest by the Soviet occupation forces joined the spontaneous revolutionary movement without hesitation. They even succeeded in organizing the extraordinary clandestine Party Congress in a Prague factory under the protection of local workers, which condemned the aggression against Czechoslovakia and set out a program for continuing the reforms of the Prague Spring. The conservative members of the Politburo, the agents of the secret police who participated from the very beginning in the pro-Soviet conspiracy, and all the old-fashioned, Stalinist "comrades" throughout the country, who were ready to cooperate with the occupiers, were desperately isolated and stigmatized as traitors.

Hannah Arendt, in an unsurpassed analysis of the phenomenon of modern revolutions, points to the three fundamental principles animating them and inspiring their participants. She calls them, *"following eighteenth-century political language... public freedom, public happiness, and public spirit."*[7] If I am to characterize the course of events in Czechoslovakia after August 21, 1968 in a nutshell, it was, indeed, as if some miraculous trigger was pulled and all three Arendtian principles, otherwise dreaming somewhere in the depth of our collective soul, suddenly woke up and were set into spontaneous, smart, and concerted action.

The higher the revolutionary emotions soared in the days after the Soviet-led invasion, the deeper the fall that followed. In fact, the retrogression from freedom back to the slavery of totalitarianism started at the very moment when the arrested leaders of the Prague Spring were finally released and returned from Moscow, after they had signed a protocol there that not only decided their own political future but sealed our national fate for the next twenty-one years.

Actually, the role of the "Men of January" – who were then for a short time on the pedestal of national heroes – in the suppression of the spirit that brought the whole nation together in a spontaneous revolutionary action, was the saddest and the most tragic part of the story of our 1968. Their repeated promises to remain faithful to the principles and ideals of the Prague Spring, their repeated appeals to the nation to understand the current difficulties, and to accept all the concessions that had to be made, supposedly in order to preserve the main objectives of the "process of renewal," turned out to be nothing but empty words and later, even sheer lies of experienced party apparatchiks.

A treaty was signed and duly ratified in Parliament under their watch to legitimize the "temporary" stay of the Soviet troops on our territory. Contrary to all their proclamations and assurances, the Soviet

---

[7] Hannah Arendt: *On Revolution*, p. 221

justification of the August intervention – that the socialist order in Czechoslovakia had to be "rescued" by "fraternal international assistance" – won recognition in the Czechoslovak Communist Party as its new official political line. It was shocking and sad, indeed, to observe the "Men of January" voluntarily playing an active role – until they themselves were forced to step down – in making this U-turn. The results of their "defense" of the legacies of post-January developments in the period that followed August 21 were simply indefensible. The measures first to limit and later to entirely eliminate the influence of "counter-revolutionary" forces began to be implemented with their explicit approval. Those in the Communist leadership who did not want or were not able to embrace again the dogmas of Marxism-Leninism and return to the old ways of thinking and familiar habits of Communist totalitarian rule were forced to resign one after another.

The conservative wing of the Communist Party got back into the saddle. The human freedom that had been discovered and grew during the previous months started to shrink again, and our short-lived revolution was, first inconspicuously, but later openly and explicitly, superseded by the long period of "normalization." Thorough screening was initiated within all ranks of the Communist Party, and later even carried out among the non-Communist silent majority of the population, with the aim of punishing all rebels and cleansing all "revisionist" and "counter-revolutionary" elements from Czechoslovak society. The law used to suppress by force the spontaneous demonstrations that broke out on the occasion of the first anniversary of the invasion was signed by Alexander Dubček himself.

I observed this regressive trend with disbelief and frustration. I had just begun my university studies in the fall and had participated enthusiastically in the students' protest strike in November 1968 and in the big students' demonstration which followed the martyr's death of Jan Palach.[8] The worst surprise, however, was that the atmosphere changed

---

[8] Jan Palach (1948-1969) was a Czech student at Charles University. His self-immolation (on January 16, 1969 on Wenceslas Square in Prague) was a political protest against the end of the Prague Spring resulting from the 1968 invasion of Czechoslovakia by the Warsaw Pact armies (https://en.wikipedia.org/wiki/Jan_Palach)

gradually under the pressure of normalization, even in the student environment. Within less than two years from August 1968, most of my colleagues at the Faculty of Natural Sciences of Charles University were also displaying a readiness to follow suit and adapt themselves to the new political situation, in order to secure for themselves tranquil professional and academic careers. They joined, one after another, a renewed official student organization loyal to the normalization regime; even worse, in all possible interviews and questionnaires – used by "normalizers" not so much to find out what people really thought, but rather to break their resistance – they were ready to express their agreement with the official criticism of "grave political mistakes" made by the "revisionists" during the "period of crisis," and their consent to the August invasion of the Warsaw Pact armies. No matter what they had said before, what they thought or felt inside, they also dumped easily the Arendtian principles of *"public freedom, public happiness, and public spirit"* discovered during our revolution, and fell in line with the changed political circumstances, accepting with little hesitation a "social contract" that was offered by the triumphant "normalizers."

I was well aware that there was still a clear and stark choice available at the time. One could either agree to play this "game" (and the vast majority of people in Czechoslovakia decided to do so), or to go into exile. In the summer of 1969, I also briefly considered taking the latter step, but in the end, I did not. My question, then, remained. Was there some other option besides emigration or adopting an opportunistic attitude? What about those who decided, for whatever reason, to stay? What about those who either did not have this choice at all, or found it unacceptable or problematic from the standpoint of their moral principles? Or those who simply did not have the stomach to swallow such an overdose of pragmatism and refused to maximize their personal benefits under the given circumstances?

1977

To evoke the atmosphere and the spirit of Charter 77 and also to clarify my personal reasons for adding my signature to this document without much hesitation, I have to depart from the end of my previous anamnetic experiment on 1968, from the depressing atmosphere of normalization of the 1970s. But first things first:

According to its original declaration, made January 1, Charter 77 was

> *"a free, informal, open community of people of different convictions, different faiths and different professions united by the will to strive, individually and collectively, for the respect of civic and human rights, both in Czechoslovakia and in the world."*[9]

What must be mentioned is, however, the connection which emerged for me in this context between the primarily political problem of human rights – violated in a specific manner by our totalitarian regime which metamorphosed in the normalized Czechoslovakia of the 1970s, as Václav Havel put it in one of his best essays from the late 1980s, from its earlier forms to its *"advanced or late stage"*[10] – and the essentially theoretical realm of European philosophy.

The man who was the most outspoken and most effective in articulating this connection was one of the first three spokespersons of Charter 77, the retired university professor Jan Patočka. And it needs to be said right away: when he was confronted with this connection in the concrete circumstances of his life under the conditions of the late totalitarian regime, he felt obliged to tackle it with adequate philosophical precision. He entered the shaky terrain of dissidence from a *polis* he belonged to as a real philosopher. He brought about an emphasis on maximum existential truthfulness and profundity.

Originally, it was perceived as quite surprising that it was Jan Patočka who assumed, of all other possible candidates – together with playwright Václav Havel and former Czechoslovak minister for foreign affairs in 1968, international lawyer Jiří Hájek – this challenging role, and stood in the forefront of the "dissidents'" revolt. Up until the creation of Charter 77, Patočka enjoyed, even among his Marxist opponents, the

---

[9] The Charter 77 Manifesto (http://www. cnn.com/SPECIALS/cold. war/episodes/19/ documents/charter. 77/)

[10] Václav Havel: *Stories and Totalitarianism.* In: *Open Letters, Selected Writings 1965-1990.* Edited and translated by Paul Wilson, Alfred A. Knopf, New York, p.331

reputation of a profound theoretical thinker and a renowned academic scholar. He was not regarded as a public intellectual accustomed to expressing his opinions in political discussions, and certainly not as a politician. He was highly thought of in the informed circles of the intelligentsia as a master in his field of study and a great teacher, endowed with exceptional capability to elucidate the history of philosophical ideas, from ancient beginnings to its present state, and to open for his students the gate leading to the wonderful world of Western philosophy. As one of the last pupils of Edmund Husserl, Patočka was perceived not only as an interpreter, but also as an original philosopher. Departing from his teacher's phenomenological method, he both worked on the history of philosophy, and lectured in his unique manner in front of students. He was simultaneously engaged in his own philosophical investigations focused on the *Lebenswelt* (the natural world of human life) and other fundamental problems of contemporary phenomenology.

For most of his life, Patočka was used to approaching his topics *more philosophico* – following his teacher in making phenomenological *"epoché"* and observing everything that "is" as phenomena. But upon accepting the role of Charter 77's spokesperson, he significantly altered his previous attitude. He decided, metaphorically speaking, to step down from his philosophical "observatory," to enter the public realm of his *polis*, which was then going through a serious crisis, and set himself in action. He therefore became one of the leading figures of a movement that openly criticized the political practices and manners in Czechoslovakia at the time, as far as respect for human rights was concerned, and announced his readiness to lead the dialogue about it with the Czechoslovak government.

From the standpoint of international politics and international law, the creation of Charter 77 was inspired by two events: a) the Final Act of the Conference on Security and Cooperation in Europe was adopted in the summer of 1975; and b) two major international human-rights treaties, the International Covenant on Civil and Political Rights and the International Covenant on Economic, Social and Cultural Rights, came into force in Czechoslovakia in the fall of 1976. All these documents provided clear information on the international obligations of the Czechoslovak state to fulfill these covenants "in good faith" and accommodate its legal order and practice to their normative framework.

The international context definitely played a very important role in Charter 77's origins and enabled the drafters of its founding document to come up with a number of strong arguments that could be used as the legal basis for its proposed dialogue about human rights with the government and for all its other oppositional activities. Nonetheless, what was crucial in bringing together a group of committed individuals, who were ready to join the initiative and to express support for it by putting their signatures on Charter 77's original declaration, was not so much Charter 77's justification, grounded in international politics or law, but the domestic situation in Czechoslovakia, the poisoned atmosphere that prevailed there in the 1970s, the deep spiritual crisis experienced by Czechoslovak society because of the policies of normalization. It was primarily this crisis and not the changed international situation that compelled philosopher Patočka to engage the Communist regime and to enter the proposed public debate between the Czechoslovak government and Charter 77 with his existential reasoning. And, one has to admit, for the majority of Charter 77's signatories – people who came from all walks of life, Christians of all denominations, Jews, ex-Communists expelled from the party for their revolt in 1968, independent liberal intellectuals and quite often just young people without any specific past, creed, goals, or expectations – the "reasons" behind philosopher Patočka's decision to publicly fight this spiritual degeneration were quite compelling even for non-philosophers.

These reasons can still be found in six short texts Patočka wrote in the last weeks of his life, shortly before he died following prolonged police interrogation in March 1977.[11] These articles defend the cause of Charter 77 against its enemies and can be regarded as Patočka's political testament. When these texts are put into the overall context of his life's work, it becomes evident that what he articulated in his capacity of spokesperson of Charter 77 was in a way nothing new, but corresponded to what he already set out as the basic mission of all philosophy in the 1930s. He argued then that the latter's task is not *in abstracto* speculation,

---

[11] Jan Patočka: *Texty k Chartě 77* [*Charter 77 Texts*]. In: *Češi I*, p. 428-447

but the ability *"to criticize life in all its components and manifestations..."*[12]

> *"...the willingness to give expression to what society still rudely wants to say, to give its voice to still mute tendencies, but also to expose what is behind them, to demonstrate their genesis, to mark cross-roads, to identify problems, even to try to resolve them."*[13]

And indeed, this idea is formulated repeatedly, though in a different way, in Patočka's Charter 77 texts: in publicly defending human rights, Charter 77 was not intended to interfere in politics *sensu stricto* – with politics conceived as a power struggle whose basic aim always is and must be to replace those who are momentarily in government. Charter 77's activities had to be strictly limited to a non-political goal, yet one that, for the sake of our humanity, was of crucial importance: by pointing to the individual violations of human rights and proposing the dialogue about it to the ruling power, to resist the devastating consequences the late totalitarianism of the 1970s had for those exposed to its *"radiation."*[14] The Charter 77 activities had to be founded, according to Patočka, on what should not be given up, even under such unfavorable political circumstances, that is, on the moral claim made on each of us to live with integrity. This claim not only turned all participants in the Charter 77 movement into political "dissidents," thus undermining the totalitarian Communist regime, but it also extracted them from the world of sheer lies, pretentions, and endless manipulations. It was a return journey on the path to truth. This claim opened for them the door into the largely forgotten and abandoned realm of classical political philosophy.

In his text explaining *"What Charter 77 is and what it is not,"* dated January 3, 1977, Patočka decided to bring in his capacity as Charter 77's spokesperson *"to everyone's clear awareness"* the *"truths of which*

---

[12] Jan Patočka: *Kapitoly ze současné filosofie* [Chapters from contemporary philosophy]. In: *Péče od duši I*, p. 96

[13] Ibid., p. 92

[14] Václav Havel: *Stories and Totalitarianism*. In: *Open Letters, Selected Writings 1965-1990*, p.349

we are all in some sense aware"[15] and also his own philosophical definition of human rights:

> *The idea of human rights is nothing other than the conviction that even states, even societies as a whole, are subject to the sovereignty of moral sentiment: that they recognize something unconditional that is higher than they are, something that is binding even on them, sacred, inviolable, and that in their power to establish and maintain a rule of law, they seek to express this recognition.*[16]

According to conventional wisdom, the concept of human rights in the international covenants to which the authors of the Charter 77 Manifesto were appealing is rooted in the European Enlightenment of the late eighteenth century. Patočka's moral argument, however, sounded rather like a voice coming to the present from a distant past, bringing to life something that did not fit well in the contemporary human-rights discourse, but instead belonged to premodern and largely abandoned spiritual traditions. His argument that respect for human rights represents a *moral foundation* without which *no society, no matter how well-equipped it may be technologically, can function*[18] – that it is our recognition of *"the sovereignty of moral sentiment"* and not just our human nature which constitutes them – shifted the focus from the modem emancipated individual who simply possesses human rights as "entitlements," to the ancient conflict between politics and philosophy. It turned the attention to the trial of Socrates, who seemed to have been the inspiration for Patočka's approach to political matters in general, and, for his own activities in the public realm, his great example and predecessor.

What is the actual source of political order? What enables a political body, asks Patočka in these texts, notwithstanding recognized customs, valid laws, form of government and all practical aspects of its daily politics, to exist as a political body? No matter what politicians

---

[15] Jan Patočka: *Čím je, a čím není Charta 77*. In : *Češi I*, p. 429. Translated as *The Obligation to Resist Injustice*. In: Erazim Kohák: *Jan Patočka. Philosophy and Selected Writings*, p. 341
[16] Ibid.
[18] Ibid.

themselves have to say on this point, their answer is from the Socratic/Patočkian perspective either insufficient or irrelevant. The adequate response to this question simply cannot come from their realm, but from the sphere outside politics. Even states endowed with the sovereignty to create binding laws, to execute them and to supervise their observance, must first honor something above them. Even sovereign states have to respect the elementary fact that being human precedes any political role one may be assigned as citizen.

> *"The distinction between the sociopolitical sphere of state power and the moral sphere.... demonstrates that Charter 77 represents no political act in the strict sense that it constitutes no competition or interference with political power in any of its functions. Charter 77 is neither an association, nor an organization."*[19]

Charter 77 was, according to Patočka just *"an outgrowth"* of the conviction of Charter 77 signatories that morality is above politics. It was *"an expression"* of their *"joy that their country, confirming the rights of humans with its signature, bestowed on this Act [the portion of Helsinki Agreement dealing with human rights – TR] the force of Czechoslovak law."* It was *"also an expression of (their) willingness... to do their part in bringing about the realization and public fulfillment of the principles proclaimed in this Act."*[20] When he said, that it was a Socratic irony that had to fly directly in the face of Communist power holders.

Considering their ferocious onslaughts against the Charter 77 signatories, it is obvious that they took Patočka's statement that *"our people have once more become aware that there are things for which it is worthwhile to suffer, that the things for which we might have to suffer are those which make life worthwhile"*[21] not as a moral proclamation, but as a kind of declaration of war.

---

[19] Op.cit., p. 341-342
[20] Op.cit. 341
[21] Jan Patočka: *What We Can and Cannot Expect from Charter 77*. In: Erazim Kohák: *Jan Patočka. Philosophy and Selected Writings*, p. 346

When the organs of state security went after Patočka openly, interrogating and trying to intimidate him day after day until he died, his speaking out was a clear act of Socratic courage.

In December 1976, I became acquainted with the text of Charter 77 through a friend, and I was invited to sign it and join others in this adventurous undertaking. I said yes without much hesitation. I did that not so much because of my personal courage, but because at that moment I had already been trapped in the realm of Patočka's philosophy. It was my response to the marasmus of normalization in the first half of the 1970s, when the entire public domain in Czechoslovakia was again fully manipulated by the totalitarian Communist government. Seeing no future for myself in the official academic institutions, or anywhere else where a declaration of loyalty to the regime was required as a kind of admission ticket, and having decided not to emigrate, I decided to forgo the career of scientist or researcher. Instead, I immersed myself in the depths of philosophical literature, reading somewhat eclectically everything from the basic writings of classical Greek philosophers to the works of their contemporary successors and interpreters.

Inspired and occasionally tutored by Patočka and his disciples of the older generations, I tried to become acquainted with the history of philosophical and political ideas: as they emerged for the first time, were forgotten, but rediscovered later, discussed again, interpreted, transformed, and often distorted in the great dialogue of mankind, which started at the very beginning of European history and went on and on over the centuries. In this context, I should add, I also came for the first time upon the names Hannah Arendt and Eric Voegelin.

Looking back from a distance of more than thirty-five years, what I chose could be called hyperbolically *consolatio philosophiae hodierna,* to paraphrase the title of the famous text by Boethius. The first thing I discovered in my search for a kind of Boethian consolation, however, had nothing to do with the content of the philosophical ideas I was keen to study.

What I realized instantly was that I certainly was not alone setting out on the journey of philosophy for this reason. On the contrary, the existential and not just academic attitude towards philosophy became quite common in the Czech intellectual environment of that period. In fact it is still preserved in a way – for better or for worse – today. I came to know a number of other philosophical apprentices and sometimes quite weird and eccentric inquisitive minds and started to circulate among various reading or lecture groups and debating societies. But most importantly, at the time my education was founded on the private lectures or seminars of Patočka who for all of us represented the highest authority in philosophical matters and became in our world a kind of genuine philosopher-king.

My signature on the Charter 77 Manifesto at that time was nothing more than one step in my journey to philosophy. I started along this road inspired by Patočka and there is little to add. All that followed after January 1977 was just the consequences of my original decision. I realized immediately that I treaded quite dangerous and risky waters. Like any other Charter 77 signatory, I had to accept the status of social pariah. It was a form of exemplary punishment for one's revolt against the ruling power. I had to get used to becoming an occasional target of the attention of repressive organs of the state. I lost my white-collar job and had no other choice than to work, first in a Prague hospital and then, after I was fired again, in a hotel, as a stoker.

But like most other Charter 77 signatories, I could not have cared less about all these matters. This decision was not only an act of liberation for me, but it enabled me to get acquainted with the most exciting group of like-minded people. Patočka died in March 1977, but an unusual body politic, later named by one of its leading activists, Václav Benda, a *"parallel polis,"* came into being.[22] It brought together not only the signatories of Charter 77, with all different convictions, faiths, and professions, but also all of those who decided to resist totalitarianism on their own terms.

Those who signed Charter 77 might have been motivated *more Socratico,* but surely, they did not take this step alone. They discovered immediately what it meant to leave the protective walls of their private lives, to step into the public space and to reach out to others. They

---

[22] Václav Benda: *Parallel Polis.* Translated by Paul Wilson. In: *Civic Freedom in Central Europe. Voices from Czechoslovakia,* Gordon Skilling and Paul Wilson, editors, Macmillan, 1991, p. 35-41

discovered the binding power of acting together. They discovered that the essential political virtue is not the one leading to immediate political success, but the readiness to build relationships of trust, the ability to act in concert, the willingness to support each other in confrontation with all dangers, to keep alive the spirit of solidarity. In short, they discovered, each and every one in his/her own way, on his/her own terms, the fact that, according to Hannah Arendt, creates an elementary precondition of political life: the fact of plurality which is essential to our human condition and which the normalized life of the totalitarian state aimed to obliterate.

This strange body politic – surrounded by the greater whole of which it was a tiny part, finding itself in a permanent state of siege by repressive organs of the state, having no territory, no protective walls, but just its self-appointed citizens – was certainly incapable of independent existence in the world, yet managed to exist until the end of the Communist regime in 1989, for almost thirteen years. Thanks to the nature of its foundation, thanks to its rules, its "citizenship," and, most importantly, because of the external environment in which it had to operate, the "parallel polis" was, indeed, a rather bizarre entity – a "merry ghetto," as it was also nicknamed. I would certainly hesitate to identify any new political idea whose emergence could be attributed to its existence and which could eventually, when the opportune moment finally came in November 1989, be considered to have inspired our revolutionary action.

As a member of this colorful crowd and becoming, in turn, one of the spokespersons of Charter 77 in 1986, I still tried, in the middle of all other independent or dissident activities, to stick to philosophy. The change after 1977 was only that our philosophical circles, operating since then in the environment of the "parallel polis" and for this reason occasionally threatened by repressive operations of the secret police, had become open to all the new instigations and impulses coming from the newly discovered public sphere. It therefore gave us the opportunity of being exposed not only to new questions and new themes, but also to so badly needed new books that were smuggled to us by our friends from abroad. It also offered us the opportunity to listen to distinguished Western philosophers who began to come to visit our "parallel polis" and gave their lectures at our "flying university."[23]

1989

The role the professional revolutionists played in all modem revolutions is great and significant enough, but it did not consist in the preparation of revolutions. They watched and analyzed the progressing disintegration in state and society; they hardly did, or were in a position to do, much to advance and direct it. Even the wave of strikes that spread over Russia in 1905 and led into the first revolution was entirely spontaneous, unsupported by any political or trade-union organizations, which, on the contrary, sprang up only in the course of the revolution. The outbreak of most revolutions has surprised the revolutionist groups and parties no less than all others, and there exists hardly a revolution whose outbreak could be blamed upon their activities. It was usually the other way around: revolution broke out and liberated, as it were, the professional revolutionaries from wherever they happened to be – from jail, or from the coffee house, or from the library.[24]

I chose to start my third anamnetic experiment with this sobering remark of Hannah Arendt concerning all "professional revolutionists" of the modem era, because I consider it reasonable advice when the role of dissidents in the Velvet Revolution in November 1989 is to be discussed and evaluated. It certainly corresponds to my own recollection. The story of the Velvet Revolution has already been told so many times, and I am not going to revisit it. What I will do, instead, is make the three following points.

Point one: What, in fact, is a revolution? According to conventional wisdom, it is a historical event *par excellence,* an event that literally makes history, one that radically and irreversibly changes the social and political condition of human life. Most important, though, is the revolution's subjective element. It is an event that has to be recognized as

---

[23] Barbara Day: *The Velvet Philosophers*, Claridge Press, London, 1999
[24] Hannah Arendt: *On Revolution*, p. 259

such, not only by its immediate participants, but by all those who are going to be affected by it. Based on my personal experience with revolution in 1989, Arendt is absolutely right that it is not something that can be "made" by men. Revolution is certainly not a man-made thing, but a radical break, a discontinuity in the human perception of time, a dramatic moment of truth, when we realize that our tomorrow will be different from our yesterday, that from this moment we are going to be living in a new world. To illustrate this point and to demonstrate the drama in our souls in a moment in which such recognition occurs, I will quote again from Arendt's *On Revolution*:

> *The date was the night of the fourteenth of July 1789, in Paris, when Louis XVI heard from the Duc de La Rochefoucald-Liancourt of the fall of the Bastille, the liberation of a few prisoners, and the defection of the royal troops before a popular attack. The famous dialogue that took place between the king and his messenger is very short and very revealing. The king, we are told, exclaimed: "C'est une revolte," and Liancourt corrected him: Non, Sire, c'est une revolution.* [25]

By recalling this conversation in the context of my own anamnesis, I certainly do not intend to place, without any further qualification, the events I was part of in Prague, in November 1989, into the same category with the events in France two hundred years earlier. And what I would least like to do is compare our own "dramatic" encounter with history at that time with the truly tragic situation of French King Louis XVI, not only bearing in mind the incomparable consequences which the confusion of the terms "revolte" and "revolution" had for him and could have, obviously in the opposite direction, for me and other "Velvet revolutionaries."

I actually remember very well the moment when I, at least intuitively, started to feel that what we were experiencing could be *"revolution,"* and not just another *"revolte"* – despite the fact that in the days ahead we had to expect realistically and to be prepared that the revolutionary process in which we played quite a significant role, could be

---

[25] Op.cit., p. 47

forcefully reversed. It happened at one of these first big demonstrations on Wenceslas Square, organized by Civic Forum, a revolutionary steering body of which I was a member. Speeches were delivered and songs sung from the balcony on the third floor of a house on the square.

The intention was to send a clear and straightforward message to the crowd, at first a little surprised, but later absolutely excited and ever-growing. It was at the third of these public rallies, if I am correct, that Alexander Dubcek arrived. Brought from Bratislava, he appeared in public for the first time after twenty years of invisibility and addressed the jubilant revolutionary gathering. I do not know why, but I decided that day not to stay with the other rally organizers in the area around the rostrum for speakers, who were quickly lining up as the revolution was progressing, but to go down and observe the scene from the square. I already knew what was approaching. In the evening twilight a singer, Marta Kubišová, appeared on the balcony and started to sing "Prayer for Marta," a song that became, as Václav Havel recently put it, a kind of unofficial anthem of 1968. People on the square, I think, most of them with tears in their eyes, started spontaneously to light candles they brought with them, without being "officially" instructed to do so. That was it. The message could not have been stronger. I realized that the revolution that had died in the streets of Prague more than twenty years ago had finally returned. To be understood correctly: as far as "ideas" are concerned, no one I know of, except for a few '68ers, desired to revive the project of "socialism with a human face," which had been once and for all buried in August of 1968. What had to be brought back to life, if we wanted liberty, and not a reformed version of illiberal order, were the three Arendtian principles of *public freedom, public happiness, and public spirit*, so easily abandoned and forgotten in the years of normalization. And what I saw on Wenceslas Square that night was that they were back, indeed, and at least for some time were ready to "inspire" Czechs and Slovaks, to wake them up, to bring them into a disciplined, well-organized and bold collective action.

Point two is the noetic dimension of revolutionary action itself and the corresponding epistemology. I will start with the observation of Petr Pithart, a leading activist of the revolution of 1989, one of the few Charter

77 signatories with some political experience and qualifications, who was to become Czech prime minister immediately after the victorious Velvet Revolution.[26] I remember that he once told me, trying to articulate the experience he had as one of the negotiators of Civic Forum with their counterparts of the *ancien regime,* the following: being in the very center of revolutionary action during the days that followed November 17, 1989, could hyperbolically be compared to being at the center of a nuclear explosion. Therefore, to continue his metaphor, dragged by forces released in a moment when two subcritical amounts of radioactive material combined, with their vision paralyzed by the blinding flash of the chain reaction, the representatives of Civic Forum – a group of hastily selected individuals, some of them certainly not very well prepared for this job – had to cope with, and prudently react to an absolutely new and largely unexpected situation. Sitting at the round table with their well-trained opponents, who were backed by the repressive organs of the state, still ready to intervene in its defense, they had to proceed without a clear democratic mandate, master plan, or strategy thoroughly prepared in advance, just feeling their way, applying trial and error, not knowing well their opponents and their real intentions. This negotiation evolved day after day, not only with all Czechoslovak citizens around and the whole democratic world watching, but also with major international actors playing their game of balancing power, communicating through their secret lines and carrying about their geostrategic "national interests." The only democratic feedback the negotiators could rely on were the daily consultations with other members of the broader leadership of Civic Forum. However, the steering body of the Velvet Revolution itself had only a very limited mandate, being composed of representatives of loose networks of civic initiative, comprising a number of self-appointed individuals who either had credentials from their past activities within the "parallel polis" or were co-opted in the course of the Velvet Revolution.

---

[26] Petr Pithart (1941) is a Czech politician, lawyer and political scientist. He was a member of the Communist Party of Czechoslovakia from 1960, was active in the Prague Spring, and left the party after the Soviet invasion. Later he became one of the most prominent dissidents against the Communist regime, including being one of the first signatories of Charter 77. In 1989 he was one of the prominent leaders of the Civic Forum, founded at the start of the Velvet Revolution.

The negotiators were obviously not only supposed to keep this body informed of their interim achievements. They also needed to obtain approval for the next steps, and that could happen only after a thorough and, for the most part, protracted but hardly productive or result-oriented discussion.

The lesson to be drawn from what I described above, using just quick brush strokes to evoke the picture of daily routines of the Velvet Revolution, is as follows: those who would like to explore the political ideas animating revolutions should first consider the inherent, or one can say, using the medical terminology, "endemic" features of the human situation in which all the "revolutionists" – either professionals aptly described and mocked by Hannah Arendt, or amateurs like most Czechoslovak dissidents in 1989, who could be in many ways ridiculed as well – were finding themselves. What should not be forgotten is the blindness that strikes all who are doomed, as Pithart, to act and make decisions in the middle of a nuclear explosion. Revolutionary action is taking place in a state of epistemological chaos and total uncertainty. To talk about a "surprising" absence of new political ideas in the European revolution of 1989, as Francois Furet and Timothy Garton Ash did,[27] may make sense from the standpoint of an outside observer of revolutionary events. However, it simply ignores the basic nature of the revolutionary's playing field. It is out of touch with the immediate experience of those who, for some reason, happened to have played the game. The question, then, is how to consider their perspective and reconcile it with that of the committed observers, *spectateurs engagés* in the sense of Raymond Aron.[28] How can one increase the participant's capacity of understanding and judgment in the context of an event primarily experienced as a discontinuity in time? And, in reality, the interchangeability of these roles does belong to human nature, doesn't it? Are we not both actors and first observers of events that comprise the history of our lives? Do we find

---

[27] Timothy Garton Ash: *The Magic Lantern. The Revolution of '89 Witnessed in Warsaw, Budapest, Berlin and Prague. With a New Afterword by the Author*, Vintage Books, A Division of Random House, Inc, New York, 1999. I deal with this problem in the fourth "exercise" *On Political Ideas in the Period of Transition*.

[28] *Spectateur engagé* is the name of famous book of his conversations with Jean-Louis Missika et Dominique Wolton (Raymond Aron *Spectateur engagé*, Julliard, Paris 1981)

ourselves suddenly caught up in these events, or, to return to Hannah Arendt, are we situated in such moments in a "gap" between our past and our future? Is it surprising that she quotes, when referring to this gap, Alexis de Tocqueville, who also apparently saw no new political ideas when he arrived in America to study its revolution? And in the conclusion of his lengthy work, which is still an unmatched masterpiece of the discipline, he had nothing more to say than to express his noetic uncertainty:

> *Although the revolution that is taking place in the social condition, the laws, the ideas, the opinions and the feelings of men is still very far from being terminated, yet its results already admit of no comparison with anything that the world has ever before witnessed. I go back from age to age up to the remote antiquity, but I find no parallel to what is occurring before my eyes; as the past has ceased to throw its light upon the future, the mind of man wanders in obscurity.*[29]

In the two previous remarks I tried to recall the direct experience of revolution – the situation we were a part of, caught in its enormous power, where the only thing we could do was wait and see where we would end up. My third point concerns my realization for the first time, in the middle of all the hectic activities, typical of the months following November 17, 1989, that our revolution was already behind us. I still remember the shock I experienced sometime in the spring of 1990 when I first read an article, written not by a professional propagandist from the previous era, trained to distort reality in conformity with its official ideological interpretation, but by someone who apparently spoke from the bottom of his heart. The author was explaining what happened in the Velvet Revolution and especially Charter 77's role in a way at odds with my own perceptions and experiences. According to this version, what happened was not revolution at all but just a plot on a large scale, a secret deal made between the forces of the *ancien régime* of the Communist Party and their Charter 77 counterparts, who only pretended to be in opposition

---

[29] Alexis de Tocqueville: *Democracy in America,* New York: Alfred. A. Knopf, 1945, p. 331

and only wanted power. Even if this particular article was crazy enough to be tossed, aside – bringing in the old and well-worn arguments of Zionism and Judeo-Masonic conspiracy – the moment I read it, I realized an inconvenient truth. Paradoxically, thanks to its success, the Velvet Revolution, as a genuine historical or, rather, history-making event, was no longer in the hands of those who had taken part in it, who had become, whether by choice or necessity, temporary "revolutionists." It was a legacy that no one could claim. In this sense, the Velvet Revolution was still "ours," but only as expressed in the aphorism of French poet and writer René Char, quoted at the very beginning of Hannah Arendt's *Between Past and Future,* where he *"compressed the gist"* of what four years in the *resistance* against the Nazis meant for those who took part in it: as *"our inheritance" that "was left to us by no testament."*[30]

---

[30] Hannah Arendt: *Between Past and Future: Eight Exercises in Political Thought,* p.3

Exercise 2

Philosophy as Personal Experience and the Others[31]

"I know all that sounds very general, very indefinite and very unrealistic, but I assure you that these apparently naive words stem from a very concrete and not always easy experience with the world and, if I may say so, I know what I am talking about."[32]

"For after that in the wisdom of God the world by wisdom knew not God, it pleased God by the foolishness of preaching to save them that believe. " [33]

In his lecture *Politics and Conscience* Václav Havel seems to touch on a fundamental conflict taking place in this age, the conflict between the principle of "the impersonal," which has come to dominate

---

[31] A contribution to *Hostina*, a volume edited by Václav Havel dedicated to the memory of Jan Patočka, composed of essays by twenty-one Czech and Slovak philosophers, both living at home and in exile,.
His motive for becoming its editor was personal. After his return from prison in the spring of 1983, where he himself discovered the power of philosophy to resist the existential tension he was exposed to during his jail time, he wrote them a letter, asking them to articulate their inner motivation for "philosophizing."
(*Hostina* was originally published as "samizdat" – Edice Expedice, 1985 – and in 1989 by Josef Škvorecký in Canada (*Hostina. Filosofický sborník*. Edited and with an introduction by Václav Havel. Sixty-Eight Publishers, Toronto, 1989, p. 189-203). The English translation was published in: *Good-bye Samizdat. Twenty Years of Czechoslovak Underground Writing*, edited by Marketa Goetz-Stankiewicz, Northwestern University Press, Evanston, Illinois, 1992, p. 256-266.)
[32] Václav Havel: *Politics and Conscience*. In: *Open Letters, Selected Writings 1965-1990*, p. 268
Václav Havel: *Politics and Conscience*, p. 249-271
[33] *1 Corinthians, 1:21, King James Bible*

the contemporary understanding of Being, and the principle of personal responsibility that man as man bears for his/her life. On the one side there is the objective knowledge of modern science and its fruit, technology and the modern concepts of human history, which present themselves no less objectively and which provide support for ideological doctrines serving to legitimize the "ground" of the modern state. On the other side there is the individual human being with his/her concrete life, finding him/herself increasingly oppressed and enslaved by the mechanisms of the impersonal. The modern crisis is the crisis of man being expelled from the natural world, not only endangered by this or that concrete thing (missiles, polluted environment, immoral political systems) but exposed to the danger that his/her intrinsic mission, his/her human identity, may be destroyed. In the name of Scientific Truth and Infinite Progress, totality, impersonality, the strange Mr. Nobody is attempting to divest humans of their individual personal responsibility and conscience; to demote them to mere executors of "objective," "historical" interests. How are we to face this sort of danger? Václav Havel says simply: by holding our human ground:

> *"The best resistance to totalitarianism is simply to drive it out of our own souls, our own circumstances, our own land, to drive it out of contemporary humankind……. A reaffirmed human responsibility is the most natural barrier to all irresponsibility."*[35]

First Gloss: The Rule of the Impersonal and the End of Philosophy

Patočka once pointed out that two influential nineteenth-century currents of thought - positivism and Marxism - contain the idea of the end of philosophy.[36] All their differences notwithstanding, the positivist and

---

[35] Václav Havel: *Politics and Conscience,* ibid

[36] In 1972, Patočka was asked by his students to comment on the Heidegger's text *Das Ende der Philosophie und die Aufgabe des Denkens* (in: Martin Heidegger: *Zur Sache des Denkens,* Max Niemeyer Verlag, Tübingen, 1969). He delivered two lectures dealing with Heidegger's argument and later edited their transcript. The final version was then published in French (*La fin de la philosophie est-elle possible?,* translated by E. Abrams, in: Jan Patočka: *Platon et l'Europe,* Lagrasse, Verdier, 1983, pp. 239–

the Marxist agree that the formulation of their respective positions was the last philosophical act in human history, that subsequently philosophy completely lost its *raison d'être*. Both came to believe that they had arrived at an attitude toward Being on which human existence as such could be based once and for all. All meaningful and legitimate questions, they said, can be posed only from this basis, and the basis itself must be accepted as the unquestionable premise of all subsequent human striving. Both positivist and Marxist replaced philosophy, the love of wisdom – that attitude of permanent receptiveness to what is, that being-in-question – with a special conception of a specific and definitive answer, or rather a predetermined conception of how to answer any question that man may ever have to face; the human being holding the scientific *"Weltanschauung"* – be it in the spirit of either of these doctrines – has presumably achieved ontological anchoring and seemingly acquired the definitive key to human life.

Positivist philosophy ended with the transition of humankind into the positive evolutionary phase (which follows the theological and metaphysical phases). The task of interpreting, uncovering, and presenting to everyday human life its laws became from that moment on the province of individual positive "sciences" built on a uniform mathematical or rather mathematico-logical basis. Because philosophy is unable to produce a subject of its inquiry, it has lost its place and meaning in today's world. Everyday scientific practice, uncovering the objective laws of a given reality, has thus become the only legitimate way by which man is able to secure for himself the "good" life, which, according to modern understanding, is life in the abundance of goods and chattels both corporeal and spiritual. It is, after all, only science that opens to man the "technical" possibilities of satisfying the individual's physical, cultural, and social needs, of optimally organizing the life of human society, of ensuring its constant movement in the direction of progress – from the worse to the better, from the less to the more, from the chaos of the natural

---

264) and German (*Das Ende der Philosophie?*, translated by F. Matula, in: Jan Patočka: *Ketzerische Essays zur Philosophie der Geschichte*, Stuttgart, Klett-Cotta, 1988, pp. 432–460)

state, *belli omnium contra omnes,* to a perfectly and thoroughly organized paradise of plenty on earth functioning in the absence of conflict.

The Marxist likewise feels no need to philosophize further, namely, to continue questioning his own assumptions. True, he regards scientific positivism with its idolatry of facts as something naive and prejudicial. In contrast to the positivist, the Marxist, as a remote heir of Hegel, knows that knowledge of facts is not absolute knowledge but always a specific answer circumscribed by the question posed. What matters most to him, then, is not a theoretical explanation of facticity, but an insight into the nature of human praxis as such, into the structure of human reality and into the laws governing its movements. And here, after all, the only true and generally binding account is already provided by the founding father of the teaching, Karl Marx. Thus, it is pointless to go on explaining and reinterpreting the world, trying again and again to raise philosophical questions. The latter signals a lack of understanding of what human praxis is all about, that is, of the fact that the time has come for the world to be changed according to the intentions of the only true, the Marxian, interpretation. After Marx, philosophy can be followed only by revolutionary ideology, by "technical" instruction based on Marx's "theoretical" teaching of how to achieve such a change and lead mankind in the direction predetermined by history, in accordance with its objective, lawful orientation, indeed with the tendency contained in the very concept of Being.

The followers of both Auguste Comte and Karl Marx assumed that the necessary evolution toward the ideal *regnum hominis,* the perfect world of human rule as they saw it, corresponds to a fundamental trend contained in human existence. It never occurred to them that it could possibly be otherwise, and therefore they considered as definitively answered also the main ontological question regarding human existence. There is no doubt that the two differed in their ideas about what this *regnum hominis* ought to look like and what would be the most appropriate way of achieving it, but they basically agreed that the aim of human history, the meaning of human life, the telos of all being is already present, within reach, and that all it takes is to set forth on the journey toward it.

Lest I be misunderstood: when in connection with positivism or Marxism I speak of the end of philosophy, I am not claiming that Comte or Marx did not tackle the deepest philosophical problems, or that it would be impossible to assert that they had genuinely philosophical followers. Questions concerning the philosophical interpretation of their work will deliberately be left aside. Rather, I want to put in context the "end of philosophy" as implied in the structure of their thought, and the actual decline of philosophy, its loss of prestige and relevance in the intellectual atmosphere of our time, its transformation into an academic institutionalized discipline preoccupied with its narrowly specialized, from the perspective of non-philosophers largely unintelligible problems, without practical responsibility for what goes on in the world. The modern world seems to have accepted this positivist/Marxist diagnosis and in fact come to feel that it can easily do without philosophy, welcoming an end to its meddlesome and tortuous questioning.

Yet when we consider the causes for our becoming thus subservient to the mechanisms of impersonality, it appears that it is exactly this – "philosophically" grounded – decline of philosophy which may be the most important of them. It is as if together with philosophy people of the technical era have given up their own personal experience as the only relevant ground in which their lives' options, their "life in truth" is rooted. Philosophers have been driven out of the human world – in part thanks to their own recent "philosophies" – and enclosed in special "cultural reservations." People have credulously given themselves to ideologies, the results of scientific research, technical achievements, "objective" laws, "objective truth" – expecting perhaps that in this way they would be safe from the mistakes and pitfalls from which personal daily life cannot be protected. But someone played them a nasty trick: they were persuaded to give up the natural world, and, simultaneously, to move into the strange kingdom of objectivity ruled by the anonymous, exact, never erring, merciless, and unforgiving Mr. Nobody.

Second Gloss: Husserl – the Rebirth of Philosophy on the Ground of Subjectivity

When, in the first decade of this century, Edmund Husserl began pointing out as symptom of the upcoming crisis the inverse relationship between the world of everyday experience and the world that manifests itself in the scientific approach and that has taken over and completely permeated human life, his speech might have impressed many as *"foolishness of preaching"* – had they lent even half an ear to it. After all, scientific objectivity was verified by daily praxis. Universal progress was taken to be a reality beyond discussion.

But Husserl is not guided by irrational and romantic visions of returning to the "lost paradise" of the natural peoples when he is proposing the primacy of the natural world over its scientific interpretation. On the contrary, he sees the way toward a restoration of respect for the natural world and for personal experience to which it gives meaning in the project of radically reconstructing philosophy and regenerating its importance for people – that is, conceiving a plan for philosophy as a "rigorous science."

Is this a contradiction in terms? Was it not science, the scientific worldview (*Weltanschaung*) that was instrumental in furthering the decline of philosophy? Is philosophy as a rigorous science at all conceivable?

The problem is resolved when we remember what Husserl considers the "scientificity" of science and, particularly, the critique he levels at the modern sciences. His objection to them is the following. The modern sciences have betrayed the original principle on whose foundation science originated in ancient Greece. They have become estranged from the: idea of purpose (*Zweckidee*) of universal science, from the demand that science be built on that absolute base.

On no account can this demand be fulfilled either by Hegelian speculation from a position of the absolute spirit or by empirical science governed by rules of "common sense." According to Husserl, the leading idea of science implies two things: first, the evidence, the necessity for establishing the proof for scientific knowledge through direct experience,[37] and, second, the apodicticity[38] of the beginning, from which alone issues that experiential knowledge which finds its evidence in observation.

The modern sciences are thus called to answer for their doings. War is declared on Mr. Nobody, who has monopolized them for himself. What is challenged to provide an account of itself, to establish whence scientific knowledge derives its meaning altogether, what entitles it to rule human life, is the myth of the objective validity of scientific knowledge, the myth of the objective description of the world that claims to be qualified to decide on everything.

For Husserl, the competent judge entrusted with arbitration is experience itself, one's own subjectivity, because it alone is qualified to satisfy the requirements mentioned above, evidence and apodicticity. "I am" is the reality whose evidence we, as subjective beings, are always living and whose negation is unthinkable: the experience of "I am" is an apodictic experience, and the only true ground on which it is possible to build a "philosophy as rigorous science." It is the gate that gives man access to reality and Being.

Phenomenology, then, attempts to reveal the structures by which in its individual acts the "I" relates to the world, to explain how in its consciousness the "I," ego, constitutes object – meaning as a correlate of its acts. This phenomenological perspective alone, according to Husserl, creates the precondition for the legitimate description of the world as performed by empirical science, or rather, the precondition for any scientific activity whatsoever.

To me one thing seems important: In describing the life of subjectivity, in seeking out the *a priori* of how the ego comes by its phenomenal contents, Husserl does not speak in a Kantian spirit; he does

---

[37] *"Evidence is, in an extremely broad sense, an 'experiencing' of something that is, and is thus; it is precisely a mental seeing of something itself."* (Edmund Husserl: *Cartesian Meditations*, Martinus Nijhoff, Den Haag, 1970, sec.5, p. 12)

[38] *"An apodictic evidence, however, is not merely certainty of the affairs or affair-complexes (states-of- affairs) evident in it; rather it discloses itself, to a critical reflection, as having the signal peculiarity of being at the same time the absolute unimaginableness (inconceivability) of their non-being."* (*Cartesian Meditations*, sec. 6, p. 15-16.)

not speak of some supra-personal subjectivity common to all that can be abstracted from the experiences of individuals. Husserl's transcendental subjectivity is unequivocally personal in nature. Eidos ego, that is, the ego that is conscious, the ego that has led itself to clarification, is still an ego, a monad, and not an abstract concept. It is "I" who perceives, meditates, considers, decides, bears responsibility. In this view, Husserl's philosophy as science is always "my" philosophy. He/she who wants to take on Mr. Nobody has always to begin with him/herself.

Third Gloss: The Charge of Solipsism and Transcendence

The classical charge frequently leveled against the radically subjectivist disposition of Husserl's philosophy – which in different variations falls also on the heads of his followers – is that of so-called solipsism: what Husserl presents is pure egology, which in essence is unable to approach the actual philosophical problems – the ontological questions. By limiting the terrain on which he moves to the subject-monad, Husserl can never grasp the being of existents and cannot interpret the world which, after all, is not only the ego's correlate but primarily the common world that every ego shares with other egos. His monadic ego is an "egoistic ego" narcissistically looking mostly at itself, having decided to create the whole world from its own resources, while haughtily overlooking everything that could deflect its glance in a different direction.

In the first place, it must be remembered that Husserl was aware of this charge. He himself was the first to raise it. Overcoming the charge of solipsism is not only the central difficulty but also the central task that Husserl's phenomenology has set for itself. The crucial concept here is not the concept of subjectivity but the concept of transcendence. Husserl's subjectivity is not divested of the concreteness given by the singularity of the specific personal "I." Husserl does not inquire into how that subjectivity "functions" generally, in all egos, how the self-aware human organism is made up "objectively."

This subjectivity is in no regard objectively given – that would be a contradiction. In its concreteness, uniqueness, individuality, this subjectivity is "transcendental" – it is endowed with capability to overstep itself. If we had directly placed the gravitational center of human existence outside the self, outside the personal "I," ego, if we had not gone the way of phenomenology, but only accepted its results (does it even have any?), we would have overlooked the decisive experience of transcendence that in fact underlies the ego's being.

In his interpretation of Husserl's *Cartesian Meditations* Paul Ricoeur contrasts two conceptions of transcendence, that of Descartes, the man who stands at the beginning of the modern era but still goes back to the medieval spiritual tradition with reference to the deepest Christian motifs and Scholastic concepts, and that of Husserl, who represents the culmination of the journey of the modern spirit while at the same time already taking decisive steps toward its overcoming.[39]

As if both were fighting the same menace – skepticism and nihilism. In the case of Descartes, its cause was the breakdown and fall – after centuries of stability – of the medieval world (Descartes writes his *Meditationes de prima philosophia* at the time of the Thirty Years War, which profoundly disrupted and changed Europe). In the case of Husserl, his source became the crisis of the modern spirit, or rather, the crisis of its most prominent fruit, *"the crisis of the European sciences"* (Husserl completes his philosophical oeuvre at the very threshold of World War II, which, according to some thinkers, marked the end of Europe as such).

> *"Whereas Descartes transcends the cogito by means of God, Husserl transcends the ego by the "alter ego," the existence of other "I"s. Having taken the first step – founding the ground of certainty in the immanence of ego cogito – Descartes immediately takes the second: referring to the idea of infinite being, on which can be built the human relation to being endangered by skepticism, and with whose help man is then able to overreach the sphere of the mere immanence of his "I.""*[40]

This idea provokes a displacement of the center of gravity of subjectivity toward the infinite being. Husserl rejects this step and claims

---

[39] Paul Ricoeur: *Études sur les Méditations Cartésiennes de Husserl*, in: *Revue philosophique de Louvain* 52, 1954, p. 75-109 and Paul Ricœur: *Husserl's Fifth Cartesian Meditation*. In: *Husserl: Analysis of His Phenomenology*, Northwestern University Press, Evanston, Illinois, 1967, p. 115-142
[40] Op.cit., p. 135

that the transcendental ego itself is capable of meeting all the tasks of the first philosophy, and that the step transcending the immanence of the ego can be taken on the ground of immanence itself – by meeting a second "I," by finding oneself in the common world.

Setting aside, for the time being, both Descartes's and Husserl's conclusions, we are, it seems to me, facing a reality of fundamental importance: In essence, man can choose from two directions of stepping out of the mere immanence of an isolated self – the direction inward, for an encounter with God, whose idea we carry somewhere deep within, and the direction outward, for an encounter with the others with whom we share the common world.

Fourth Gloss: "I" and the Other

I will now try to analyze the twofold movement of transcendence in somewhat more detail. Thus, on the one hand there is the movement of "inward" transcendence, the movement by which "I" overreaches its immanent experience in an inward direction – I shall call it thinking. On the other hand, there is the movement by which I transcend myself in an outward direction, going into the world I share with others. This movement I shall call acting.[41]

The first characteristic of the movement of thinking is that it means withdrawal from plurality, from the life with others to the solitude of the meditating "I." To think presupposes, as Hannah Arendt says, "to stop and think:" to cease at least for a moment with all the movements of which our lives consist and return to that interior dwelling where "I" retreats to in order to reach out to the state of unity with one's "self."

From this follows the second characteristic of thinking. Thinking is a movement that is essentially bodily. To think does not mean to get rid of the body and move in the spheres of pure mind; to think means to leave the world of mere appearances and perceive the ideas that determine the existence of existents from one's own corporeal perspective,

The third characteristic of thinking testifies about the experience of thinking as such. Thinking, it is true, takes place in the solitude of man's

---

[41] I depart here from Hannah Arendt's principal opus *The Human Condition*

"internal abode," but is felt as a silent inner conversation of the soul with itself (TES PSYCHÉS PROS HAUTÉN DIALOGOS ANEU FÓNÉS), as Plato defined thinking in *The Sophist)*,[42] as a silent dialogue between me and myself. Thinking is a way toward the truth in the company of an invisible partner – someone before whose face and in whose questions all internal life of "I" takes place.

Acting is the opposite movement, being directed from the singularity of the "I" toward the common world. Its first characteristic is that it marks the entrance into plurality, into a meeting with those who are essentially other than "I," but who create and share this world with me.

The second characteristic is based on this: Whereas the "I" in isolation basically means "two in one," the "I" that has entered the world becomes "one alongside others," a unique, independent participant therein. A person cannot furnish himself with a personality but, on the contrary, receives it from the others before whom he steps forth.

The third characteristic: Acting is fundamentally connected with speech. That with which "I" turned to a person enters the shared world, its "marketplace."

The fourth characteristic: The guiding principle of acting is freedom. In the movement by which "I" enter the world the thing that matters most is the preservation of the same opportunity for others (it is they who create the personhood of my person in the first place). It is the protection of the freedom of that movement as such that matters. In this shared world the issue of concern is successfully to defend the shared freedom.

Last, the fifth characteristic: The demarcation and successful defense of the shared space is a *conditio sine qua non* of acting – and it is also the fundamental meaning of human laws. Acting as such, as a manifestation of human freedom, however, is not entirely under the rule of law. It can manifest itself in the human world as the capacity of humans to love one another and to forgive, i.e. to give preference not to the "what"

---

[42] Plato: *Sophist*, 263e2,3, quoted from *Plato in Twelve Volumes, Vol. 12*. Translated by Harold N. Fowler. Cambridge, MA, Harvard University Press; London, William Heinemann Ltd. 1921, https://www.perseus.tufts.edu/hopper/text?doc=Perseus%3 Atext%3A1999.01.0172%3Atext%3DSoph.%3Asection%3D263e

of an occurrence but to the "who," to the guilty person. It is endowed with the power to release that person from the consequences of his/her past actions. It means a possibility to value the other "I" more highly than the simple fact of its deeds.[43]

Philosophy articulates both inner experience of thinking and public activity (political, in the original sense of the word), which are complementary to and inseparable from each other. If it is possible now to appeal to Plato's definition of the human soul as that which is self-moving, or rather that which itself is that movement, then it seems to me that this rhythm of twofold transcendence, as roughly outlined above, is what this movement is all about, is the lot in which all other human life potentialities are rooted and from which, in the final analysis, they derive their origin.

Fifth Gloss, Concluding

To unite politics and conscience, as Václav Havel demands in the conclusion of his essay, means to understand that both the movements by which the "I" transcends itself belong together; it means to show that it was Mr. Nobody who separated them – making conscience into a privatissimum and politics into "technical" or bureaucratic attendance on the monstrous mechanisms of the modern state. If "I" wants to remain true to itself, if it does not want to risk becoming nothing, it must say No to this separation. Should this happen – and, no doubt, it requires courage and entails considerable risks – it may turn out that the denouement of the story, similar to the one we find in Tolkien's myths, does not have to belong only to the realm of fairy tales and imaginary stories.

---

[43] Hannah Arendt: *The Human Condition*, p. 236-242

Exercise 3

Jan Patočka versus Václav Benda[44]

I

Independent citizens' initiatives, independent culture, independent church structures, and so on, represent a radically new phenomenon which in the past twelve years has become a part of the Czechoslovakian reality that cannot be overlooked. Even if much of what we would include in this category – a wide range of cultural activity, for instance – has a prehistory of its own, it is undeniable that the declaration of Charter 77 in January 1977 was the decisive impulse towards independent activity of all kinds. In Czechoslovakian society – which at that time had been controlled by a Communist regime for almost thirty years and had been paralyzed since the late 1960s by the "normalization process" – the emergence of the Charter was extremely important: it meant the restoration of a certain public space that was independent of the ruling power and unmanipulated by it. A "parallel polis" was constituted within a society that had been formed by totalitarianism.

Against the expectations of the skeptical, this community has proven to be an unusually vigorous social phenomenon. It has managed, so far, to defend its own existence, in the face of almost overwhelming odds, against the attempt by the organs of power to destroy, or at least curtail it. Vasil Biľak, for all his talk about "the rubbish heap of history"

---

[44] This text was my contribution to the Charter 77 debate published originally in 1988 in Czech "samizdat" that started in the early 1980s in the circles of dissent. Its English version was published in *Uncaptive Minds*, II, 5 (9), November-December 1989, p. 36-40 and in: H. Gordon Skilling and Paul Wilson (eds.): *Civic Freedom in Central Europe*. MacMillan, 1991, p. 121-128; and again in: F. Flagg Taylor IV (ed.): *The Great Lie, Classic and Recent Appraisals of Ideology and Totalitarianism*. ISI Books, Wilmington, Delaware, 2011, p. 519-527

and the express train that would crush the legs of those foolish enough it get in its way, has finally had to retire without seeing the "final solution" of the dissident question. It is highly probable that neither his colleagues who are still in power, nor their eventual replacements, will ever see their dream of crushing dissent come true. The fact is that the cause for which this parallel community came into being in the first place, and which remains its fundamental *raison d'étre* – the defense of human rights and freedoms – has taken on an unexpected urgency. Regardless of the reasons for this – whether it was the activities of those in the parallel communities, or the fact that at the same time, the Americans elected President Reagan to a second term and Mikhail Gorbachev assumed power in Moscow, or simply because of the logic of historical development – the question of human rights is no longer just the concern of isolated groups of eccentric individuals and the humanitarian problems that constantly arise around them, but it is a domestic political question of the first order, and therefore one of the key elements on the agenda of international politics.

II

The philosopher Jan Patočka, one of the prime movers and ultimately one of the first spokesmen of Charter 77, wrote several texts in which he outlined what, in his opinion, the activity of Charter 77 was based on, what goals it ought to set for itself, and what means it ought to use to achieve those ends; in other words, "what the Charter is and what it is not." Patočka's exegesis seems to me the best place to start if we wish to find our bearings in the independent community that the Charter opened up.

According to its original declaration, Charter 77 saw itself as a

> *loose, informal, and open community of people of different convictions, different faiths, different professions, who are joined together by the determination to work, as individuals and together, for the respecting of civic and human rights both in our own country and in the world.* [45]

---

[45] The Charter 77 Manifesto (http://www. cnn.com/SPECIALS/cold. war/episodes/19/ documents/charter. 77/)

But the appearance of Charter 77 cannot be understood as a political act, and therefore its significance cannot be measured by the usual political measurements. According to Patočka, what its signatories had in common was not anything political, but a certain moral stance, the conviction that human society cannot function satisfactorily if it does not rest on a moral foundation. Not only that, but without this moral foundation, society finds itself in danger of losing its integrity altogether, of losing that from which springs the very meaning of its existence. The point is, Patočka said,

> *to assure not the functioning of a society but the humanity of humans. Humans do not invent morality arbitrarily, to suit their needs, wishes, inclinations, and aspirations. Quite the contrary, it is morality that defines what being human means.*[46]

According to Patočka, the citizens who sign the Charter declaration are saying to those who run the state: Govern, make sure the vital functions of the social organism run smoothly, but on one condition: that you unconditionally subordinate the exercise of that power to morality! Do not infringe upon the legal rights of those who, from your point of view, are powerless! And you must maintain this stance even when, and especially when, it is not in 'the interests of the state' to do so. You must recognize, at last, that the supremacy of morality over power is what makes human society human; it is the state's most elementary *raison d'étre*; it represents the only possible basis for that 'social contract' posited by the founders of modern political theory.

Patočka's conception of Charter 77, which in my opinion is generally accepted as "canonical" to this day, has left something essential unsaid, for obvious reasons, since Jan Patočka died in March of 1977, and therefore could not have analyzed the experiences undergone by Chartists in their effort to live out the consequences of this "moral stance" under totalitarian conditions. What is missing is an answer to the question: in what new situation does this event place both those who take direct part in

---

[46] Jan Patočka: *The Obligation to Resist Injustice*. In: Erazim Kohák: *Jan Patočka. Philosophy and Selected Writings*, p. 341.

it, and the rest of society, particularly the power structure, which was compelled to respond in some way to the existence of Charter 77, and still has to?

One of the first to attempt such a response was Václav Benda, who in 1978 published his essay on the parallel polis.

Benda argues that Patočka was right in pointing out the absolute preference for a moral stance over practical political considerations: a demand to act not opportunistically, but *sub speciae aeternitatis,* was the basis on which the Charter stands. If, however, the Chartists, now that their cause is in motion, wish to find a guide that would allow them to keep their bearings and to act and make responsible decisions in the new situation, then Patočka's point of departure – because of its timeless abstraction from a concrete temporal horizon – is inadequate. According to Benda the task of the Chartists, and of all like-minded people regardless of whether they signed the Charter or not, is this: to continue building the independent community that has thus come into being, to defend in every possible way the space it has managed to wrest lor itself from the powers that be, and not to waste a single opportunity to expand it. How can this be achieved? By creating all kinds of independent parallel structures – that is, structures unmanipulated by totalitarian power: parallel information networks, cultural and educational institutions, parallel foreign contacts.

On the one hand, therefore, we have Patočka's perspective: the Charter is purely apolitical, a matter for *inner* decision of all those who take part; it appeals to something elementary and prepolitical, something that forms a basis for political behavior, but which is not in itself political. On the other hand we have Benda's point of view: in signing the Charter, each signatory in effect joins *other* signatories, and this, in effect, is a political act. Even though the Charter entered the world with unpolitical assumptions, it established a parallel polis, which is a political community, and this fact cannot simply be ignored or glossed over. Moreover, the intrinsically political nature of the Charter represents its most powerful weapon, enabling it to confront totalitarian power and realize its moral ideals even in unfavorable circumstances.

III

Patočka's exegesis of the Charter is strongly reminiscent of the Socratic point of view, of Socrates's way of coming to terms with social and political crisis in the Athens of his time. Before concerning yourself with public matters, Socrates urged his fellow citizens, pay heed to *"wisdom and truth and the perfection of [their] soul."*[47] His concern for prepolitical matters is, in a certain sense, more important than political activity. According to Socrates, only a man alert to the truth, a man of inner discipline, integrity and responsibility, is capable of being a good citizen, or rather a politician.

It seems to me that something quite similar echoes from the words of Patočka's conversations on the nonpolitical character of Charter 77. Anyone who publicly supports the Charter with his or her signature has, in effect, sent this message to those who hold power: I hereby retire from the game you've been forcing on the people of this country. It is a false and immoral game, and I've simply had enough.

Just as Socrates did not take part in the degenerate political life in Athens, but instead spent his time talking with his fellow citizens, mainly the young, examining the assumptions on which some future political action might be based, so Patočka claimed that the Chartists have nothing to do with politics, as it is generally understood, a politics that thinks only of power and acts from motives of success and fear.

> *The participants in Charter 77 do not seek any political role or privilege for themselves, and least of all do they wish to be any moral authority or social conscience. They condemn no one and judge no one. Their sole concern is to purify and reinforce the awareness that there is a higher authority, binding on individuals in virtue of their consciences, and on governments in virtue of their signature on important international treaties, placing them under an obligation not only when it suits them, not only within the limits of political*

---

[47] Plato: *Apology,* 29e. Quoted from *Plato in Twelve Volumes,* Vol. 1 translated by Harold North Fowler; Introduction by W.R.M. Lamb. Cambridge, MA, Harvard University Press; London, William Heinemann Ltd. 1966, https://www.perseus. tufts.edu/hopper/text?doc=Perseus%3Atext%3A1999.01.0170%3Atext%3DApol.

*convenience and inconvenience, but by their commitment,
represented by their signature, to subordinate politics to
justice, not vice versa.*[48]

But let us carry the analogy a step further. The figure of Socrates is far more paradoxical, for although he refuses to take part in politics, although he, figuratively speaking, retreats from the public square of Athens into the back streets, where he carries on conversations that have nothing to do with the political agenda of the day, it is he who, in the end, comes to embody Athenian virtues that are, in the true sense of the word, political. Such virtues had been gradually disappearing from Athenian public life. Socrates towers above the grey Athenians around him because he has an active interest not just in private matters, but also in matters he believes to be important to the community. It is Socrates, and not those who condemn him, who is capable of the activity which puts him in danger of losing his life. Nor does he retreat, but prefers death to giving up his cause.

*Therefore I say to you, men of Athens, either do as Anytus
tells you, or not, and either acquit me, or not, knowing that
I shall not change my conduct even if I am to die many times
over.*[49]

Perhaps it will not sound like an exaggeration if I say that Jan Patočka, too, ended his life as a philosopher in the Socratic mould; as a philosopher who withdrew from the *Agora,* from the place that represented the center of political life, not because he surrendered it to irresponsible usurpers and politicians blinded by power, so he could go on philosophizing somewhere in peace, but in order to reveal, and even at the cost of his life, once more to make public the meaning of political activity, the only thing that can become the cornerstone of any future political sphere.

There is only one sense in which our analogy falters. Whereas Socrates was unsuccessful in his political reform of Athens, and instead became the founder of a European philosophical tradition, Patočka's

---

[48] Jan Patočka : *The Obligation to Resist Injustice*. In: Erazim Kohák: *Jan Patočka. Philosophy and Selected Writings*, p. 342
[49] Plato: *Apology*, 30b

philosophical act changed the public face of his society in a genuinely essential way. Within a community that had been paralyzed for decades by totalitarian mechanisms, and whose citizens appeared to be asleep, enchanted by some black magic, a new community was awakened, independent of the first one. It is this fact, this heritage, left behind by the philosopher, to which Václav Benda turns his attention with such urgency.

IV

Regardless of how influential Patočka's thinking was, the independent community that arose from it is in no sense a community of philosophers. On the contrary, the great majority of those who live in it don't think philosophically, nor are they in any particular way interested in philosophy. To the question what is keeping them together, then, despite vast individual differences, a single answer may be given: it is precisely what the totalitarian system denies them in the first place – freedom.

Are we not offered a prototype, through which we can come close to the events in that polis which Benda described by the adjective "parallel," precisely in the polis of ancient times, in the ideal of civil freedom on which it is based, and in the political action for which it opens up space?

But today there is one basic difference. If we mention freedom, we almost automatically assume that it means freedom of will, that quality of an individual who is free to the extent that he acts according to his own lights, his own decisions, and, on the contrary, resists submitting to arbitrary decisions forced on him from outside. Whether this will is conceived of as mere willfulness (i.e., the power to do whatever one wants), or whether one sees it as the capacity to submit voluntarily to a higher principle and act in accord with one's responsibilities, either to God, or to oneself, or to one's humanity – in one aspect the same thing is always involved.[50]

For man to be free, he must disengage himself from all external things, the course of which he cannot influence anyway, and withdraw into himself: this is what the Stoic philosopher advises.

---

[50] Hannah Arendt: *What is Freedom.* In: *Between Past and Future,* p. 143-171

Do not love this world, take no care for its fleeting glories, rewards or wisdom, and cleave entirely to eternal truths, to one's God, in expectation of His Kingdom. Only that will make you free: this is what Christian faith says.

Freedom is primarily freedom from politics, and consists in the guarantees that every individual must have, so that he may in peace and security devote his energies to his private affairs: this is what the theoreticians of liberalism claim.

Don't get mixed up in anything and look out for yourself: this is the decadent opinion of modern bourgeois man.

However different these points of view are, the point on which they agree is obvious: freedom is something that is directed inwards, away from a world that has succumbed to vanity, from the labyrinth of the world to the paradise of the heart, to the cultivation of one's immortal soul, from public affairs towards private interests.

I would say that the Greek notion of freedom was just the opposite. The citizen of Athens was not free when he was by himself, his own master, among his possessions, in private, where, in our modern view of things, he could do what he wanted. On the contrary, he became free the moment he left this private space and went out into the community – when he spent his time among those who were not subordinated to his power, but among his equals, his fellow citizens, with those who were as free as he was. It was important not just that he had the right to take part in public affairs, that he could speak in the agora or do what he thought was to the good of the community, but also the fact that he did so in the presence of others, who at the same time could see him and hear him, and judge his actions and his words; who could either agree with him, or oppose him, yet always recognizing him as a person capable of free action.

Unlike our conception, this notion of freedom was essentially political. It was not free will, but rather free initiative. It did not depend merely on the abilities or qualities of isolated individuals, on their private possibilities or outlooks, but it was conditional on the freedom of others around him. It was not a matter of the state of one's soul, but rather of the state of the world.

It seems to me that precisely here is the core of the argument that Benda opposes to Patočka's conception of Charter 77. For Benda, what creates the identity of the "dissident," what differentiates the citizen of the independent community from the other members of society, does not consist in any higher morality or greater love of truth, nor in his ability to carry on a philosophical dialogue, but in his conception of freedom. There are people who have ceased to perceive freedom, as those around them do, as free will (which one can cultivate in private) and have once again begun to understand it in the Greek way: as something essentially political, as initiative. These are not apolitical people, as Patočka stressed; far from it. On the contrary, they are people who, thanks to their experience with totalitarianism, which utterly deprived them of a political dimension to their lives, have rediscovered and are now experiencing that which politics originally was. They have experienced the meaning of free behavior.

In this situation, the decision to create a parallel polis cannot be understood as a step away from the world, as an escape from the contemporary crisis, which is first and foremost a political crisis. On the contrary, it is a step into the world, to the very focus of what is happening, into politics, a step taken in the belief that it is only personal risk and personal initiative, regardless of how meaningless and unimportant it may seem to the powers that rule this world, that can bring about a cure.

The place of the independent community in the wider context of Czech history can be determined only by the future. Perhaps much of what today seems important and fascinating to us, the things we talk and worry about, will prove to be merely marginal and will, in time, be forgotten. And on the contrary, perhaps something we are overlooking, something that is quietly and secretly at work among us, may with the distance of time become apparent. But there is one thing I believe can be said with certainty now: that the motives which brought the parallel polis into existence and thanks to which those who live in it have been moved to action, which changed the course of their lives in decisive ways, will certainly remain. For I believe that these motives are, at least from the human perspective, eternal.

Exercise 4

On Political Ideas in
the Period of Transition

The point of departure of this text is a controversy I got into a long time ago with Timothy Garton Ash. It bears on a question whether the revolutions of 1989 produced some new political ideas. We met several times in the hectic days of late November 1989, inside Prague's Magic Lantern theater, the temporary headquarters of the Civic Forum, the principal organ of our "Velvet Revolution." We spent hours debating the events that were evolving around us – I was their participant, he a "committed observer" – not knowing what their outcome was going to be, unable to grasp fully the fundamental fact that this frenzy around us was, indeed, a revolution, i.e. the process of history in the making.

A few months later Timothy Garton Ash published his account of the recent East Central European revolutions in the book *The Magic Lantern.*[51] Elaborating on a remark uttered by the French historian Francois Furet – *"With all the fuss and noise, not a single new idea has come out of Central Europe in 1989"*[52] – Ash stated in the last chapter of his book:

---

[51] Timothy Garton Ash: *The Magic Lantern. The Revolution of '89 Witnessed in Warsaw, Budapest, Berlin, and Prague,* Random House, New York, 1990. The edition quoted here: Timothy Garton Ash: *The Magic Lantern. The Revolution of '89 Witnessed in Warsaw, Budapest, Berlin, and Prague. With a New Afterword by the Author,* Vintage Books, A Division of Random House, Inc, New York, 1999.

[52] Furet's remark is quoted in Ralf Dahrendorf's seminal *Reflections on the Revolution in Europe,* the first major reflection on the events of *annus mirabilis* 1989, written in the spring of 1990. I am quoting here from its second edition (Ralf Dahrendorf: *Reflections on the Revolution in Europe,* Transaction Publishers, New Brunswick (U.S.A) and London (U.K), 2005, p. 27

> *The ideas, whose time has come are old, familiar, well-
> tested ones. (It is the new ideas whose time has passed.)*[53]

When I read this diagnosis, I intuitively disagreed. It was, however, the only thing I could do about it. The basic argument of Ash and Furet seemed to be unbeatable (if you believe that some new political ideas have emerged in 1989, tell me what these new ideas are!).

Nevertheless, observing what was happening after Communism's sudden collapse, my doubts were rising. History certainly did not end with the final victory of Western liberalism, as Francis Fukuyama speculated already in his famous article from the summer of 1989,[54] but its new chapter has begun, carrying all planetary mankind from the 20th to the 21st century.

Would it be possible to say that one of the fundamental problems of the transitions begun 1989 is the endemic deficiency of the epistemological perspective of Ash and Furet? Shouldn't we admit that the political ideas which emerged in the European revolutions, were in a certain sense "new?" That it is exactly their novelty that still needs to be grasped, thought through and properly articulated?

Several times I tried to share my concerns with my distinguished British colleague, but without much success. Here is one of his reactions:

> *One claim I made in the last chapter of The Magic Lantern
> has been the subject of controversy. This is my assertion
> that the revolutionaries, or postrevolutionaries, brought to
> the new Europe of the 1990s "no fundamentally new
> ideas." (That was, incidentally, another reason Furet gave
> for not considering it to be a proper revolution.) I have been
> challenged on this by old friends and participants in the
> revolutions, including Czech philosopher Martin Palouš.
> They have not yet, however, managed to reveal to me what
> major new idea about the arrangement of human society
> emerged from 1989.*[55]

---

[53] Timothy Garton, Ash, op.cit., p. 154
[54] Francis Fukuyama: *The End of History*, National Interest, 1989, pp. 3-18
[55] Timothy Garton Ash: *The World Turned Right Side Up*, Hoover Digest, 2000, No. 1. The same argument is repeated in *Ten Years After: Afterword to the Vintage edition* (Timothy Garton Ash: *The Magic Lantern. The Revolution of '89 Witnessed in*

I am aware that what has been at stake here are not just the methodological differences between an Anglo-Saxon empiricist and a Central European phenomenologist, as Ash once put it. The core of this difficulty has its *fundamentum in re* – articulated more than half century ago by Hannah Arendt, who pointed in her seminal work on modern revolutions to the fact that the political ideas inspiring revolutionaries usually got lost *"through the failure of thought and remembrance"*[56] in the post-revolutionary aftermath!

And here are my questions: Is this loss an unavoidable consequence of any revolutionary action? Could it be prevented? What actually were the principal political ideas igniting the European revolution of 1989? Are these ideas still relevant in our new historical situation? Can they be retrieved from their oblivion?

Dahrendorf's "Reflections" Read Again in 2016

When Dahrendorf wrote his *Reflections on the Revolutions in Europe* in March 1990, the political processes in East Central Europe initiated by the events of 1989 were only in their early stage. The fall of Communism brought a new energy to the whole region, and the euphoric atmosphere of sudden liberation was still prevailing. In the postscript to the 2nd edition of his book Dahrendorf explained how it came into existence:

In February of 1990, he participated at a conference in Warsaw with a number of current revolutionaries and distinguished political theorists in attendance. Unexpectedly, they received an invitation to visit Polish President Jaruzelski – a man who declared martial law in Poland in 1981, sent thousands of Solidarność activists to jail, but agreed in the end to hold the Round Table Talks with the non-Communist opposition and enabled the peaceful transfer of power. His invitation was accepted. When the meeting started, President Jaruzelski opened the conversation:

What does it all mean, and where is it going to lead.....? Are

---

Warsaw, Budapest, Berlin, and Prague. With a New Afterword by the Author, Vintage Books, A Division of Random House, Inc, New York, 1999, p.162)
[56] Hannah Arendt: *On Revolution*, p. 221

> *we not witnessing a process of dissolution without anything
> taking place of the old and admittedly dismal structures?*

And he literally "showered" his visitors with a stream of follow up questions.[57]

As soon as Dahrendorf – who, according to his own words, *"felt rather ashamed to be unable to give sensible answers"*[58] to President Jaruzelski's questions – returned back to the *"quiet of his Oxford study, "*[59] he immediately started to work on them in writing. Looking for a proper genre for his reply, he decided on the form of *"a letter to a gentleman in Warsaw "*[60] – seeking inspiration in Edmund Burke, a conservative British thinker who wrote a similar letter in 1790, *to a very young gentleman at Paris.*[61]

Here is Burke's central point concerning the actual course of the French Revolution:

> *You see, Sir, by the long letter I have transmitted to you, that
> though I do most heartily wish that France may be animated
> by a spirit of rational liberty, and that I think you bound, in
> all honest policy, to provide a permanent body in which that
> spirit may reside, and an effectual organ by which it may
> act, it is my misfortune to entertain great doubts concerning
> several material points in your late transactions.* [62]

Dahrendorf's treatise soon became a seminal work of "transitology" – a kind of branch of political science born as a consequence of the revolutions of 1989, developed in the following years by the armies of scholars of all ideological orientations. For the further later editions Dahrendorf wrote a new postscript in 2004 and added also a short introduction. Here he raised a question: *"Should the analysis not*

---

[57] Ralf Dahrendorf : *Reflections on the Revolution in Europe*, the 2nd Edition, Transaction Publishers, New Brunswick (U.S.A) and London (U.K), 2005, p. 4

[58] Dahrendorf, op. cit., p. 167

[59] Op.cit., p. 3

[60] Op.cit. p. ix

[61] Edmund Burke: *Reflection on the French Revolution*. In: *Selected Works of Edmund Burke, Volume 1*, Methuen and London, 1905, p. 14 (quoted from https://www. files.ethz.ch/isn/125465/603.pdf)

[62] Ibid.

have been updated, or revised in the light of later evidence?" And he answered to himself:

> *This would have been impossible. The book itself has become a document of the time for which it was written and its argument remains as reminder of the power and the limitations of social analysis applied to contemporary events.*[63]

It is exactly Dahrendorf's awareness of his own limitations that makes his book a valuable reading still today. Nowhere else is his epistemic humility better demonstrated than in its end where he expressed the hope that in the light of his candid arguments the actors in the current European revolution would be willing *"to reconsider some of (their) less persuasive ambitions:"*[64]

> *I have little to recommend my opinions, but long observation and much impartiality........I also like the way Burke winds up his epistle by describing himself as one who "when the equipoise of the vessel in which he sails may be endangered by over-loading it upon one side, is desirous of carrying the small weight of his reason to that which may preserve its equipoise." Is there a more measured way of describing a countercyclical view of things? Liberty above all is what I believe in. The goal may be obvious, but the path to it has many pitfalls. We can help overcome some of them, but for the most part our own energy and sense of purpose are called for. The rest is luck. I keep my fingers crossed and hope for the best. This I do with all my heart.*[65]

What can be said about Dahrendorf's book when reread in 2016? There are two points to be made on the positive side of the balance sheet:

First, it is Dahrendorf's general evaluation of 1989 which profoundly differs from the one offered by Ash and Furet:

> *The revolution of 1989 has changed Europe. It has changed the world. In my own life, and in my understanding of the*

---

[63] Dahrendorf, op.cit., p. vii
[64] Op.cit, p. 164
[65] Ibid.

world, it marks a turning point as important as 1789.[66]

The collapse of the bi-polar political architecture has not only fundamentally changed East Central Europe, but had a much bigger impact: it brought the whole "short" 20th century – the "age of extremes," as Eric Hobsbawm put it – to its end.[67]

If this premise is accepted, its consequences for "transitology" are enormous. What swept through East Central Europe in the :year of miracles had to be conceived as other big modern revolutionary transformations.

If we can agree with Hannah Arendt that *"the revolutions of the modern age appear like gigantic attempts to repair these foundations, to renew the broken thread of tradition, and to restore, through founding new political bodies, what for so many centuries had endowed the affairs of men with some measure of dignity and greatness,"*[68] we should use the same yardstick also for the phenomena that can be observed in the connection with our 1989.

What must be analyzed is not only what has been so far achieved by the "post-totalitarian" societies in East Central Europe themselves in their "return to Europe," and what preconditioned these achievements: their geopolitical determinants; their economic potential and actual performance; their mentalities, cultures and spiritual traditions; their bigger or smaller capacity to conform in their new social and political life to the rules of Western democracy.

What must be also studied are the broader horizons within which their journey from Communism has been taking place; a crisis that has stricken European civilization in the 20th century; the current process of globalization in which we all – both Europeans and non-Europeans, all global mankind - are finding ourselves in the beginning of the new millennium.

---

[66] Op.cit., p. 178

[67] Eric Hobsbawm: *The Age Of Extremes, A History of the World 1914-1991*, Vintage Books, , New York, 1996

[68] Hannah Arendt: *What is Authority*. In: *Between Past and Future. Eight Exercises in Political Thought*, p. 140

Second, what has clearly passed the test of time is Dahrendorf's Burkeian liberal conservativism. Indeed, nothing much has changed between 1790 and 1990. The central problem of post-Communist countries was, indeed, the one of Edmund Burke and linked with *"spirit of rational liberty"* he was so much concerned about that he decided to write *"a letter to a very young gentleman at Paris"* – *"entertaining great doubt concerning several material points"* in *"late transactions"* of French revolutionaries: how *"to provide a permanent body in which that spirit may reside?"* How to create a new body politic, after an outlived, "ancient" regime has been displaced or simply fell apart? How to transform the profoundly negative force of revolution into the architectonic power of lawmaking and city-building? How to follow the American rather than the French example and found a new political order *"without violence and with the help of a constitution?"*[69]

As far as this fundamental question, Dahrendorf's answer was stern, clear and absolutely right:

East-Central Europeans could only succeed in their efforts to free themselves from their totalitarian yoke by reintroducing the rule of law in their countries; by recreating all institutions of freedom in their societies; by restoring the political culture based on civic values. What had to be strongly rejected in the moment of revolutionary change were all proposals based upon utopian visions of a "just" society – ending usually in a temporary reign of terror and virtue and followed by restoration of some form of illiberal order.

If the revolutions of 1989 were really to constitute the order of liberty, the main trust should have been put in free republican institutions. It was not the *"pure ethics of conviction,"*[70] what should have driven the politics of transition forward, but the *"practical ethics of responsibility."*[71] It was the political will to moderate revolutionary radicalism; to follow the advice of common sense and start the standard democratic political processes as soon as possible. It was the readiness of revolutionaries to reintroduce the habits and practices of the established Western

---

[69] Ibid.
[70] Dahrendorf, op.cit., p. 11
[71] Op.cit., pp. 10-11

democracies, in spite of all their imperfections, difficulties and problems. It was their conscious return to *"old, familiar, well-tested ideas"*[72] and among them to the idea of the *"open society"* of Dahrendorf's teacher Karl Popper.

Let's look now at the situation after 1989 on the ground. What can be said now about the concrete policies of transition launched after the European revolutions of 1989? The main message of Dahrendorf's candid recommendations was a warning against too much of revolutionary zeal.

The revolutions of 1989 clearly demonstrated the will of the people to get rid of Soviet totalitarianism. The will itself, however, could not have provided directions how to turn freedom, miraculously re-gained, into worldly – i.e. stable and lasting – realities.

Exactly for this reason the liberation struggle was far from over according to Dahrendorf when he was writing his letter to a gentleman in Warsaw. The removal of Communists from power has not terminated the fundamental conflict accompanying European history from its beginning until today – the conflict *"between advocates of systems (side of illiberalism) and defenders of the open society."*

"Defenders of the open society" should have kept struggling after the European revolutions of 1989 in the battle of ideas. They were advised by Dahrendorf *"to go back to the 1780s, to the lessons of the great transformations of that time"* and to use *The Federalist Papers, as an " manual of liberal democracy. "*[73] And they should have been principled in this matter:

> *"The choice between freedom and serfdom is stark and clear, and it offers no halfway house for those weaker souls who would like to avoid making up their minds. "*[74]

What was to be distinguished and executed separately in the confrontation with "illiberals" – *"those weaker souls"* that were still around after the recent round of European revolutions – were three

---

[72] Op.cit, pp. 27,28
[73] Op.cit. p. 30
[74] Op.cit. p. 62.

different tasks of politics of transition that should be undertaken in the proper order, one after another.

The first task was the democratic constitution. What came right after the revolution was the *"hour of constitutional lawyers"* who had the task to lay down the foundations of a new democratic state.

Then *"normal"* politics was to burst in, *the hour of politicians –* where there are literarily a *"hundred ways and we can forever learn from one another in framing our own – your own, my own, everybody's or at least every country's own – pattern of economic or social progress."*[75]

The economic reform should be designed and successfully implemented on in its political context. There is no pattern or even a system to be just replicated or copied.

The key and the lengthiest process, however, was connected with the third problem: the emerging civil society. The *"hour of citizens"* had to come after the *"hour of constitutional lawyers"* and the *"hour of politicians."*

> *The third condition of the road to freedom is to provide the social foundation which transforms the constitution and the economy from fair-weather into all-weather institutions capable of withstanding the storms generated within and without, and sixty years are barely enough to lay these foundations.*[76]

There is no doubt that different nature of the three different tasks on the agenda of post-Communist transitions was more than once confirmed in all post-Communist countries. In reality, however, these tasks were usually not coming in an orderly sequence. They had to be rather carried out simultaneously – with constitutional lawyers, politicians and citizens not having separate "hours" for their "solo" actions, but doomed to cooperate, influencing each other, arguing with each other, leading dialogues together, correcting their specific missteps in the light of their common, shared transitional experience.

It is quite significant what Dahrendorf himself openly recognized in his postscript from 1999: *"that the weakest part of the Reflections is*

---

[75] Op.cit. p. 66
[76] Op.cit., p. 100

that about the European and international context. "[78] It is here where one could have observed things happening in the post-revolutionary period that simply could not have been foreseen in the first stage of the reopening of closed societies of East and Central Europe and as such were not factored into Dahrendorf's interpretative framework.

The problem that seemed to be entirely omitted by him was the close interaction between the changes taking place at home and in the international domain. What was happening in the region liberated after Communism's sudden collapse was not just the process of democratization, but the multiple transitions – not only *"one transition, but rather the conjuncture among domestic, regional and international systems in transition."*[80]

The collapse of the regimes in East Central Europe was accompanied by the collapse of an empire! As result of that, three states – Czechoslovakia, Yugoslavia and the Soviet Union – fell apart and were replaced – under different circumstances, with different outcomes and further consequences – by their successors.

With respect to all these fragmentations, some questions have arisen: Is the agenda of state or nation-building compatible with the agenda of democratization? Is it not true that these two processes have only rarely gone hand-in-hand in Europe's past? What actually is the consequence of this "hard" fact for the process of post-Communist transitions?

And more questions can easily follow based on observations of the current situation. If we want to analyze the post-totalitarian development in its entirety – if we want to understand the basic patterns of post-totalitarian political culture and behavior – we certainly should also pay attention not only to the revolutionary ideas, but also to the bulk of collective historical experience; to that "state of mind" in which the post-totalitarian societies were finding themselves after their glorious "reopening" to the rediscovery of complicated East and Central European history; to the impact of their reawakened national sentiments! We should seek to understand the basic "mental" condition of postCommunism – the

---

[78] Op. cit., p. 175
[80] Cf. Valery Bunce: *Leaving Socialism a Transition to Democracy*, in: Contention, vol. 3, no. 1, Fall 1993, p. 35-47

reinvention of politics after the demise of the last version of the 20th century totalitarianism – on the one hand rooted in the past; but at the same time confronted with the new uncertainties and threats coming to our world from the unknown future.

To summarize my argument here: the developments which followed after the collapse of Communism have simply shown that Dahrendorf's sharp distinction *"between serfdom and freedom,"* the concept of post-totalitarian politics as a conflict *"between advocates of systems (side of illiberalism) and defenders of the open society,"* proved also to be an ideological simplification. Interpreting the post-Communist transitions just as reopenings of temporarily closed societies, and seeing the principal problem of the societies of East Central Europe in transition as a "stark choice" between just two options, with no "third way" between them, Dahrendorf simply missed what was and still is at stake.

The return to Europe of post-Communist countries has from the very beginning had not only its local or regional aspects, but also its universal, or rather global dimensions connected with the spiritual and political crisis of the West in general. It has never been just a question how to get rid of an already very rusty and entirely unattractive version of European Communism. It was not only the matter of homecoming of post-totalitarians, their sometimes relatively easy, sometimes toilsome march from the "Babylonian captivity" in the Soviet Empire to the European "paradise" of plenty, but the beginning of a new era in the history of mankind; the arrival of "the post-European age" – the age of globalization characterized by the definitive end of European hegemony in worldly matters accompanied by the resurgence of other, i.e. non-European civilizations.

My personal experience with the process of post-Communist transition

I was a freshman at Charles University in Prague in the fall of 1968 and was looking – as anybody else at the age of eighteen – for some basic orientation in his adult life. The spring of that year brought the breeze of fresh air to Czechoslovakia, but the promising attempt of the Communist reformers to democratize socialism and "endow it with a human face" was terminated by the invasion of Warsaw Pact armies on the night from August 20 to 21. As a result of this act of aggression, Communist orthodoxy returned to Czechoslovakia and a loyal, ideologically "correct," but highly opportunistic "normalization" regime was reinstalled step by step. The initially-declared intention of the Communist leadership to preserve the "ideals" of January and continue the process of "rejuvenation" of socialism turned out to be a plain, "tactical" lie from the very beginning. The people's will to resist this reversal – demonstrated in an unprecedented manner during the protests in the days after the occupation – was marvelous, fascinating, soul-breaking, but all in vain. Within a couple of months it was evident that every Czechoslovak citizen would have to make one of three elementary choices in the new situation: to stay in the country and get in line with the restored totalitarian order; to go into exile; to resist the process of normalization at home on one's own terms and suffer the consequences of this resistance.

Since neither the acceptance of the "social contract" the normalizers were offering, nor emigration were attractive to me, only the third choice was left. Its consequence, however, was that I had to reconcile myself with the fact that under the given circumstances, the academic career I was preparing myself for was gone; that the only option left for me was a kind of "inward journey" from the outside world poisoned by current politics, into the internal sphere where I could enjoy at least certain fundamental inalienable personal freedoms – first of all freedom of conscience, the freedom of thought and, to a certain limited extent, the freedom of expression.

Setting myself on this road, I discovered the world of classical philosophy, literature and art. I became a devout disciple of Jan Patočka who continued teaching in private/semiclandestine seminars after he had definitively lost his position in the Philosophical Faculty of Charles University.

The decision to resist the pressures of normalization hadn't opened only the world of philosophy and classical thought for me, but also introduced me to a group of like-minded people who were also determined not to yield – composed mostly of all sorts of intellectuals and artists who had participated in the revival of the free spirit in Czechoslovakia during the 1960s and were being expelled again from official public life for their non-conformist attitudes. On the one hand I renounced my ambition for a life in academia, but at the same time I established a number of new friendships. I got involved in various forms of underground activities, dialogues and communications taking place out of the reach of state control or its ideological supervision.

Having made my choice freely, I could hardly be blackmailed anymore and lured by the prospects of professional development in the framework of a society being normalized. When I was acquainted in December of 1976 with the text of Charter 77, I signed it without hesitation – inspired by Patočka's Socratic arguments and his personal example – and voluntarily accepted, together with other several hundred individuals, the lot of being connected with the "citizenship" in the nascent body of political "dissidents" that Václav Benda a year later called the "parallel polis."

For more than a decade then I was living surrounded by its inhabitants, participating at all sorts of forms of its "parallel," i.e. essentially free and independent activities. It was there that I experienced my third encounter with freedom when a real opportunity for profound historical change of the European political architecture finally occurred.

Looking back now at my overall 1989 experience it is obvious that from the very beginning of this "year of miracles" there were growing signs around us that a profound political transformation was on the way. I was still utterly unaware of what was coming, unable – as many others, including Václav Havel – to realize what this would mean for our lives. And when the things started to happen, I was, I have to admit, again and again, taken by surprise.

For sure, I was actively participating in more and more political forms of life of Charter 77 – originally constituted only as an open space for "human rights dialogue" and for other independent activities resisting the practices of the totalitarian state, but not conceived originally as a platform for formulation and implementation of political alternatives.

I was used – already for a couple of years – as its spokesperson in 1986 – to the significant intensification of contacts with Western diplomats in the context of the so-called "Helsinki process," affected in the second half of the 1980s by both Gorbachev's "perestroika" and Reagan's more assertive policies towards the East, forcing the Soviet leader to open a new round of talks between two main nuclear superpowers guaranteeing the status quo on the divided European continent.

I participated in several street demonstrations during that year, beginning with Palach Week where I got my first opportunity to address briefly the gathered crowd of people.

I took into consideration that our regular philosophical "symposion" at Václav Havel's country-house had to be cancelled in 1989, because of other more timely commitments of its participants.

I had a chance to meet in Prague the Polish dissidents, already in power and coming for a visit as members of the Sejm, with their brand new diplomatic passports.

I observed the German exodus in Prague, and took note of the fall of the Berlin Wall.

I marched with students at their demonstration on November 17.

As a member of Charter 77's inner circle I was among the founders of Civic Forum created two days later and immediately got involved in its hectic, indeed revolutionary activities.

But it was only in the weeks that followed I started to realize that we might have really made it; that what was going on around me was a real revolution; that my tomorrow was going be qualitatively different from my yesterday; that I was finding myself in an entirely new situation, at the beginning of a new chapter of our national history.

My general experience concerning the way Civic Forum, a self-appointed steering body of the Velvet Revolution, operated, only further illustrates my previous comment. The political events we were part of kept surprising us again and again. They were always somehow faster than our ability to understand them. There was no time and no space for revolutionary political ideologies or utopian plans. Our actions were always sheer improvisations, and certainly not premeditated steps to implement well-defined policies with clearly-stated goals

The daily consultations after Civic Forum had been founded in the late evening of November 19 in the Činoherní klub theater – first taking place in a small art gallery "U Řečických," then in Mánes, then in Laterna

Magica, and finally in so-called Špalíček – were all marked by our quite specific and unforgettable collective mindset – on the one hand determined and unscared, but at the same time more playful and relaxed than stern and deadly serious; a mindset formed in the years of the collective existence of most members of our "revolutionary team" within the "parallel polis."

First we were a group of no more than 30-40 individuals permanently debating, being overwhelmed by all the news coming. We were constantly pressed by time and needed to make quick decisions on the spot, prepare responses to the actions or proposals of our opponents; organize our own activities in the immediate future – usually in the next day, but sometimes within the next hours; trying to learn how to improvise "in concert," but always exposed to some new unexpected challenges, dilemmas, and opportunities. Here are the basic clusters of "questions" we had to deal with:

What should be the basic demands of Civic Forum, whose negotiators started to communicate with the representatives of the Czechoslovak Government only a few days after the outbreak of the revolution?

How to keep alive the jazzy atmosphere that attracted more and more people to the squares and streets and keep enlarging the spontaneous public support for our demands?

How to disseminate the basic messages of Civic Forum all over the country, because it was Prague where the revolution started and which became the central locus of all its most important, and most visible activities?

How to keep the cooperation between Civic Forum and the students' Strike Committee strong and effective? How to keep pushing things forward based on our own deliberations and at the same time respect the fact that what was going on was primarily a students' revolution?

How to deal with the fact that the cooperation between Czechs and Slovaks in the days of the Velvet Revolution immediately brought back some of the old national habits and long-sleeping dichotomies?

What message was to be conveyed to the Armed Forces which decided, in spite of dangerous hopes of certain factions of the Communist leadership to stay in their barracks and let the political communications between the Government and Civic Forum go on at their own pace and direction?

What kind of technical international assistance should we ask for? How to use effectively the presence of Western journalists and all channels of communication with our international partners created in the past decade in the context of the Helsinki Process?

Maybe the biggest challenge to which we were exposed as the founders of Civic Forum, however, was not so much its external operations, but this entity itself, its own development and expansion. The power of improvisation characterizing our first steps was astonishing, but it certainly had its limits. Within days it was obvious that the independent spirit of the "parallel polis" of the dissidents that brought Civic Forum into existence would have to be replaced by, or at least complemented with, more efficient methods of political work, communications and institution-building. The more weight and power Civic Forum was getting, the more urgent was the necessity to change its whole *modus operandi*. But it had to be achieved democratically, i.e. not by means of directives coming from a close circle of revolutionary leaders, but after proper deliberation and by consensus of all the participants!

As the revolution progressed and the prospects for success were rising, there were not only more and more people joining Civic Forum all over Czechoslovakia. All of a sudden here were important players on the scene arriving from the world very different from our "parallel polis," having their own specific expectations and subscribing to their own institutional culture. There is no doubt that the appearance of Václav Klaus, Valter Komárek, Vladimir Dlouhý, Miloš Zeman and other economists from the Institute of Scientific Prognosis meant for us a tremendous boost. Maybe it was even one of the decisive moments sending out a clear message to the public: that it was not just a bunch of the "usual suspects" in action here; that a serious political game was in progress; that a real transformation was already knocking at the door; that the times in Czechoslovakia were really changing.

Based on my own observations and participatory experience I would argue: those who say today that the main leaders of the Velvet Revolution – and first of all Václav Havel, who played a special and the most visible role in the whole drama – were inspired by and tried to implement some utopian ideas of a new political order, are simply wrong. The vision of a democratic political system dominated by popular movements voicing directly the people's will – existing without standard Western political parties acting within the framework of parliamentary democracy – was never on the table during our discussions. The subject of our debates during the revolutionary weeks was not a final desirable outcome of our efforts – a vision of democracy to be achieved – but our daily strategic goals: first, the concrete steps, which resulted within two weeks in the demise of the "ancien regime," and then, after its representatives decided to yield to our demands, the basic framework and the first priorities of the coming post-Communist transformation.

The tasks theoretically defined by Dahrendorf and their practical solutions in real life turned out to be two different things. As I have said earlier they were certainly not coming one after another, but had to be rather carried out simultaneously, in a process specifically tailored to the concrete circumstances of the Czechoslovak case, with all the necessary players – including those who were sitting on the other side of the negotiating table – cooperating!

The sequence in which the transition of power took place in Czechoslovakia during the Velvet Revolution – a solution of the social and political crisis negotiated between the representatives of Civic Forum and the Government in the weeks after November 17 – is well known, so I will repeat here only its principal milestones:

On November, 24, the whole leadership of the Communist Party stepped down.

On December 3, based on the proposal sent to the National Assembly by the Government, Article 4 about the leading role of Communist Party in Czechoslovakia, was removed from the socialist constitution.

On December 10, the Government of National Understanding was formed. President Husák announced the same day his abdication.

On December 28, the Law on the Co-optation of New Deputies was passed by the National Assembly; based on this legislative act the first group of new deputies was co-opted as a replacement for those deputies who had resigned their seats in the previous weeks; and finally one of them, Alexander Dubček, the leader of the reform wing of the Communist Party during the Prague Spring, was elected President of the National Assembly.

On December 29, Václav Havel was elected President of Czechoslovakia.

January – February of 1990, the process of further co-optations continued and changed profoundly the composition of all principal legislative organs of Czechoslovakia (the National Assembly, the Czech and Slovak National Councils), in order to reflect the new power constellation and enable the beginning of the process of political transformation.

At this time Civic Forum obviously had a quite different structure and composition than it had at its beginning. It had its Coordination Center in Prague (with tens of employees, a bunch of commissions and other organs in charge of various agendas). A network of its regional offices existed all over the country, staffed with local activists and future regional politicians. Its parliamentary clubs, both on the federal and the national levels, were formed and working.

At the same time, however, it was still a revolutionary body with a specific *modus operandi* and an uncertain future. The fundamental question was: should it be transformed into a real democratic political entity (a political party with its specific program and ideological identity) or rather be diffused somehow into the whole system of future Czechoslovak democracy which was still in the process of making?

During the first half of 1990 I was fully engaged in its activities. In spite of all the attractions and prestige connected with becoming, all of a sudden, a new politician, my personal plans for the future were somewhat different: with regard to my basic life orientation, I intended to free myself from the daily political engagement at the right moment and go to Leuven in Belgium to work on my doctoral thesis in phenomenological philosophy at the Husserl Archives. During the previous revolutionary phase I was one of Civic Forum's founders and became a member of its Steering Council, where I oversaw foreign relations. At the end of January I was co-opted into the Czechoslovak

Federal Parliament and served on its foreign relations committee. In spite all of that I decided not to run for a parliamentary seat in the June election, because I planned to start my philosophical studies. But things turned out differently for me. In the end I never made it to Leuven, and got trapped instead in the complicated new Czechoslovak political realities.

And here is the explanation. Already during the first half of 1990, many prominent activists of Civic Forum started to serve in various high state functions. Václav Havel and his closest team left for Prague Castle. Others were appointed members of new executive or legislative bodies or occupied vacant positions in the various institutions within the state administration. Others returned to their original professions, not being inclined to become politicians.

I was also a member of the Federal Parliament for the time being, but felt at the same time that somebody still needed to stay at Civic Forum's Coordination Centre and take responsibility for the continuation of its activities. So, I did. Its position within the hectic political life of the country in the first half of 1990 gained immense political gravity, but was becoming more and more precarious and challenging. The first months of political transformation based on the acts of new legislative bodies were bringing not only new freedoms for everybody, but created many new opportunities, especially for the people well connected with the "ancien regime," and logically generated also some bad feelings, disagreements and frustrations within the population at large. Those who remained at the Coordination Center of Civic Forum were finding themselves in a "perfect storm" situation – in daily contact with all sorts of local politicians coming from all over the country, messengers of bad news, various petitioners or just grumbling individuals trying to bring into the current fast political processes sometimes healthy, but often quite crazy and incoherent points of view.

The prospect of the first democratic election planned for June set the stage for a new round of political competition and, for obvious reasons, this was the priority number one among our political tasks in this period. Communication between the center and the regions turned out to be the biggest challenge. The political debate concerning the future of Civic Forum's ideological orientation was bursting out in this context, fed by the emerging experts in a "new science of politics" (the fast evolution of this "science" was certainly a very interesting part of the realities of transition), and first of all, by the aspiring politicians who tried to attract public attention and present themselves as the only right persons for the job.

The revolutionary unity of the first weeks after November 17 quickly disappeared, and the necessity foreseen by Dahrendorf to make the choice *"between freedom and serfdom,"* was presented by many as the central issue of the day. It was becoming more and more obvious that another round of the Velvet Revolution – this time the battle of ideas to lead the process of post-revolutionary transformation – was still to come.

It was no surprise then that the victorious election that legitimized the leading position of Civic Forum in Czechoslovakia's political life after the Velvet Revolution, didn't bring reconciliation to the parties to this conflict. On the contrary, it rather accelerated the process of the Civic Forum's internal polarization. During the summer of 1990, two antagonistic tendencies could be observed:

On the one side, there were intensive efforts – I was personally involved in them – not to unnecessarily bring any ideology into the internal debates within Civic Forum at the given moment and first to complete its institutional reform; to transform this revolutionary body composed of people with a variety of ideological points of view and life experience into a democratic political body able to perform its tasks and responsibilities based on the mandate given to it in the June election; to turn it into an efficient, action-oriented entity able to fulfil its election program.

On the other side, there was an increasingly vocal tendency, especially in the regions, to accelerate the transformation of Civic Forum into a "standard" ideologically defined right-wing political party; to win first the internal battle of ideas – first of all, with the group of "sixty-eighters" who were departing in the on-going internal Civic Forum debates about the direction and pace of transformation on their own political experience and orientation; who were subscribing in this context to their own "old-fashioned" concepts and visions.

The conflict between these two schools of thought culminated in the fall in the election of the Civic Forum's leadership. I ran for the position of chair of Civic Forum, representing the first of them, against

Václav Klaus, the Minister of Economy and the main proponent of fast economic liberalization. Because Klaus had launched a quite efficient campaign all over the country during the summer and enjoyed – as a seasoned, shrewd politician – the support of a strong faction of right-wingers elected on the Civic Forum ticket to the Parliament – several influential people around Václav Havel were also on his side – the result of this election was unsurprising: he won by an overwhelming majority of votes and I lost.

The election of Václav Klaus to the post of Civic Forum's chair, however, was – as could have been easily predicted – the beginning of its end. Six months later, the political body that carried the weight of the Velvet Revolution ceased to exist, splitting into the Civic Democratic Party, which fully identified itself with the new chairman's ideology, and the "rest." The time of unity in a broad revolutionary movement – a necessary condition for the revolution's success – came to its end and the era of "standard" political parties dominating the political scene of the re-born Czech democracy ever since, had begun.

What can be said about it today? The decision to go the way Václav Klaus and his associates and supporters chose in 1990 certainly cannot be reversed. A system of parliamentary democracy – with the "standard political parties" playing central role in it – has become a reality and it is a good thing. But the question, whether it was the only choice to achieve this goal – especially with regard to what we can observe more than quarter century later – still remains open, and my frank opinion is that this question deserves to be occasionally re-visited.

The special area of transition that needs to be at least mentioned in this account of my personal experience with it, is the domain of international relations. As I have already said, I was actively participating in the current on-going international debates already during the 1980s as one of the spokespersons of Charter 77 in the context of the "Helsinki Process," launched in 1975 to secure the "peaceful relations between the states with different social and political systems" in Europe.

The results of the Helsinki Conference contained in its Final Act were originally perceived by many as a victory of the Soviet leader Brezhnev, and the confirmation of the Soviet domination over East and

Central Europe formed after World War II. Its agreed human rights clauses (its "third basket"), however, had a surprising side effect. In spite of the fact that they were carefully formulated in perfect harmony with the principle of "non-intervention in the domestic matters" of the state-parties, they inspired a strong response "from below" in the whole East and Central European region, they led to the creation of Charter 77 and other similar initiatives in the countries of the Soviet bloc and opened a way out of the existing ideological stalemate.

First, there was hardly any visible change of our situation after the "Helsinki Process" started in the second half of the 1970s, but its immediate positive effects were twofold. It created at least some protective shield against the worst forms of human rights violations by the totalitarian Communist regimes and helped the further erosion of their monolithic power. It offered an opportunity to those who tried to resist their refined manipulatory devices developed in the past half century to keep the East and Central European nations in servitude, to internationalize their human rights struggle; to become a kind of "third party" in the current European inter-state discussions; to acquire at least some international legitimacy for their primarily domestic activities; to open for them new, essentially important and surprisingly efficient channels of international communication.

In the first revolutionary weeks our international relations were still evolving within this tradition. As "Head of the International Relations Department" of the Coordination Center of Civic Forum I kept regular communication with the key Western embassies and the international media covering Czechoslovak events. Especially, I remember the visit of the group of members of the US Congress in mid-December. Together with Ivan Gabal and Jan Urban, two other members of our team, we gave them a briefing in a hotel on Wenceslas Square and after that were asked to walk with them, surrounded by the CNN crew and at least twenty agents of the Czechoslovak secret police, who just observed what was happening and apparently had no instruction to place us under arrest, on Wenceslas Square, full of signs, posters and inscriptions indicating the omnipresence of the Velvet Revolution.

After the situation started to stabilize and the new political order was taking shape, it was obviously no longer Civic Forum, but the state institutions in transition where the first steps bringing us back to the free world were being made: the Government of National Understanding where Jiří Dienstbier, former dissident, political prisoner and Charter 77 spokesperson in 1979 and again in 1985, served as the Minister of Foreign Affairs; the re-constructed National Assembly, chaired at that moment by Alexander Dubček, which was in charge of legislative acts necessary to dismantle the "iron curtain" and for our international reopening; and, of course, President of the Republic Václav Havel, who was adored internationally as the uncontested leader of our Velvet Revolution and respected as a world statesman whose words and opinions really mattered and had tremendous weight at the current historical crossroads.

There is no doubt that it was Václav Havel's role at the given moment which was crucial for our way out of the Babylonian captivity we had been living for the long four decades. I still remember several of his first official visits abroad as President of Czechoslovakia, which I helped to arrange in my capacity in Civic Forum. The first one, on January 2 of 1990 went to the two German states (to Berlin and Munich), and the second one in February, went to Iceland, Canada and the United States, where Václav Havel met President Bush and addressed a joint session of the US Congress. Both trips carried the specific signs of the new era. The official delegations were much too big, measured by the "normal" standards of inter-state relations: President Havel and his closest entourage; an unusually large number of ministers with their advisors and assistants; artists; former dissidents previously involved in the Velvet Revolution; the representatives of students; the university rectors.....

The result was that the program in both cases was too complicated for a regular state visit, because everybody was keen to play a role in it and be part of what was perceived as a celebration of our freedom rather than an opportunity to open new relationships with our Western counterparts. A somewhat bizarre aspect of these trips was the fact that protocol and diplomatic formalities had to be taken care of by the individuals of the past, the diplomats, still working in their posts, loyal during their careers to the "ancien regime." Regardless of all sorts of

complications and eventual hiccups, the responses of all our partners –
most importantly of the Government of the United States – were
unambiguous and hopeful: they expressed their readiness to assist us in the
fulfilment of the basic objectives of our democratic transition.

Since the beginning of February, I also worked in the Foreign
Relations Committee of Czechoslovak Federal Parliament. In this capacity
I attended a regular meeting of the Inter-Parliamentary Union which took
place in Bonn, Germany in May. Again, I had an opportunity here to
communicate with several "old-timers" – for instance, the Czechoslovak
Ambassador to Germany Milan Kadnár or Bohuslav Kučera, the former
chair of the Socialist Party, who was the head of the Czechoslovak
delegation at this meeting – and to get familiar with their quite impressive
professional behavior and diplomatic skills. It was quite an interesting
message that I brought with me from Bonn to Prague, still living in the
heady atmosphere of the Velvet Revolution. The representatives of many
countries of the Global South certainly didn't share our current enthusiasm
and were observing the "happy" resolution of the East-West problem with
a certain suspicion.

But my most important exposure to the problems of Czechoslovak
international relations started when I accepted the offer after the June
election – originally I thought just for a couple of months – to become an
advisor at the Ministry for Foreign Affairs. Because that was the main
locus of all daily foreign political activities.

I need first to recall here once more what I have already stated in
other contexts: there was no clear preconceived plan, based on someone's
utopian visions (articulated, for instance, in Jiří Dienstbier's *Dreaming of
Europe*[81]), just to be turned into reality and implemented after our
victorious revolution. It was experience on the ground that was our
principle guide. Whatever idea the main architects of new Czechoslovak
foreign policies were coming with had to be tested against and
accommodated to the changing international realities; carefully thought
through and in consultation with all our strategic partners: in our

---

[81] Cf. Jiří Dienstbier: *Snění o Evropě* [Dreaming of Europe], Nakladatelství Lidových
novin, Praha, 1990

neighborhood; in Europe, now entering a new phase in the process of her integration; in the area of trans-Atlantic cooperation.

It is true that the "Helsinki Process" that had turned out to play a pivotal role in the historical turn just experienced, attracted our attention. What was tested first was the idea of its uses in the new situation, first of all its further institutionalization. The idea of NATO's and the EU's enlargements came, for obvious reasons, much later. It was certainly not for us, "post-totalitarians," just making the first steps on our way back to the Free World, to start this conversation.

One of the greatest challenges of the Foreign Ministry was actually again at home: How should it be transformed it from what it was in the past into an efficient, competent and at the same time democratic institution capable of fulfilling its tasks in the context of post-Communist transition? How could it use effectively its existing potential, both human and material, contained, for instance, in its archives? What should its new organizational chart look like? Who should stay and who had to go? What should be the requirements for the newcomers – in 1990 often the rehabilitated former diplomats expelled in the purges during the period of "normalization," or people in one way or another connected with the Velvet Revolution?

My fate was sealed in the fall when I lost to Václav Klaus in the election of President of the Civic Forum. Less than two weeks later – after one of Jiří Dienstbier's deputy ministers, Luboš Dobrovský, became the new Minister of Defense – I was offered this position by Minister Dienstbier. I accepted and thus committed myself to stay there for the next two years and to participate in all the main tasks of our new foreign policies. My plan to go to the University of Leuven and gain there the doctorate in philosophy was shelved, at least temporarily, and it has never been fulfilled.

My belated response to Timothy Garton Ash

In conclusion I will return to the controversy I have departed from in this text. First, I do not think that revolutions produce ideas. It is other way around: they are inspired by them. In our case the animating ideas were quite simple: We wanted to free ourselves from the moral devastation of late totalitarianism. What we asked for was the respect for human rights. If there was something specific, and maybe new in our concept of human rights in comparison with their version within the project of European Enlightenment, it was the way they were understood by Jan Patočka, Czech philosopher and one of the first spokespersons of Charter 77: not so much as a series of entitlements of their holders, but as a fundamental human duty to stand up and speak out for the rights of others; an act by which human beings confirm their unity with themselves and their solidarity with all "others" around them in their natural world.

Second, our revolution was fundamentally a non-violent one: not driven by utopian visions of a perfect, just society and poisoned by the "ethics of virtue," but determined to achieve the objective of our liberation, by the process of democratization, by reintroducing the rule of law into the environment devastated by the Communist tyranny and building all the institutions of liberty necessary for this task.

And third and last: It happened at the moment of culmination of a world crisis; at the moment of transition from the 20th to the 21st century, when the Eurocentric modern age was coming to its end and the Post-European era of globalized mankind was announcing its arrival. Finding ourselves at the historical crossroads and surrounded by a growing number of unknown, unprecedented phenomena, we had no perfectly functioning models available to guide our actions, no place to return to, in spite of our strong, well-justified desire to integrate our new state into the old European and transatlantic institutions. We tried to follow the example of the West and to integrate our post-totalitarian societies into the existing Western structures, but had to proceed step by step, guided first of all by our experience and learning by the mistakes we were making on the way.

Observing the changing situation in the world, it is still an open question whether we will succeed in the end or fail in one way or another in our efforts. When it comes to the political ideas to inspire and direct our actions, it may be a good opportunity now to remind ourselves that there is a much older concept of them than the one originated in the European Enlightenment.

What I have in mind are political ideas of ancient Greek poets and playwrights. So let me conclude this essay with a quotation from one of them. This is what Aischylos – a reading inspired by Eric Voegelin[82] – put into the mouth of King Danaos, when he was getting ready for his, by its very nature, tragic action concerning a group of female refugees, "suppliant maidens" who were begging for protection in his city:

> *I cannot aid you without risk or scathe/ Nor scorn your prayers – unmerciful it were/ Perplexed/distraught I stand and fear alike/ the twofold chance, to do or not to do/....A deep saving counsel here there needs/ An eye that like a diver to the depth/Of dark perplexity can pass and see/Undizzied, unconfused/[83]*

So here is my ultimate question for Timothy Garton Ash: aren't we now, at the current moment of our transition – together with all others who have been assisting us in our journey and offered us examples and models to be followed – exactly in this situation? Don't we also need – as ancient King Danaos needed and prayed for – not just *"old, well tested"* ideas of European modernity, but *"saving counsels,"* which we don't seem to have right now easily at our disposal?

---

[82] Eric Voegelin: *Tragedy.* In: *Order and History Volume II. The World of Polis,* p. 317-340
[83] Aischylos: *Suppliant Maidens,* Verses 407-409, translated by. E. D. A. Morshead https://en.wikisource.org/wiki/Four_Plays_of_Aeschylus_(1908)_Morshead

Exercise 5

Common Sense and the Rule of Law: Returning Voegelin to Central Europe[84]

Athanatoi thnétoi thnétoi athanatoi, zóntes ton ekeinón thanaton, ton de ekeinón bion tethneóntes (Mortals are immortals and immortals are mortals, the one living the others' death and dying the others' life.)[85]

The "Immortalization" of a Philosopher

An elementary fact in the history of thought is the emergence of philosophical schools around prominent thinkers. The disciples of a Master strived to preserve his work for the future, to carry through his basic intention and to continue in the implementation of the task pursued, but unattained by him in his lifetime. Nevertheless, there is another elementary fact in the history of thought. Such schools did not last usually more than one generation. After some time, the most talented disciples started seeing through the limitations of the standpoint from which their teacher approached philosophical problems and realized the unattainability of the tasks he had set for himself. At a certain moment in time, they came to the conclusion that it was not possible to continue on the road marked out by him; that they were finding themselves at a new

---

[84] This text was written in 2004, during my tenure as the Czech Ambassador to the United States as my contribution to the edited volume honoring the 70th birthday of Ellis Sandoz (*Common Sense and the Rule of Law: Returning Voegelin to Central Europe.* In: Embry C. R. and Cooper B. (eds.): *Philosophy, Literature, and Politics. Essays Honoring Ellis Sandoz.* University of Missouri Press, Columbia and London, 2005, pp. 258-284.

[85] Heraclitus, B62. The English translation is from John Burnet's *Early Greek Philosophy*, London, 1920, quot. from *www.randyhoyt.net/projects/heraclitus*

crossroads where they had to take new decisions, to unveil the open questions and issues behind all the answers the Master's philosophical "teaching" contained. By paradox, this moment of destruction of the teacher's legacy, however, does not necessarily mean its absolute end, its retreat from the human world and its fall into oblivion. On the contrary, it is exactly here where we can find the key to his potential immortality, and this is the third elementary fact in the history of thought. Only when overcome and problematized, when – to use a figure of speech – struck from the heavens to the earth, does the philosopher gain his place in the dialogue engaged in by great, "immortal" thinkers across the borders of civilizations and centuries.

To guess at this point of time what place in the overall spiritual context of the twentieth century will belong to Eric Voegelin (1901-1984), whether it will be namely he who will be given the credit for the fundamental shift in the sphere of political thinking – as his disciples and followers seem to believe – would in my opinion be somewhat precipitate. At the same time, however, let it be stated that it is to their credit that the open-ended process of Voegelin's possible immortalization has started. Voegelin is undoubtedly one of those contemporary thinkers who – probably against their will and in spite of their own warning that philosophy will not allow itself to be closed into any systematic philosophical teaching – did create a kind of philosophical school. During his academic career in the United States and later in Germany, Voegelin influenced decisively a significant group of philosophers, theologians, political scientists, cultural anthropologists, etc. – now finding themselves at the summit of their professional careers – who are convinced that the principal task of their own work is to keep Voegelin's philosophical legacy alive. They publish the collected works of Eric Voegelin, organize Voegelin conferences and write studies or even whole monographs on him. They founded the Eric Voegelin Society, which has held since 1985 its annual meetings as a part of the annual conventions of the American Political Science Association.

All this demonstrates more than clearly that Voegelin was indeed an exceptionally successful and influential teacher, and that his legacy represents a very powerful inspiration. In the course of years, a global network of Voegelinians has been created, a chain of people as if united by a single philosophical will, sharing Voegelin's fundamental conviction that it is still Plato, Aristotle and other classical thinkers who should teach us what is (and what is not) philosophy; and that it is philosophy in this classical sense that remains at the moment of contemporary European crisis as the single most important weapon to be used "in defense of civilization." The aim which these contemporary Platonists (a kind of Platonic Academy operating in the post-modern environment of today's globalizing world) strive for, seems to be guided by a single intention: to initiate a Renaissance of classical political thought, to rediscover the liberating power of classical political ideas, to retrieve the dimension of philosophical dialogue for our current political discourse.

Nevertheless, time and tide wait for no man. First-generation Voegelinians have already reached their "acme," and one might pose the question of the further fate of their project. What will become of Voegelin's legacy in the long-term perspective, from the point of view of the dialogue of mankind across the borders of civilizations and centuries? Despite all the disciples' endeavor to disseminate the ideas of their Master, the "Voegelinian Revolution" in political thought, as announced in 1982 in a book of the same name by Ellis Sandoz,[86] one of the most prominent American followers of Voegelin and today apparently the main guardian of the Voegelin legacy, seems yet to be completed. It is realistic and fair to admit that Voegelin's influence on the current mainstream political thought remains limited. This state is actually illustrated by texts on Voegelinian themes produced, presenting almost exclusively a positive, i.e. accordant interpretation of Voegelin's teaching. The fact that Voegelin is still usually presented in the role of great guru and unrivaled Master in matters of thought, demonstrates that the destructive, critical phase of work on his philosophical legacy – the true test of his actual greatness and key phase of the process of his "immortalization" – has not yet arisen, and if it has, then it is evidently still at a very timid, initial stage. Where will the Vogelinian debate and research be, let us say, thirty years from now? Can we imagine that? Will Voegelin be still recognized as a great, truly

---

[86] Elis Sandoz: *The Voegelinian Revolution: A Biographical Introduction*, Louisiana State University Press, Baton Rouge, 1981

"revolutionary" philosopher of the period at the great turn of history as his immediate disciples believe? Or, will this image be whittled by the passage of time, and Voegelin "only" remembered as one of those educated Central Europeans, born at a tragic time, uprooted from their domestic environment, living their lives on the periphery of the big world, leaving behind only faded photographs, collected volumes of their works, and gradually disappearing traces of their personal struggles, which were heroic and that is why respectable, but did not make a real difference from the point of view of the universal history of the spirit?

Anamnesis

Raising all these hardly answerable questions, I am well aware of my serious limitations as far as my possible contribution to the on-going Voegelinian debate. To clarify my perspective, I have to depart from my own personal anamnesis. I will begin in the socialist Czechoslovakia in the 1980s when my own introduction to the world of Western philosophy and my first encounters with Eric Voegelin's thought took place. Then I will focus on the radical change brought by the Velvet Revolution of 1989 that has reopened our society kept closed for more than four decades, and offered to all its members an opportunity to take part in the political process of rebuilding democracy. In the light of new experience, I have been forced to reexamine my approaches to and my reading of the fundamental problems of classical political philosophy, and last but not least, enabled to start communicating with the international Platonic Academy of Voegelinians.

I ran across the name of Eric Voegelin for the first time in the early 1980s, in the meetings of "Kampademia," a small group of friends who got together with a bold, and somewhat quixotic intention to "revive" the tradition of Socratic/Platonic thought in the midst of a "small" Czech society stricken in the second half of the 20th century by the totalitarian plague. Our common teacher was Jan Patočka, one of the last students of Edmund Husserl and undoubtedly the greatest Czech philosopher of the 20th century. He decided to take a bold, genuinely Socratic step toward the end of his life. Almost seventy years old, he became one of the first three spokespersons of Charter 77 and died only two months after the Charter's original declaration on January 1, 1977 due to a heart attack he suffered after a series of prolonged police interrogations. Patočka's phenomenological research of the *"natural world of human existence"* (Husserl's Lebenswelt)[87] and especially his philosophy of history – elaborated step by step in his private lectures in 1970 and finally sketched in the form of six "heretical essays"[88] – represented one of the principal points of departure and maybe the most frequent topic of our disputes and conversations. Through Patočka and under his guidance, we were all introduced not only to the basic ideas of phenomenology formulated by his great teacher, but also studied and discussed the works of many other contemporary philosophers and political thinkers: for instance Hannah Arendt, Eugen Fink, Martin Heidegger, Karl Jaspers, Emanuel Levinas, Paul Ricoeur, Leo Strauss, and last but not least Eric Voegelin. I remember well lively exchanges after the presentations of Pavel Bratinka who gave us the introduction to Voegelin's *New Science of Politics*, or Zdeněk Neubauer who talked about the "Voegelinian Revolution," inspired by the above-mentioned book by Ellis Sandoz. I also made my own contributions to this debate, being the lucky one in our group and having in my private holdings the first four volumes of *Order and History*. I received them thanks to the Jan Hus Foundation that not only sent us many books in the 1980s, but also sponsored the visits to Prague of dozens of renowned Western scholars (including Charles Taylor, Roger Scruton, David Levy, Jurgen Habermas, Ernst Tugendhat, Richard Rorty, Norman Podhoretz, Paul Ricoeur, Jacques Derrida, Jean-Pierre Vernant, Jean-François Lyotard, Emmanuel LeRoy Ladurie, André Glucksman, Alain Finkelkraut and Pierre-Jean Labarriere) to give lectures and to challenge our naïve and sometimes uninformed enthusiasm for philosophy that was conceived by

---

[87] Jan Patočka: *Přirozený svět jako filosofický problém*. In: *Fenomenologické spisy I*, p. 127-261; Jan Patočka: *The Natural World as a Philosophical Problem*.
[88] Jan Patočka: *Kacířské eseje o filosofii dějin*, In: *Péče o duši III*, p. 11-144; Jan Patočka: *Heretical Essays in the Philosophy of History*. Translated by E. Kohák. Edited by James Dodd. Open Court, Chicago and La Salle, 1996

Patočka as *"new possibilities of life in that shaken situation,"*[89] by their professionalism and expertise.[90]

How then did the philosophy of Voegelin fit into our "academic" context at that time? What were we searching for in our on-going dialogue? What were the main questions we were occupied with during the last years of European Communism? Some of our seminars from 1983-1984 were recorded, transcribed and published.[91] I re-read them recently when I was collecting all necessary background materials for this piece. With all the reservations and doubts that such a *"recherche du temps perdu"* can raise twenty years later, it was, indeed, an interesting reading. To characterize the inquisitive atmosphere of our seminars and the fundamental aim of our philosophizing, I can use the blunt formulation used as the title of one of the chapters of Voegelin's *Autobiographical Reflections, "Why Philosophize? To Recapture Reality!"*[92] We all would have subscribed to Voegelin's blunt statement that the motivations of his work arose "from the political situation:"

> *Anybody with an informed and reflective mind who lives in the twentieth century since the end of the First World War, as I did, finds himself hemmed in, if not oppressed, from all sides by a flood of ideological language – meaning thereby the language symbols that pretend to be concepts, but in fact are unanalyzed topoi or topics. Moreover, anybody who is exposed to this dominant climate of opinion has to cope with the problem that language is a social phenomenon. He cannot deal with the users of ideological language as partners in a discussion, but he has to make them the object of investigation. There is no community of language with the representatives of the dominant ideologies. Hence, the community of language that he himself wants to use in order to criticize the users of ideological language must first be discovered and, if necessary, established.*[93]

---

[89] Jan Patočka: *Heretical Essays in the Philosophy of History*, p. 41

[90] The Prague activities of Jan Hus Foundation in Prague are described in Barbara Day: *The Velvet Philosophers*. London: Claridge Press, 2000

[91] T. Korder: *Voegelin a Patočka*. Athanaeum Rozmluvy vol. 45, 1988

[92] Eric Voegelin: *Autobiographical Reflections*. In: *Autobiographical Reflections. Revised Edition with a Voegelin Glossary and Cumulative Index*, 2006, p. 118

[93] Ibid.

We certainly were not resisting only *"a flood of ideological language,"* but also its political incarnation in the form of an *"advanced or late totalitarian regime."*[94] This regime tried desperately to preserve its power in the changing international environment in Europe – influenced first by the so-called "Helsinki process," and since 1985, by the policies of "perestroika" of the new Soviet leader Mikhail Gorbachev – and in this context, to destroy our "parallel polis," founded by the declaration of Charter 77, by all available means. No matter how complicated and sometimes even dramatic the circumstances might have been, we were trying to do in our regular "academic" meetings what Voegelin suggested in the above quoted passage: to discover, and if necessary to establish an alternative *"community of language"* in order to recover and explore our place on the spiritual map of emerging global mankind and to connect our personal stories (under the influence of Patočka) to philosophy.

The reason why I threw myself into the study of Voegelin's *Order and History* was simple: I was struck from the first pages by the power of his arguments and found the way he worked with the classical texts and ideas congenial with and complementary to the style of the philosophical work of our teacher. Both Patočka and Voegelin pursued their own philosophical projects by summoning up all their education and spiritual strength. They both formulated their big questions and proceeded on the original paths of thought that ran quite close to each other – *"lying,"* in the words of Parmenides, *"far from the beaten paths of humans."*[95] Nonetheless, as genuine philosophers, they both were excellent interpreters of the history of ideas, true guardians of the authenticity and integrity of philosophical language, originating in the efforts of concrete men and women of the past to articulate their finite experiences of encounter with the transcendent source of order within their concrete historical societies. Under their guidance, we were being introduced to a philosophy that was not a metaphysical doctrine consisting of true

---

[94] Václav Havel: *Stories and Totalitarianism.* In: *Open Letters, Selected Writings 1965-1990,* p. 331

[95] Parmenides: *On Nature (Peri Fyseos)* . Originally in Herman Diels: *Die Fragmente der Vorsokratiker,* English translation, edited by Allan F. Randal), quoted from The Classic Internet Library

(http://home.ican.net/~arandall/Parmenides/

propositions about eternal and unmovable Being, but a way of life, a kind of movement of human existence, whose aim was to *"live in truth,"* to keep open the possibility of human life to *"escape one's own ignorance."*[96] In other words, both Patočka and Voegelin were able to open, even for a layman or dilettante like me, the forgotten and largely unnoticed layers of the Western spiritual tradition. They helped me to rediscover the meaning of basic concepts and symbols used in philosophical discourse. They shook me out of the shell of my presumed certainties to realize the metaphysical depth under the surface of facts and data that had to be explored and known by anyone who wished to understand and to articulate meaningfully his/her concrete situation within the universal horizon of human history.

Reexamining the contributions I made in our seminars from 1983/4, I certainly cannot have any illusions about their quality or even the originality of their message. On the contrary, their language betrays not only the lack of skill and experience of the contributor, but the power of Baconian *"Idols of the Market Place"* – the case when *"the ill and unfit choice of words wonderfully obstructs the understanding"*[97] – no matter how strong my desire to overcome them or at least get them under control. Being inspired and taught by genuine philosophers like Patočka or Voegelin, we were invited – in spite of all flaws, imperfections and the evident amateurism of our academic conversations and in the context that was determined by our current political existence in Central Europe – to the society of classical thinkers like Socrates, Plato and Aristotle and many others. Thanks to this apprenticeship, we could participate, in our own way, using our modest resources and capabilities, in the never-ending dialogue of mankind initiated in ancient Greece and other centers of the civilized world many centuries ago. The Socratic appeal to care not so much about *"money and honor and reputation"* but rather about *"wisdom*

---

[96] Cf. Aristotle's Metaphysics, book I, 982b19-20 (DIA TO FEUGEIN TÉN AGNOIAN EFILOSOFÉSAN), trans. W.D. Ross, The Classic Internet Library

[97] Francis Bacon: *The New Organon* (*On True Directions Concerning the Interpretation of Nature*), XLIII, in: *Selected Works of Francis Bacon*, *http://www.constitution.org/bacon/bacon.htm*

and truth and the greatest improvement of the soul"[98] meant in the interpretation of Patočka or Voegelin much more than a superficial invitation to take up moral philosophy caricatured by Hegel in his in his *Lectures on the History of Philosophy*:

> *"Because Socrates in this way gave rise to moral philosophy, all succeeding babblers about morality and popular philosophy constituted him their patron and object of adoration, and made him into a cloak which should cover all false philosophy. As he treated it, it was undoubtedly popular; and what contributed to make it such was that his death gave him the never-failing interest derived from innocent suffering."* [99]

What was clearly at stake here for us was the future identity of Europe's "heart," the power of great ideas and symbols of the past to be mobilized in the concrete situation of our "polis" that was finding itself in the 1980s in one of its spiritual crises.

The Velvet Revolution in November 1989 brought a radical change into our world. Thanks to the collapse of Communism, Central Europe reemerged as an active player in the field of international relations and her fragmentation, in the decades of the Cold War's "frozen" system of national societies, had been offered a new opportunity: to set out on a journey from totalitarianism to democracy. The new situation terminated for obvious reasons the existence of the dissidents' "parallel polis" and brought a new challenge to what I have always considered the most important part of my public engagement: to assist the rebirth of classical political ideas in our current context and to enhance with their help our capacity of understanding.

The new social and political context shaped by the newly gained freedom could not let my reading of Voegelin go untouched. On the one hand, I have had the chance to become acquainted with the activities of a

---

[98] Cf. Plato, Ap. 30a-30b, quot. from the English translation by Benjamin Jowett, The Internet Classical Archive, Apology by Plato, *http://classics.mit.edu/Plato/apology.html*

[99] Georg Wilhelm Friedrich Hegel: *Lectures on the History of Philosophy*, E.S, Haldane (transl.), Routledge & Kegan Paul Ltd., London, repr. 1955, Vol. I, p. 388, *www.gutenberg.org/files/51635/51635-h/51635-h.htm#c384*

global network of Voegelinians and have benefited greatly from it. I have gained an opportunity to study Voegelin's "Opera Omnia" volume after volume, to read the abundance of the secondary Voegelinian literature, to participate in the on-going Voegelinian dialogue within a group of distinguished scholars, and to present my own insights, comments and eventual "discoveries" at the regular annual meetings of the Eric Voegelin Society. On the other hand, being pushed forward in the irreversible historical time – growing older and becoming more and more perplexed not only by all the difficulties of our own transition to democracy, but by all the intricacies of the New World Order emerging from the ruins of the Old One – I had to realize that my perception of political ideas has also been changing. I had to admit that in the current situation I am simply unable to read Voegelin in the way I had originally; that I have some difficulties with my original understanding of the Voegelinian project aiming at the *"defense of civilization;"* that in spite of the indisputable fact that it is among Voegelinians where one can find a living political thought today, there is something problematic, at least from my own point of view, in the prevailing focus and style of the current Voegelinian research.

Struggling with my personal loss of direction, I have started looking for a new point of departure. Surprisingly, I did not find it in the realm of ideas, among Voegelin's fascinating insights into their history, that made him without any doubt one of the greatest philosophers of the 20th century, but in his *Autobiographical Reflections*, that could be published only thanks to the persistence of Ellis Sandoz, one of his most talented students and undoubtedly the most influential herald of the "Voegelinian revolution." Voegelin's escape from Central Europe and his encounter with American "common sense" have lead me to raise the following questions: Is it not here, in Central Europe where Voegelin's anabasis – that began in the 1930s when totalitarianism, once characterized by him as a *"cadaveric poison"* released by Western civilization and now *"spreading its infection through the body of humanity,"*[100] was on the rise – must come to its end? Is not this potential homecoming – rather than all these efforts to summarize the results of Voegelin's Herculean search for

---

[100] Eric Voegelin: *The Origins of Totalitarianism.* In: *Published Essays 1953-1965*, p. 15

order – that represents the biggest challenge for the Voegelinian legacy at the beginning of the 21st century? Is it not in the midst of singular, passing human matters, and eventually not only in Central Europe, where we should be looking for Voegelin's proverbial Rhodos and where the question of the potential immortality of his teaching must be tested?

Escape from Central Europe and Discovery of American Common Sense

Let us depart from the known facts of Voegelin's biography. Born on January 3, 1901 in Cologne in Germany, in 1910 he moved with his parents to Vienna. This is where Voegelin received his education – first at the Gymnasium and then at the University of Vienna where he studied political science at the Faculty of Law with Hans Kelsen. International events led to a radical change of the Viennese scene during the course of Voegelin's studies. At the time of the monarchy, Vienna had the relatively liberal, cosmopolitan atmosphere of a world metropolis. Defeat in the First World War, however, resulted in the disintegration of the Austro-Hungarian Empire and in the emergence from its ruins in 1918 of a republic – albeit one lacking the free republican spirit. The liberalism typical of the Viennese imperial era was replaced by petit bourgeois narrow-mindedness and grievances over historical injustice. Instead of the cosmopolitan tolerance typical of the "world of yesterday" of the former rulers of Central Europe (described so persuasively from a Jewish perspective in Stefan Zweig's autobiography), there was the rise of small Austrian chauvinism, xenophobia, ideologically motivated encounters of antagonistic social classes and general spiritual decline and loss of direction. There were, of course, deeper reasons for this transformation; it was not merely the hangover of military defeat resulting in the retreat from the position of power, but also the omen of deep spiritual and social crisis which in the post-war period started engulfing the whole European continent, culminating in the assumption of power by totalitarian political movements and resulting in another world war. It was namely this shift that framed Voegelin's political experience and the elementary existential point of departure of his philosophy.

The academic environment – and Voegelin moved around almost exclusively in that environment – was, of course, relatively more resistant to the general decline. Reading about the way in which he planned his academic training, all the names of the people who taught him, all the places where he studied and the different disciplines, one cannot but be amazed by all the possibilities which were available to a young scholar, by the quality of contemporary spiritual life, and by the criteria of university education in Austria of those days, a country politically and spiritually in decline. Nevertheless, the "decline of the West," as clearly implied in Voegelin's reflection, was felt not only as a political problem, but was becoming increasingly apparent in the intellectual milieu, too. Maybe that is one reason why Voegelin's intellectual striving was so inseparably linked with private seminars held within a circle of friends calling itself "Geistkreis." The group included, for instance, Alfred Schütz, with whom Voegelin exchanged a written discussion of Husserl's phenomenology, as well as a number of others whom Voegelin later met again in American exile. "Geistkreis" was nothing more than a group of young enthusiasts who discussed everything that aroused their inquisitive minds, yet the mere existence and mission of the group reflected the shifts occurring in the world of Austrian academia, inconspicuously at first, but later moving slowly the center of authentic intellectual life into the private sphere, still free from any manipulation by the state.

Despite the fact that Voegelin received the core of his education from an impressive line of German and Austrian professors who introduced him to the world of European learning, a major influence in Voegelin's academic maturing was apparently his trip to the United States in 1924-1925. As a Laura Spellman Rockefeller Fellow, Voegelin was given his first opportunity to become acquainted with the American university environment and compare it with his hitherto European experience. The encounter with America became his destiny. This is where he encountered "common sense," which "spoiled" him, according to his own words, to such a degree that from that time onwards he was no longer able to exist non-problematically in Central Europe and within the framework of her venerable and cultivated philosophical traditions. Whereas the European discussion of political and social phenomena turned round in the vicious circle of contending philosophies and schools (mainly of neo-Kantian provenance) and de facto neglected the increasingly gloomy contemporary political situation, the American manner of political thinking was quite different. It did not lean primarily on one or another philosophical school and tradition but let itself be inspired by concrete political events, namely the foundation of the American republic, the adoption of its Constitution, which from that time onwards became the source of the "good life" of American citizens and whose further development and protection were generally perceived as the basic guarantee of freedom and human dignity. In brief, America presented itself to Voegelin as an amazing synthesis of classical thought, which he had striven in vain to restore in his Central European environment, and of the best components of the Christian tradition which European Modernism, in his view, was also desperately lacking. The pragmatism of William James and John Dewey, the philosophy of George Santayana, Whitehead's lectures at Harvard University, and also solid American theory of law or government, consciously abstaining from the attainment of heights of philosophy – all that had such a strong impact on Voegelin that he returned to Europe – to use his own expression – a changed man, unable to exist further in the increasingly restricted, increasingly narrowing, increasingly philosophically sterile European environment.

Voegelin's philosophical diagnosis of the crisis of European civilization in the twentieth century turned him into an open, uncompromising critic of emerging totalitarian movements and especially of national-socialist policy. His reputation in this respect, however, placed him at the time of the Austrian Anschluss in immediate jeopardy. If it was originally his conversion to Anglo-Saxon "common sense," that made Voegelin, to quote his own words, *"unfit for further existence in Central Europe,"* it was the German Nazis with their project of "the Thousand-Year Reich" that forced him to leave Vienna and become an exile. In March 1938, he fled under rather dramatic circumstances to Switzerland, and from there after a short time he departed for the United States.

Why did American "common sense" alienate Voegelin not only from contemporary European politics, but also from a certain tradition of

European political thought which became dominant in the last three centuries, i.e. in the modern period of European history? Why was it in the United States of America – in a democratic republic of the "New World" which took upon herself more than once in the twentieth century the burden of the defense of Western civilization against the totalitarian barbarity that originated on the "old continent" – where Voegelin rediscovered the liberating power of classical, i.e. pre-modern political thought?

To answer these questions, let us look briefly at the way in which the problem of "common sense" is approached by one of the great figures of American "pragmatism," William James. In his lectures of 1906-1907 (published in 1907 under the title *Pragmatism: A New Name for Some Old Ways of Thinking*),[101] James stated clearly what he understood as "common sense:" *"our fundamental ways of thinking,"* discovered already by *"exceedingly remote ancestors, which have been able to preserve themselves throughout the experience of all subsequent times,"* used till now and forming *"one great stage of equilibrium in the human mind's development."*[103]

The fundamental philosophical question analyzed by James was the problem of noesis, the problem of knowledge and knowing: What does it mean to know something? What kind of relationship is established between *"knower"* and *"things to be known?"* What ontology is commensurate with the world in which man is able to live as a rational being? Can the classical philosophers who for the first time formulated the great ontological questions and discovered the fundamental ideas of our Western thought, help us in our efforts to understand better our contemporary situation and improve our capacity to use our own "common sense?" According to James, there are two alternative approaches to the problem of noesis: monism, which corresponds to the perennial philosophical quest for the world's unity, or pluralism. In his lecture *The One and the Many* James says:

---

[101] William James: *Pragmatism: A new Name for Some Old Ways of Thinking*. Longmans, Green &Co., New York and London, 1907. All quotations in this essays are from *The Writings of William James, A Comprehensive Edition*, edited with an Introduction, by John, J. McDermott, Modern Library, New York, 1968
[103] Op.cit., p. 420

The great monistic Denkmittel for a hundred years past has been the notion of the one Knower. The many exist only as objects for his thought – exist in his dream, as it were; and as he knows them, they have one purpose, form one system, tell one tale for him. This notion of an all-enveloping noetic unity in things is the sublimest achievement of intellectualist philosophy. [104]

The hypothesis of the universe's *"oneness,"* the hypothesis of one world consisting of things seen by an omniscient knower *"as forming one single systematic fact,"* the hypothesis of the actual world being present to the senses of a human spectator always within the finite horizon of his mortality, but *"complete eternally,"* has important implications. Its discovery and conscious acceptance signal a genuine revolution in the historical process of human self-understanding. From this moment on, any theory of knowledge, any plausible answer to all concrete questions emerging from the fact that man is endowed with the capacity of reasoning – that he is able to distinguish in his own noetic activities between pure reason (dealing with matters of truth and untruth), ethical, i.e. practical reason (working primarily with the distinction between good and bad) and aesthetic reason (attributing the qualities of beautiful and ugly to the things in the human world) – has no other choice but simply to take the "monistic" hypothesis into consideration. The "knowing" man must get rid of everything that does not comply with it. He has to leave, as if forced by its coercive power, his pre-critical past behind and enter into a new universalistic era dominated and wholly permeated by his modern "science." In short: the necessary consequence of the "Copernican turn" made in European history by Immanuel Kant, is the birth of the modern European spirit with its progressivist understanding of human history, the most important implication of which is the ontological degradation or even conscious denial of all human knowledge which previously was helping man to orient himself in the world, known as his "common sense."

The stance of pragmatic American philosophers must be seen as a gentle and thoughtful rejection not of the value of Kantian arguments, which were praised highly by William James, but of that absoluteness with

---

[104] Op.cit. p. 411

which the monistic philosophy was presented. Against the ontological hypothesis which enthrones the one Knower *"conceived either as an Absolute or as an Ultimate,"* the pragmatists raise *"the counter-hypothesis that the widest field of knowledge that ever was or will be still contains some ignorance...Some bits of information always may escape:"* [106]

> *This is the hypothesis of noetic pluralism, which monists consider so absurd. Since we are bound to treat it as respectfully as noetic monism, until the facts shall have tipped the beam, we find that our pragmatism, though originally nothing but method, has forced us to be friendly to the pluralistic view. It may be, that some parts of the world are connected so loosely with some other parts as to be strung along by nothing but the copula "and." They might even come and go without those other parts suffering any internal change. This pluralistic view, of a world of additive constitution, is one that pragmatism is unable to rule out from serious consideration. But this view leads one to the farther hypothesis that the actual world, instead of being complete "eternally," as the monists assure us, may be eternally incomplete, and at all times subject to addition or liable to loss.* [107]

When we adopt a pluralistic view of the world, several fundamental things will change. First of all, we will lose from our sight the systematic, i.e. static conception of noesis, seen by the one omniscient knower, consisting of individual pieces, the validity of which has been "scientifically" tested and which are assembled into a coherent, i.e. non-contradictory whole. Instead, we will tend to focus more on the problem of noesis as a process, on the dynamic aspects of the life of the mind we are part of, in spite of our finite bodily existence. We will start discovering the temporal dimensions of the fundamentally human situation which was discovered first by Socrates and two generations later philosophically analyzed by Aristotle, who defined humans as those who do not possess the divine knowledge of the One Knower, but are always striving to escape

---

[106] Op.cit. 418
[107] Ibid.

their ignorance they are aware of, because *"by nature (they) desire to know."*[109]

> *Our minds [or knowledge as it is stated previously in the text, remark by MP] thus grow in spots; and like grease spots, the spots spread. But we let them spread as little as possible: we keep unaltered as much of our old knowledge, many of our old prejudices and beliefs, as we can. We patch and tinker more than we renew. The novelty soaks in; it stains the ancient mass; but it is also tinged by what absorbs it. Our past apperceives and co-operates; and in the new equilibrium in which each step forward in the process of learning terminates, it happens relatively seldom that the new fact is added raw. More usually it is embedded cooked, as one might say, or stewed down in the sauce of the old.*[110]

This figurative description of the process within which human knowledge is acquired, grows and is altered in the course of time, clearly implies an utterly different, much more positive attitude of the "pragmatist" towards "common sense," than was the position of monism. At the same time, pragmatism has an incomparably higher appreciation for the singular facts given in the immediate experience of individual human beings, living in the presence of the known past, but open towards the unknown future. In short: pragmatism as a noetic stance is much more embedded in the concreteness of human life than in the abstract generalities apprehended by those who subscribe to a "monistic" school of thought. It simply respects the fundamental fact of our noesis, that the bulk of our knowledge is inherited from our ancestors, from our family or tribe, from the society, culture and civilization we were born into. At the same time, however, pragmatism is ready to test the truths that we received from the past and believe in, against the changing realities of our life, against all these challenges we are exposed to as free human beings, who had no

---

[109] PANTES ANTHRÓPOI TOU EIDENAI OREGONTAI FYSEI (All men by nature desire to know)
(Aristotle, *Metaphysics*, 980a21, trans. W.D. Ross, The Classical Internet Library, http://classics.mit.edu/Aristotle/metaphysics.html
[110] William James, op.cit., p.419

choice but to act on their own, to use their own capacity of judgement and to make, at the right time, the right decisions.

In this regard, the distinction made by James between the use of "common sense" in practical talk – as man's *"gumption and good judgement – and in philosophy which understands by common sense"* the *"use of certain intellectual forms and categories"* inherited from the past – is not as great as it might look from his own distinctions and definitions. Pragmatists are indeed sincerely interested and want to explore what *"our fundamental ways of thinking"* are *"which have been able to preserve themselves throughout the experience of all subsequent times"* – as customs or habits of thought, as our beliefs – because they are well aware that without these discoveries, sometimes of our *"exceedingly remote ancestors,"* our capacity for good judgement and good action would be seriously damaged or even utterly paralyzed. Truth as the supreme noetic category and "good" as the basic orientation point of our practical life, come in the pragmatic perspective together again, bridging the gap between them and other "transcendentalia" (esse, verum, bonum, pulchrum), which opened in Western civilization with the advent of the Modern Age.

> *Truth is one species of good, and not, as it is usually supposed, a category distinct from good, and coordinate with it. The true is the name of whatever proves itself to be good, in the way of belief and good, too, for definite, assignable reasons.* [111]

> *'What would be better for us to believe?' This sounds very much like a definition of truth. It comes very near to saying 'what we ought to believe': and in that definition none of you would find any oddity. Ought we ever not to believe what it is better for us to believe? And can we then keep the notion of what is better for us, and what is true for us, permanently apart?* [112]

To sum up in the context of analysis: It is this shift from the "monistic" perspective, which has long dominated modern European

---

[111] Op.cit. 388
[112] Op.cit. 389

thought, to the point of view adopted by American pragmatism, that can heal, according to Voegelin, our contemporary spiritual disease. It is so because the move from monism towards pragmatism opens the door again to classical political thought, which can help to restore the impaired balance of the European political mind. From the pragmatic perspective, one can rediscover under the conditions of modernity the classical Socratic question concerning the human good and making humans *"give an account"* of their lives and care about *"the greatest improvement of the soul,"* to repeat once more the above-quoted passage from Plato's "Apology;" one can recapture for contemporary use the meaning of the classical concept of politics as a form of life of free human beings, the meaning of the classical concept of law, the only ruler capable of making all citizens equal, the meaning and scope of natural rights which are inalienable because they are not the product of human activity but have been established by God.

All this explains why pragmatism is a genuine American philosophy and why it is a pragmatic attitude that characterizes more than anything else the frame of the American political mind. But more than that: It is my conviction that it was the rediscovery and new pragmatic reading of Aristotle and of the other classical political philosophers by American "founding fathers," that served as one of the major spiritual inspirations for the American Revolution.

Whereas the fundamental orientation of Voegelin's philosophy remained the same as in his Viennese period, the political circumstances of his work – Voegelin already became an American citizen in 1944 – dramatically changed. (The United States, according to Voegelin, was the only country which could save politically the threatened Western civilization and whose reality at the same time offered a solution for that civilization's spiritual rebirth.) Whereas residence in crisis-stricken Central Europe called for an existence of a more Socratic type, life in America made him adopt a Aristotelian perspective, trying to explore the phenomenon of the crises of European civilization in its full scope and with all ontological implications, and penetrate to the very heart of contemporary problems. In order to understand the blind alley in which mankind was finding itself in the middle of the 20th century, and to help to cure the illness destroying the European spirit, Voegelin was ready to study the vast amount of material belonging to the discarded spiritual heritage – both European and non-European – using not only all the instruments he brought with him to America from his Central European past, but also the American inspiration of "common sense" which served him as a beam of light in the Dark Times of European civilization. His task, however, was enormous. Not being designed as a regular academic project, but rather as an emergency operation in defense of civilization, it can evoke in the mind of a pessimist the memory of eternal punishment of mythical king Sisyphus, or at least – in the mind of a more optimistic observer – one of the legendary heroic labors of Heracles.

Relentlessly and earnestly, Voegelin tried to battle his way through the whole history of mankind, and finish his work on the new science of politics, on the new philosophy of history, the central theme of which is the never-ending struggle within human society between the forces of order and disorder. What we see, however, when we examine the results of his efforts, is not the hero returning victorious from his battles, but an excellent, really profound philosopher whose results are endowed with power to generate insights. But alas, when they are built into an opus, they seem to be disintegrating in the author's hands. Voegelin returns humbly, again and again, to his point of departure and tries to embrace the accumulated material mastered with such unparalleled "bravura" into his grandiose thought-construction. Instead of the originally planned history of political ideas, he produces a study of the relation between history and order. But even this project he does not finish. The never-ending search for order is increasingly interrupted by the classical philosophical theme of preparation for death and meditation aimed beyond the sphere of ephemeral human affairs.

Common Sense and the Rule of Law

Let us go through Voegelin's intellectual biography once more, with special focus on the question of the law. It is my contention that it is exactly here, where the need to reflect on Voegelin's life experience and return Voegelin to Central Europe is indeed topical. It is the realm of jurisprudence, where Voegelinian ideas should be studied and possibly applied in the first place, if Central Europeans want to understand better their totalitarian past, to reexamine their historical identity and vision of the world, to reformulate their political programs for the transition from the 20th to the 21st century.

Voegelin studied law at the University of Vienna under Hans Kelsen, who was undoubtedly one of the most important European jurists of the 20th century and, as the author of *Pure Theory of Law*, the founder of a school of legal thought of enormous influence, especially in Central Europe.[113] Sharing with Voegelin the fate of political refugee, Kelsen also spent the second half of his life in America, but intellectually their paths diverged. Voegelin, however, never committed real "parricide" and did not fully abandon his great teacher who represented for him the end of a certain European tradition, a tradition that had to be properly understood within its own historical context, within its own limits. This is, however, exactly the reason why, according to Voegelin, it is Kelsen's "pure theory of law," where we should start the search for the way out of the current impasse; where we should start testing our capacity to understand our own situation as far as the idea of law and its place in human society is concerned; where we should be looking for *"a point of departure for an advancement towards the reconstruction of a complete political science."*[114]

From the American perspective, wrote Voegelin in a small article published in 1927 with the aim of introducing Kelsen's *Allgemeine Staatslehre* to the American public,[115] the least comprehensible trait of Kelsen's legal thought is its foundations in neo-Kantian positivistic logic. In his basic arguments Kelsen departs from the Marburg School of Simmel and Windelband. What determines the character of data we are primarily

---

[113] In the Czech Republic, Kelsen's students (František Weyr, Ota Weinberger, Václav Chytil, Vladimír Kubeš, Zdeněk Neubauer, Karel Engliš, Jaroslav Kaláb, Jaroslav Krejčí, Josef Kepert, Adolf Procházka, Jaromír Sedláček, just to name the most accomplished ones among them) formed so-called "Brno School of Theory of Law" (Brněnská škola právní teorie). Its influence is still remarkable and has a profound effect on our current post-Communist jurisprudence and constitutional discussion.

[114] Eric Voegelin: *Pure Theory of Law and of State.* In: *Published Essays 1922-1928*, p. 98.

[115] Eric Voegelin: *Kelsen's Pure Theory of Law.* In: *Published Essays 1922-1928*, p. 182-191

dealing with in the realm of law – be it legal codes or statutes, procedural rules, case-law, etc. – is according to him not their material content, but a form in which they are given, their specific *a priori*, in Kantian terminology, antecedent to all forms of experience. Before studying or eventually constructing any positive legal system one must be aware of the fundamental distinction between the "original categories" of *Sein* (being, Existence, referring to the realm of what is) and *Sollen* (ought, Essence, referring to the realm of what should be). This point of departure becomes clearer when we move from the ontological to the epistemological level: The distinction between *Sein* and *Sollen* is translated into the distinction between the causal method of natural sciences (studying the causal relations between existent things), and the normative method applied in cultural sciences (dealing with all various aspects of cultural objectification).

The basic aim of Kelsen's "pure theory" is to approach the law strictly as a positively given normative system, i.e. as a structured, hierarchically (i.e. top-down) organized and complete whole, composed of elementary legal rules (maxims) derived from the basic norm (*Die Grundnorme*), the first and supreme legal maxim, articulating the primordial will of the sovereign, i.e. the state. The simplest analytical element of this system, the norm, must have a clear formal structure corresponding to the normative *a priori* of *Sollen*. The norm, *Rechtsatz* must be, explains Voegelin to his American readers,

> *composed of two parts: The first contains a statement concerning unqualified human behavior, the second makes a statement concerning the coercive behavior (Zwangsakt) of the state official. The complete rule is a hypothesis making the coercive behavior of the state official dependent on the previous occurrence of the behaviors and events stated in the first part of the rule.*[116]

Consequentially, Kelsen's concept of the state, laid down and developed in his *Staatslehre*, also departs from the neo-Kantian paradigm. The state is fully identified with its law. It is conceived as a materialization

---

[116] Op.cit. p. 185

of the will of a concrete human society to erect the protective walls of legal order around all manifold forms of its life. The state should not be built, justified, explained as a shelter of its national, i.e. religious, cultural or linguistic identity, but only as the sole source of its law and the guarantor of its sovereignty. According to Kelsen, the theory of the state has to cope first with the question of its origin and its position within international society under international law; then it proceeds to its basic law, the state constitution, whose task is to provide the overall composition or anatomy of the state body; then to the state organs performing their diverse functions in the process of creation of norms and their enforcement; then to all concrete forms and procedures of how the principle of *"Rechststaat"* is realized in all diverse relations between the citizens and the state and between the citizens themselves.

From the beginning, however, it is evident that the above-indicated reduction of legal orders to *"a system of postulates in the realm of Sollen"*[117] – that can indeed, as Voegelin pointed out, *"surprise the American lawyer who is accustomed to a wealth of rights, duties, privileges, powers, liabilities, and disabilities..."*[118] – was problematic and in a way self-defeating. No matter how purified Kelsen's theory could be from any non-normative content and from any remnants of state doctrines originating in natural law, it never could be fully dissociated from the reality of human society it was supposed to form and order. The legal theories of his predecessors – German jurists such as von Gierke, Laband, Gerber or Jellinek – reflected the rise of Bismarck to power and went along with his ambition to unify Germany and to rebuild it as a modern constitutional federal state. For Kelsen, the main point of reference was the reality of dismemberment of the Austro-Hungarian Empire, defeated in the Great War 1914-1918. His "pure theory of law" based on the categorical distinction between *Sein* and *Sollen*, pretending to isolate normative legal order from any undesirable interference of the supreme echelons of "naturally ordered" human society, simply could not remain isolated from the real events happening in the human world. Can one imagine a better illustration of the fundamental problem of the neo-

---

[117] Op.cit. p. 184
[118] Op.cit. p. 185

Kantian foundations of Kelsen's legal doctrine than the fact that Kelsen, who had been asked to draft the new Austrian Constitution and proceeded as much as possible in conformity with the principles of his "pure theory," had to see his finished *magnum opus* affected profoundly by the empirical, historically determined Austrian political reality?

Nonetheless, no matter whether the final result of the genesis of the Austrian constitution was "pure" or rather "tainted," in 1927, Voegelin still speaks about it in unambiguously positive terms. He evaluates Kelsen's practical achievements not only as *"the most important event in the modern history of constitutions from the point of view of legal technique,"* but *"with its background of the pure theory of law,"* as *"a remarkable contribution to the development of democracy."*[119]

He concludes his article with a kind of summary of Kelsen's position that does not seem to be showing any sign of the approaching spiritual crisis:

> *By transferring the legal system into an ideal realm of meanings and reducing it to an instrument, Kelsen destroys any undue respect for existing legal institutions. The content of law is shown to be what it is: not an eternal, sacred order, but a compromise of battling forces – and this content may be changed every day by the chosen representatives of the people according to the wishes of their constituencies without fear of endangering a divine law.*[120]

> *No state entity hides behind the law and issues the legal rules; every rule can be traced back to its origin in a definite governmental agency, which again is but a part in the machinery set up for turning out legal rules in accordance with the desires of different social groups. The pure theory of law thus signifies not only an important progress in legal analysis and technique, but also a development from the half-absolutistic philosophy of the German empire towards the spirit of the new democracy.*[121]

---

[119] Op.cit. p. 190
[120] Ibid.
[121] Op.cit. p. 191

"The spirit of the new democracy," prevailing in the years after World War I, did not have a long duration in Europe, however. The totalitarian movements seized power first in Italy than in Germany, and in both countries such a profound change of form of government took place by means of constitutional amendments, i.e. in the continuity of the existing legal order. Austria was first transformed from a democratic republic into an authoritarian state and, a couple of years later, annexed to Germany. Both Kelsen and Voegelin had to escape from Central Europe and found new homes in America. Kelsen devoted his time to the new international law initiated by the creation of the United Nations. Voegelin focused on the history of political ideas and tried to elaborate the foundations of his *"new science of politics."* He returned to the fundamental questions concerning the nature of the law and jurisprudence in his courses taught at the Louisiana State University from 1954 to 1957.

The historical events that took place in the world during the three decades that passed between the publication of Voegelin's article about Kelsen in 1927 and the appearance of the mimeographed *"temporary edition exclusively for the use of students"* registered in Voegelin's course on the nature of the law in 1957,[122] changed substantively the situation of mankind, and consequently, influenced his thought heavily.

The world after Auschwitz could not, as it was plainly stated by Karl Jaspers, become the same again as it had been before the German Reich started implementing its hegemonic plans and waged war upon anyone who dared to oppose them – in the end upon the whole world of Western, i.e. Judeo-Christian civilization. The unprecedented crimes against humanity committed by the Nazi regime showing total disrespect for elementary human compassion and the absence of "common sense," had a mobilizing effect and catalyzed a strong international response. As Voegelin put it in his famous review of Hannah Arendt's "Origins of Totalitarianism:"

> *What no religious founder, no philosopher, no imperial*
> *conqueror of the past has achieved – to create a community*
> *of mankind by creating a common concern for all men – has*

---

[122] *Editor's Introduction.* In: Eric Voegelin: *The Nature of the Law and Related Legal Writings*, p. xiii

> *now been realized through the community of suffering
> under the earthwide expansion of Western foulness.* [123]

But what happened after the war was also far from satisfactory. On the one hand, the main war criminals were tried before the International Court of Justice and a new international organization of the United Nations was created with the intention to eliminate wars and to enhance peaceful relations among all nations of the world. The problem, however, was that the Soviet Union, one of the winners of the war, was one of the main disseminators of the totalitarian disease. The new internationalism under the aegis of the United Nations – raising hopes in many people that mankind was finally finding itself on the way to the realization of Kant's old project of *"perpetual peace"* – was simply not based on a realistic assessment of the emerging international situation because it did not reflect at all its crucial aspect: the Soviet threat. For a political realist like George Kennan, who was the first to make this point in his famous long telegram from the American Embassy in Moscow, and who was later assigned to formulate the basic principles of US postwar foreign policy, the right response to the emerging challenge was not a utopian belief in the persuasive power of Kantian ideals, but a very clear message to be sent to the Soviet enemies of American values and Western civilization: the policy of "containment." The result was what was realistically achievable, i.e. the "bipolar political architecture" in Europe with the following implication for Europeans: the inhabitants of her Western half enjoying freedom and gradually progressing from the painful postwar reconstruction towards prosperity under the American security umbrella; the nations of her Eastern half (including a large part of what used to be Central Europe) being deprived of freedom and united with the Soviet Union "forever," as one of the favorite ideological slogans of totalitarian rulers went, sentenced to life in the totalitarian prison under Soviet domination.

In short: observing the international developments in the 1950s, when Voegelin was teaching in Baton Rouge, there was only one evident conclusion if one did not want to abandon the requirements of "common

---

[123] Eric Voegelin: *The Origins of Totalitarianism.* In: *Published Essays 1953-1965*, p. 15

sense:" World War II did not bring the solution to the world crisis caused by the emergence of totalitarianism. Soviet Communism was definitely not a partner for the countries of the Free World to be appeased and invited to participate in the dialogue concerning the new world order, the dialogue of mankind that has been constituted *"through the community of suffering under the earthwide expansion of Western foulness."* On the contrary, the rise of the Soviet Union to the position of world power was an ominous sign, demonstrating how challenging it was going to be to protect the spiritual foundations of Western civilization for the future.

In 1924 Voegelin was a young, talented and well-educated man, whose basic aim was to build a bridge between his Central European background and the newly discovered American experience, and who still could believe optimistically that the Great War of 1914-1918 gave a historical opportunity to *"the spirit of the new democracy."* Thirty years later, he was already an accomplished and respected scholar in the field of political science and philosophy, whose own life experience demonstrated clearly the depth of the current spiritual and political crisis of European humanity; a classicist par excellence whose fundamental objective was to reexamine the richness of classical political ideas and symbols of the past and bring them back to life, to start with their help a new chapter in the dialogue of mankind. He was in the middle of a successful academic career in America and discovered in the United States not only a promised land of pluralistic common sense practiced in American politics and jurisprudence. Being confronted with various aspects of life in his new home, it was here, where Voegelin gained, according to his own words, *"an understanding...of the plurality of human possibilities realized in various civilizations, as an immediate experience, an experience vécue."*[124] It was exactly his enlarged understanding of American common sense that opened before him a vast field of never-ending search for order as it unfolds and exists in human history. When he distributed the mimeographed synopsis of his course among his students – *"Voegelin's only comprehensive and systematic text on law"* – he already had an articulate knowledge of both method and objective of his own research.

---

[124] Eric Voegelin: *Autobiographical Reflections.* In: *Autobiographical Reflections. Revised Edition with a Voegelin Glossary and Cumulative Index* , p. 60

As it is stated clearly in the editor's introduction to Volume 27 of Voegelin's collected works:

> *It is a product of the mature Voegelin. He wrote it at a time when he had settled upon the necessity of abandoning his original plan of writing a history of political ideas, published "The New Science of Politics," and the first three volumes of "Order and History," and taught the course of jurisprudence four years. He had to come to realize that ideas do not have a history, that only people do, and that their history consists of their successes and failures in the differentiation of their noetic and pneumatic experience of life under God. For the same reason, he had to come to realize that law cannot have a history apart from the history of the society whose order it articulates, and that its essence, or nature, is the structure of the society whose law it is.* [125]

The way in which Voegelin opened his inquiry into the nature of the law had to be surprising for an average American student unprepared for philosophical arguments and accustomed to standard pragmatic America jurisprudence, where the meaning and content of all concepts were perceived primarily in relation to their ability to organize the thought of practicing lawyers. What makes the law the law, what is its essence, in spite of the fact that there is *"a plurality of legal orders accepted as valid in a corresponding plurality of societies?"* [126] In order to answer this question, however, we are not advised to start directly comparing different laws and legal systems, but depart from the phenomena of law, as they are given in our daily, pre-analytical experience, as they exist in the world in which we live and understand ourselves with the help of our "common sense."

Voegelin starts his quest accepting for the moment Kelsen's view that the law is a system, *"an aggregate of rules,"* enforced in a concrete historical society, but characterized by their timeless validity. Observing how a legal system functions, we see immediately that the validity of its

---

[125] *The Editor's Introduction.* In: Eric Voegelin: *The Nature of Law and Related Legal Writings,* p. xiii

[126] Op.cit. p. 7

rules does not stay the same but rather *"comes and goes,"* appears and disappears in time. The legal order is not a static system, but rather an entity that finds itself in the permanent process of change. It obviously cannot change all its parts at once. When we say "it changes," it necessarily means that its own "essence" is of a "historical" nature; that *"there is always, from one change to another, an unchanged corpus of rules, sufficiently large to retain the identity of the order."*[127]

Formerly valid rules (rules that have been derogated or abrogated by new ones) and rules that are going to be valid (rules *de lege ferenda*) simply cannot be treated as invalid rules without further qualification, argues Voegelin. The identity of legal order, the source of validity of its norms is inseparably connected with the fundamental fact that it has not only its presence as *"an aggregate of rules,"* but also its past and its future.

The temporal character of legal order becomes even more obvious when we raise the question of its validity not *in abstracto*, but in the context of a concrete legal action, let us say a concrete decision of some court. *"The court decision is the point at which the law becomes valid for the concrete case."* If we started from the law as an aggregate of valid norms and had to cope with the problem of its change, here we would be confronted with the problem that reminds one of the paradoxes of Zeno:

> *If we remember the aura of uncertainty that surrounds every serious litigation, we must admit that we never know what the aggregate of valid rules is as long as the court has not handed down its decision in the concrete case. Once the court has reached its decision, the particular aggregate whose validity has become complete with the decision, and thereby incorporates the decision itself, already belongs to the past. If therefore, validity is 'of essence of the law' and if every aggregate of rules in the series called legal order belongs either to the past in which it is no longer valid or to a future in which it is not yet valid in the decisive concrete case, then "the law" seems to have disappeared altogether from the realm of existents.*[128]

---

[127] Op.cit. p. 12
[128] Op.cit. p. 16-17

So, what is the law? Just to sum up once more again Voegelin's answer to his American students: The law cannot be conceived as a separate entity. It must be always analyzed and understood in the context of social order. The attention that is usually paid only to the content of norms or eventually to their practical use in concrete situations should be directed also, and maybe primarily, to those structures within which the law is given to us on the pre-analytical level of our experience. The law in the sense of the aggregate of valid rules that has come into existence in the process of lawmaking defined and regulated by the highest, i.e. constitutional norms, must be reconnected with the pre-analytical understanding of the law within a concrete historical society that is being ordered by the law; a society that respects and guards the law as the very substance of its order, as its fundamental value and *conditio sine qua non* of its own existence.

Such a reconnection between the law and the pre-analytical experiential basis in the context of which the law is originally given opens a new field of inquiry and generates a new set of questions. If the above mentioned Zenonic argument brings to our attention the temporality of the law – the fact that it is not primarily a static aggregate of norms but a process whose fundamental objective is to order a society and to make its individual members free and equal – the emphasis on the phenomenological approach in the field of jurisprudence points to the problem to be singled out in Voegelin's examination: *"the equivocal use of 'the law' in the sense of valid rules made by organs of government and 'the law' that somehow pervades the existence of man in society."*[129]

> *What is preserved in this pale equivocation of our everyday language is the profound insight, rarely to be found in contemporary legal theory, that 'the law' is the substance of order in all realms of being. As a matter of fact, the ancient civilizations usually have in their language, a term that signifies the ordering substance pervading the hierarchy of being, from the God, through the world and society, to every single man. Such terms are the Egyptian maat, the Chinese tao, the Greek nomos, and*

---

[129] Op.cit. p. 24

the Latin lex.[130]

One does not need to keep going in the train of thought well known to Voegelin's reader, which only demonstrates what was the central message of his jurisprudential course: to realize that one cannot inquire into the nature of the law without being able to raise the fundamental questions concerning Western history that can be formulated only by means of Western philosophy. I have no way of knowing how Voegelin's American students reacted to this turn from the realm of experience they could examine with the help of the American brand of "common sense," to the vast area of ontological problems that can be identified within the open field of the universal history of mankind. Nonetheless, what is evident is that their teacher was a genuine philosopher who did not want to miss a single opportunity to challenge the way in which people he had some business with become used to perceiving and understanding their matters, to shake them out of their shells; to lure them from the *terra firma* of their alleged commonsensical certainties to the depths that open by virtue of fundamental philosophical questions; to tell them that they should "care for their souls," i.e. not to have opinions only, but to seek true knowledge, if they wanted to act prudently, to serve the "common good" of their societies and to keep them open and free.

Looking back on what has happened in and with Central Europe in the past fifteen years, one has to admit, first of all, that the situation has gotten much more complicated, the impact of the collapse of Communism being much wider and farther reaching than it looked in the heydays of the revolutions that set the whole region on the path of democratization. We certainly need to accept the "rule of law" as the main principle to rebuild our states and the whole region to complete our return from our Babylonian captivity to Europe – to reintegrate ourselves into the transatlantic community of open societies, respecting inalienable human rights and freedoms, allowing our economies to be regulated by market forces and not by governments, accepting the culture and form of democratic government. We certainly need "common sense" to overcome or at least to reconcile ourselves with all these unfortunate Central

---

[130] Ibid.

European traditions, – dying hard and changing slowly – that caused us a lot of troubles and individual suffering in the past century. We desperately need it to make the right choices here and now, on the current historical crossroads, in the context of new threats to the Western freedom that global mankind is confronted by at the beginning of the new millennium. However, to absorb and "metabolize" the novelty of our situation we need a renaissance of classical philosophy in Central Europe, as it is gravely needed in the rest of the world. We need to listen attentively and to respond to that call that is connected with the great Central European philosophers of the 20th century, such as Jan Patočka and Eric Voegelin. Their greatness and their potential immortalization are based on the fact that they both were classicists and understood the message that is conveyed in the fragment of Heraclitus that is used as epigraph in this essay: mortals are immortals and immortals are mortals. How should we understand this cryptic statement? What does it mean? It turns our attention to the middle term between mortality and immortality. It does not turn us away from our transient political matters. It just reminds us, as old Socrates did, that we should care first for something that is more important than *the greatest amount of money and honor and reputation:" "wisdom and truth and the greatest possible improvement of the soul."*[131] Whether this message with which he himself failed, when tried by the Athenians, is persuasive enough to be taken seriously by a sufficient number of Central Europeans, still remains to be seen. But it is certain that if it were missed altogether and fell only on deaf ears, our hope for freedom and all the efforts to reintroduce democracy to our region after the collapse of Communism in 1989 would be in vain.

---

[131] Plato: *Apology*, 29d7-e1

Exercise 6

What Kind of God
Does Human Rights Require?[132]

For as I went through the city and looked carefully at the
objects of your worship, I found among them an altar with
the inscription, 'To an unknown god.' What therefore you
worship as unknown, this I proclaim to you. [133]

The organizing question of this volume – *Do Human Rights Need
God?* – can be reversed: "Does God Need Human Rights?" The matter is
the relationship between God and Man; the problem of whether respect for
human rights – generally recognized as a *conditio sine qua non* of any
form of democratic governance and politics – can be used as a kind of
proof of God's existence, proving that despite modern secularism and all
the atheistic inclinations of our "enlightened" times, the realm of the
divine and the realm of the human, in any open society, belong essentially
together.

I have organized my reflections on the issue of God and human
rights into four parts. In the first two parts, I will remind us of two
fundamental distinctions, or rather tensions, that must be recognized in any
attempt to explore what Aristotle called *filosofia peri ta anthrópina*, to
inquire into the philosophical foundations of our "human condition."

---

[132] This text was written in 2004 as my contribution to an edited volume, based on the
series of conference organized by the Divinity School at University of Chicago in
2003 (*What Kind of God Does Human Rights Require?*. In: Bucar, E.M. and Barnett
B. (eds.): *Does Human Rights Need God?*, William Erdman's Publishing Company,
Grand Rapids. Michigan and Cambridge, U.K., 2005, p. 243-268

[133] *Acts, 17:23, New Revised Standard Version*

First, I will focus on the distinction between two elementary *modi* of human existence, the *vita activa* and the *vita contemplative.*

Second, I will look at the polar relationship arising within human existence between its finiteness and historicity on the one hand, and its openness towards transcendence or eternity on the other.

Third, I will mention the classical political "virtues" – such as self-control, respect for common sense, generosity, moderation, etc. – and I will use Cicero as an outstanding example of a moderate politician. I will argue that the Ciceronian attitude towards public matters, the Ciceronian moderate state of mind, should be recommended as the point of departure in our contemporary debate concerning politics, God and human rights.

In my fourth and final remark, I will try to apply the previous points to our present situation. I will comment briefly on the current perception of human rights issues in Central Europe – influenced by Central European experiences with totalitarianism in the 20th century and tested today against sometimes odd realities of post-Communist transitions. I would like to use this case as a concrete illustration of how the *vita contemplativa* can eventually inform and shape the *vita activa*. I want to emphasize the healing power of "common sense" and the importance of Ciceronian "moderation" in our current spiritual and political crisis. I will conclude by raising the question concerning the possible role of "divine" transcendence in the process of "globalization" that has been accelerated after the fall of Communism in 1989, and has become the main characteristic of our human situation in the world at the beginning of the 21st century. Thanks to this trend – that is perceived as necessary and unavoidable on our current historical crossroads – all members of the human species, living in historically, culturally and religiously heterogeneous communities, have been brought closer together than ever before and have been made, despite the plurality and diversity that belongs to our human condition, a part of one planetary mankind.

I

Let us start from the Aristotelian distinction between two fundamental ways of human life, *vita activa* and *vita contemplativa*, so powerfully and creatively used in the political thought of Hannah

Arendt.[134] On the one hand, there is our being in the world which we share – engaged in three fundamental human activities: *"labor, work, and action"*[135] – with the plurality of others. On the other hand, there are the noetic activities of man, taking place in the soul, in the *interior domus* of his/her *"self,"* *i.e.*, in that inner space, where each of us can temporarily

---

[134] Her point of departure is the idea that political thought within our Western tradition has been formed primarily from the perspective of the "thinking ego;" that all its concepts and habits have been constituted as if disconnected from the experiential basis of *vita activa* where they are originally coming from: *"I suspect,"* she wrote to her teacher and life-long friend Karl Jaspers in 1956, *"that Western philosophy has never had a clear concept of what constitutes the political and couldn't have one, because, by necessity, it spoke of man the individual and dealt with the fact of plurality tangentially."* (*Hannah Arendt Karl Jaspers Correspondence 1926-1969*. Edited by Kotte Kohler and Hans Saner. Translated from the German by Robert and Rita Kimber, Harcourt Brace Jovanovich Publishers, New York, San Diego, London, 1992, p. 166).
The key thing in our current situation and the major task of our own political thought then is, according to Arendt, to bring *"the fact of plurality"* back to our attention. She suggests reexamining and rethinking our elementary political concepts, brought to us from the past, from the perspective of the "acting ego" (her analysis of the dichotomy between the *vita activa* and the *vita contemplativa* can be found in the Prologue and in the first chapter of her fundamental work *The Human Condition*, The University of Chicago Press, 1958, p. 1-21).
[135] *"With the term vita activa, I propose to designate three fundamental human activities: labor, work, and action. They are fundamental because each corresponds to one of the basic conditions under which life on earth has been given to man.*
Labor is the activity which corresponds to the biological process of the human body, whose spontaneous growth, metabolism, and eventual decay are bound to the vital necessities produced and fed into the life process by labor. The human condition of labor is life itself.
Work is the activity which corresponds to the unnaturalness of human existence, which is not imbedded in, and whose mortality is not compensated by, the species' ever-recurring cycle. Work provides an 'artificial' world of things, distinctly different from all natural surroundings. Within its borders each individual life is housed, while this world itself is meant to outlast and transcend them all. The human condition of work is worldliness.
Action, the only activity that goes on directly between men without the intermediary of things or matter, corresponds to the human condition of plurality, to the fact that men, not Man, live on the earth and inhabit the world. While all aspects of the human condition are somehow related to politics, this plurality is specifically the condition – not only the conditio sine qua non but the conditio per quam – of all political life." (Hannah Arendt: *The Human Condition*, p.7).

withdraw from the common world of appearances.[136] As humans – belonging to the species ZÓON LOGON ECHÓN, *animal rationale*, according to the Aristotelian taxonomy[137] – we are able to interrupt temporarily all activities we have been busy with and to "think," *i.e.*, to see our own situation in the world as if from a distance.[138] In the fleeting moment of contemplation we are able to discover the abyss lurking behind and beyond TA PHAINOMENA, the appearances of things around us, things given to us in our experience. The fundamental, and always awful, *i.e.*, awe- and wonder-evoking, difference between Being and Nothingness (between "is" and "is not") not only reveals the nature of things

---

[136] There is, for sure, the whole tradition of Western philosophy and theology, both in its classical Greek form or in its later Christian modifications, which can be consulted here. What I would like to recommend here instead, as a primary source in the search for the constitution of that inner world we dive into in the moment of contemplation, is the corpus of "fragments" of Pre-Socratic philosophy (their classical edition in English is available under the title *Ancilla to the Pre-Socratic Philosophers, A Complete Translation of the Fragments in Diels Fragmente der Vorsokratiker* (Cambridge, Massachusetts, Harvard University Press 1983). The Pre-Socratic fragments can obviously be read in different ways. No matter what they say about the "origins" of the cosmos or how they explain the processes either taking place in the human world or belonging to "physis," they bear testimony to prima facie encounters with that space that opens for a "philosopher" who has embarked on adventures of *vita comtemplativa* and descends, leaving all "things" he is busy with in his daily life behind, to the inner world of his thoughts. Perhaps the two greatest examples of this descent: the way of truth embarked upon by Parmenides; and Heraklitus's explorations of divine *Logos* and of the *apeirontic* (infinite) depth of immortal soul (the concise and reasonably short interpretation of elementary noetic problems of Parmenides and Heraklitus can be found in Eric Voegelin's *Order and History Volume II. The World of the Polis*, p. 274-313).

[137] The Aristotelian "definition" was in fact formulated only later by Porfyrios, but its real source can indeed be found in Aristotle's *Politics: LOGON DE MONON ANTHRÓPOS ECHEI TÓN ZÓÓN FYSIS She [nature]… has endowed man alone among the animals with the power of speech)*, 1253a9-10. Translated by E.T.Sinclair. Revised and re-presented by Trevor Saunders (quoted from Penguin Books, 1981).

[138] This distance can again be measured in all sorts of ways and discussed in all sorts of contexts, but it is basically the distance of 'spectator,' mentioned in the following anecdote from the life Pythagoras reported by Diogenes Laertius ("Life of Pythagoras," *Lives of the Philosophers*, trans. C.D.Yonge): "Having been asked by Leon, the tyrant of the Phliasians, who he was, replied, 'A philosopher.' And added, that he used to compare life to a festival. 'And as some people came to a festival to contend for the prizes, and others for the purposes of traffic, and the best as spectators; so also in life, the men of slavish dispositions,' said he, 'are born hunters after glory and covetousness, but philosophers are seekers after truth.'" (8:VI).

experienced, but also makes us aware of our own finite existence in time, of our life that will pass away at the moment of our death and still cannot be lived well, without being directed by *nous* or reason; without being informed by knowledge that is permanently tested against the horizon of the divine eternity.[139]

The importance of this distinction cannot be overestimated. Its discovery, whose history can be traced back to the origins of "politics" and "philosophy" in ancient Greece, brought into existence European (Western) civilization with its "open" political culture (whose very essence is human freedom) and its "rationalistic" concept of science. It is obvious, however, that what is at stake here is not just a matter for historians, professional philosophers or other experts interested in the past lives of Western philosophical or political ideas. The discovery of "self" that enables man to share the public space with the plurality of others, and at the same time to put one's own opinions and beliefs under the test of reason – bringing its light into the "young" mind, born into this world, protected by parental care and guidance – is an event to be understood originally on the elementary, existential level of human life. Here, we are confronted with a fundamental question that is tied to our own pursuit of self-understanding. And this is a hermeneutical problem that cannot be tackled properly by any of our modern historical, social, legal or political sciences; a problem that must be approached in the way the classical political thinkers of ancient Greece were employing when leading their dialogues with contemporary politicians and studying, *more Socratico*, the political ideas and practical politics of their own times.

Is it not here – in the context of the question of who we are – where the concepts whose relations are to be analyzed in this volume, God and human rights, should first be approached and rediscovered? Is it not true that all other contexts in which they are commonly used and should be studied – the theological context for the former and legal/political context for the latter – are derivative? Is it not true that without careful clarification

---

[139] The scope of the problem referred here to is enormous within our Western civilization, to say nothing of the conceptions of "eternity" in the non-European traditions. I limit myself here consciously to the short but inspiring analysis concerning the dichotomy "eternity versus immortality" in Hannah Arendt, *The Human Condition*, p. 17-21.

of how these terms are constituted on the existential level, all answers to the question "what kind of God does human rights require?" could lead us astray and leave us lost in all sorts of metaphysical fallacies and perplexities?

II

Bringing the problem of the relationship between God and human rights to the existential level we have obtained a basic clue in our inquiry: The relation of a person to the transcendent pole beyond his own activities cannot be separated from his relationship to himself, to his own finite existence in the human world. The bond between man and God is essentially "anthropomorphic." We cannot move forward in our efforts to answer the question "what kind of God does human rights require?" unless we are able to understand that there is a kind of mirror linkage here; *i.e.*, unless we are able to grasp our own human existence in the light of our experience with the divine. With that in mind, we can take the second step. The conflict between *vita activa* and *vita contemplativa*, the never-ending quest for the meaning of finite human life, does not take place in a vacuum, but always is a matter of concrete human beings finding themselves in concrete places and in concrete times. The context we have to pay attention to when reflecting on the relation between man and God is the open field of human history. Here we are touching upon an essential and important problem. The human openness towards transcendence and eternity introduces the element of movement into the human world. It is the conflict between *vita activa* and *vita contemplativa* itself where human history in fact begins.

The consequences of the fact that not only we mortals but also the world into which we were born and are going to leave at the moment of death, is not stable, but ever-changing, are enormous. The ever-present element of divine transcendence in it cannot be separated from our finiteness and must be treated as a historical problem. Both human rights and God are concepts that have their own history. Both God and human rights, by their very nature, transcend our finite being-in-the-world,[140] "are

---

[140] I am consciously borrowing this term from Heidegger's *Sein und Zeit* (Martin Heidegger: *Sein und Zeit.* Max Niemeyer Verlag Tubingen, 1993). Heidegger's

not from this world," but both at the same time represent historical phenomena. *"All men are created equal"* in the famous words of the American Declaration of Independence, and, indeed, *"they are endowed by their Creator with certain inalienable rights."* At the same time, such a statement could not have been pronounced except under very specific historical circumstances, for a very clear purpose and with very significant political implications. On the one hand one can say that human rights needs God in order to be declared "inalienable;" to gain the status of a principle that transcends the field of current *realpolitik* and the existing rule of man; to help to form a government that accepts the finiteness of human existence or nature and institutionalizes human freedom. On the other hand, the answer to the question why human rights "needed" God in the particular case of revolting American colonies – to justify why it became necessary to dissolve the *"political bands"* which had tied them to the British Crown – is presented in the form of *"facts"* to *"be submitted to a candid world"* demonstrating that *"the history of the present King of Great Britain is a history of repeated injuries and usurpations."*[141]

In this sense even our current inquiry cannot be conceived from the position of a detached observer, but must be conscious of its own historical context. It should be driven first of all by our own inner need to seek truth about ourselves, as well as our need to act in such a way as to ensure that our concrete, historically conditioned society will remain free and open. It is certainly true that human rights, as we know and recognize them today, were discovered and declared under unique circumstances of great revolutions: English, French and American. It is also true that these three history-making events of the seventeenth and eighteenth centuries indeed became "turning points" and started the transition of mankind from the Middle Ages to Modernity. Our own current situation, at the beginning of the twenty-first century, however, is also "revolutionary." The central position of Europe and European civilization in the context of universal

---

"Frage nach dem Sinn des Seins" and the following *"Fundamentale Daseinsanalyse,"* where the concept *In-der-Welt-Sein* is introduced, represent, in my view, the basic point of departure for any serious attempt to think through the relationship between God and human rights.

[141] *The Declaration of Independence.* Quoted from: *The American Republic. Primary Sources*, ed. Bruce Frohnen (Liberty Fund, Indianapolis, 2002) p. 189.

human history is not taken for granted any more as it used to be in the past. The fundamental fact today is that all nations living on the Earth have become parts of one globalized humanity. All of us, whether we like it or not, whether we live somewhere in the "center" or on a distant and isolated periphery, are finding ourselves in one interconnected, interdependent, multicultural, and multireligious "post-modern" world. What about the future of "monotheism" we have gotten used to within our Western, *i.e.*, predominantly Christian tradition? How should we accept the highly unpleasant and puzzling fact that even our faith in one God has to struggle today with the problem of plurality? Is our concept of human rights, as we perceive, discuss and use it today, really completely "inalienable," or are we doomed to rethink it again and again, forced by unpredictable historical events, such as the fall of Communism in 1989 or the tragedy of 9/11?

To understand the "essence" of our current human rights discourse and politics requires more than reminding ourselves of the spirit of great modern revolutions. In order to know "who" we are today, we also need to go back to the crucial moment at the beginning of Western history, to the emergence of the Greek city-state. The very concept of human rights and its relation to God cannot be properly understood without taking into consideration the ethos and experience of the *polis*, historically the first state that was based on the principle of the equality of its citizens and ruled not by the will of a deified Emperor or Pharaoh but by "law." Again it is Aristotle who provides us with the most analytical and most systematic account of Greek politics.

"Observation tells us," reads the first sentence of his *Politics*, *"that every state (POLIS) is an association (KOINÓNIA), and that every association is formed with a view to some good purpose (AGATHOU TINOS HENEKEN)."*[142] And a little further: the *polis* must be conceived as *"the final association (KOINÓNIA TELEIOS)."*[143] With its creation, *"for all practical purposes the process is now complete; self-sufficiency (AUTARKEIA) has been reached and while the state came about as a means of securing life itself (TOU BIOU HENEKEN), it continues in being*

---

[142] Aristotle, *Politics*, 12521-2, trans. W.D. Ross, The Classic Internet Library
[143] Op.cit, 1252b28

to secure the good life (TOU EU ZÉN)."[144] On the individual level, *EU ZÉN*, to lead a *"good life"* means to commit oneself, consciously and voluntarily, to the service of *"practical wisdom and virtue (FRONĚSEI KAI ARETÉI)."* On the level of the state, it means to guard *"law (NOMOS)"* and to serve *"justice (DIKÉ):" "for justice is the arrangement of the political association (POLITIKÉS KOINÓNIAS TAXIS), and a sense of justice decides what is just (HÉ DE DIKAIOSYNÉ TOU DIKAIOU KRISIS)."*[145]

Obviously it is impossible to discuss here the whole corpus of Aristotle's political thought. Nonetheless, the lines quoted from the first book of *Politics* illustrate my point more than clearly. In *Politics*, Aristotle put himself consciously into the position of unbiased observer of political matters. Nonetheless the way he deals with the topic shows the underlying Greek political experience and the Greek spirit that were born with the emergence of the *polis*. The *polis* came into existence at the moment when those who were managing their "private" households (*oikiai*) as autocratic despots decided to create a common space to deal with common matters. Transferred from the possession of one, the rule (ARCHÉ) was put *"into the midst of the people" (ES MESON TÓI DÉMÓI).*[146] The might of the Emperor or Pharaoh, so far the only recognized ultimate source of order in the human world, was to be replaced by law (NOMOS). A *"final human association" (KOINÓNIA TELEIOS)* in Aristotle's terms came into existence. It was the POLIS, a community not ordered hierarchically, as was the case of all previous state bodies – *"empires with complicated hierarchies and bureaucracies, and yet be essentially no more than a giant*

---

[144] Op.cit. 1252b29-30

[145] Op.cit. 1253a37-39

[146] Cf. for instance Herodotus, *Historiai*, III:142, where a well-meant but unfortunately in the end rather unsuccessful attempt to establish a "democratic" form of government on the island of Samos is described by Maendrius who "had taken hold of the rule entrusted him by Polycrates," as follows: *"To me, as you too know, the scepter and all the power of Polycrates has been entrusted and it is possible for me to rule you, but what I for my part rebuke my neighbor for, I myself will not do according to my ability; for neither Polycrates pleased me by being lord over men similar to himself nor any other who acts like that. Now, Polycrates fulfilled his portion, but* I put the rule in your midst and proclaim the equality before the law for you.*"* (In: *Lost Trails*, translated by Shlomo Felberbaum, *www.losttrails.com* (emphasis added).

household or aggregate of households gathered around the central cell of the royal house"[147] – but horizontally, based on the plurality of free and equal men. ISONOMIA, equality before the law, conferred freedom on the citizens of the *polis*, gave them the right to act and to speak freely before the assembly of their peers, and shielded them against the excessive and arbitrary uses of state power.

Citizens should have felt themselves free of the risk of being killed, imprisoned, enslaved, or otherwise harmed in their daily lives by the actual ruler. The elementary intention of the "rule of law" was to give them freedom and to protect them against willful tyrants and usurpers, those inclined to overstep their human lot and to seek their own aggrandizement. Conflicts and disputes in the *polis* could not be resolved by intervention of absolute power from above, but strictly within the limits of political justice (POLITIKON DIKAION). Binding decisions in all disputed matters could be taken only by the proper judicial organ of the POLIS in "due process." With freedom and equality in the sphere of justice, members of the POLIS had the right to submit accusations and, when sued, were entitled to a fair and public trial. Elected jurors sat in judgment of their fellow citizens, sworn to listen impartially to both sides and to vote strictly on the issue at hand.

Aristotle, observing the political processes throughout *Magna Graecia*, was of course well aware of the difference between the ideal and reality, between the perfect constitution of the state (POLITEIA ARISTÉ) and the constitutions of various concrete city-states of the past and the present, often in the hands of bad rulers and finding themselves in the constant process of change. What is crucial for him, however, is the ability to make such a difference and to be aware of the underlying distinction between the state as *"a means of securing life itself,"* and the state that achieves *"self-sufficiency"* (*AUTARKEIA*) and *"continues in being to secure the good life"* – the distinction between the state organized as a grand household and a *POLIS*; between autocratic and non-autocratic forms of government; between the bad political regime, where the ruler seized power just to promote his self-interests and to satisfy his *libido dominandi*, and the good one where the ruler promotes the common

---

[147] Jan Patočka: *Heretical Essays in the Philosophy of History*, p. 28-29.

interest (TO KOINON SYMFERON) and acts strictly as *"a guardian of what is just and hence of what is equal."*[148]

As we have seen, Aristotelian political thought is based on concepts of "political justice," "common interest," "equality," "the rule of law,"[149] and moreover, on the underlying conviction that "the good life" of the *polis* is, in spite of all the uncertainty and danger connected with its freedom, preferable over the life lived merely for the *"continuous preservation of life through work and production."*[150] Nonetheless, it seems, at first sight, that Aristotle was unable to address satisfactorily the question that is topical for our inquiry concerning the relation between God and human rights. So far we have talked about the *POLIS* from the perspective of citizens – free men and privileged holders of "civil rights" – those few within any concrete KOINÓNIA of ancient Greeks who were distinguished from all others by their *"participation in giving judgment and holding office"*[151] (a POLIS is *"a number of such persons large enough to secure a self-sufficient life"*).[152] But what about all other inhabitants of a "city-state," women, children, old people, craftsmen, slaves, foreigners with permanent residence, etc.? What is their situation within a *polis*, which is *"an association of free men?"*[153] Do they have (or can they hope to achieve) a legal status that would confer on them at least

---

[148] *ESTI D 'HO ARCHÓN FYLAX TOU DIKAOU, EI DE TOU DIKAOU, KAI EI DE TOU ISOU* (Aristotle, *Nichomachean Ethics*, 1134b1-2, trans. Terence Irwin, (Hackett Publishing Company, Indianapolis, 1985). The famous Aristotelian classification of correct and deviated constitutions can be found in the third book of *Politics* (1279a22-1279b10): *"Sovereignty necessarily resides in one man, or in a few, or in the many....The usual names for right constitutions are as follows: (a) Monarchy aiming at the common interest : kingship (BASILEIA). (b) Rule of more than one man but only a few: aristocracy (ARISTOKRATIA).... (c) Political control exercised by the mass of the populace in the common interest: polity (POLITEIA)...The corresponding deviations are: from kingship tyranny (TYRANIS); from aristocracy oligarchy (OLIGARCHIA); from polity, democracy (DÉMOKRATIA)."*

[149] *"The laws, if rightly established, ought to be sovereign"* (*DEI TOUS NOMOUS EINAI KYRIOUS KEIMENOUS ORTHÓS*), Aristotle, *Politics*, 1282b1-2.

[150] Jan Patočka: *Heretical Essays in the Philosophy of History*, p.29.

[151] *METECHEIN KRISEÓS KAI ARCHÉS* (Aristotle, *Politics*, 1275a23)

[152] *POLIN DE TÓN TOIOUTÓN PLÉTHOS HIKANON PROS AUTARKEIAN ZÓÉS, HÓS HAPLÓS EIPEIN* (Aristotle, *Politic*, 1275b20-21)

[153] *POLIS KOINÓNIA TÓN ELEUTHERÓN* (Aristotle, *Politics*, 1279a21)

some rights? Can they hope that their inferior position will end one day, and they will be also free and equal?

It is important to note that Aristotle is quite ambivalent or even fuzzy on this point. On the one hand, he is inclined to say that women and slaves are unsuited by nature to become citizens. Therefore, they do not and cannot belong to the POLIS, and their natural place is within households or villages[154] on its territory.[155] On the other hand, when we take into consideration the whole corpus of Aristotle's anthropology (FILOSOFIA PERI TA ANTHROPINA)[156]– and one has to read his *Politics* in this context – it is evident that it aims towards a different concept of human nature. *"All men aim at happiness and the good life,"* says Aristotle later in *Politics*[157] when discussing the conditions within an ideal or perfect state. And again *"all men by nature desire to know"*[158]

---

[154] The Household (OIKIA) is the *"association of persons, established according to nature for the satisfaction of daily needs" – HÉ MEN OUN EIS PASAN HÉMERAN SYNESTÉKIA KOINÓNIA KATA FYSIN ESTIN* (Aristotle, *Politics*, 1252b12-14. The village is the "association of a number of houses for the satisfaction of something more than daily needs. It comes into being through the process of nature in the fullest sense, as offshoots of the households are set up by sons and grandsons." (Aristotle, *Politics*, 1252b15-18)

[155] What is especially disturbing from our modern perspective in Aristotle's descriptive account of Greek *koinónia* is the natural conception of the institution of slavery. It seems to be unthinkable for Aristotle that the household, serving the satisfaction of all needs connected with the physical being of man and the continuation of human life in the succession of generations within a family or tribe, could exist without the relation between master and slave (DESPOTÉS KAI DOULOS). In the several chapters of Book I of *Politics* when speaking about "economics" (PERI OIKONOMIAS, the matters of household), Aristotle seems to accept entirely the conventional beliefs of his times concerning this topic: *"These considerations will have shown what the nature and functions of the slave (HÉ FYSIS TOU DOULOU KAI TIS HÉ DYNAMIS) are: any human being that by nature belongs to another (HÓ GAR MÉ AUTOU FYSEI ALL' ALLOU ANTHRÓPOS ÓN) is by nature a slave (HOUTOS FYSEI DOULOS ESTIN); and a human being belongs to another whenever, in spite of being a man, he is a piece of property (HOS AN KTÉMA É ANTHRÓPOS ÓN), a tool having a separate existence and meant for action (ORGANON PRAKTIKON KAI CHÓRISTON)."* (Aristotle, *Politics*, 1254a13-17)

[156] Aristotle, *Nicomachean Ethics*, 1181b15.

[157] *TOU TE EU ZÉN KAI TÉS EUDAIMONIAS EFIENTAI PANTES* (Aristotle, *Politics*, 1331b39)

[158] *PANTES ANTHRÓPOI TOU EIDENAI OREGONTAI FYSEI* (Aristotle, *Metaphysics*, 980a21, trans. W.D. Ross, The Classic Internet Library

reads the famous opening sentence of his *Metaphysics*. Already these formulations indicate that his ethical teaching – which represents the basis of his political thought, introducing the distinction between *"virtue of character"* and *"virtue of thought"*[159] – has a strong noetic component. And as such, it is not "elitist," "racist," "sexist," or in any other way "supremacist," to use the expressions from our current political vocabulary, but essentially "egalitarian," "non-discriminatory" and "democratic."

First of all, one has to take into consideration that Aristotle is an "empiricist." The concepts used by him, mostly his own creations, describe the social and/or political reality observed. The Aristotelian descriptions, however, are far from being "value-free" in our modern sense, but are inseparably connected with his ethical point of departure – with his underlying conviction that the human "good" and the freedom of the POLIS belong essentially together; that the recognition of a distinction between *"life for life's sake"* and a *"good life"* is the origin of the POLIS and everything political. It is this conviction that inspired Aristotle to give his account of human associations, pre-political and political, forms of constitutions, citizenship, regime changes, state education, etc. What one should keep in mind is the fact that the Greek POLEIS, which as *"associations of free men,"* enjoying their "civil rights," were formed by a tiny minority of the overall population, were preceded and surrounded by grand empires managed as *"aggregates of households"* where all were in the position of slaves. No "rule of law" was recognized and only the divine ruler could be considered free. Furthermore, what can be observed in the Greek world – and Aristotle gives great attention to this phenomenon – is what we would call in our modern terminology the process of "emancipation." More and more individuals were liberated to enter the public space and become citizens. The domination of pre-political gentilitian structures (GENÉ) based on blood relationships – having their own cult-places, priesthood, an assembly house, a common

---

[159] *DITTÉS DÉ TÉS ARETÉS OUSÉS, TÉS MEN DIANOÉTIKÉS TÉS DE ÉTHIKÉS* (Aristotle, *Nichomachean Ethics*, 1103a14-15)

treasury and, of course, ruler as a chief executive (ANAX or ARCHÓN)[160] – was step by step broken and replaced by the political power stemming from the new administrative units of the emerging POLIS.[161] This "emancipation," which brought sometimes hardly manageable dynamism into Greek political life, had, nonetheless, its cultural and historical limits. As clearly stated by Eric Voegelin:

> *The pathos of the polis was the pathos of a dynamic participation of the people in the culture that originated in the aristocratic society. The dynamics were on the side of the 'people.*[162]

> *The individual never gained the personal status in his political unit which, under the influence of the Christian idea of man, characterized the political formations of Western civilization; it always remained in a status of mediation throughout the fictitious tribal and blood-relationships within the POLIS.*[163]

We must also remind ourselves in this context of the Aristotelian distinction between *vita activa* and *vita contemplativa*, which we discussed in the previous chapter. *"Philosophy and the spirit of the polis are closely linked,"* states Patočka in the context of his explorations of the beginning of European history.[164] It is this link that one has to focus on to understand, what is the real source of dynamism so evident in the patterns

---

[160] Cf. Erich Voegelin: *The Hellenic* Polis. In: *The World of the Polis*, p.181-194 or Jean-Pierre Vernant: *Les origines de la penseé grecque*, Quadrige, 4ieme edition, 1981
[161] Voegelin demonstrates this trend on the constitutional reform of Cleisthenes from 508, B.C. which *"divided the Attic territory into ten regions and constituted their inhabitants as ten new phylai. Each of the ten phylai was subdivided into ten districts, the demoi. Citizenship was now made dependent on membership in one of the demoi… the net effect was a successful democratization of the constitution breaking the power of the old gentilitian structure."* (p. 184). *"Nevertheless,"* he notes a couple of lines later, *"only the power of the aristocratic gene was broken, not the gentilitian spirit of the institutions. It is true that demos as such had to have its territorial basis. But it was a corporation of persons just like the older blood relationships. The Athenian still had his citizenship, not through the legal act making his person a member of the polis, but by the virtue of his membership in demos."* (p. 184)
[162] Eric Voegelin: *Order and History Volume II. The World of the Polis*, p. 183
[163] Op.cit., p.188,189
[164] Jan Patočka: *Heretical Essays in the Philosophy of History*, p. 39

of Athenian constitutional history; this problem is connected with the Aristotelian concept of human nature.

"For it is owing to their wonder that men both now begin and at first began to philosophize," reads the famous dictum from Aristotle's *Metaphysics* about the origin of philosophy.[165] The impulse to set out on a journey *"to know for the sake of knowing,"*[166] *"in order to know and not for any utilitarian end"*[167] is that awesome and shocking moment when *"a man who is puzzled and wonders thinks himself ignorant,"*[168] desires *"to escape from ignorance."*[169] It is exactly this moment when the philosopher is born. Because we already said that all men by nature desire to know – in order *"to escape from ignorance"* that they are aware of – it is obvious that the opportunity to think freely and to pursue *"this as the only free science"*[170] is open to everybody. The possibility of *vita contemplativa* must be conceived as universal. To be a philosopher is a matter of "quality" of individual noetic life and it depends neither on aristocratic origin nor on one's current status within the POLIS – whose institutions were, as we have seen, still decisively influenced by the gentiitian traditional spirit of Greek society, by the fact that Greek egalitarian political culture originated in the milieu of aristocratic society.

It must be always emphasized: Such an act of liberation is not, and has never been, an easy thing. It requires courage and determination, because as a free thinker, man finds himself by definition in the situation of one standing against many. *"Aristotle,"* says Patočka, when arguing

---

[165] *DIA GAR TO THAUMAZEIN HOI ANTHRÓPOI KAI NYN KAI TO PRÓTON ÉRXANTO FILOSOFEIN* (Aristotle, *Metaphysics*, 982b12-13, trans. W.D. Ross, The Classic Internet Library)

[166] *TO D'EIDENAI KAI TO EPISTASTHAI AUTÓN HENEKA* (Aristotle, *Metaphysics*, 982a30-31

[167] *DIA TO EIDENAI TO EPISTASTHAI EDIÓKON KAI OU CHRÉSEÓS TINOS HENEKEN* (Aristotle, *Metaphysics*, 982b20,21)

[168] *HO D'APORÓN KAI THAUMAZÓN OIETAI AGNOEIN* (Aristotle, *Metaphysics*, 982B17-18)

[169] *TO FEUGEIN TÉN AGNOIAN* (Aristotle, *Metaphysics*, 982b20)

[170] *AUTÉN HÓS MONÉN OUSAN ELEUTHERAN TÓN EPITHÉMÓN* (Aristotle, *Metaphysics*, 982b27)

that philosophy and the polis have a common origin, *"to be sure, also tells us that the lover of myths is also a philosopher in a way"*[171]

> *...though he will be one only if he seeks to awaken a sense of wonder, or awe over what actually is; the wonder of being is no fable, it manifests itself only to those who dare come to the boundary of night and day into the gate to which DIKÉ holds the key, and such a daring one is at the same time EIDÓS FÓS, the human being who knows.*[172]

To summarize: The POLIS was brought into being as a body whose members were not only endowed with certain rights and privileges, but also had a duty to participate actively in the maintenance and protection of its order. The *conditio sine qua non* for the *polis's* survival was the existence of citizens determined not only to mind their private business, but also to be actively involved in public matters; to let the law (NOMOS) emerge in the never-ending process of law-giving. It was not the law in books or in stone but exactly this collective legislative activity which made citizens free and equal. The POLIS consciously renounced the previous aspirations of divine rulers to secure to the "state" they were administering the status of immortality. It based its original social contract, distinguishing between the good life of free men and the life focused fully on its maintenance and self-preservation, on the acceptance of the tough reality of human finiteness and historicity of the human world.

It was the resulting tension between the condition of plurality characterizing the life of citizens in the public space of the POLIS, and the

---

[171] *KAI HO PHILOMYTHOS PHILOSOPHOS PÓS ESTIN* (Aristotle, *Metaphysics*, 982b18-19)

[172] Patočka refers here (*Heretical Essays in the Philosophy of History*, p. 40, citing Aristotle, *Metaphysics*) to Parmenides, the Eleatic philosopher who in his famous poem describes the travel of a thinker to *"the well-spoken path of the Goddess"* (*ES HODON POLYFÉMON DAIMONOS*), the road *"lying far indeed from the beaten paths of humans"* (*TÉND'HODÓN – HÉ GAR AP'ANTHRÓPÓN EKTOS PATOU ESTIN*), where he can "learn all things (*panta*), both *"the persuasive, unshaken heart of (Objective) Truth"* (*ÉMEN ALÉTHEIÉS EUKYKLEOS ATREMES ÉTOR*), and *"the (subjective) beliefs of mortals, in which there is no true trust"* (*ÉDE BROTÓN DOXAS TAIS OUK ENI PISTIS ALÉTHÉS* (Parmenides, *Peri Fyseos*. In: Hermann Diels: *Die Fragmente der Vorsokratiker*, (Zweite Auflage Berlin 1906). English trans. and ed. Allan F. Randall, The Classic Internet Library).

requirement, imposed separately on each of them, to achieve personal integrity through the thinking activities taking place inside the "soul," that constituted human matters, which preoccupied the POLIS and set them into permanent motion. And it was this tension, whose purest articulation was the conflict between POLIS and philosopher that burst out in the world of the ancient Greeks, bringing European mankind into existence and pushing it on the path of its universal history. Once more we can refer here to the *Heretical Essays in the Philosophy of History* of Jan Patočka:

> *These reflections should not be understood as an idealization of the Greek polis, as if it arose from the spirit of selfless devotion to "the common good," analogous to the perspective of the guardians, as it is postulated – not described – in Plato's Republic. For one, the genesis of the polis is not a process that can be precisely localized, attributed to these or those individuals; anonymous assumptions, contingencies and particular situations play the role here that cannot be quantified. Until the Persian Wars, for instance, the Athenian polis is something that crystallizes gradually in conflicts with its neighbors, as well as in the struggles of political parties in which tyrannis, opposed to the spirit of the polis, plays anything but a minor role. Yet, precisely the circumstances that the polis arises and sustains itself amid internal and external struggles, that it is inter arma that finds its meaning and that long-sought word of Hellenic life, is characteristic for the new formation and new form of life. Here, in very specific conflicts on a modest territory and with minimal material means is born not only the Western world and its spirit, but, perhaps, world history as such. The Western spirit and world history are bound together in their origins: it is the spirit of free meaning bestowal, it is the shaking of life as simply accepted with all its certainties and at the same time the origin of new possibilities of life in that shaken situation, that is, of philosophy. Since, however, philosophy and the spirit of the polis are closely linked so that the spirit of the polis survives ultimately always in the form of philosophy, this particular event, the emergence of*

the polis, has a universal significance.[173]

What does all this have to do with our question concerning the relation between God and human rights? In my view, there are three preliminary conclusions here to be taken into further consideration:

First, what must be clarified in this debate is the relation between its substance and its political context. This tension that becomes obvious whenever we want to speak, for instance, about human versus civil rights. It is the existence of a POLIS with its ideals of the "good life" and the "rule of law" that allows this question. The POLIS, the first body in world history whose inhabitants had the courage to institutionalize freedom as the substance and purpose of their "good life," was certainly not able even remotely to realize our standard of human rights. At the same time, without this Greek "origin" the question of human rights could never be raised and would be devoid of any meaning.

Second, the question of human rights is not solely inseparable from its concrete political context. Pointing to the more fundamental problem of human nature, it seems to represent the major dynamic factor dismantling all static structures produced in the flow of human history and bringing about historical change. What we can observe from the empirical Aristotelian perspective in the classical world of the Greek POLIS is the series of reform steps whose aim was to amend existing constitutional frameworks to keep pace with the process of liberating more and more individuals from the shackles of servitude and bringing them into the POLIS; in our modern language, the process of social and political emancipation. We should never forget this dynamism when we try to understand and bring into the debate of God and human rights Aristotelian political and ethical thought, the whole corpus of FILOSOFIA PERI TA ANTHRÓPINA.

And third comes the impact of conflict between *polis* and philosopher. It is the realm of *vita contemplativa,* the realm we enter when we think, which generates the most powerful impulse for our liberation, which is the strongest equalizer as far as our human nature is concerned. It is the Socratic turn from the fascination with power and glory of his

---

[173] Jan Patočka: *Heretical Essays in the Philosophy of History*, p 41.

great and beloved city to the *"care for the soul"*[174] that can help in the moment of decay and crisis. The question of human nature acquires different and not only empirical meaning here, and we can discover all implications that human rights are indeed universal; we can reflect on what it means that all men – belonging to different POLEIS in different times and spaces, but always under God – are equally endowed with their natural and inalienable rights.

III

In our efforts to analyze the relationship between God and human rights, we have departed from the distinction between our *vita activa* and our *vita contemplativa.* As a tension experienced between who we are in the external world and our interiority, this distinction does not seem to be conditioned by or tied to any specific culture or civilization, but rather belongs to our human existence as such, to our human nature. At the same time, it is true that the most distinct and observable materialization of this aspect of the human condition belongs to European (or Western) civilization, where it has gained the form of irreconcilable conflict between POLIS and philosophy. It is this conflict where European history as such – or Europe's historicity – has its origin, according to Czech philosopher Jan Patočka. It is here that the never-ending search for order in human society has begun, striving to counteract all forces destabilizing and disordering any historical human community. EPIMELEIA TÉS PSYCHÉS, the care for the soul – the appeal to obey first that inner "oracle" (DAIMONION) Socrates had, according to his own testimony, since he was a child, [175] and that each of us can discover within him- or herself thanks to our human nature – was offered by classical philosophers as the only available cure for all the diseases of the "good" but open and therefore unsecured life of the POLIS.

This appeal of classical philosophers undoubtedly represents the strongest possible moral argument why all men (and women), created equal, should be guaranteed the fundamental right to have rights and to take care for the soul. At the same time, the outcome of the trial of Socrates

---

[174] Plato: *Apology*, 30a8-30b1
[175] Plato: *Apology*, 31d1

and all the following lessons that classical philosophers learned from their interactions within the political sphere, illustrates clearly the depth of the problem that has emerged for any future political body that has come into existence in the course of universal European history. The very existence of "lovers of knowledge" after the conviction of Socrates by his fellow-citizens and their primary preoccupation with invisible things and that *"mysterious good,"* to be sought primarily not in politics but in "academic" philosophy,[176] clearly betrays new dangers to which the identity of the free citizen is exposed to, especially in the moments of political crisis: The separation of the realm of thought from the realm of action; the de-politicization of philosophy, and the elimination of philosophy from politics; the situation in which humans caring for their souls can hope to achieve inner unity with themselves by withdrawing from public matters and finding themselves in a state of alienation in their relation to the external world.[177]

---

[176] *EN AKADÉMEIAI TO SIÓPÓMENON AGATHON ZÉTEIN KAI DIA GEÓMETRIAS EUDAIMONA GENESTHAI* (*to look for an undisclosed good in Academy and to became happy with the help of geometry*). These references come from one of the most hilarious but also very illuminating descriptions of the clash between the philosophical way of life and leadership in the political domain , Plutarch's account of the life of Dion, a relative of and an adviser to the Sicilian king Dionysios II. Dion brought his teacher Plato to Sicily twice in order to educate and to convince the ruler to subordinate his activities as statesman to the guidance of philosophy. (Plutarch, *Lives, vol. VI,* Translated by. Bernadotte Perrin. Harvard University Press, reprint 1970, *Dion,* XIV:1-6, p.29

[177] There is no space here to look more closely at this phenomenon that has influenced substantively the whole tradition of Western philosophy and seems to have always played an important role in the human rights discourse. As a rather anecdotal illustration of how estranged the relationship between POLIS and philosopher in the post-Socratic era can be, let us take the example of Diogenes of Sinope (412 - 323 B.C.). The eccentric life of this Cynic philosopher (cf. Diogenes Laertius, *Life of Diogenes.* In: *The Lives and Opinions of Eminent Philosophers*, trans. C.D. Yonge, *http://classicpersuasion.org*), who allegedly lived for years in Athens in a large tub, shows more than clearly what is at stake. Philosophy was transformed by him into a colorful mélange of often provocative opinions of both stateless and homeless persons, showing, first of all, the distance of their holder from all ephemeral political matters, his disdain not only for his fellow-citizens, but also for his fellow-philosophers, his disenchantment not only about Athens or any other concrete political body, but about the whole of human civilization. From the records of his numerous conversations with various interlocutors, it is apparent that he believed that as philosopher he was doomed to remain a stranger in the world of the Greek POLIS. This estrangement, however,

One can rightly object that classical philosophers themselves were well aware of this split. Not only Socrates himself, but both his greatest disciples, Plato and Aristotle, considered the achievement of balance between *vita activa* and *vita contemplativa* to be one of the major tasks, maybe the major task, of their thought. Let us follow in the next step of our analysis the example of a man who, on the one hand introduced the basic Greek concepts into his own Roman environment and was at the same time a great and accomplished statesman: Marcus Tullius Cicero.[178] For sure, he is certainly not the only one who belongs to this category. Nonetheless, his moderate, generous, open-minded, but at the same time realistic approach to the problem of the link between the requirements imposed on us by philosophy, and the responsibilities we have to the political order, which guarantees our freedom, including the freedom of thought and the freedom of expression, is definitely worth our attention.

Whereas the efforts of Socrates to save the spirit of the POLIS from the forces of disorder and disintegration, with the help of "care for the soul," did not succeed – and it was the unstoppable decline of Greek POLEIS that brought Greek philosophers into the state of alienation – the Roman republic in the times of Cicero (106-43 B.C.) was still on the ascent to world supremacy. In this sense, Cicero's primary source of inspiration was the historian Polybios (205-123 B.C.),[179] who, unlike his predecessor Thucydides, did not need to cope with *"the greatest movement yet known in history,"* which destroyed Hellenic civilization from within in the deadly conflict of the Peloponnesian War.[180] Polybios was *"seeking an*

---

could be overcome (the adherents of Hegel's dialectics might be inclined to say *aufgehoben*) according to Diogenes by making resort to man's place in the cosmos, by making the claim that the ultimate source of human dignity is not in citizenship, a good passport in our modern terminology, but in human nature. One of these conversations recorded by Diogenes Laertius, is particularly telling in our context: *"The question was put to him what countryman he was, and he replied, 'A Citizen of the world (KOSMOPOLITÉS)'"* (op.cit.)

[178] In the following paragraphs I will be following the analysis of Cicero's political thought by James.E. Holton (In: *History of Political Philosophy*. Edited by Leo Strauss and Joseph Cropsey. University of Chicago Press, Third Edition 1987, p. 155-175).

[179] Polybios, *The Histories*, trans. W.R. Paton, *The Loeb Classical Library*, 1927

[180] Thucydides, *The History of the Peloponnesian War*. Translated by Richard Crawley, The Internet Classics Archive, http://classics.mit.edu

explanation for the extremely rapid, almost unprecedented expansion of Roman power. "[181] The might and political success of a state that once was just a poverty-stricken village on the periphery of the civilized world; the fact that its mixed regime (combining in a judicious mixture the elements of monarchy, aristocracy and democracy), passed successfully the test of time; the Roman sophisticated law, which grew gradually from the rustic customs of ancestors and amalgamated into the balanced composite of old and new legal norms – all these observations of Polybios were adopted by Cicero and became the firm, indubitable point of departure for his own philosophical reasoning and argumentation in the political realm.

Whereas for the great majority of philosophers in the post-classical period – for Academic Skeptics or Epicureans, for instance – the *vita contemplativa* gained absolute supremacy, Cicero, who is considered by many *"a dilettante rather than a serious student of philosophy,"*[182] belongs among those few thinkers who were firmly convinced by the opposite. For mainstream Western political thought, the phenomena linked to the *vita activa* can be rightly understood only when observed from a distance by an impartial, safely disengaged observer, who simply *"left aside,"* as Hannah Arendt remarked, the fundamental aspect of the political realm – *"the condition of plurality."* Cicero, on the contrary, set for himself the task to restore the primacy of the political sphere in Roman political thought and firmly believed that *"the practical life ought to be preferred to the contemplative life."*[183] He was very well aware that Greek thought was perceived as an alien element in Rome and was treated, especially because of its speculative tendencies, by the pragmatic Roman spirit with a certain disdain and suspicion. But in spite of that, he was deeply convinced that it was of key importance for the healthy development of Roman culture to open it to Greek political ideas and insights made by the classical philosophers coming from the Socratic tradition.

As an Academic Skeptic, Cicero shared the fundamental Socratic view concerning the limited value of any particular human knowledge. He

---

[181] Strauss and Cropsey, *History of Political Philosophy*, p. 164
[182] Op.cit., p. 155
[183] Op.cit., p. 159

believed that it was the dialogue that must be recommended and intentionally cultivated as the principal tool of human cognition relevant in the public sphere. The dialogue as a literary form

> *lends itself to the presentation and examination of conflicting opinions, it permits the writer to focus on the relative merits of the positions being examined while at the same time suggesting, rather than revealing, the content and direction of his own thought. The form of dialogue permits the writer to guide the discussion, but places the burden of following the argument upon its conclusion upon the reader.*[184]

And it is exactly here where philosophy can, according to Cicero, render enormous service to the city. Even though the dialogue does not produce decisive evidence that is ultimately right or wrong, it can – leaving aside each individual dialogue's reader to make up his/her mind – at least cultivate and humanize public life and shed some light on otherwise obscure, confusing and necessarily conflicting situations. One does not need to add that such an instrument of public policy can obviously be especially useful in moments of crises, when the basic values and principles of a political order become questionable and are sometimes ruthlessly examined in public; when the whole political body has to reexamine its foundations and use its collective prudence and common sense to navigate safely through the narrow pass between the past and the future; between the Scylla of fundamentalism and the Charybdis of relativism, between the rule of the iron fist and anarchy, both being deadly enemies of civic freedom.

As a realist, Cicero was well aware that not everybody in the state can become a philosopher; that not everybody can actively contribute to balanced judgement, addressing the open issues as they have been identified in the process of deliberation. So, he set for himself a kind of minimalistic goal. He introduced the alien Greek philosophy to Rome, to inspire and strengthen within the city the group of decent, open-minded individuals. He promoted the Socratic culture of dialogue and never-ending search for the public good to give voice to the middle class,

---

[184] Op.cit. p. 157

respecting and praising gentlemanly behavior, tolerating conflicting opinions, and recognizing the civic virtues Aristotle so eloquently analyzed in the context of his FILOSOFIA PERI TA ANTHRÓPINA: to remain always sober, temperate and self-reflexive in one's own words and actions; to be ready to lead others but never to forget that what makes a great leader is not his large ego or strong hand but his prudence and moderation; to know that what is just and right should be always sought for as a kind of middle term between two extremes.

Only where there is such a climate of ideas, *cultura animi*, which Cicero tried to evoke when inviting his readers to the environment of his philosophical friends – his contemporaries or the members of the older Scipionic circle[185]- is it possible to hope that the basic intention driving these conversations – *"to promote the firm foundation of states, the strengthening of the cities, and the curing of the ills of peoples"*[186]– can be taken seriously. Only thus can the challenges connected with the historical existence of Western civilization be tackled in good faith, and have, at least some hope for success. Only in this context, it makes sense, in my view, to raise the question of the extent to which Cicero's political ideas applied only to the specific experience of Rome, or could be generalized to apply to other political situations in different periods and in other states or cities. Only in this context, should one read the fascinating debates between the interlocutors of Cicero's dialogues, offering very clear and classical formulas about the nature of law, which might be seen as quite relevant in the later debates on civil rights versus human rights. Is the law a man-made thing and justice just the product of this or that human society? Are all rights to be granted to the members of a political community nothing more than creations of legislative organs of the state? Or should we delegate the principal legislative initiative to the Almighty

---

[185] The dialogue described in *The Republic* (Cicero, *The Republic*, trans. C.W.Keyes, The Loeb Classical Library (Harvard University Press, 1928) allegedly took place during a Roman holiday in 129 B.C. among members of the Scipionic circle; the dialogue recorded in the *Laws* (Cicero, *Laws*, trans. C.W. Keyes, The Loeb's Classical Library (Harvard University Press, 1928) was to take place among Cicero himself, his brother and an Epicurean friend.

[186] Cicero: *Laws*, I.. Quoted from Strauss and Cropsey, *History of Political Philosophy*, p. 171

God, in agreement with one of the participants of the three-days-long dialogue in *Republic*:

> *True law is right reason in agreement with nature; it is of universal application, unchanging and everlasting; it summons to duty by its commands, and averts from wrongdoing by its prohibitions. And it does not lay its commands or prohibitions upon good men in vain, though neither have any effect on the wicked. It is a sin to try to alter this law, nor is it allowable to attempt to repeal any part of it, and it is impossible to abolish it entirely. We cannot be freed from its obligations by senate or people, and we do not look outside ourselves for an expounder or interpreter of it. And there will not be different laws at Rome and at Athens, or different laws now and in the future, but one eternal and unchangeable law will be valid for all nations and all times, and there will be one master and ruler, that is God, over us all, for he is the author of this law, its promulgator and its enforcing judge.* [187]

Let us leave all these questions open and let us try, in conclusion, to sum up the Ciceronian lesson. To what extent is his argument relevant for our own human rights dialogue or conversation?

When observing contemporary political phenomena and trying to delimit the content and scope of our human rights discourse, we should be conscious of all dangers and ideological fallacies that can stem from the fact that many eloquent preachers or activists of this cause are voicing primarily their state of alienation. What must be identified as a great danger for any meaningful dialogue on this topic is the ongoing conflict between the requirements and appeals of *vita activa* and *vita contemplativa*; the loss of spiritual balance within our political culture; the collapse of our common sense, that seem to be one of the most warning symptoms of our current political crisis. And what should be recommended as the remedy for this deficiency, which is often lurking behind the abundance of good will and self-professed altruism of so many human rights activists and defenders? The Ciceronian courage and

---

[187] Cicero: *The Republic*, III, 33. Quoted from Strauss and Cropsey, *History of Political Philosophy*, p.169

determination to revive in our messy situation in the contemporary world the tradition of Socratic philosophy; to enlighten our politics, absorbed in daily factional strives and power struggles, with a healthy dose of Aristotelian moderation. Is it not the case, even today, that the cause of human rights can be served well only in an environment of quiet generosity, gentlemanly behavior and balanced judgment, an environment that can emerge only as a result of productive conflict of different opinions brought together in dialogue? If there is a God who can be recognized and eulogized as the good patron and guardian of Ciceronian tradition in Western politics, is it not exactly him whom human rights does need?

IV

In the last section of this treatise, I am going to return from the past to the present and comment briefly on some current originally Central European issues in the ongoing human rights debate. I will analyze here – using the example of Czechoslovak Charter 77 – the concept of human rights that emerged in the dissidents' struggle against totalitarianism. In conclusion, I plan to wrap up the arguments elaborated in the previous sections in the light of our current experience at the beginning of the 21st century, and summarize once more my answer to the central question of this volume.

In order to present the case of Charter 77, the Czechoslovak human rights movement active in the final stage of Communist rule over Central and Eastern Europe, I have to start with a concise overview of some basic historical facts concerning Czechoslovakia and to attempt to explain them. The fundamental problem of Czechoslovakia was that it came into existence as an independent state with *"the help of nineteenth-century ideas"* that informed, according to Patočka, *"the explanations of the war of 1914/1918"* and *"proved incapable of explaining the central phenomenon of the twentieth century"*[188] – the profound crisis of European civilization whose most visible and most destructive manifestation became the rise of totalitarianism.

---

[188] Jan Patočka: *Heretical Essays in the Philosophy of History*, p. 120

"The history of Europe since the eighteenth century," wrote Masaryk, the founding-father of the Czechoslovak state and its first president, in the book whose intention was to render an account of his "foreign action" during the war years,

> *proves that given democratic freedom, small peoples can gain independence. The World War was the climax of the movement begun by the French Revolution, a movement that liberated one oppressed nation after another, and now there is a chance for a democratic Europe and for freedom and independence of all her nations.*[189]

This quotation shows clearly the conviction of its author that the world after the World War would be moving in the same direction as it had been before, during "the Golden Age of Europe" of the 19th century; that all dominant modernization trends of this era – the gradual increase of quality of life in all European societies, the dramatic enhancement of their possibilities with the help of scientific discoveries and technical innovations – would continue; that in spite of all possible regressive movements, temporal troubles and aberrations, European civilization, guided by reason and being filled with the "ideals of humanity," would keep marching on the path of progress. The Czechoslovak democratic "nation-state" was supposed to take its place next to other free and democratically ruled nation-states, to become a part of a new, *i.e.*, "progressive" political architecture, shaped by the newly emerging democratic spirit, more integrative approaches, and the development of a peaceful international legal order, which would eliminate war from the realm of international politics.

Masaryk was well aware that the nation whose cause he tried to promote was small; that international politics, in spite of all Wilsonian ideals gaining at least temporary predominance in the world of the day, was primarily a domain of power. He realized that Czech smallness did not mean only the lack of resources, the disadvantage that results from

---

[189] Tomas. G. Masaryk: *The Making of a State* (New York, 1969) p. 372. Quoted from *The Spirit of Thomas G. Masaryk 1850-1937.* An Anthology edited by George J. Koftun with foreword by Rene Wellek, St. Martin's Press, New York in association with Masaryk Publications Trust, 1990, p. 219

small numbers and the fragile geostrategic position of Central Europe, being sandwiched between Germany and Russia. He knew that it was also a kind of "quality" connected with the parochialism and often pusillanimity of current Czech society, reflecting the spirit of "liberated servants," which characterized its rebirth from the oblivion of its "dark times" (that had started with the debacle in the Battle on White Mountain in the early 17th century[190]) into its enlightened modern existence. Masaryk's greatness as a thinker and his statesmanship were based on his personal courage to address and challenge this endemic smallness in a conscious, straightforward manner. Already in the 1890s, he tried to challenge his fellow-citizens and formulate the Czech question in worldly terms ("as a world question," as he himself put it.)[191] World War I offered him a unique opportunity to make a great step forward in his efforts to shake modern Czechs out of their "shells." The gaining of political independence was supposed to be just the beginning of a further process of national maturation, to be accomplished – after the life-and- dead struggle between "reactionary" theocracies and "progressive" democracies was decisively won by the latter – in the next forty or fifty years.

Masaryk's great political vision, based on his belief in progress and the power of human reason, however, was nothing but a great illusion. The 20th century turned out to be not just an extension of the previous period, a continuation of processes, initiated by the Enlightenment and liberating *one oppressed nation after another.* The ideas of the 19th century were insufficient to offer a clear guidance and spiritual orientation in the new situation. Given the international constellation that arose after the war and the both spiritual and political crisis that became more and more manifest all over Europe in the 1930s, Masaryk could only dream and pray that history would give his newly independent country a break to grow and to mature in peace, but he simply could not get it.

---

[190] The Battle on White Mountain took place on November 8, 1620. The armies of the revolting Czech Estates were defeated there by the armies of Austrian Emperor Ferdinand II and as a result the Czech lands were under their absolutist rule for the next three centuries.

[191] Cf. Tomáš G. Masaryk: *Česká Otázka; Naše nynější krize* [The Czech Question; Our Current Crisis]. 6th ed. Prague, 1948

The rise of Hitler to power in Germany and the ambitions of his Nazi movement to gain world supremacy first destroyed Czechoslovakia. Then the German Reich unleashed World War II. Liberation in May 1945 brought only temporary relief and evoked false illusions. Only ten months later, Churchill announced in his famous Fulton speech that he saw the iron curtain coming down in Europe. In February of 1948, the Communist Party, backed by Stalin's Soviet Union, came to power. Germany and Europe seemed to be divided irreversibly, and Czechoslovakia became a part of the "Eastern bloc," building its "radiant socialist future" under the total control of Moscow that would remain in place, as the propagandists of the new regime liked to repeat again and again, "forever."

The society of Czechs and Slovaks had to endure and survive all sorts of methods and social experiments to be brought under the control of totalitarian leaders and kept closed to comply with the blueprints of their ideology. First, the 1950s with the unlimited, merciless reign of Stalinist terror, executing its opponents, sending thousands of free-minded individuals to jails or concentration camps, organizing regularly all sort of witch-hunts and "party purges," pursuing the draconian processes of nationalization and collectivization, destroying systematically all non-conformist social and civic institutions and replacing them by the web of Potemkin villages and totalitarian "façade organizations."

Then came the "Golden Sixties." They brought, under the label of de-Stalinization and the policies of "peaceful coexistence of the countries with different social systems," undoubtedly at least some relief. Most of the surviving political prisoners were released. The people experienced a certain "thaw," enjoyed the fresh air coming into the poisoned and stuffy environment of the "socialist system of government," started to slowly raise their heads again and cherished hope that the Soviet iron grip could be at least loosened and socialism "reformable." The Prague Spring of 1968, an attempt to endow the existing totalitarian system with a "human face," arose with the greatest possible expectations of this kind and opened at least temporarily a door to the West. Nonetheless, the Soviet-led invasion of Czechoslovakia on August 21 sent a clear message not only to the Czechs and Slovaks but to all Central Europeans. The hopes for a more open future were futile. Their region was not only under the full control of the Soviet Union, but abandoned by the West, in the name of Cold War stability and political realism. This was exactly the moment when things really turned around for us. What happened was not only the deepest crisis endangering the socialist system of government, as it was later put by the ideologues of the "normalization era" that followed immediately, but it was also our own crisis. Central Europeans had to realize that their future would depend not only on the lot prepared for them by others, but also on their own judgment.

Here is how the transition of totalitarianism from its "young years" to its "advanced stage" – to the situation in the period of "normalization" when the Communist Party tried to consolidate again its shaken power in the 1970s and apply the "lessons from the years of crisis" – is described by Václav Havel, undoubtedly the brightest Czech analyst of the normalization regime and the most consistent critic of the totalitarian state of mind. Because Havel's approach to this indeed peculiar metamorphosis of totalitarian rule is in my view unrivalled and has become "classic," I dare to quote from him at unusual length:

> *In the fifties there were enormous concentration camps in Czechoslovakia filled with tens of thousands of innocent people. At the same time, building sites were swarming with tens of thousands of young enthusiasts of the new faith singing songs of socialist construction. There were tortures and executions, dramatic flights across borders, conspiracies, and at the same time, panegyrics were being written to the chief dictator. The President of the Republic signed the death warrants for his closest friends, but you could still sometimes meet him on the streets.* [192]

> *The past twenty years can almost serve as a textbook illustration of how an advanced or late totalitarian system works. Revolutionary ethos and terror have been replaced by dull inertia, pretext-ridden caution, bureaucratic anonymity, and mindless, stereotypical behavior, all of which aim exclusively at becoming more and more what they already are.*

---

[192] Václav Havel: *Stories and Totalitarianism.* In: *Open Letters, Selected Writings 1965-1990*, p.331

The songs of zealots and the cries of the tortured are no longer heard; lawlessness has put on kid gloves and moved from the torture chambers into the upholstered offices of faceless bureaucrats. If the President of the Republic is seen in the streets at all, he is behind the bulletproof glass of his limousine as it roars off to the airport, surrounded by the police escort, to meet colonel Qadaffi.

The advanced totalitarian system depends on manipulatory devices so refined, complex, and powerful that it no longer needs murderers and victims. Even less does it need fierce Utopia builders, spreading discontent with dreams of a better future. The epithet "Real Socialism" which this era coined to describe itself, points a finger at those for whom it has no room: the dreamers. [193]

No surprise that the Czech population's most common reaction to the normalization practices imposed on them from above corresponded to their deeply rooted political habits and "traditions." Masaryk's statues re-erected in 1968 were removed again. Masaryk's spirit was quickly dumped and forgotten. Czechs rediscovered once more their infamous Švejkish qualities: opportunism beyond the grave, readiness to play with a serious face, but duplicitous thoughts, all the games proposed by totalitarian rulers who were ready to offer the ruled a smart "social contract:" a relatively undisturbed private life and even some personal benefits in exchange for loyalty to the "normalization regime."

Nonetheless, one should not be surprised either, that this situation – when nothing or almost nothing wrong was visible on the surface, but the "normalized" society was day after day disintegrating and demoralized by an endless chain of lies and deception – was diagnosed by people like Václav Havel as leading to a serious spiritual and political crisis. If Central Europe was not to accept her lot, to which Milan Kundera tried to draw attention to when he published his famous article about its "tragedy,"[194] the 1970s in Czechoslovakia was certainly the moment that called for a kind of Socratic action. And it was Charter 77, originally a group of 242

---

[193] Op. cit. , p. 331-332
[194] Milan Kundera: *The tragedy of Central Europe*, *The New York Review of Books*. April 26, 1984

individuals, who decided to step into the public space, to speak up and to accept this uneasy and in all sorts of ways risky role.

There are two key moments that inspired the creation of Charter 77 and in fact served as the legal basis of its argument with Czechoslovak authorities – the adoption of the Final Act of the Conference on Security and Cooperation in Europe on August 1, 1975, which launched so-called Helsinki Process, and the entry into force in Czechoslovakia of two major human rights instruments of the United Nations on March 23, 1976.[195] In a moment, I will touch upon this aspect of the international environment in which Charter 77 came into existence and pursued its activities. First, I suggest we examine briefly the primary motives that made the vast majority of signatories of this document get on board and examine the experience they started as soon as they became a part of this quite unusual human rights adventure. Do not Charter 77 and similar cases of resistance against totalitarianism demonstrate that any substantive human rights debate needs more than to focus on valid law, domestic and international, more than a rigorous examination of whether states in their legal actions – administrative, civil or relating to questions of criminal justice – comply with their human rights obligations? Is not the very concept of human rights of such a nature that it is very difficult or almost impossible to separate it from its original (extralegal) existential basis?

According to its declaration from January 1, 1977 Charter 77, was a *"free, informal, open community of people of different convictions, different faiths and different professions united by the will to strive, individually and collectively, for the respect of civic and human rights,"*[196] both in Czechoslovakia and in the world. Coming from all walks of life – Christians of all denominations, Jews, Marxists and expelled Communists, free thinkers, independent liberal intellectuals and quite often just sheer eccentrics and adventurers – those who decided to sign the Charter 77

---

[195] International Covenant on Civil and Political Rights and International Covenant on Economic, Social and Cultural Rights
https://www.ohchr.org/en/professionalinterest/pages/ccpr.aspx
https://www.ohchr.org/en/professionalinterest/pages/cescr.aspx
[196] This and the following quotations are quoted from the English version of the Charter 77 Manifesto (http://www. cnn.com/SPECIALS/cold. war/episodes/19/ documents/charter. 77/)

document were sending to the authorities and to the general public one single but all-important message. They found it impossible to keep silent any more in the situation when hypocrisy became a generally recognized social norm, all basic human rights existed *"regrettably on paper only"* and a large number of people became *"victims of a virtual apartheid."* To challenge that situation, they did not create an organization for oppositional political activity. They got together only to adopt a clear, unambiguous moral stance in public matters. The vast majority of people may have found this type of behavior quixotic or even silly. What, however, was immediately obvious to everybody who had the ears to hear and the capability to listen, was that with Charter 77 Czechoslovak society regained not only the voice of conscience and freedom but also the voice of common sense. The human rights dialogue with the government, suggested in the original declaration, never started and most likely never could because of the nature of a totalitarian regime. The deadening silence of normalization was nevertheless broken and there were many other and maybe more valuable candidates to enter the proposed public debate, to exchange opinions on relevant matters, both in Czechoslovakia and abroad. The whole new discourse became a social reality whose aim was to start to ask meaningful questions again; to reexamine who we really were, who we had become in our current situation; to document the cases of the unjustly persecuted and express solidarity with them and with their families; to search for the truth in the whole range of public issues, whose treatment was for decades dominated by all sorts of ideological distortions, bureaucratic mindlessness, opportunistic manipulations, and very often sheer lies.

The way in which Charter 77 launched its human rights initiative reopened under the conditions of an *"advanced or late totalitarian system"*[197] the central question of classical political philosophy: What is the highest good that should be the ultimate aim of our actions? All Socratic philosophers in the ranks of Charter 77 certainly gained an excellent opportunity to re-read the texts of old classics in the light of their own experience. What was at stake here was indeed the matter of personal

---

[197] Václav Havel: *Stories and Totalitarianism.* In: *Open Letters, Selected Writings 1965-1990,* p.331

integrity in the political environment poisoned by the Ciceronian *morbus animi*, the spiritual disease caused by the *aspernatio rationis*, the contempt of reason.[198] The question was the existence of the man of reason – who does not have the truth in his possession but lives with the Platonic problem of *"care for the soul"* – in the *polis* struck by a totalitarian plague, having a government whose only aim was its self-preservation, whose story was, to use one of Eric Voegelin's favorite Shakespearean quotations, *"a tale told by an idiot, full of sound and fury, signifying nothing."*[199]

At the same time, however, there was another important thing that those who decided to devote themselves to *vita contemplativa* had to accept as a part of their bold philosophical exercise within Charter 77: The argument of plurality as the elementary condition of *vita activa*, with which Hannah Arendt entered into the dialogue about Western political thought. There were not only individuals with their lonely heroic internal struggles to live according to the Socratic appeal, in unity with themselves; but others were here, too, who shared the same experience, who had to endure the same harassment from the authorities, who were exposed to the same type of questions and existential tensions, who were ready to express in concert their solidarity. The participants in Charter 77, seeking the *"general public interest"* were not only contributing to the restoration of moral consciousness of society, but also were recreating and rediscovering its absent and, for so long paralyzed public space. It was due to the emergence of what was called the dissidents' "parallel polis"[200] that the totalitarian regime lost a substantive part of its magic, after the Declaration

---

[198] Cf. Marcus Tullius Cicero : *Tusculan Disputations* IV : 23-32 (a reference made by Eric Voegelin in *Wisdom and the Magic of the Extreme*. In: *Published Essays 1966-1985,* p.322

[199] William Shakespeare: *Macbeth*, V:5. in *The Complete Works of William Shakespeare*, Rex Library, 1973, p. 843

[200] The concept of "parallel polis" comes from Václav Benda, whose seminal essay on this topic published in early 1980 initiated an important and substantive discussion in the dissidents' circles. Benda's essay "The Parallel Polis" and other contributions to this debate (including my text "Jan Patočka versus Václav Benda," which is being used here as my own point of departure) can be found in *Civic Freedom in Central Europe: Voices from Czechoslovakia*, ed. H.G. Skilling and Paul Wilson (Macmillan, 1991).

of Charter 77 was published; why the cause of human rights was not only perceived as a strong moral appeal coming from lonely voices calling from the desert, but became in the course of time a political matter of great importance and also got the necessary domestic and international visibility and recognition.

My reference to the Socratic philosophers participating in Charter 77 may have raised some eyebrows or brought smiles to readers' lips, but there was one among Charter 77's founding fathers who was undoubtedly worthy of this name: one of its first three spokepersons, who died in March 1977 (only two months after its pronouncement), one of the last students of Edmund Husserl, Jan Patočka. He published in the last weeks of his life six short, but important texts related to his Charter77 experience.[201] It seems to me quite appropriate to conclude the debate on the philosophical significance of Charter 77 with his thoughts.

The central theme of this text is morality as a necessary condition of human existence, something which escapes by its very nature any state control, no matter how much power and control can states have.

> *No society, no matter how good its technical foundation is, can function without a moral foundation, without a conviction that has nothing to do with opportunism, circumstance, and expected advantage. Morality, however, does not exist just to allow society to function, but simply to allow human beings to be human. Man does not define morality according to the caprice of his needs, wishes, tendencies and craving; it is morality that defines man.*[202]

The respect for human rights is, according to Patočka, nothing else but recognition of this plain truth:

> *The idea of human rights is .... the conviction that even states, even society as a whole, are subject to the sovereignty of moral sentiment: that they recognize something unconditional, that is higher than they are, something that is binding even on them, sacred, inviolable,*

---

[201] Jan Patočka: *Texty k Chartě 77.* In: *Češi I,* p. 423-447
[202] Jan Patočka: *The Obligation to Resist Injustice.* In: Erazim Kohák: *Jan Patočka. Philosophy and Selected Writings,* p. 341

*and that in their power to establish and maintain a rule of
law, they seek to express this recognition.*[203]

Patočka's explanations and conclusions give away the solid dose
of Socratic irony. The fact that governments, including the government of
socialist Czechoslovakia, are concluding and signing international
agreements on human rights, that international human rights conventions
are becoming now a part of their legal order, marks the beginning of a new
era in the history of mankind in which governments subordinate their own
sovereign authority to the claims and dictates of morality. They confirm
by these acts to all citizens that

> *there is a higher authority, binding on individuals in virtue
> of their consciences, and on governments in virtue of their
> signature on important international treaties, placing them
> under an obligation not only when it suits them, not only
> within the limits of political convenience and
> inconvenience, but by their commitment, represented by
> their signature, to subordinate politics to justice, not vice
> versa.*[204]

Charter 77 is, according to Patočka, nothing else but an outgrowth
of this conviction. It is an expression of the joy of Czechoslovak citizens
that their government has decided to recognize and participate in this
epochal change. It is their positive response, their solemn and public 'yes'
approving that decision. It is, indeed, a great and very welcome thing,
Patočka concludes:

> *Not simply or primarily fear or profit, but respect for what
> is higher in humans, a sense of duty, of the common good,
> and of the need to accept even discomfort,
> misunderstanding and a certain risk, should henceforth be
> our motives.*[205]

For the reader who is experienced in international law and politics
it is immediately evident that the author of this text is not a lawyer, but a
philosopher. Yet it is Patočka's argument that brings me back to the legal

---

[203] Ibid.
[204] Op.cit. p. 342
[205] Op.cit., p. 342-343

context within which the initiative of Charter 77 emerged. The question was whether international obligations of state – be they just political commitments, such as participation in the Helsinki Process, that was triggered by the Final Act of the Helsinki Conference, or legal obligations created by the signed and ratified international conventions, whose fulfillment could be required and violations sanctioned under international law – could be recognized as a new source of the rights of individual citizens. The moral reasoning of Patočka, emphasizing the existential basis of human rights discourse, highlighting the fact that its current participants – the signatories of Charter 77, whose spokesperson he became – were ready to take upon themselves *"even some discomfort, misunderstanding, and a certain risk,"* was not a particularly strong legal argument and could hardly convince either the Biblical scribes and Pharisees, or contemporary experts on international law. What does it actually say about the nature of human rights that the patient endurance of the inhabitants of the "parallel polis" managed to convince in the end even these experts, that it was the dissidents, and not their opponents, who were right and won decisively their extraordinary legal case?

Patočka's philosophical contribution to our human rights debate in the seventies had another important consequence. It was developed in the context of his philosophy of history and offered a new perspective on the Czech political program, partly continuing in Masaryk's tradition, partly departing from it, exactly in those aspects where Masaryk – as the Czech experience earlier in the 20th century demonstrated – failed. Patočka agreed with Masaryk that Czech parochialism and smallness must be constantly challenged by powerful universal ideas; that the Czech question must be always thought through and conceived as "a world question." On the other hand he did not agree with Masaryk's progressivist concept of world history. He realized that European superiority in global matters ended with the totalitarian horrors of the 20th century; that mankind needs, after the European path of progress to the radiant future collapsed, *"a new political principle,"* which Hannah Arendt called for in the Preface to her *Origins of Totalitarianism*:

> *a new law on the earth, whose validity this time must comprehend the whole of humanity, while its power must*

> *remain strictly limited, rooted in and controlled by newly
> defined territorial entities.*[206]

Patočka distinguished between two legacies which European civilization left to the emerging post-European world: the imperial, self-assured and assertive way of conquest whose most powerful weapon is the instrumental, scientific reason of the Modern Age; and the much older and by definition more uncertain way of internal transformation, whose guiding principle is the "care for the soul," the never-ending quest for inner truthfulness, a really human – always finite and never complete – wisdom or knowledge (HÉ ANTHRÓPINÉ SOFIA of old Socrates). And there is no doubt that the cause of human freedom and human rights, threatened maybe more than ever before in the post-European – multicultural, multireligious and more and more interconnected – world, exhorts us to set out on the second path, to accept its Socratic principle with all implied challenges and difficulties.

The miraculous change of 1989 put Central Europe back on the map of the Western world. The short 20th century ended with the collapse of Communism. In the period that followed, first our region, then the whole of Europe, and now even the whole world have been undergoing a profound transformation. With the beginning of the 21st century, and especially after 9/11, a new era is clearly announcing itself, the age of planetary mankind and globalization. What is the burden we are carrying with us from the past? How can we protect our freedom that seems to be endangered again, when totalitarianism does not reside any more in well-defined states or other clearly distinguishable territorial entities, but has acquired a new form of loose, fuzzy and as if entirely invisible international terroristic networks? What kind of God does human rights need in our current situation?

I tried to offer at least some answers to this question throughout this treatise, based mainly on my Central European experience. So let me conclude by praying to this God, having, for sure – if he or she exists at all – many different faces and speaking in many different languages, and

---

[206] Hannah Arendt: *The Origins of Totalitarianism*, p. ix.

asking him for what Hannah Arendt, one of the greatest Central Europeans of the 20th century, had in mind when she wrote:

> *the old prayer which King Solomon, who certainly knew something of political action, addressed to God – for the gift on an 'understanding heart', the greatest gift a man could receive and desire – might still hold for us. As far removed from sentimentality as it is from paper work, the human heart is the only thing in the world that will take upon itself the burden that the divine gift of action, of being a beginning and therefore being able to make a beginning, has placed upon us. Solomon prayed for this particular gift, because he was a king and knew that only an 'understanding heart' and not mere reflection or mere feeling, makes it bearable for us to live with other people, strangers forever, in the same world, and makes it possible for them to bear with us.*[207]

---

[207] Hannah Arendt, *On the Nature of Understanding*. In: *Essays in Understanding 1930-1954*, p. 322

Exercise 7

Amicus Brief sent to the Court of Appeals of the District of Columbia[208]

First I would like to state the reasons that lead me to make this motion. I am a citizen of the Czech Republic, former dissident (I was a spokesperson for Charter 77, the leading civic initiative in the 1980s in Czechoslovakia that strived to promote the cause of human rights against the totalitarian Communist regime), now a diplomat working for the Czech Government and a lawyer involved right now in extensive academic research in the area of freedom of expression. Between 2001 and 2005 I served in Washington as Ambassador Extraordinary and Plenipotentiary of the Czech Republic to the United States. Right now I am starting my new mission in New York, as the Czech Permanent Representative to the United Nations. In my former capacity as the "guardian" of the bilateral relations between the Czech Republic and the United States, I had an opportunity to be part of the transatlantic dialogue in all its multifaceted dimensions, sometimes smooth, sometimes less easy, as we all know, between Americans and Europeans, both heirs of one Western civilization, going through and coping with all the challenges of our turbulent times at the beginning of the 21st century. Representing one of the nations of "New Europe," that have returned only after the wave of democratic revolutions in 1989 from the Babylonian captivity in the Soviet Communist Empire, I had a single message to send to all our partners in the United States, based on our national interests, historically proven and bitterly tested throughout

---

[208] I discussed the topic of "freedom of expression," and especially the differences between the US and European case law in this matter, with my friend William Dansie, a Washington attorney and he suggested to me that I write this letter to support the case of one of his clients.

the 20th century: America and Europe have to work together to protect our common values, to defend our common civilization, to preserve the freedom of our common world. The anti-Americanism of Europeans and anti-Europeanism of Americans, being so easily generated today above all because of our inability to find quick solutions and fixes to the global problems we share, need to be overcome. It can be done only through the illuminating power of genuine ideas and not with the help of cheap, superficial ideologies. If freedom, prosperity and security are what we all want, the spirit of constructive, magnanimous and imaginative transatlantic cooperation must prevail. The West needs to stand united in defense of its civilization.

Given our own historical experience in Central Europe, one of the central themes of such cooperation is human rights. The country I represented in Washington and now represent in New York at the United Nations, the Czech Republic, has always been active in this area – Václav Havel, our first president after the fall of Communism, has become a great symbolic figure in this tradition – in making use of our past experience and speaking up on behalf of those whose fundamental rights and freedoms are still being seriously and systematically violated, be it in Belarus, Burma, China, Cuba, the Middle East or anywhere else in the world. Nonetheless, the human rights dialogue, in order to be effective in protecting the victims of continuing oppression by the dictators and their repressive governments, has also other dimensions as well. In order to cope with all the subtle and sometimes certainly not trivial questions emerging also in our free societies due to all the complexities, uncertainties and tensions of our more and more interconnected and interdependent post-modern world, we need not only to fight dictators, international terrorists and other "enemies of open society," but also to do "fine tuning" of our own democratic machines. For sure, we all do it "in our own way," but to be able to guarantee to all individuals under the jurisdiction of our governments their fundamental rights and freedoms, we need to seek the advice not only of our own legal traditions and common sense, but also of comparative law, to exchange views, to craft precise legal arguments in communication with our friends and allies in the democratic world.

While in Washington, I tried to do a little more than the daily routines of my profession, my diplomatic mission conceived as business as usual. I have enjoyed tremendously living in the environment still animated by the basic spirit and political ideas that Tocqueville found so fascinating more than one hundred and seventy years ago, when studying "democracy in America." As an academic turned temporarily into a diplomat, I have established links of communication with a number of American lawyers, political theorists and public intellectuals in order to get acquainted with the US instruments and approaches to human rights protection especially in my field of study, which is, as I stated above, freedom of expression. In this context I have run across the case now being submitted to your review. This case has drawn my attention to the extent that I decided – in the spirit of friendly cooperation between our countries and as a strong believer in the power of open transatlantic dialogue – to write an *amicus brief* and to bring to your attention a couple of legal arguments and questions you might find interesting or even relevant for your considerations. I am certainly not an expert in any area of American law and I am not able, and I even do not want to argue the case in a way that American legal professionals would, if they were writing this text. My point of reference will be European human rights law, namely *Article 10 of the European Convention of Human Rights* and the case-law of *the European Court of Human Rights in Strasbourg*. In presenting the arguments I have arrived at when studying the facts and the law of this case and comparing it with the similar instances in the European case-law, I would like to articulate what my general intuition keeps telling me. From what I have learned it is obvious that American and European systems of human rights protection are, in spite of differences in the origins of their legal traditions, very close. Actually, I dare to say, they are like-minded. Are we not offered here an important instrument of transatlantic cooperation? I believe that a meaningful communication based not on rivalry, but our like-mindedness (Greek HOMONOIA, being-of-one-mind) is maybe more needed today than ever. I am even convinced that it represents the necessary condition for the realization of the basic goal we share on both sides of Atlantic: to save the best of our Western legacies for future generations; not to take from them the opportunity to "live well" in the old Aristotelian sense, i.e. as members of political bodies whose affairs are run by courageous, decent, tolerant, open-minded and self-disciplined people, in a world which is maybe sometimes rough and full of uncertainties, but still ruled by the law and not by men enslaved by their own lust for power, enabling its inhabitants to enjoy their inalienable rights, to participate in the public lives of their nations, to make their own contributions to the "common good," to pursue happiness according to their own choice and to be free.

The case of Mr. Potts concerns his premeditated action at the stairs of the Supreme Court plaza by which he and other plaintiffs intended to publicly express their views concerning a burning political issue, that was at that moment – and still is – intensively debated in all sorts of public forums, both national and international. Because political demonstrations at the Supreme Court Building and Grounds are forbidden by law, Mr. Potts and others were arrested by a law-enforcement officer at the scene. They were charged with violating the relevant statute (40 USC para 6135), found guilty and sentenced by the Superior Court of the District of Columbia. The questions presented for your review in the appeal of the plaintiffs are:

First, does the Superior Court of the District of Columbia have jurisdiction in this case?

Second, do the facts of the case meet the criteria for the application of the above-mentioned federal statute? Can an isolated act of a dozen individuals, even if premeditated and announced previously via e-mail, be assessed as an act of a "movement?" Can the hood used by Mr. Potts to express his opinion concerning the treatment of individuals suspected of terrorist activities by United States military forces, be perceived by a court applying this statute in its reasoning, as a *device designed to bring a political movement into public notice?"*

Third, does not the case of Mr. Potts and others rather demonstrate that there is something wrong with the federal statute applied? What is the underlying concept of *"political movement"* in it? What is the underlying definition of *"device designed to bring a movement into public notice?"* Is the statute precise enough to make a distinction between a political movement and a free individual initiative, between a device purposefully created by a political movement and used for its promotion and a form of expression, chosen by an individual citizen or a group of citizens to articulate in public his/her/their opinion concerning a matter of public interest and/or common good?

And lastly: even if Mr. Potts and others were found guilty of violating the above-mentioned federal statute, does not their punishment for their action constitute a violation of their fundamental constitutional rights: The Redress of Grievances Clause and the Freedom of Speech Clause of the First Amendment and The Privileges and Immunities Clause of the Fourteenth Amendment? Cannot the fact that there is no notice warning the visitors that demonstrators are subject to arrest on the steps of the United States Supreme Court constitute a violation of the principle of due process of law in their case?

As I have stated earlier, I have no qualification and no ambition to step into the realm of American law and jurisprudence. But allow me to ask now. What would a judge of the European Court of Human Rights do in your place? What arguments would he or she have to consider and weigh, if asked to assess the facts and the law of this case? For obvious reasons, I have to skip the argument concerning the Superior Court's jurisdiction. And I am also not going to discuss the application of the principle of due process of law, even though the European Court of Human Rights would obviously have to examine the case in this regard. In this *amicus brief* I want to focus on the basic material problem in the case of Mr. Potts and others, as if it were to be supervised by the European Court of Human Rights, on the question of whether the right to freedom of expression guaranteed by *Article 10 of the European Convention of Human Rights* was violated here or not. This provision says:

> *1. Everyone has the right to freedom of expression. This right shall include freedom to hold opinions and to receive and impart information and ideas without interference by public authority and regardless of frontiers. This article shall not prevent States from requiring the licensing of broadcasting, television or cinema enterprises.*

> *2. The exercise of these freedoms, since it carries with it duties and responsibilities, may be subject to such*

> *formalities, conditions, restrictions or penalties as are
> prescribed by law and are necessary in a democratic
> society, in the interests of national security, territorial
> integrity or public safety, for the prevention of disorder or
> crime, for the protection of health or morals, for the
> information received in confidence, or for maintaining the
> authority and impartiality of the judiciary.*[209]

The basic difference between this formulation and the language of the First Amendment of the American Constitution is immediately obvious. Article 10 of the European Convention on Human Rights does not only define positively the scope of the right to freedom of expression, but also mentions *"formalities, conditions, restrictions or penalties"* that can be imposed by the state, as long as they are *"prescribed by law,"* are *"necessary in a democratic society"* and follow one of the enumerated *"legitimate aims,"* (including the one which would be at stake if the case of Mr. Potts and others were reviewed by the European supervisory organs: *"maintaining the authority and impartiality of the judiciary"*).

At the same time, however, the case-law of the European Court shows that, as far as the basic approach to the right to freedom of expression is concerned, there is practically no difference between Europe and the United States. In both cases freedom of expression is considered to be a principal value essential for the life of open, i.e. democratic society, to be guarded by the courts of justice on all levels and protected against all possible breaches and intrusions. The case *Handyside versus the United Kingdom* from 1976, frequently quoted in the case-law of the European Court of Human Rights, states: *"Freedom of expression constitutes one of the essential foundations of democratic society, one of the basic conditions for its progress and for the development of every man."*[210] For sure, the right to freedom of expression cannot be conceived as "absolute," its exercise *"carries with it duties and responsibilities"* and as such *"it may be subject to ...restrictions."* However, even democratic governments may have, and frequently do have a tendency, let us suppose in good will to

---

[209] https://www.echr.coe.int/Documents/Convention_Eng.pdf

[210] *Handyside versus The United Kingdom*, 1976, para. 49. The information concerning all the cases before *the European of Human Rights* court mentioned in the letter can be found at: https://www.echr.coe.int/Pages/home.aspx?p=caselaw&c=

protect other legitimate interests, to impose restrictions on freedom of expression that are too severe, too broad, even capable, in the long run, of paralyzing its fundamental role in democratic society. That it is why the task of the European Court of Human Rights in enforcing Article 10 of the European Convention is to perform a very strict review in each concrete case whether the restriction imposed is justifiable. *"Freedom of expression, as enshrined in Article 10 is subject to a number of exceptions which, however, must be narrowly interpreted and the necessity for any restrictions must be convincingly established."* (*Observer and Guardian against the United Kingdom*, 1991, para. 59). If the restriction is found excessive, substantively weakening the role of freedom of expression as one of the essential foundations of democratic society, the European Court adjudicates the violation of Article 10 of the European Convention. Its wording indicates that there are three formal criteria, three questions raised by the Court when examining the concrete cases submitted to its review: whether restrictions imposed are *prescribed by law*, whether they follow *a legitimate aim* and whether they are *necessary in a democratic society*. As far as the general scope of freedom of expression, Article 10 protects not only *"information"* or *"ideas"* *"that are favorably received or regarded as inoffensive or as a matter of indifference, but also those that offend, shock or disturb the State or any sector of the population.;"*[211] not only *"the substance of ideas and information expressed, but also form and means by which they are conveyed."*[212]

So, what would be the debate in the European Court of Human Rights about if Mr. Potts and others filed a complaint about the violation of their right to freedom of expression that would fall under its jurisdiction? (To be able to further elaborate the argument of my *amicus brief*, I have to pass, for obvious reasons, the problem of admissibility related to the exhaustion by the applicant of all domestic remedies and to take the Superior Court's ruling as the hypothetical final domestic position in this matter.) The first question would be whether the facts of the case

---

[211] Ibid.

[212] *Human Rights Practice, June 2000, Article 10: Freedom of Expression) including non-verbal expressions such as through one's dress, musical performances, street protests, graffiti, etc.*

prove that the issue at stake is a restriction imposed by a state organ on the complainant's freedom of expression. Based on the facts presented in the appeal by the attorneys of Mr. Potts and others, I am convinced that the Court's answer would be yes.

The second question would be whether the restriction imposed on the right to freedom of expression of Mr. Potts and others was *prescribed by law*. The formal answer would have to be clearly yes – the statute 40 USC para 6135 is undoubtedly the law applied – but the character and quality of that law would have to come under detailed scrutiny. The law imposing restrictions on fundamental rights has to meet two requirements:

> *Firstly, the law must be adequately accessible: the citizen must be able to have an indication that it is adequate in the circumstances of the legal rules applicable to a given case. Secondly, a norm cannot be regarded as a "law" unless it is formulated with sufficient precision to enable the citizen to regulate his conduct: he must be able – if need be with appropriate advice – to foresee, to a degree that is reasonable in the circumstances, the consequence which a given action may entail.* [213]

A serious question would then arise in the context of the reviewed case: is the statute 40 USC para 6135 capable of making necessary distinctions between possible breaches of law whose intention is to secure the undisturbed functioning of a judicial organ, and the exercise of fundamental constitutional rights in traditional public forums; between a *"political movement"* and an individual civic initiative; between a *"device designed to bring a movement into public notice"* and devices so common in our ordinary lives as garments, dresses and all other things of this kind used eventually by non-organized individuals to articulate in public their feelings, emotions, state of mind, opinions, ideas?

The third question would concern the existence or non-existence of *a legitimate aim* for the restriction. And again *"maintaining the authority and impartiality of the judiciary"* would be certainly found as one of the protected public interests enumerated in Article 10.2. of the Convention. The fact that a legitimate aim is given without any reasonable

---

[213] *The Sunday Times versus the United Kingdom*, 1979, para. 49

doubts in the case of Mr. Potts and his fellow-plaintiffs would be the strongest argument in favor of the judgment by which they were found guilty of violating the above-mentioned federal statute. However, it still would have to be argued more specifically and proven beyond reasonable doubt, if the European Court were to accept this argument, that their act was indeed jeopardizing the *"authority and impartiality"* of the Supreme Court, especially in the light of the fact that there was no proceeding there that day.

The fourth and, I believe, the most important question to be examined would be whether the restriction imposed on the right of Mr. Potts and others to freedom of expression was *necessary in a democratic society*. The European Court would have to evaluate whether the sentence for their alleged breach of the federal statute 40 USC para. 6135 was *pertinent and proportionate* to the legitimate aim pursued. Because the action of Mr. Potts and others would be undoubtedly characterized by the Court as their political expression – *"there is no warrant in its case-law for distinguishing...between political discussion and discussion of other matters of public interest and concern"*[214]– it would warrant the highest level of protection under Article 10, since *"freedom of political debate is at the core of the creation and development of a democratic society."*[215] What would have to be carefully looked at, would be the balance between the negative impact of the restriction imposed on one of the core values, essential for the very existence of democratic society (materialized in the moment of free political debate, without which such a society could not flourish and rather would quickly deteriorate), and its positive impact attached to the protection of another public interest or common good that also has its intrinsic value. When deciding whether such and such restrictive measures against fundamental rights and freedoms are really necessary or not in a democratic society, the European Court has pointed out many times: *whilst the adjective "necessary," within the meaning of Article 10 para.2 of the Convention, is not synonymous with "indispensable," neither does it have the flexibility of such expressions as "admissible," "ordinary," "useful," "reasonable" or "desiderable;"*

---

[214] *Thorgier Thorgeirson against Iceland*, 1992, para. 64
[215] *Lingens against Austria, 1986, para. 42*

rather it implies a "pressing social need."[216] Was anything like *"a pressing social need"* present when the restriction on the right to freedom of expression was imposed on Mr. Potts and others by penalizing them for the violation of the statute 40 USC para 6135, *Parades, Assemblages, and Display of Flags in the Supreme Court and Grounds*? My honest conviction is: no. It leads me to the conclusion that the decision consistent with the existing case-law of the European Court of Human Rights would be very clear: the restriction imposed in the case of Mr. Potts and others was not necessary in a democratic society, and their punishment for their action on steps of the Supreme Court has to be considered as a breach of Article 10 of the European Convention.

I am well aware that all my thoughts, reflections and eventual conclusions come from a different legal system and have no direct precedent for your own assessment of the facts and the law of this case. Nonetheless, when I was studying the argument presented by the attorney of Mr. Potts, I was amazed how many similarities and parallels can be discovered here. First, the questions concerning the statute applied and allegation of its general *"vagueness"* that can easily lead to its abuse and that is why it calls for rather *"lenient"* narrow interpretation. Then the concepts to be clarified if this statute is to fulfill its *"legitimate aim"* to protect the Supreme Court of the United States from undue influence: *"political movement," "device designed to bring it into public notice."*

Second, the overbreadth doctrine under the First Amendment: I looked at several articles analyzing *Broadrick v. Oklahoma*, 412, US and other cases leading to its formation (for instance *Wisconsin v. Mitchell*, 113 S.Ct. at 2194, 1993 and *R.A.V v. City of St. Paul*, 122, S. Ct. at 2538, 1992):

> *In freedom of expression cases, the Court has often held that a statute or ordnance, even though it could be constitutionally applied to the specific conduct of the party before the Court, can nonetheless be held unconstitutional if it also could be applied to a substantial amount of protected expressive activity. The Court's reason for this seemingly strange result lies in the societal interest in*

---

[216] *Barthold against Germany*, 1985, para. 55

protecting the full and robust exercise of free expression, uninhibited by any fear that some individuals will think their conduct might be punishable under the statute at issue [217]

And Justice White's concurring opinion in *R.A.V v. City of St. Paul*, referring to the overbreadth doctrine formulated in *Broadrick v. Oklahoma*:

A defendant... being prosecuted for speech or expressive conduct....may challenge the law on its face if it reaches protected expression, even when that person's activities are not protected by the First Amendment. This is because "the possible harm to society in permitting some unprotected speech to go unpunished is outweighed by the possibility that protected speech may be muted." [218]

Is this persuasive for the case under your review? I would say, yes, indeed, and it also reminds me a lot of the approach to the basic ideas of human rights protection practiced by the European Court of Human Rights.

Third, the discussion concerning the concept of public forums, the places for public discourse: traditional, designed and limited. Indeed, a fascinating question, very relevant for our European human rights debate today, and I already can think about the several instances in the case-law of the European Court of Human Rights where the doctrine capable of making coherent distinctions between them and, first of all between public forums as such and non-public forums, *"reserved exclusively for its intended purposes, as long as the resulting regulation on speech is reasonable and not an effort to suppress expression merely because public officials oppose the speaker's view"* could be distilled from, but I will stop here and leave it open for future considerations.

I hope I have not overstepped the limits of good manners and good taste, by writing to you such a lengthy *amicus brief*. I have no interest here, no agenda, but I am interested in the subject itself, and in enhancement of communication, for the reasons, stated above, between Europe and

---

[217] H.J. Bourguignon: *The United States Supreme Court and Freedom of Expression*, October Term 1992, *Human Rights Law Journal*, Vol. 15, No.4-6, 1994, p. 137-149.
[218] *R.A.V v. City of St. Paul*, 122 S. Ct. At 2558, White, J. Concurring

America in legal matters, particularly in the field of human rights protection with special focus on the right to freedom of expression. I myself, in fact, used, hopefully not abused, this right by writing to you this brief, knowing well that I cannot have any influence on the decision in this case you are to make. But as an observer who has a real passion for the ideas at stake here, I confess I am very curious what this decision is going to be and what kind of legal arguments you will make in support of it.

With deep respect for the American justice system, believing that American and European legal traditions are like-minded in spite of all their differences, convinced that we all who live on both sides of the Atlantic Ocean belong to one Western civilization whose freedom needs to be protected today as it was the case in the past and will be the case in the future,

Faithfully Yours,
Martin Palouš

Exercise 8

Nyack College
Commencement Speech, 2010

President Scales, Board of Trustees, Faculty, Students, Ladies and Gentlemen!

First of all, I want to express my thanks and gratitude for the degree that has just been conferred upon me. Becoming Honorary Doctor of Laws at Nyack College – which *"seeks to…fulfill its mission by being socially relevant; academically excellent; globally engaged; intentionally diverse; and personally transforming"* – is an honor. I am receiving this distinction not only in recognition of my modest contributions to the implementation of Nyack's five core values, but also as a challenge and a great responsibility. Let me say on this occasion a few words addressed to the main protagonists of this ceremony: to the students, who have fulfilled all requirements prescribed by their study programs and will shortly receive their diplomas certifying their academic qualifications.

The very name of this event – commencement – dear Graduands soon to become Graduates – invites our attention. This Commencement is held on the occasion of the successful completion of your studies and marks the end of an important period of your life. Looking back now, you may realize how hard it was, at least from time to time, to carry out successfully all the tasks your teachers were imposing upon you, to overcome all the obstacles you faced during your years at Nyack. How important the support of your families and friends was in the moments of stress, failures or personal crises! But you made it and now you can rejoice and celebrate! Congratulations! The Latin phrase *finis coronat opus,* applies to all of you gathered here today!

Nonetheless, as the linguistic meaning indicates, commencement rather points in the opposite direction. It does not denote "end," but on the contrary "beginning" or "initiation." It designates a forward-oriented transition, a bridge between your past and your future. It evokes not only memories, but most of all opportunities before you, choices you will be making. Allow me to stay for a moment with this element of novelty contained in the etymology of the noun "commencement," and think aloud about it from a more general perspective.

Let me begin with a contemporary thinker, Hannah Arendt. She approached the world of politics primarily through the lens of her own Jewish experience and saw the emergence of totalitarianism as the central event of the 20th century. She considered it something that did not strike European civilization like a bolt out of blue, but rather emerged as *the subterranean stream of Western history....that has finally come to the surface and usurped the dignity of our tradition.*[219] But if we accept Arendt's view that the main task of our political thought is to resist the temptation to resort to totalitarian solutions for practical problems emerging today in the realm of increasingly globalized politics, what does it mean from the standpoint of Christian anthropology?

In several texts written against the background of our current crises, Arendt keeps calling on us to rethink the fundamental political idea of Saint Augustine's *City of God* , where he speaks *"from the background of specifically Roman experiences,"* and conceives freedom *"not as an inner human disposition but as a character of human existence in the world:" "Initium ut esset, creatus est homo, ante quem nullus fuit,"* (*"that this beginning therefore might be, the first man was created."*)[220] And it is this original creation of Adam that should serve us as the elementary point of departure of Augustine's political philosophy:

> *In the birth of each man this initial beginning is reaffirmed because in each instance something new comes into an already existing world...Because he is a beginning, man can begin; to be human and to be free are one and the same.*

---

[219] Hannah Arendt: *The Origins of Totalitarianism*, p.ix
[220] Hannah Arendt: *What Is Freedom?* in: *Between Past and Future*, p. 167

God created man in order to introduce into the world the faculty of beginning: freedom.[221]

Don't we have here in a nutshell a sufficient or even the only reason why – as read in *The Declaration of Independence* that gave birth to the American nation – *"all men are created equal... and are endowed by their Creator with certain inalienable Rights?"* Doesn't this Augustinian anthropology offer us a sufficiently convincing explanation that, despite modern secularism and the atheistic inclinations of our "enlightened" times, the realm of the divine and the realm of the human in an open democratic society belong essentially together? Can we not infer from this that human rights cannot be perceived as a set of entitlements stemming from human nature, but should be recognized as a seal of dignity of man as God's most valuable creation? Isn't it thanks to this divine beginning, that human rights – belonging to every man *"without distinction of any kind, such as race, color, sex, language, religion, political or other opinion, national or social origin, property, birth or other status"* [222] – should be unconditionally protected? By individuals led by their reason and moral conscience, by states through their sovereign power to establish and maintain the rule of law within their societies, and by all the bodies and organs of international society embracing planetary mankind?

And on the contrary, isn't this capability of beginning something new, inherently present in each individual human being, what all preachers and disseminators of totalitarianisms would like to paralyze or entirely dispose of? Isn't this miraculous capacity of action interrupting the chains of causality in the human world and making each and every one of us unique and irreplaceable, exactly the thing that should be replaced, according to designs of totalitarians, by their seemingly rational blue prints, plans and projections of "radiant futures?" And don't we already know too well – informed by the tragic experience of mankind in the 20th century – that such utopias will not open for us anything like an earthly paradise, but rather will send us directly on "the road to the hell" – sometimes "paved," but often not even that – "with good intentions?"

---

[221] Ibid.

[222] https://www.un.org/en/universal-declaration-human-rights/

There is a special area, Arendt once wrote, where the *"fact that we have all come into the world by being born and that this world is constantly renewed through birth"*[223] requires a special attention to be paid to education:

> *Education is the point at which we decide whether we love the world enough to assume responsibility for it and by the same token save it from the ruin which, except for renewal, except for the coming of the new and young, would be inevitable. And education, too, is, where we decide whether we love our children enough not to expel them from our world and leave them to their own devices, nor to strike from their hands their chance of undertaking something new, something unforeseen by us, but to prepare them in advance for the task of renewing a common world.*[224]

I would like to wish you all the best in your future endeavors whatever they may be. I know that not everyone among you will become a teacher, but all of you will keep in your memories this day of Commencement celebrations. So please, remember also this Arendtian appeal and when exposed to various phenomena connected with *"the fact of natality"*- no matter how bizarre and incomprehensible they might appear to be – do not to miss a chance in your concrete, always unique and thus unprecedented situation, to make a right decision. In this sense let me conclude my exhortation with a prayer, Hannah Arendt mentioned in the conclusion of one of her essays. It is *"the old prayer which King Salomon, who certainly knew something of political action, addressed to God – for the gift of an 'understanding heart', the greatest gift a man could receive and desire."* The human heart, Arendt continues, is namely

> *the only thing in the world that will take upon itself the burden that the divine gift of action, of being a beginning and therefore being able to make a beginning, has placed upon us. Solomon prayed for this particular gift because he was a king and knew that only an 'understanding heart,' and not mere reflection or mere feeling, makes it bearable for us to live with other people, strangers forever, in the*

---

[223] Hannah Arendt: *The Crisis in Education,* in: *Between Past and Future,* p. 196
[224] Ibid.

same world, and makes it possible for them to bear with us. [225]

So let the Almighty God give you this Solomonic wisdom, and let His Blessing be always with you wherever you go and whatever you do. What other than mutual understanding and relationships of love and friendship do we need if we want to "live well" in the postmodern world today, to preserve in it our basic values, our personal integrity, our political freedom, our fragile, – but always endowed with the divine gift of action – humanity?

---

[225] Hannah Arendt: *Understanding and politics.* In : *Essays in Understanding 1930– 1954*, p. 322

Exercise 9

Jan Patočka's Socratic Message for the 21st Century[226]

It is a distinct honor and a great challenge for me to take part in this conference assembled, thirty years after the death of Jan Patočka, for the purpose of *"exploring the significance of his work and its continuing influence on contemporary philosophy."* I intend to avail myself of this opportunity to take a look at a few short texts dealing with Charter 77, written by Patočka in the last weeks of his life. I will be focusing on the following questions: What is the place of these texts in the corpus of Patočka's works? How do they fit into the overall context of his philosophical investigations, inspired essentially by Husserl's phenomenology? What is the message of his Socratic teaching for us today, at the beginning of the twenty-first century?

Before I continue, I wish to thank publicly all those who, in the past decades, have worked resolutely and unrelentingly to preserve Patočka's philosophical heritage: up through 1989, under the difficult conditions of a totalitarian regime, and since then as editors of the *Collected Works*, now appearing through the meticulous care of *the Patočka Archive* in Prague. It is thanks to all these courageous and hard-working people that we may now study the whole of Patočka's philosophy, delve into the deep, wonderful, and adventurous world of his thought. There are surely quite a few names meriting mention here. I believe, however, that Ivan Chvatík deserves the highest credit and appreciation as the main architect and genuine founding father of the project.

---

[226] Published in: Ivan Chvatik and Erica Abrams (eds.): *Jan Patočka and the Heritage of Phenomenology. Series: Contributions to Phenomenology, Volume 61*, Springer Dordrecht Heidelberg London New York, 2011, p.163-174

According to its founding declaration dated January 1, 1977, Charter 77 was created as

> *a loose, informal and open association of people of various shades of opinion, faiths and professions, united by the will to strive individually and collectively for the respecting of civic and human rights in our own country and throughout the world.* [227]

Signatories came from all walks of life – Christians of various denominations, Jews, ex-Communists expelled from the party for their revolt in 1968, independent liberal intellectuals and quite a few young people with no specific background, creed, goals or expectations. They may have had different motives for signing, and most did not pay much attention to the legal reasoning of the founding declaration, yet all sent one and the same message to the Czechoslovak authorities: we cannot remain silent, with hypocrisy as an accepted norm in today's Czechoslovakia, where all basic human rights *"exist, regrettably, on paper alone"* and many people have become *"victims of a virtual apartheid."* Patočka not only joined this Central European "tea party," but agreed to assume the role of one of the three Charter 77 spokespersons. In this capacity, he wrote a series of texts which – as he died shortly afterwards of a stroke suffered following prolonged police interrogations – are now regarded as a kind of political testament.

Do these texts, now included in Volume 12 of Patočka's *Collected Works*, have something to say that should not escape our attention here? It is clear that Patočka did not write them in an environment that would generally be considered as opportune for philosophizing: in tranquil isolation, given a chance – to paraphrase Parmenides' ancient poem – to set out upon the *"well-spoken path of the Goddess"* (ES HODON POLYPHÉMON DAIMONOS), *"lying far indeed from the beaten paths of humans"* (TÉN D'HODÓN HÉ GAR AP' ANTHRÓPÓN EKTOS

---

[227] The Charter 77 Manifesto (http://www. cnn.com/SPECIALS/cold. war/episodes/ 19/documents/charter. 77/)

PATOU ESTIN).[228] Quite the contrary, he wrote them in the midst of the most serious political struggle he had ever engaged in, interrogated daily by the secret police and threatened by the State Prosecutor with charges of subversion and "antisocialist" activities. When one reads these texts thirty years later, it is nonetheless obvious that, in spite of their focus on actual matters connected with the extremely difficult first weeks of existence of Charter 77, it is a philosopher who is speaking: a philosopher well aware that his audience is not the usual academia, but the entire polis, all of his fellow citizens, whom he must address accordingly, i.e., not as a Parmenidian or Platonic scholar, with his spiritual eye turned to the sphere above the heavens, but after the fashion of Socrates, the first, as Cicero put it in his *Tusculan Disputations*, calling *"philosophy down from heaven, and placed it in cities, and introduced it even in homes, and drove it to inquire about life and customs and things good and evil."*[229]

In his first text written in his capacity as one of the first spokespersons of Charta 77, dated on January 3, 1977, Patočka wrote, trying to bring *"to everyone's clear consciousness"* *"the truths of which we are all in some sense aware:"*

> *The idea of human rights is nothing other than the conviction that even states, even society as a whole, are subject to the sovereignty of moral sentiment: that they recognize something unconditional that is higher than they are, something that is binding even on them, sacred (inviolable), and that in their power to establish and maintain a rule of law, they seek to express this recognition.*[231]

The concept of human rights in the international covenants the authors of the Charter 77 manifesto were referring to, has its roots in the

---

[228] PARMENIDES, *"Peri physeos,"* in Herman DIELS (ed.), *Die Fragmente der Vorsokratiker*; English version, ed. and transl. A. F. Randal, quoted from The Classic Internet Library.

[229] M. Tulius CICERONIS, *Tusculanarum disputationum*, ed. C. F. W. Müller (Leipzig : Freytag, 1904), Lib. V, § 10: *"Socrates autem primus philosophiam devocavit e cælo et in urbibus conlocavit et in domus etiam introduxit et coegit de vita et moribus rebusque bonis et malis quærere."*

[231] Ibid.

European Enlightenment of the late eighteenth century. Patočka's moral argumentation, his invocation of *"the truths of which we are all in some sense aware,"* sounds, however, more like a voice out of a distant past, reviving something that does not really fit into the contemporary human rights discourse, but rather hearkens back to premodern, largely abandoned spiritual traditions. His argument that respect for human rights represents the moral foundation of all human societies (and no society, he says, can function without such a foundation!) – that such rights are constituted, not simply by human nature, but through our recognition of the sovereignty of moral sentiment – shifts our focus from the modern emancipated individual, perceived as their bearer or "owner" (possessing them simply as something he or she is "entitled" to), to the age-old conflict between politics and philosophy. It turns our attention to the trial of Socrates, who seems to have been the main source of inspiration for Patočka's approach to political matters in general, his great example and precursor with regard to his own activities in the public realm.

The similarity between Patočka and Socrates calls for some comments. Let me quote what Hegel has to say about certain widespread Socratic "traditions" in his *Lectures on the History of Philosophy*:

> *Because Socrates in this way gave rise to moral philosophy, all succeeding babblers about morality and popular philosophy constituted him their patron and object of adoration, and made him into a cloak which should cover all false philosophy. As he treated it, it was undoubtedly popular; and what contributed to make it such was that his death gave him the never-failing interest derived from innocent suffering.*[232]

Patočka's Socratic appeal in his Charter 77 texts escapes, without a doubt, Hegel's taunting remarks. He is a genuine philosopher, speaking from the apeirontic depth of his thought.

One could draw another parallel, inasmuch as Socrates, in the *Apology*, states that he felt, since childhood, the call to obey *"a sort of*

---

[232] Georg Wilhelm Friedrich Hegel: Lectures on the History of Philosophy, E.S, Haldane (transl.), Routledge & Kegan Paul Ltd., London, repr. 1955, Vol. I, p. 388, www.gutenberg.org/files/51635/51635-h/51635-h.htm#c384

voice that comes to me."[233] Patočka's Socratism too is something that was present throughout his philosophical life, long before his open conflict with the Czech polis. From his early writings in the 1930s to the 1977 Charter texts, Patočka grappled with the problem of *"negative Platonism,"*[234] the problem of returning from Plato's positive doctrine of separately existing ideas to the essentially negative and dialectic wisdom of his master. He repeatedly expressed his conviction that the real beginning of philosophy does not lie in Socrates' words, in his *logos*, but in his deed – *"Socrates is this deed."*[235] In this sense, philosophy's most important task is not to speculate *in abstracto* but, as Patočka wrote already in 1936, at age twenty-nine, *"to criticize life in all its components and manifestations;"*[236]

> *to express what society has hitherto wanted without being*
> *aware of it, to put into words its unvoiced tendencies, but*
> *also to show what is behind them, to clarify their essence,*
> *their genesis, their intricacies and problems, and to attempt*
> *then to resolve them.*[237]

The figure of "Socrates the philosopher" – whether he be *"a literary myth or a historical reality"*[238] – plays a prominent role in Patočka's thought. *"Socrates,"* he wrote in an unpublished text from the late 1940s, *"is the inventor of the question of good,"*[239] a question that is not meant to *"give way to an answer."*[240] What Socrates asks of us, in raising this question, is not to escape it through an answer, but to let it prevail: *"to stick with it and understand its meaning."*[241] Consequently,

---

[233] Plato: *Apology*, 31d1

[234] Jan Patočka: *Negative Platonism: Reflections concerning the Rise, the Scope, and the Demise of Metaphysics—and Whether Philosophy Can Survive It.* In: Erazim Kohák: *Jan Patočka. Philosophy and Selected Writings*, pp. 175-206.

[235] Jan Patočka: *Kapitoly ze současné filosofie* [Chapters from Contemporary Philosophy]. In: *Péče o duši I*, p. 98

[236] Ibid.

[237] Ibid., p. 92

[238] Jan Patočka: *Negative Platonism*. In: Erazim Kohák: *Jan Patočka. Philosophy and Selected Writings*, p. 180

[239] Jan Patočka: *Věčnost a dějinnost* [Eternity and Historicity], in: *Péče o duši I*, p. 143

[240] Ibid.

[241] Ibid., p. 144

the adequate philosophical response to the question of good is not a philosophical doctrine – a set of metaphysical propositions claiming the status of eternal truths – but a new orientation of human life, philosophy as *"caring for the soul."* Patočka sums up:

> *Socrates discovered man as the being most different from all others – the human being as originally unfinished, yet committed unto his own hands in order to understand his essential will and to give meaning to his life. For such a being, the events of life must take on significance; and a being for whom events have significance is a historical being. Socrates is the discoverer of human historicity.*[242]

This is the point. It is precisely this discovery that contemporary philosophy – after all its confusions, willfulness, and erratic moves, all its fruitless efforts to do away with or seemingly overcome the metaphysics of the past – should choose, according to Patočka, as its starting-point. It is to Socrates and his finite human wisdom, HÉ ANTHRÓPINÉ SOFIA,[243] that we look today for guidance and inspiration at our historical crossroads, at this moment of deep spiritual and political crisis in Western civilization. Patočka concludes:

> *Si licet parva comparare magni, philosophy is starting over again with Socrates.*[244]

What does this statement mean? If what the Socratic beginning is all about is not Socrates' word alone, but his deed, where do we begin?

I will come back later to the Socratic element in Patočka's Charter 77 texts. Let me first digress from this theme to comment on a viewpoint which seems clearly to have had a significant influence on Patočka, at least in the final stage of his philosophical life: the point of view introduced into contemporary philosophical discourse on political matters by Hannah Arendt.

"I avoid the expression 'political philosophy,'" Arendt remarked to Günter Gaus in a radio interview in 1964, later published in a collection

---

[242] Ibid., pp. 146-147
[243] Plato: *Apology*, 23a6
[244] Jan Patočka, *Věčnost a dějinnost* [Eternity and Historicity], in: *Péče o duši I*, Translated by MP p. 214

of her essays, because it is *"extremely burdened by tradition,"*[245] by a deeply rooted conviction of philosophers that political matters can be approached *"philosophically,"* from the standpoint of a thinker who isolates himself from all his fellows in order to think. If politics and philosophy are to be brought together, what must serve as a starting-point is their tense relationship, the *"vital tension between man as a thinking being and man as an acting being."*[246] Given this tension, the human matters here at issue cannot be dealt with from a neutral, objective perspective, as when speaking of nature, as if one were to become all of a sudden a spokesperson for the whole of humankind. Human matters are always given us as something relating to our own lives, in the unique situation in which we find ourselves, in our concrete existence, in our concrete historical society.

In the same vein, Arendt wrote in 1956, in a letter to her teacher and lifelong friend Karl Jaspers:

> *I suspect that philosophy is not altogether innocent in this fine how-do-you-do.....that Western philosophy has never had a clear concept of what constitutes the political, and couldn't have one, because by necessity it spoke of man the individual and dealt with the fact of plurality tangentially.*[247]

These two quotations, in my view, aptly characterize the basic task Arendt set for her own in-depth investigations of *vita activa* and *vita contemplativa,* pursued with unmatched clarity and precision in *The Human Condition* and *The Life of the Mind*: to return from empty political categories and concepts to "things themselves" in the realm of politics; to view political matters primarily through the lens of our own personal experience in the tragic twentieth century; to try to understand totalitarianism as its central event, as something that did not strike European civilization like a bolt out of the blue, but rather emerged, as she

---

[245] Hannah Arendt: *"What Remains? The Language Remains:" A Conversation with Günter Gaus.* In: *Essays in Understanding 1930-1954*, p. 2
[246] Ibid.
[247] Hannah Arendt and Karl Jaspers: *Correspondence 1926-1969.* Edited by Lotte Kohler and Hans Saner. Translated by Robert and Rita Kimber. Harcourt Brace Jovanovich Publishers, New York, San Diego, London, 1992, p. 166

puts it in the Preface to the first edition of *The Origins of Totalitarianism*, as *"the subterranean stream of Western history"* that *"has finally come to the surface and usurped the dignity of our tradition."* [248]

Arendt's starting from her own political experience, from what she held to be her *"personal problem,"* [249] did not mean, however, that she intended to remain forever chained to her own, however painful or persistent, idiosyncrasies. What she was seeking in her work as a *"political theorist,"* as she called herself,[250] was to offer a "political theory" transcending her personal point of view, a theory erected as a bridge between past and future, opening a new perspective, an opportunity to begin anew "after Auschwitz." Her insights and political ideas were not to be framed in the Platonic vision of a "perfect state," but to "function" as acts of reconciliation, "saving counsels" of ancient drama, helping us, as members of planetary humanity constituted by the unprecedented tragedies of the twentieth century,[251] to understand totalitarianism, *"to come to terms with and reconcile ourselves to....a world in which such things are possible."* [252] This did not mean blindly applying the French proverb *tout comprendre, c'est tout pardonner*, but rather cultivating the only *"inner compass we have,"* [253] our understanding, our common sense, our common capacity for healthy judgement. If we are determined to avert

---

[248] Hannah Arendt: *The Origins of Totalitarianism*, p. ix

[249] Cf. Hannah Arendt: *"What Remains? The Language Remains:" A Conversation with Günter Gaus.* In: *Essays in Understanding 1930-1954*, pp. 10-11: *"First of all, the generally political became a personal fate when one emigrated. Second . . . friends collaborated or got in line. The problem, the personal problem, was not what our enemies did, but what our friends did."*

[250] Ibid., p. 1: *"My profession, if one can even speak of it at all, is political theory."*

[251] Cf. what Eric Voegelin said in his review of Arendt's *Origins of Totalitarianism* about the emergence of totalitarian mass movements in the twentieth century: *"The putrefaction of Western civilization, as it were, has released a cadaveric poison spreading its infection through the body of humanity. What no religious founder, no philosopher, no imperial conqueror of the past has achieved—to create a community of mankind by creating a common concern for all men—has now been realized through the community of suffering under the earthwide expansion of Western foulness."* (Eric Voegelin: *The Origins of Totalitarianism*. In: *Published Essays 1953-1965*, p. 15.)

[252] Hannah Arendt: *Understanding and Politics*. In: *Essays in Understanding 1930-1954*, p. 308

[253] Ibid.

the possibility that similar or even greater horrors than Soviet gulags or Nazi "death factories" may one day happen again:

> *if we want to be at home on this earth, even at the price of being at home in this century, we must try to take part in the interminable dialogue with the essence of totalitarianism.*[254]

There is an essential prerequisite if future totalitarian tendencies in our thought are to be averted. What must be overcome, as Arendt emphasized in her conversation with Günter Gaus, is the extreme burden of the tradition of Western political philosophy. Does this mean that this tradition is to be discarded? No. What Arendt suggests is that Western political philosophy should be examined in a new way. In the realm of the political, we should first of all free ourselves of the perspective of *"One Omniscient Knower"* that dominates our Western epistemology.[255] We should adopt a worldview springing from the primordial tension between acting and thinking, politics and philosophy. What should be rediscovered, or rather constituted anew, by the proposed Arendtian turn is, as she wrote to Jaspers, the *"pure concept of the political"* that *"Western philosophy has never had, and could not have."* What should be carefully thought through is what this philosophy has *"dealt with tangentially"* and passed by without proper attention: *"the fact of plurality,"* i.e., the fact that plurality is a fundamental aspect of the human condition.

Patočka seems to have discovered the thought of Hannah Arendt only in 1970, when working on his last big project, *Heretical Essays in the Philosophy of History*. He summarizes, for his own analyses, Arendt's elementary distinctions between labor, work and action – *"three fundamental human activities,"* each of which corresponds *"to one of the basic conditions under which life on earth has been given to man"*[256] – referring these concepts back to the part of the *Nicomachean Ethics* where Aristotle differentiates between various forms of free human life – the life

---

[254] Ibid., p. 323.

[255] I borrow this term from the founder of American pragmatism, William James, Cf. my essay *Common Sense and the Rule of Law: Returning Voegelin to Central Europe* in this volume

[256] Hannah Arendt: *The Human Condition*, p. 7

of gratification or enjoyment (BIOS APOLAUSTIKOS), the life of politics or action (BIOS POLITIKOS), and the life of contemplation or study (BIOS THEÓRETIKOS).[257] There is no doubt that Patočka used Arendtian distinctions, in a coherent and creative manner, in his search for the origins of European history. Nonetheless, in going through all his references to her analyses and observations, not only in the final text of the *Heretical Essays*, but also in the preparatory manuscripts and lectures from this period,[258] I was puzzled by his total silence as concerns Arendt's central point: human plurality as an essential aspect of our human condition, neglected by Western political philosophy. How can he have accepted some of her greatest insights, while at the same time closing his eyes to core elements of the revolution she wrought in contemporary political thinking? Does this mean that Patočka, in spite of his own deep insights into the origins of European politics and philosophy, articulated with great intellectual strength and passion in his *Heretical Essays in the Philosophy of History*, remained a captive of the Western tradition which Arendt saw as an *"extreme burden?"* That, despite all his efforts to restore *"the link between philosophy and the spirit of the polis"*[259] in his investigations of Europe's origins, Patočka simply missed what, according to Arendt, is the living heart of political phenomena? That he too is one of those philosophers who have no *"pure concept of the political,"* and by whom the *"fact of plurality"* has been *"dealt with tangentially?"* The answer is clearly no.

To clarify this point, we would need a precise and sufficiently detailed comparison of Arendt's and Patočka's interpretations of the relation between politics and philosophy, of the *"tension between man as a thinking being and man as an acting being."* I cannot broach this subject in the framework of today's short talk. What I can and shall do instead – to defend Patočka against possible questions and critiques on the part of Arendtians – will be based solely on my experience with Charter 77 and my re-reading of his texts about it. His resort to moral argument, to *"the truths of which we are all in some sense aware,"* proves clearly that

---

[257] Aristotle, *Nicomachean Ethics*, 1095b-1096
[258] Published in Jan Patočka: *Péče o duši III*, p. 147-514
[259] Jan Patočka: *Heretical Essays on the Philosophy of History*, p. 41

Patočka remained, to the end of his life, a Socratic philosopher, forced rather by circumstances than by a desire for political engagement to assume an active role in public affairs. There is, in these texts, a good deal of evidence that he was indeed always a thinker and never a politician; he went public, in a Czechoslovakia sick with the totalitarian plague, not to engage himself in politics properly speaking, but to think out loud and publicly inquire into the roots of our political crisis with the philosophical help of his old Socratic questions and ideas. Surprisingly, regardless of his possible neglect of human plurality in his philosophy of history and his reflection on Europe's foundations, his Socratic action contributed substantially to the opening of a new public space where human plurality could re-emerge in the specific phenomenon of a "parallel polis."[260] It was precisely this body politic, destined to live a mere thirteen years – certainly not just a courageous and virtuous, but in many ways a bizarre and problematic community of the *"shaken,"* composed not only of the signatories of Charter 77, with their various opinions, faiths and professions, but also of many others, resolved to resist totalitarianism on their own terms – that has remained as part and parcel of Patočka's spiritual legacy to future generations.

Rereading Patočka's Charter 77 texts thirty years after the facts, I had to struggle, for obvious reasons, with my own idiosyncrasies. While a bygone world has left its mark on these documents, when read as a whole – six short pieces, in chronological order – they may be compared to Socrates' three consecutive speeches before the Athenian court which, if we can trust Plato, go to make up his *Apology*. These six texts either articulate Patočka's own views on Charter 77's essence and mission, or react to different instigations – the malicious media campaign against Charter 77, the threats of the State Prosecutor, questions raised by foreign journalists or circulating among the general public. They reflect the events of the last weeks of Patočka's life, yet all deal with one and the same old question: what, apart from its recognized customs, its valid laws, its form of government and all the practical aspects of daily affairs, enables a body politic to exist qua body politic? Whatever politicians themselves may

---

[260] Cf. *Exercise 3 Jan Patočka versus Václav Benda* and *Exercise 13 Charter77 – a Retrospective* in this volume

have to say to this point – whether they appeal to religion or to ideology, to enlightened self-interest or to collective well-being as the elementary *raison d'être* of a state – their answers are, from Patočka's Socratic perspective, either insufficient or irrelevant. The adequate response to this question cannot come from their realm, but only from a higher sphere, above, or shall we say rather outside of politics. Even states, having the power to enact and enforce binding laws, must first and foremost honor the rule of law. Even sovereign states are obliged to respect the elementary fact that our humanity has precedence over any political role we may be assigned or pressed to play as citizens. Not only individual human beings, but states and society as a whole are, by necessity, *"subject to the sovereignty of moral sentiment."*[261] Sticking to this simple premise, signing Charter 77 cannot be perceived, according to Patočka, as a *"political act in the strict sense."*[262] Charter 77 *"constitutes no competition or interference with political power in any of its functions;"*[263] hence, it is *"neither an association, nor an organization,"*[264] but a simple *"outgrowth of the conviction"*[265] that no society *"can function without a moral foundation."*[266]

There is, however, one argument advanced by Patočka in his Charter 77 texts that compels further examination:

> *Charter 77 never sought more than to educate. But what does that mean? Each individual must learn for himself, though he can often be affected by examples, warned by bad results, or taught by dialogue and discussion.*[267]

We all recall the exchange, in the *Apology*, between Socrates and his accusers concerning the problem of the education of youth. Who is a good educator and, on the contrary, who corrupts the young? In Ancient

---

[261] Jan Patočka: *The Obligation to Resist Injustice*. In: Erazim Kohák: *Jan Patočka. Philosophy and Selected Writings*, p. 341

[262] Ibid., p. 342

[263] Ibid.

[264] Ibid.

[265] Op.cit., p. 341

[266] Ibid.

[267] Jan Patočka: *What We Can and Cannot Expect from Charter 77*. In: Erazim Kohák: *Jan Patočka. Philosophy and Selected Writings* p. 346

Athens, the polis itself was held to be the best educator,[268] but what happens, then, in times of crisis? Is the best teacher still the mass of law-abiding citizens, the polis as a whole, with its dubious customs and decadent culture, or rather the philosopher? Socrates' answer to this question, and the verdict of the Athenians, are well known. From that point on, polis and philosophy went their separate ways.

This divorce brings us back to Arendt's argument that plurality is a fundamental aspect of the human condition and that today, perhaps more than ever before, our thought should include a *"pure concept of the political."* Does the Socratic choice – the choice of being in unity, in agreement with oneself, over being in *"harmonious relations"* with all others in the polis – always lead to philosophy's profound alienation from public affairs, as was apparently the case in all the Socratic schools, starting with Plato's Academy, after the death of Socrates? Or is there still a chance that the polis may, after all, be reformed, or even saved, through the force of the Socratic deed? With the same proviso Patočka made when speaking of this deed – *si licet parva comparare magnis* – I believe he himself, through his own Socratic action, proved that the answer to this question need not always be negative. Though the dissident parallel polis was an unusual and imperfect body politic – totally dependent on the bigger whole it was but a tiny part of, living under state repression, in a permanent state of siege, just a bunch of self-appointed citizens with no territory or protective walls – surprisingly enough, it did manage to start something genuinely new. It was a vulnerable, colorful, bizarre entity, yet a new beginning!

Those who signed the founding declaration of Charter 77 may have been initially motivated *more Socratico*, by the desire to live in peace with their own souls, in unity with themselves. They discovered, however, in the course of events, that launching into this adventure was not a mere matter of personal integrity, constituted in the *"silent dialogue between me and myself."* They discovered what it means to leave the protective walls of one's private life, to step into the public arena and call on one's fellows. They discovered the binding power of acting together. They

---

[268] Cf. Pericles' *Funeral Oration*, in THUCYDIDES, *The History of the Peloponnesian War*, 2.41: *"In short, I say that as a city we are the school of Hellas."*

discovered that the essential political virtue is not success in the struggle for power, but rather the building of trust, the ability to take concerted action, the readiness of each and every one to support the others in the face of danger, to maintain the spirit of solidarity. In short, they discovered, each in his or her own way, on his or her own terms, the same fact that Arendt held to be a fundamental prerequisite of political life: the fact of plurality, essential to our human condition, yet dangerously absent from the basic concepts of our political thought.

With this quite simple, yet practical discovery in mind, I shall in conclusion go back once more to human rights. When we read Jan Patočka's Charter 77 texts, it is immediately obvious that the author is not a lawyer, but a philosopher. His assertion that the obligation of states to respect human rights can be inferred from their being subject in general to the *"sovereignty of moral sentiment"* is simply too fuzzy for jurisprudence. In order to be understood in the context of contemporary public international law, it would have to be translated into "legalese," and would certainly need to be more specific – for instance, regarding international responsibilities ensuing from the violation of this obligation and possible compulsory measures that could be brought to bear on a non-yielding, "unrepentant" violator. The question of the legal subjectivity of individuals in contemporary international human rights law is also, without a doubt, a great deal more complicated than Patočka's straightforward view of self-defense in the field of human rights as the civic duty of individuals, stemming from their moral beliefs and convictions.

Lawyers, of course, have the full right to raise their professional questions, as they were invited to do in the early stages of Charter 77, when Patočka was writing his last texts. They are, however, at risk of missing the main point of Patočka's Socratic deed and legacy – as actually happened in the days following the publication of the Charter 77 manifesto on January 5, 1977, some being blinded by juridical rigor, others acting simply out of fear and opportunism. In actual fact, the focus on human rights is not only an outgrowth of the moral conviction of isolated individual citizens. It is also the main content of their "non-political politics." It is the only political program, the only political objective their "parallel polis" ever had, other than the general call for governments to obey their own laws: the strengthening of respect for a new principle, a new rule of conduct in the international realm, which is slowly gaining ground in the contemporary phase of human history, i.e., the rule of law instead of a mere balance of power in international relations – the conviction expressed by Patočka, in his first text on Charter 77, that here also, and not only in the domestic affairs of nation-states, politics *"should be subordinated to justice, not vice versa."*[269]

The world has undeniably changed in the past thirty years. Since 1989, Communism is a bygone thing in Europe. Charter 77 has retired from active business a long time ago, and only three aging former spokespersons now guard its legacy. Czechoslovakia has disappeared from the map, but both the Czech Republic and Slovakia are free countries, members of NATO and the EU. Europe is reunited, the old bipolar stability irretrievably gone. Everything seems to be in flux. What would Jan Patočka have to say to all this? It's hard to guess. Observing the political processes we are part of, endeavoring to understand the world around us with its new opportunities, its dangers and challenges, our best bet is to hearken anew to his questions, renewed from a distant past: such is Patočka's Socratic message for the twenty-first century.

---

[269] Jan Patočka: *The Obligation to Resist Injustice.* In: Erazim Kohák: *Jan Patočka. Philosophy and Selected Writings* p. 342.

Exercise 10

Edvard Beneš:
A Bridge Builder Who Failed[270]

Introduction

To speak about US policies towards Europe in the years after the end of World War II from the Czech perspective is to re-visit the time of

---

[270] This essay is an adapted version of my paper *The Policy of Containment from the Perspective of the Contained*, presented at The Truman Legacy Symposium on Foreign Aid which took place in Little White House in Key West, Fl. (a branch of Truman's Presidential Library) in May, 2012.

And a word of warning in this context: I am not a professional historian and, as result of that, what is presented here should not be read as my contribution to the contemporary Czech historiography dealing with the topic which is – and still will be in the times – a source of our painful, emotionally loaded Czech national conversations. It is nothing more than a testimony of my own encounters with Eduard Beneš, first of all as an avid reader of Patočka, then through the sources mentioned below and also in the private conversations I have had with family members and friends in the past five decades.

Here is a somewhat eclectic selection of my primary and/or secondary sources:

The Czech sources: Edvard Beneš: *Paměti. Od Mnichova k nové válce a novému vítězství*, Orbis Praha 1947, Edvard Beneš: *Paměti I, II, III*. Edited by Milan Hauner, Academia Praha 2007; Eduard Beneš: *Demokracie dnes a zítra*. Čechoslovák, London 1944; Eduard Táborský: *Prezident Beneš mezi Západem a Východem*, Mladá Fronta, Praha 1993; *Formování československého zahraničního odboje v letech 21938-1939 ve světle svědectví Jana Opočenského*, Arenga Praha 2000; Antoine Mares: *Edvard Beneš. Drama mezi Hitlerem a Stalinem*, Argo Praha, 2016; Georges-Marc Benamou: *Mnichovský přízrak*. Translated from French (*Le Fantome de Munich*) by Zuzana Tomanová, Paseka Praha-Litomyšl, 2007;Jiří Koftun: *Republika v nebezpečném světě. Éra prezidenta Masaryka 1918-1935*, Torst, Praha 2005.

The English Sources: Eduard Beneš: *Democracy Today and Tomorrow*, The MacMillan Company, New York, 1939; *From the Hussite Wars to NATO Membership. The Czech Contributions to Peace and War in Europe*. Editor ELK, Prague 2002; Hugh Agnew: *The Czechs and the Lands of the Bohemian Crown*,

our illusions, confusions, false expectations and miscalculations. It calls for re-examination of the origins of the tragedy of Central and Eastern European nations finding themselves on the wrong side of the Iron Curtain descending, as Churchill observed already in the spring of 1946, on the European Continent. Why and how did it happen? Who should be blamed for Czechoslovakia losing its independence – three years after having regained it after the German occupation – being turned into a Communist satellite state and doomed to remain in the Soviet sphere of influence until the revolutions of 1989?

There are two different sets of facts and actions which bear on troubling questions. On the one hand, there is the reality of the postwar global order and the place of Central Europe in it as seen from the United States, the state that emerged from World War II as a leading world power championing Western liberal principles and values.

On the other hand, there are Czech contributions to the state of international public affairs that was created in Europe and in the world in the second half of the 20th century – in the first place, the policies pursued by the second Czechoslovak President Edvard Beneš, the heir of the political legacy of Tomas Garrigue Masaryk, Czechoslovakia's founding father, in the times of critical political transitions.

My intention as author of this article – who was born in 1950 as a citizen of the then socialist Czechoslovakia – is not to engage in a traditional blame game and accuse Beneš from my perspective of someone who already knows what was coming and what really happened in the next decades. The purpose of my reflections presented here is not just to criticize Beneš's political mistakes that were an important part of the chain

Hoover Institution Press, Stanford University, Stanford, California, 2004; Jaroslav Pánek and Odlřich Tůma (eds.): *A History of the Czech Lands*, Charles University, Prague 2009; Betty Miller Unterberger: *The United States, Revolutionary Russia, and the Rise of Czechoslovakia*, Texas A&M University Press, 2000; Igor Lukeš: *On the Edge of the Cold War. American Diplomats and Spies in Postwar Prague*, Oxford University Press, 2012; Madeleine Albright: *Prague Winter. Personal Story of Remembrance and War*, 1937-1948, Harper Collins Publishers, 2012; Mary Heimann: *Czechoslovakia. The State that Failed*, Yale University Press, New Haven and London, 2009; Anne Applebaum: *Iron Curtain. The Crushing of Eastern Europe 1944-1956*, Doubleday New York-London-Toronto-Sydney-Auckland, 2012; John Lewis Gaddis: *George F. Kennan. An American Life*, Penguin Press New York, 2011

of events that brought another round of miseries on his own nation. What must be considered as more important here is the careful examination of the root causes of what now belongs to our Czech contemporary history; which should serve today as an important lesson not only for our own contemporary politicians, but for everyone willing and able to learn from our common past. This is the sole purpose of this text.

Foundation, Rise, and Fall of Masaryk's State

The idea of independent Czechoslovakia was born in the turmoil of the Great War 1914-1918. Its spiritual father and most energetic proponent was university professor of philosophy and sociology Tomas Garrigue Masaryk. Not only an academic but also a politician, Masaryk had been actively involved in Czech public life for decades. He was known for his vocal defense of many politically controversial issues and for his stubborn readiness to challenge the parochial, petit-bourgeois mentality of his compatriots.[271]

The reasons Masaryk decided in the fall of 1914 to abandon the political doctrine of "austroslavism" – the belief that the "national interests" of Central European Slavonic nations would have been served best within the federalized Austro-Hungarian Empire – and started his campaign for independence, are important. Masaryk's political deeds and actions were always inspired by his philosophy. As a true philosopher Masaryk did not see the flow of current international events just in terms of power and "Realpolitik." He perceived them through the lens of his "ideas" – in the context of universal history unfolding in the transition from the 19th to the 20th century. For him, the war that had started after the assassination of Archduke Franz Ferdinand, in Sarajevo on June 28 1914, and spread quickly all over the world, was a manifestation of a deep, endemic conflict between two opposing principles of the social organization of modern mankind – between "reactionary" theocracy and "progressive" democracy. The contending geostrategic ambitions of different powers might clash on the battlefields, but far more was at stake:

---

[271] There are many sources available to present Masaryk's spirit to the reader in English, but my highly recommended source is Gordon Skilling: *T.G. Masaryk. Against the Current, 1882-1914*, Macmillan, 1994

the whole spirit of relations between nations, the political culture that would dominate human affairs in the future. A revolution similar to one that had given birth to the United States and established in the last decades of the 18th century on the territory of the British colonies a "New World Order," (*Novus Ordo Seclorum*), burst out now also on the old continent. A "New Europe," a Europe of free, democratically governed nations was striving to defend her cause against the traditional European order that had been created by the power politics of theocracies.[272]

No surprise that such an intellectual approach to politics brought Masaryk's "foreign action" close to another visionary, who had already been endowed with a real, and, indeed, robust political power: American president Woodrow Wilson. Wilson's assertion from the spring of 1917 that the United States did need to go to war in order that the world *be made safe for democracy,"*[273] and his famous "Fourteen Points Address" at the joint session of the US Congress on January 8, 1918[274]- stating that *"the peoples of Austria-Hungary, whose place among the nations we wish to see safeguarded and assured, should be accorded the freest opportunity to autonomous development"* (Point 10)[275] and further on that *"...a general association of nations must be formed under specific covenants for the purpose of affording mutual guarantees of political independence and territorial integrity to great and small states alike."* (Point 14)[276] – was surely sweet music to Masaryk's ears. It was in fact the most authoritative confirmation of the rectitude of the solution of the "Czech question" for the 20th century he himself was relentlessly working for; a clear signal that the Czechs and Slovaks were taking the right decision at this critical historical juncture. Their desire to gain independence, after three dark centuries of enslavement under the Habsburgs, would be finally heard by the powers-to-be and become reality.

---

[272] T.G. Masaryk: *New Europe.* In: *Masaryk 1850-1937.* An Anthology edited by George J. Koftun with foreword by Rene Wellek, St. Martin's Press, New York in association with Masaryk Publications Trust, 1990, p. 205-217

[273] President Wilson's speech before the US Congress on April 2, 1917, historymatters.gmu.edu/d/4943/

[274] https://www.britannica.com/event/Fourteen-Points

[275] Ibid.

[276] Ibid.

Masaryk's "foreign action" turned out to be a spectacular success. Four years after he had left his country, he returned home as a national hero, the founding-father of the modern Czechoslovak political nation and the first president of its independent democratic state. His Czechoslovakia became the "favorite child" of the Paris "peacemakers"[277] and her borders were confirmed by the system of peace treaties.

Masaryk's closest cooperator in the liberation struggle was his disciple and devoted supporter Edvard Beneš. A trained sociologist, Beneš was not a thinker of Masaryk's caliber and reputation. He assumed the role of Masaryk's messenger and turned out to be an exceptionally skillful diplomat and dauntless implementer of Masaryk's policies. Throughout the war he played an indispensable role in promotion of the Czechoslovak cause, especially the effort to gain international recognition of the Allies for the Czechoslovak National Council as the interim Czechoslovak government in exile. During the Paris Peace Conference Beneš took the lead in all key negotiations on behalf of the Czechoslovak delegation and eloquently defended its positions, first of all concerning the borders of the emerging state, at the meetings of the Conference's "Supreme Council." After all the peace treaties had been signed and Czechoslovakia was recognized as a sovereign nation-state, Beneš returned home, and as Foreign Minister in all Czechoslovak governments under Masaryk's presidency, became the principal architect and chief strategist of Czechoslovak foreign policy.

Beneš was not only an ardent Czechoslovak patriot, but also a strong believer in the new forms of international politics and multilateral diplomacy brought into existence under Wilson's leadership. During the whole interwar period he played an active and visible role in the Geneva-based League of Nations – a new universal interstate organization created

---

[277] Besides Patočka's perspective, articulated in his *Heretical Essays on the Philosophy of History*, there are several sources I am relying on in my own reading of the significance and impact of World War I: Eli Halevi: *The Era of Tyrannies*, trans. By R.K. Webb with a note by Fritz Stern, Anchor Books, Doubleday & Company INC, Garden City, New York 1965; Margaret MacMillan.: *Paris 1919*, Random House Trade Paperbacks New York, 2003; MacMillan M.: *The Road to 1914. The War That Ended Peace*, Random House Trade Paperbacks New York, 2014; Modris Eksteins: *The Great War and the Birth of the Modern Age*, Lester & Orpen Dennys Publishers, 1989

at the Paris Peace Conference, introducing the concept of collective security as a basic instrument to avoid war which the sovereign states in the past resorted to when seeking resolution of their international conflicts, – and based his Czechoslovak foreign political doctrine on the Wilsonian vision of a "new" – an in his view quintessentially peaceful – world order.

At the same time, however, he considered himself an "idealistic realist." In the area of bilateral relations he strived to build a reliable system of treaties for Czechoslovakia to secure its position in the fragile heart of Europe. As Great Britain followed after the war the example of the United States and adhered to its traditional isolationist attitude, the corner stone of Beneš's European policy was the strategic partnership with France (a bilateral "treaty of alliance and friendship," signed in 1924) and the "Little Entente" (a pact created in 1920 between Czechoslovakia, Romania and Yugoslavia, concluded under French supervision, the rudimentary aim of which was the collective defense against possible Hungarian irredentism). In 1935, Beneš negotiated and signed – following the French example – one more "treaty of alliance" in order to offer Czechoslovakia sufficient security guarantees against the rising German threats: with the Communist government of the Soviet Union.

The central element of the "idea" of Czechoslovakia that Beneš sold successfully at the Paris Peace Conference – the concept of a Czechoslovak political nation comprised of two ethnic branches, Czechs and Slovaks – turned out to be, however, Czechoslovakia's "Achilles heel." The creation of the Czechoslovak state was, indeed, an exceptional achievement of a philosopher who managed to use the window of opportunity in the historical moment. At the same time, however, Masaryk's philosophical deed was somewhat at odds with the ethnic composition and the real distribution of power established historically in the middle of the European continent.[278] Those who engineered it didn't sufficiently weigh the consideration that the war's results only temporarily deflected the European power balance and underestimated grossly the political potential of national sentiments in the countries where the Versailles system was not perceived as a just solution leading to "perpetual" European peace. World War I simply didn't bring a permanent

---

[278] Around 30% of the total population of Czechoslovakia were Germans

solution to the "crisis of European mankind" in transition from the 19th to the 20th century, but rather marked its beginning.

The New Realities of New Europe in the 1920s and 1930s

It was first Italian fascism and later German national socialism that became the most dynamic element in European politics in the next two decades. Under their influence "Czechoslovakism" coined by Masaryk and Beneš and their fundamental political ideas came under fire. And when it turned out that not only the Czechoslovak Germans, Hungarians and Poles, but a significant number of Slovaks never fully identified themselves with the idea of Masaryk's state, and when they had an opportunity, immediately started to look for "solutions" of their national question that would better suit their ever increasing radical nationalist aspirations. The consequence was that the international position and prestige of Czechoslovakia as a successful example of Central European democracy started to deteriorate.

The most sensitive and potentially explosive question for Czechoslovakia, was its relationship with Germany. Already the Locarno Treaty concluded in 1925 had clearly indicated what the German strategy was going to be to undo the Germany's humiliation at the Paris Peace Conference and weaken as much as possible the Versailles system that was established there. In the 1930s, after Hitler had seized power in Germany, and German European policy became increasingly more and more assertive under his leadership, Czechoslovakia, and first of all its president Beneš, quickly became Hitler's main enemy and the most frequent target of his direct vitriolic attacks. The fact that there was a strong German minority in the territory of Czechoslovakia enabled Hitler to make constant accusations that the rights of Sudeten Germans were systematically and grossly violated by the Czechoslovak government, as well as explicit threats that the German Reich, if necessary, was ready to intervene by force on their behalf. Using carrots and sticks at the disposal of a totalitarian ruler, he managed easily to get the overwhelming majority of Sudeten Germans on his side and used it as an opportunity to stir up a serious international crisis – "either me or Herr Beneš" – which could easily turn the European peace achieved twenty years earlier into another destructive all-out world war.

Ignoring all security guarantees given to Czechoslovakia, the leading democratic European powers, France and Great Britain, were unprepared and unwilling to fight a new war with Germany just for its defense in the dispute caused by the situation of its national minorities. After months of unsuccessful search for an amicable solution of the Sudeten German problem during 1938 – no surprise, because for Hitler the only acceptable alternative was the dismemberment of Czechoslovakia – their prime ministers Chamberlain and Daladier agreed at the Munich Conference held on September 29 with Hitler and Mussolini to save the "peace of our time" by calling on Czechoslovakia to cede the territories inhabited by Sudeten Germans to the German Reich. Cornered and stripped of the support of its major allies, the Czechoslovak government decided to make the ultimate sacrifice in the name of European peace and yield. President Beneš, being aware of his principal role in the confrontation with Germany, resigned – following *salus rei publicae* as he later put it in a letter sent to his friends at home in January 1939 – and left the country. His departure only confirmed the tough reality that Czech society had to accept: the island of democracy at the heart of Europe surrounded by the stormy seas, built on Masaryk's political ideas and moral authority, was washed away.

Political philosophy of Edvard Beneš

Before we look at Edvard Beneš' political tragedy that unfolded as a result of his heroic efforts to reverse the misery that fell upon his nation as a consequence of Hitler's rise to power in neighboring Germany, we have to look first at the philosophical underpinnings of his actions. Inspired by the example of his teacher and predecessor Masaryk, he also chose his philosophy as his principal guide for his policies during World War II that brought the whole world within a few years to a devastating war that no peacemakers were able to avert, we have to look first at the philosophical underpinnings of his actions. Inspired by the example of his teacher and predecessor Masaryk, he also chose his philosophy as his principal guide for his policies during World War II his philosophy. But his philosophical deed turned out poorly in the actual course of human history: whereas Masaryk's "foreign action" led to the successful foundation of a democratic state, Beneš's attempt to repair its foundation by his liberation action in the second phase of the "world revolution," which according to him burst out in the beginning of the 20th century, but was not over yet, tragically failed.

Where should we be looking for its basic inspirations? From the beginning of his political career – and in this sense he went far beyond his teacher Masaryk – Beneš considered himself "socialist." He believed deeply that the emancipation of men of labor – the "fourth" estate of peasants and workers – represented the central challenge of modern democracy and was convinced that democracy was finding itself in the process of transformation from its current version into more progressive forms of democratic rule, containing essential cultural, social and economic elements – first of all by enabling the effective participation of members of hitherto suppressed and exploited social classes. As a convinced democrat – and at the same time an ardent defender of the sovereignty of small nations – Beneš was rejecting the main Marxist-Leninist premise that the way forward to the "radiant futures" of socialism and people's democracy had to start with the "dictatorship of the proletariat." He supported a unique, peculiar, evolutionary path for socialism of each of them. He opposed revolutionary violence and stood for gradual progress towards the final goal, based on permanent deliberations aiming to tame the existing social antagonisms and to achieve step by step the harmonic development and well-being of all people living in a sovereign territorial nation-state, big or small, connected by their common destiny in one national political community.

Despite its violence, the Russian Revolution of 1917 was for him an epochal event of the same caliber as the French Revolution of 1789. It made the social question the center of attention and should have been perceived internationally as an urgent appeal to all democracies of the world to look for reasonable solutions. It was, in fact, the failure of the West to react positively to the new realities of the 20th century which contributed more than anything to the rise of fascism and Nazism in the 1920s and 1930s. On the international level this mistake of the Western democracies arose, according to Beneš, because of their reluctance to normalize relationships with the Soviet Union and to isolate it from European affairs. The failed policy of appeasement of Hitler which resulted in the unleashing of the Second World War was just the culmination of this profound misjudgment and a key symptom of the spiritual crisis of modern man. The barbarity of its conduct on the German side inspired by Hitler's mad dream about New Europe offering *Lebensraum* to members of his Aryan "master" race, and his ruthless totalitarian rule highlighted the urgent need for relief.

What Beneš suggested as a future political solution of the crisis was the broadest possible cooperation between the liberal West and the socialist Soviet Union, not only during the current war but also in the post-war period; a cooperation perceived as a strategic choice that corresponded to the progressive and thus inevitable direction of human history. He believed that the military defeat of Nazism – inevitable after first the Soviet Union and then the United States entered the war against Germany – would bring the "world revolution" begun in the First World War to its successful end. This would lead to the general acceptance of "people's democracy" as a form of government corresponding best to the needs of a modern society of emancipated individuals, regardless of their social standing or class origin.

In the context of the final victory of the world revolution, he also anticipated a re-birth of Wilsonianism in the area of international relations: the revitalization of the failed League of Nations (or its eventual replacement by a new, potentially universal international organization of sovereign nation-states), eliminating once and for all the use of force in international relations, enhancing development and fair economic cooperation between all members of the international community, and guaranteeing fundamental human rights to all members of the family of man.

Following this vision, Benes designed his new Czechoslovak policies. His country at Europe's heart was to assume the role of a bridge between the East and the West, facilitating their peaceful coexistence, in spite of existing and historically conditioned ideological differences. Appealing to the spiritual legacies of Masaryk ("President-Founder" of the

Czechoslovak state), his successor Beneš ("President – Builder" as he was called in the Czechoslovak political hagiography) became the most vocal supporter of the United Big Three carrying the main burden of military operations. He ardently opposed German efforts to negotiate a separate peace with the West. He was known as the strongest advocate of Stalin, downplaying all allegations of his ruthless murderous behavior and openly imperialistic ambitions of the Soviet Union as sheer Nazi propaganda lacking any foundation in reality. He even behaved as if there were a genuine bond of trust and personal sympathy between him and Stalin; that he could, thanks to his transparent, principled policies and diplomatic skills, not only cultivate friendly relations between Czechoslovakia and the Soviet Union, but act, if necessary, as a middleman in negotiations between the Soviet leader and the other parties.

The key element of Beneš's liberation plan was *"the undoing of Munich"* – the nullification of all legal acts, both domestic and international, enacted after September, 19, 1938 – and the international recognition of the continuous, uninterrupted existence of the prewar republic in its pre-Munich borders. Any viable solution of Czechoslovak national and/or territorial problems – including the question of co-existence between the majority population of Czechoslovakia and its minorities, including German – would have been conceived on this basis.

Throughout the war years Beneš was pretty good at foreseeing the course of future events. He rightly predicted its beginning. He rightly prognosticated that in spite of the pact just concluded between Stalin's Soviet Union and Hitler's Nazi Germany, conflict between them was inevitable. He rightly foresaw that the United States was going to enter the war sooner or later. After the coalition of Great Britain, the United States and the Soviet Union had been formed, he rightly concluded that Hitler's fate was sealed and Germany's defeat was unavoidable.

Why was he so terribly wrong in his conclusions about what it all meant for Europe's future, especially what consequences the postwar power constellation in Europe might have for the restored Czechoslovakia? As the war was nearing its end and the ominous signs in the operation zone of the Red Army on the Eastern front multiplied, no doubts occurred to him, and thus no efforts to adjust his policies to the changing circumstances. The proverbial finger was already writing on the wall its "mene tekel upharsim," yet Beneš, widely respected as one of the most seasoned European politicians, seemed to be entirely unable (or unwilling?) to read. Why?

The *"Undoing of Munich"*

When Beneš left Prague on October 22, 1938, it looked as if his political career was over. Six months later, however, he was back as the leader of his nation. Exactly as he had predicted, the appeasement policies didn't save the peace in Europe, and first of all didn't secure the continued existence of Czechoslovakia. On March, 15, 1939, even the "Second Republic," that remained from Masaryk's state after the "Munich dictate," disappeared. The day before, the Slovak separatists were given the green light in Berlin to create their own "independent" state and the Czech Lands became the German "Protektorat Böhmen und Mähren." Reacting to this development, Beneš – at this moment in the United States as a visiting scholar at the University of Chicago lecturing there about the future prospects of democracy[279] – sent a cable to the highest representatives of France, Great Britain, the Soviet Union and the United States protesting as *"former president"* of Czechoslovakia against the *"unacceptable violation of sacrosanct rights"* of Czechs and Slovaks and called on them not to recognize this unlawful act.[280] The following day, responding to the appeal of Czech and Slovak organizations in the United States, Beneš announced that with regard to the fact that the German Reich itself had dishonored its Munich Treaty obligations he was ready to resume his political responsibility. He agreed to become the head of a new liberation action and committed himself to start working immediately for the restoration of Czechoslovak sovereignty and independence.[281]

Here are the basic elements of Beneš's master plan drafted in the aftermath of Nazi occupation, but to be implemented as soon as the war

---

[279] Eduard Beneš: *Democracy Today and Tomorrow,* The MacMillan Company, New York, 1939
[280] Edvard Beneš: *Paměti III,* p. 297
[281] Op.cit., p. 321-323

broke out (it was to happen within months as he predicted, and indeed, it did on September 1, 1939 when Germany attacked Poland):

1. This is fundamental position from which we are not going to yield under any circumstances: The Czechoslovak state has never ceased to exist. Everything that happened after September 19, 1938, happened unlawfully and unconstitutionally and thus from both the domestic and international legal perspectives is "null and void."

2. The "foreign action" that led to the creation of Czechoslovakia after World War I will be repeated in the coming conflagration. The Czechoslovak national army will be created under the authority of the Czechoslovak Government-in-Exile and incorporated into the military operations of the emerging anti-Nazi coalition.

3. The most important task of the Czechoslovak Government-in-Exile will be to secure its full international recognition. The whole governmental and administrative machinery will be built on the allied territory, and thus fully restore – for the time being operating from foreign soil – not only *de lege*, but also *de facto*, the international existence of the Czechoslovak state – with all the ensuing consequences for the nation at home.

4. An official consultative, semi-parliamentary body will be created to supervise the activities of the Czechoslovak Government-in-Exile, and all parts of the Czechoslovak political emigration will be invited to join.

The Persistent British Reservations

When formulating the Czechoslovak wartime objectives, Beneš didn't seem to doubt for a second that there was a Leibnizian *"harmonie préétablie,"* between the restoration of the Czechoslovak state and the idea of a new world order to be born of the life-and-death struggle between democracy and totalitarianism. He felt, as during the First World War, to be on the side of progress, empowered not only by the fact that the cause he struggled for was just, but by historical necessity.

Immediately after the war broke out at the beginning of September 1939, Beneš and his ambassador to Great Britain and future foreign minister Jan Masaryk, a son of the President-Founder, started their campaign for seeking international recognition of the Czechoslovak state, which according to them didn't cease to exist. In London, however, their efforts to *"undo Munich,"* at first ran into difficulties. It was impossible for the British Government, Beneš and Masaryk were told by their British counterparts, to nullify an agreement His Majesty's Government had entered with three other parties in conformity with the established norms of international law, no matter how grave a political mistake it might have been with regards to future developments. The British Government was willing to enable the legitimate activities of the Czechoslovak Government-in-Exile on British soil, but only in the context of its opinion that the German military action against Czechoslovakia in March 1939 was a plain violation of the Munich Agreement. This recognition, however, should not be tied to any specific British position as far as the legal continuity of the Czechoslovak state that had existed before the war, and especially with regard to the recognition of any borders that may appear in Central Europe in the future.

Within two years, however – after the situation on the ground started to change dramatically and the Soviet Union and the United States entered into war against Germany and the foundations for the cooperation between the Big Three (Great Britain, the Soviet Union and the United States), were being laid – the British evaluation of Munich changed.

On July 26, 1941, Foreign Minister Masaryk was officially informed in the note sent to him by British Foreign Secretary Eden about the King's decision to accredit an Envoy Extraordinary and Minister Plenipotentiary to Dr. Beneš as President of the Czecho-Slovak Republic. President Beneš's juridical position was thus regarded as *"identical with that of the other Allied heads of State and Governments established in this country,"* but, as seen from the lens of Beneš's *"war aims,"* still non-committal. More than a year later (on August 5, 1942) Eden wrote Masaryk another note, with the aim to *"dispel any possible misunderstanding on the Czechoslovak side:"* Because Germany decided to disrespect all the arrangements concerning the Czechoslovak state reached in Munich in 1938, the British Government considers itself free from any obligation in this regard. When the final settlement as far as the

Czechoslovak borders will be decided, the British position will not be influenced by any decision made in and since 1938.

Beneš rightly celebrated these British "shifts" of opinion – achieved without any doubt thanks to the fact that his government became, indeed, a respected member of the anti-Nazi coalition – as unmistakable proofs that his strategy was working and as important steps leading to the restoration of Czechoslovak independence. However, he had a tendency to grossly overestimate the impact of his legalistic reasoning. Would it not be more appropriate to look at the British moves not so much from the perspective of legal continuity of prewar Czechoslovakia, but rather in light of the developments on the ground as the war progressed? Was it not clear that even a British Government led by Winston Churchill, a staunch critic of the appeasement policies of his predecessor, was formulating and implementing its war policies following primarily its own aims in the spirit of the legal and political traditions of the British Empire? Wasn't it obvious that the Czechoslovak question was perceived in London from a much larger perspective than was Beneš' obsessive insistence on the question of continuity of Czechoslovak statehood? Wasn't it his desire to *"undo Munich"* and return to the *status quo ante* – motivated undoubtedly by the most sincere patriotic emotions – that in the end caused his failure to avert catastrophes that were still to come in the future? Wasn't the unwillingness of the British Government to recognize Czechoslovak borders as they existed before Munich and to give support to any solution of the Czechoslovak question prior to the postwar peace conference of the principal allies, a clear signal that the future of Czechoslovakia would depend on a new power constellation in the world that was in the process of formation in the course of the war?

The Trans-Atlantic Bond

The United States assisted in the creation of the Czechoslovak state after the First World War in 1918 and Beneš hoped that in spite of America's original reluctance to interfere in European affairs, he would find there natural support for his efforts to achieve Czechoslovakia's restoration. He travelled there twice during his years in exile and on both occasions he had an opportunity to meet President Roosevelt. The first meeting took place at the end of May 1939, when he was a professor at the University of Chicago invited to deliver lectures on the state of democracy in the world. It was two months after he had announced his decision to become the head of the Czechoslovak liberation movement. He was invited, thanks to the mediation of one of his American friends, for a lunch at Roosevelt's private residence and here is how Beneš described this encounter in his Memoirs.

Having greeted him as if he had still been President of Czechoslovakia and Munich had never happened, the American President expressed his interest in Beneš's opinion about the political situation in Europe and even asked him what he expected the United States to do. Beneš gave him *ex promptu* his usual – i.e., quite long and detailed – expose and predicted that the United States would enter the war sooner or later, in spite of its current neutrality, because the European democracies would not be able to win in this confrontation with the totalitarian dictatorships without American assistance. As far as the Czechoslovak cause, Beneš explained his plan to repeat the "foreign action" taken under Masaryk's leadership during the First World War. He concluded by expressing his hope that his request for recognition of the Czechoslovak "revolutionary" government would not be rejected by the US government when a right moment for its recognition would come in a foreseeable future, and declared his full respect for current U.S. neutrality.

> *I left Roosevelt's house convinced that he understood very well what was at stake in the coming war crisis; that he was aware of the task which would necessarily fall on the United States in this conflagration; that he rightly understood the problem of both European dictatorships, as well as the position of the Soviet Union.........I was finally sure that he was ready to help us, wherever it would be possible.*[282]

This conviction became apparently even stronger after Beneš met Roosevelt for the second time in May 1943. At that moment the United States was already at the state of war with Germany and U.S. military operations were in full swing. The Czechoslovak Government-in-Exile

---

[282] Edvard Beneš: *Paměti II*, p.91

was recognized by the Government of the United States, and Beneš was invited to pay an official visit to Washington as the head of state to exchange views concerning the actual state of the war.

Beneš wanted to go on his second wartime US trip, according to his own words, *"well prepared."* The major topic he wished to open with his American counterpart was the future of Czechoslovak-Soviet relations. He felt obliged to inform him about his intention to sign a treaty of cooperation and friendship with the Soviet Union, believing that this move was fully consistent with fundamental American war aims. By sharing this information with Roosevelt in advance, he wanted to demonstrate that Czechoslovakia was a trustworthy American ally endorsing the same values and ideals, standing firmly on the side of human progress.

But in practice for Beneš these preparations meant that in order to present his own positions about Czechoslovakia's postwar future he first consulted the Soviet Government. Before he set off over the Atlantic, he had inquired in London with the Soviet Ambassador to the Czechoslovak Government-in-Exile Bogomolov about Soviet *"general viewpoints as far as the essential basic elements of the allied wartime policies."*[283]

According to his Memoirs, Beneš's visit to Washington went smoothly and only confirmed the excellent state of bilateral relations between Czechoslovakia and the United States. The fact that he was even invited to participate as an equal among equals at a working meeting of Roosevelt and Churchill, who happened to be visiting at the same time, proved he enjoyed high status among the top allies. Believing that he achieved what he came for – the American green light for his policies towards the Soviet Union – Beneš was returning to London in an even better mood than in 1939. In summarizing the results he was bringing back from the US capital, he did not spare superlatives:

> There are only a few examples in history when the policies
> of a small state in such stormy and cataclysmal times were
> given such a great acknowledgement of the rightfulness of
> its actions, as it was the case of my American trip.[284]

---

[283] Op.cit. 184
[284] Op.cit. p. 191

A Friend in Moscow

No matter how historical Beneš's Washington visit in May 1943 might have been, its preparation indicated who was the key player in his eyes, on the current crossroads. It was neither Great Britain nor the United States but the Soviet Union – the only country, which supposedly didn't betray him at the critical moment of the Munich crisis. It had been ready then to fulfill its treaty obligations and was now decisively winning on the battlefields. Beneš's unfailing faith in the good intentions of the almighty Soviet dictator feared for his ruthless cruelty, known for his obsessive mistrust even of his closest collaborators and the readiness to kill anyone who could potentially stand in his way, became almost proverbial. It wasn't shaken even by the pact concluded between Stalin and Hitler in the summer of 1939 which led immediately to the destruction of Poland and its division between Germany and the Soviet Union. And when it turned out that Beneš was right again in predicting that this pact would not last long; that Germany would attack the Soviet Union at its first convenience and the Soviet Union would ally with the democratic West in its "Great Patriotic War," his pro-Soviet attitude even strengthened. It became the fundamental premise of his overall wartime policies, not just advised by his pragmatic analysis of the situation on the ground based on the distribution of real power, but anchored firmly in his overall "philosophical" understanding of what was going on and what was at stake in the current phase of human history.

With all that in mind, Beneš travelled in December 1943 to Moscow to sign a new treaty of alliance with the Soviet Union. He had been planning this trip for some time. The Soviet Union was the first among the allied countries to declare unambiguously the Munich agreement "null and void," and Beneš kept intentionally using the "Soviet card" to push the British and American governments to make similar steps in this direction – in spite of the fact that there was a concord reached between all three principal war allies not to conclude any agreements with the exile governments concerning their future borders before their primary aim in Europe, the unconditional surrender of Germany, was achieved.

When he finally set off on this journey in the end of 1943, the war was far from over. Beneš, however, was still firmly convinced anyways that it was the right time for him to act. The Foreign Ministers of Great Britain, the Soviet Union and the United States had already met in Moscow in the second half of October, and the Teheran Conference of Churchill, Roosevelt and Stalin had taken place between November 28 and December 1, with the intention not only to intensify their war cooperation, but also to start discussions about the post-war political order.

Beneš believed, in spite of having been repeatedly warned by his British counterparts not to go too far with Czechoslovak-Soviet friendship that the treaty with the Soviet Union would be an important step in the right direction not only for Czechoslovakia, but for the whole world. He perceived it as an integral part of a new security system to be created in cooperation with the Western allies and also an essential contribution to the collective efforts of Slavonic nations to eliminate forever any future danger of German *"Drang nach Osten."*

His trip to Moscow – crowned by a glamorous treaty-signing ceremony at the Kremlin during which Stalin *"greeted Beneš like an old and close friend"*[285] and unambiguously declared that *"the Soviet Union would never interfere in the internal affairs of Czechoslovakia"*[286] – was, Beneš believed, another great success. In the context of international relations in process of profound "revolutionary" transformations it was in fact, he wrote in his typical self-laudatory manner, a *"sensational event:"*[287]

> *Our treaty – first of its kind during the war – broke, at least partially, the wall existing between the Soviet Union and the Western world observing our move as an experiment, a "test-case," the aim of which was to demonstrate the intentions the Soviet Union had after the war in its relations with its smaller neighbors.*[288]

Summarizing his encounter with the reality of the Soviet Union at the end of 1943 in his Memoirs, Beneš concluded – contrary to all skeptics

---

[285] Igor Lukeš: *On the Edge of the Cold War. American Diplomats and Spies in Postwar Prague*, Oxford University Press, 2012, p. 29
[286] Op.cit, p. 30
[287] Edvard Beneš: *Paměti II*, p. 274
[288] Op.cit., p. 274

still stubbornly seeing in Soviet Bolshevism not an essentially progressive force, but an oppressive, tyrannical form of government and a great threat to European freedom – that the "Great Patriotic War" completed a profound positive change of the Soviet Union. It was no longer a country, he firmly stated in his analysis, torn apart by the Manichean struggle between the old and the new, the good and the evil, trapped in the chain of violence where the government was forced to use its repressive apparatus excessively to achieve the desired social transformation, to suppress all the exponents of the old regime and smash mercilessly all "enemies of the state." United in its heroic struggle against German Nazism and entering voluntarily in the coalition with the democratic liberal West, the Soviet Union turned in the course of the war into a strong, self-confident, responsible and reliable member of international society. It had gained both military strength and political authority and it now expected the recognition of others for its own political methods and means to achieve its aims and visions. At the same time it was going to respect all others pursuing their goals and realizing their policies in their own way, because it was painfully aware that there was no other way to the improved future of the world than the peaceful coexistence and cooperation between all the members of the international community.

The second trip of President Beneš to Moscow during the war took place in March 1945. He was invited to Moscow with other members of the Czechoslovak Government-in-Exile to join the leaders of the Czechoslovak Communist Party who had been in the Soviet Union throughout the war, to form with them a Government of national unity and begin the process of relocation to liberated Czechoslovak territory. It was just a month after Churchill, Roosevelt and Stalin had met again at the Yalta Conference to discuss the actual issues connected with the final stage of the war and the emerging post-war world order. There were two concrete questions which troubled Benes and his collaborators when they were about to leave London and set out on their home journey: the status of the Polish Government-in-Exile and the situation in Sub-Carpathian Ruthenia. Both issues signaled that Soviet policies towards Czechoslovakia might not be as friendly and respectful.

The problem of Sub-Carpathian Ruthenia – the easternmost part of prewar Czechoslovakia – was its cession to the Soviet Union. On the one hand Beneš himself entertained this idea at the beginning of the war, when he predicted wishfully that Czechoslovakia and the Soviet Union would be neighbors in the future, and he even announced his readiness to consider this step in his talks with Stalin in December 1943. At the same time, however, he insisted in the negotiations with all his partners, including the Soviet Union, on the territorial integrity of Czechoslovakia and in the *restitutio ad integrum* of its sovereign power as an essential element of the *"undoing of Munich."* Consistent with his master-plan, Beneš expected that the question of Sub-Carpathian Ruthenia would be settled on the basis of an international agreement concluded between the two sovereign governments only after the Czechoslovak state was fully reconstituted and its administrative functions restored.

It was no surprise he was shocked when he received the information on what was happening, before such agreement could be reached, in Sub-Carpathian Ruthenia after the Soviet victory, when the representatives of Czechoslovak civilian authorities appointed by his government tried to fulfill the tasks assigned by the Czechoslovak Government-in-Exile. The self-appointed leaders and functionaries of the local population who emerged suddenly, in close and by no means covert cooperation with the organs of repressive Soviet might arriving in the territory abandoned by Germans with army troops and other non-combatant forces, effectively blocked any efforts of Czechoslovak administrators to renew the basic functions of the state. Appealing to the "will of the people" they began immediately to set up their own rule. First, they arrested the traitors and enemies of the Soviet Union, opened their own channels of communication and spread heavily biased information and Bolshevik propaganda. The Red Army was recruiting or pressing into its ranks people who should have been treated by the Soviet authorities – at least through the lens of Beneš's legal construction – as Czechoslovak citizens. He tried to protest against this Soviet behavior, which was blatantly disrespectful to the letter and spirit of the bilateral Czechoslovak-Soviet Treaty signed a little more than a year before, using the Communist leader Gottwald residing in Moscow as his messenger, but to no avail.

Then he got, likely to his surprise, a written reaction by Stalin to his complaints[289] and in a move typical for Beneš, he immediately changed his mind. In his answer he expressed his satisfaction with all Stalin's arguments in an extremely diplomatic, polite, even subservient manner. Trying literally to appease Stalin, Beneš agreed with Stalin's opinion that the disturbing recent events in Sub-Carpathian Ruthenia were only *"local and a matter of local functionaries."*[290] He continued that it never entered his mind that *"the Soviet government would intend to resolve this issue unilaterally,"* because he was very well aware of the *"principles of the policies of the Soviet Union"* and asked Stalin *"to be true to his words."*[291] In conclusion, he declared his firm consent to Stalin's proposal: the Czechoslovak government was ready, wrote Beneš waiting humbly in his Canossa, to arrive at an *"amicable"* bilateral solution of the future status of Sub-Carpathian Ruthenia as soon as possible – outside of the agendas of upcoming multilateral peace conferences, in fact *ex post* legally confirming *the status quo*, i.e. the new realities on the ground based not on a previous decision taken in conformity with public international law, but on Soviet victory and subsequent military occupation.

The Soviet Liberation of Prague

No matter how disturbing this encounter with the practical application of the *"principles of the policies of the Soviet Union"* was, a more serious blow for the self-appointed bridge-builder between the West and the East was still to come. When Beneš decided, in spite of the warnings of some of his collaborators, to start his home journey to the liberated Czechoslovakia from Moscow, the Western diplomats accredited to the Czechoslovak Government-in-Exile in London were supposed, in conformity with the diplomatic protocol, to accompany him and secure uninterrupted communication with their capitals during the last weeks of war. Because they planned to leave Great Britain by sea, they were informed from Moscow, that they needed to apply for transit permits to pass through Romanian territory. These permits could be obtained only

---

[289] Stalin's Letter to Benes, in: Edvard Beneš: *Paměti III*, p. 581
[290] Beneš' Answer to Stalin, in: op.cit., p. 583
[291] Ibid.

from the Soviet occupation authorities in Bucharest. On the day of their ship's planned departure, however, at the moment when President Beneš was already with his entourage in the Soviet Union, they were shocked by the information that that this request was denied by the Soviet authorities with regard to the *"volatility of the military situation in the East."*[292] This unexpected Soviet move was obviously embarrassing for everybody involved. Washington protested and demanded the quick resolution of this unpleasant conflict so that the Americans diplomats *"could proceed at once to the seat of the Czechoslovak Government."*[293] But for the Czechoslovak government its consequence was potentially disastrous: Beneš's government, enlarged in Moscow by representatives of the Communist Party headed by the Party's chairman Gottwald, was forced to conduct its official business on their trip home – first in a luxurious train magnanimously supplied by the Soviet government and later at its temporary seat in Košice in Eastern Slovakia – always *"surrounded....by Soviet officials, bemedaled generals, and the security apparat,"*[294] *"inside a Soviet security bubble"*[295] and *"out of contact with the West."*[296] With regard to the fact that the liberation of Czechoslovakia from the German yoke reached its critical phase at this moment, when strictly military and broader political components of allied cooperation had to be handled together and could not be separated from each other – first in the hands of commanders of allied armed forces, second in the hands of allied statesmen and politicians – the entire dependence of the Czechoslovak government in the process of its relocation to Prague on Soviet information channels was a highly symbolical and quite ominous sign, indeed. And this symbolism soon materialized in the final phase of military operations.

Till today, the decision of the commander-in-chief of US armed forces in Europe, General Eisenhower, to let the Soviet Union liberate the Czechoslovak capital only a day after the German unconditional surrender was already signed, in spite of the fact that American contingents arrived

---

[292] Igor Lukeš: *On the Edge of the Cold War. American Diplomats and Spies in Postwar Prague*, p. 34
[293] Op.cit , p.35
[294] Ibid., p. 35
[295] Op.cit., p. 36
[296] Ibid.

in Western Bohemia already on April 17 and could have been in Prague within hours if given respective orders – way ahead of the units of the Red Army coming from Berlin – haunts the minds of Czech politicians. Was it just a matter of technical agreement between allied generals not to interlock and hamper their separate military operations, or was it rather a result of agreement reached on the highest level between allied politicians – most likely in Yalta – that Czechoslovakia would belong after the War to the zone of influence of the Soviet Union and now implemented by American armed forces?

The answer to this question isn't easy and should remain open. As Lukeš mentions in his excellent book describing the beginnings of the Cold War which serves as one of the key sources of information for this study, there was an alternative option, attempting to reverse Eisenhower's orders, vehemently pushed forward by the British Prime Minister Churchill and seriously considered in political circles in Washington. On May 5, 1945, the day when the Prague Uprising broke out, the State Department sent a cable to President Truman, who only a few weeks before replaced suddenly deceased President Roosevelt, containing the following recommendation:

> *Prague is an excellent ground to test the promise of the Soviet Government of tripartite cooperation as it is the only one of the capitals of Eastern and Central Europe which has not as yet been occupied by the Soviet Army, and which could probably be occupied by us before the Soviet forces arrive there. The success or failure of cooperation in Prague will have a profound effect on our entire position in Central Europe which would be immeasurably strengthened by our occupation of Prague. The Department of State firmly believes that the interest of the United States will best be served by the immediate occupation of Prague and supports the urgent request made to this effect by Prime Minister Churchill and Foreign Secretary Eden.*[297]

The last minute intervention, however, failed and the existing perspective of the US military prevailed. The consequences of the

---

[297] Op.cit., p. 45.

unfortunate decision of General Eisenhower, who stated adamantly *"I shall not attempt any move I deem militarily unwise merely to gain a political prize unless I receive specific orders from the Combined Chiefs of Staff"* in his memo reacting to the State Department's initiative,[298] on future developments in Czechoslovakia, are well known now. One question, however, remains pending. What about President Beneš in this situation? Was he informed properly what was going on? Wasn't he the only person endowed with enough authority who could step into this debate on the Czechoslovak side and at least try to change the course of things?

Beneš, as we can read in the book written by his personal secretary and legal advisor Edvard Táborský, sincerely rejoiced in Košice when he was reached by the news that the Third Army of General Patton crossed Czechoslovak borders and sent him a cable with greetings and congratulations.[299] However, what did he do after he learned later that thanks to Soviet pressure, Patton received an order from Eisenhower, to stop in Pilsen and not to proceed to Prague? Sitting in the *"Soviet security bubble,"* he did nothing. If he had at least tried to communicate at this critical moment of current Czechoslovak history with Washington on the highest possible level, he was the only one who might still have had the chance to start building a real bridge between the East and the West. Relying too much on his blueprint prepared in advance – the grand concept or "philosophy" of the Second World War perceived as the final part of world revolution in which the Soviet Union played a highly positive role – he simply missed his opportunity and let others act on his behalf.

The Continuity of the Prewar Republic and the Sudeten Germans

The issue which stood high on Beneš's agenda of *"undoing Munich"* was obviously its original cause: the position of the German minority in Czechoslovakia, the problem built into her foundations after World War I that brought on its breakup in 1938 and that had to be dealt

---

[298] Op.cit., p. 42

[299] Eduard Táborský: *Prezident Beneš mezi Západem a Východem* [President Beneš Between the West and the East]. Mladá Fronta, Praha 1993, p. 242

with in a way consistent with his vision of Czechoslovakia's future. In the months before the Munich Conference Beneš tried hard to accommodate the ever mounting demands of the Sudeten Germans and was ready to meet their calls for limited autonomy. At the same time he made absolutely clear what was the fundamental prerequisite for any peaceful solution of the Sudeten German problem: members of Czechoslovakia's German minority would have had to be willing to identify themselves with the Czechoslovak state and align themselves with its fundamental democratic values against the emerging totalitarian threat; they would have had to respect the existing Czechoslovak constitution as the only legitimate basis for any negotiation concerning their status.

The Sudeten Germans, however, decided on a different path. Seduced *en masse* by Henlein and his radical nationalistic associates, they linked their cause with the main European opponent of prewar democratic Czechoslovakia and European political architecture built on the Versailles foundations, Adolf Hitler who became German Chancellor in 1933. They turned themselves voluntarily into an instrument of his aggressive policies, aiming at destruction of the Versailles system, the rise of Germany to the position of world power capable of securing a necessary living space (*das Lebensraum*) for members of the "master" Aryan Race. By the requirement to "return to the Reich," they pronounced loud and clear in the end of the "hot" summer of 1938 what their own choice was: to break their bonds with the Czechoslovak democracy and enlist themselves into the columns of the German Reich marching – united behind their Fuhrer – either towards their final victory or doom.

This fatal decision changed irreversibly relations between Czechs and Germans in Czechoslovakia. If the fundamental aim of Beneš's war policies was restoration of the democratic Czechoslovak state based on Masaryk's "ideals of humanity" in its prewar borders, as far as its German minority was concerned, *restitutio ad integrum* was according to Beneš – in conformity with the absolute majority of Czechoslovak people, subjected daily to the brutality of the Nazi occupiers – simply impossible. The horrifying crimes committed in the name of the German Reich could be neither "undone," nor "forgotten," but only punished. There was no return to the *status quo ante*, and the Sudeten German problem therefore required a radically new solution. Its final version was stated in *Memorandum of Czechoslovak Government on the Problem of the German Minority in Czechoslovakia* from November 23, 1944,[300] describing the Czechoslovak position not only with regards to the current conflict and its immediate causes, but in a larger historical context. Its resumé consists of the following six points:

1. After the past experiences between the two wars, and particularly after the unexampled barbarity committed by the Germans against the Czechoslovak people during the present war, it is unthinkable that the state of affairs which existed in Czechoslovakia before Munich in respect of the German minority, should be allowed to remain.

2. It is solely by a radical reduction in the number of Germans in the Czechoslovak Republic to a figure which would not involve any menace to the security of the Czechoslovak State and people, and which could ultimately be merged with the latter, that there can be any positive settlement of the German (and similarly of the Magyar) question in the Czechoslovak Republic.

3. In this way, Czechoslovakia will be able to attain the requisite homogeneity, which is in the obvious interest of the security, internal peace and prosperity of every State. At the same time, however, one of the most serious causes of international conflicts and disputes will be removed, thus promoting international peace.

4. It is proposed to achieve these aims by a transfer of Germans (including, of course, all disloyal elements among them), which will not leave more than 800 000 of them in Czechoslovakia. (As regards Magyars, the problem can largely be settled based on an exchange of population.)

5. The transfer must be carried out on organized lines, within the shortest possible period, i.e. about two years. The short period and effective organization will reduce the hardships of those transferred to a minimum, and at the same time will render possible rapid restoration and stabilization of the political, economic and social conditions in liberated Czechoslovakia.

6. To achieve these aims, it is essential, a) that Germany should be obliged by the capitulation terms to admit on her territory Germans transferred from Czechoslovakia, to recognize them as

---

[300] Edvard Beneš: *Paměti III* , p. 562-580

German citizens and to attend to their permanent settlement on her territory; b) that the relevant Allied bodies in occupied Germany should see to it that Germany conscientiously fulfils these obligations; these Allied bodies should likewise promote the realization of the scheme by their appropriate means at their disposal.[301]

How was this proposal of the Czechoslovak Government-in-Exile actually perceived by its major wartime allies? Were individual members of the Big Three entirely supportive of the plan that the majority of Sudeten Germans should be forcibly transferred to Germany, or did they voice some concerns, questions or even objections? Were they more or less united in their approach or did they substantively differ in their response? Were their opinions concerning this issue stable or changing in the course of time?

For Czechoslovak wartime allies, the quoted *Memorandum* issued when the war was drawing to a close, was not at all surprising. President Beneš used to open this theme practically in all his private and later official wartime consultations. From his *Memoirs* we learn how eloquent and pushy he was to convince his counterparts about the rightfulness and feasibility of his suggestions and what conclusions he drew from these conversations. And here are disturbing questions their reader today cannot escape.

With regard to what was to come in the postwar period, was Beneš's fundamental demand – ethnic "homogenization" of liberated Czechoslovakia – really helping his own cause, the essence of which was restoration of Masaryk's state, based on faith in democracy and in the ideals of humanity? Wasn't actually his anti-German zeal – incited by the current Czechoslovak experiences with Nazism, but quickly complemented by his overall interpretation of Czech history starting in the 13th century with the so-called "German colonization" of Bohemia – one of the main reasons why he was so terribly wrong in his postwar policies? What utterly disqualified him for the role he assigned to himself on the current historical crossroads – the role of builder of a democratic Czechoslovak state at Europe's heart; a state based on its prewar spiritual

---

[301] Op.cit., p. 571-572

traditions and in the prewar borders, but at the same time acting as a bridge between the West and the East; a state open to all emerging challenges of the postwar period, strong enough to resist not only any future German pressures or threats, but also its possible subjugation by the victorious Soviet Union?

The solution of the Sudeten German question proposed by the Czechoslovak Government-in-Exile and confirmed again after it moved its activities to liberated territory in the spring of 1945 was, as we know, approved by Allies at the Potsdam Conference. The results of this meeting of the Big Three – the first after the end of war in Europe and the last before the outbreak of the Cold War – were summarized in the *Protocol* attached to *the Potsdam Agreement*. Its point twelve, titled *Orderly transfer of German Populations* reads as follows:

> *Three Governments, having considered the question in all its aspects, recognize that the transfer to Germany of German populations, or elements thereof, remaining in Poland, Czechoslovakia and Hungary, will have to be undertaken. They agree that any transfers that take place should be effected in an orderly and humane manner....*[302]

Based on this explicit international approval, on August 3, 1945 – only a day after the Potsdam Conference had been closed – President Beneš signed into law his Decree No. 33 removing from members of the German (and Hungarian) minority their Czechoslovak citizenship, opening thereby the way to their *"orderly and humane"* expulsion. As a Czech nationalist and believer in the unique role of Slavonic nations in the current phase of world history, he was most likely deeply convinced in the moment of the signing ceremony, that with this step historical justice was served and the *"undoing of Munich"* was brought to its successful completion. As a self-proclaimed *"idealist realist,"* however, he had every reason to be sober and cautious when evaluating the context and the consequences of this achievement.

The ethnic "homogenization" of the restored Czechoslovak state was a part of a larger geopolitical process taking place not only in Europe,

---

[302] https://en.wikipedia.org/wiki/Potsdam_Agreement#Protocol

but worldwide. The decision to divide Germany was agreed in Potsdam: to prevent German aggression, German *Drang nach Osten* from happening again. The way this decision was implemented, however, laid the foundations for the emerging bipolar political architecture. It turned divided Germany in a few years into the main turf for future ideologically motivated competition between two non-European superpowers, the Soviet Union and the United States, operating on European soil and guaranteeing Europe's peace with weapons of mass destruction which they possessed thanks to the arrival of the nuclear age.

The fundamental task of Beneš was to find a place for Czechoslovakia in it, consistent with the basic ideas inserted after World War I into her foundations. With regards to the emerging power constellation – with Stalin as one of its main architects – it might have been a mission impossible no matter what Beneš had decided to do. The trouble is that Beneš, fully absorbed by his desire to resolve the Sudeten German problem once and for all, didn't even try.

As evidenced even in his own records, and especially in his communications with the leading Sudeten German social democratic politician, Wenzel Jaksch,[303] who also found asylum in London during the war, Beneš was given multiple opportunities to think it through. He certainly could have devised an alternative strategy well in advance of the stage of its implementation, when he was discussing the Sudeten German problem practically in all his meetings with the representatives of the Big Troika during the war. Unfortunately, he evidently didn't want, or rather was not able, to change his mind.

It is the irony of history, but no surprise, at the same time, that it was the Soviet Union that seemed to be the most loyal and understanding partner of Beneš's Czechoslovak Government-in-Exile in this matter. Stalin, in contrast to Roosevelt or Churchill, was, for sure, used to punishing whole ethnic or national groups for their real or invented disloyalty to the Soviet state by their resettlement. The Soviet Union

---

[303] Wenzel Jaksch (1896 – 1966) was a Sudeten German Social Democrat politician opposed to the growing influence of Nazis in Sudeten German Politics. After Germany invaded Czechoslovakia in March 1939 he escaped to Poland, and after the German invasion of Poland to Great Britain, where he represented the interests of the Sudeten Germans in the Czechoslovak Government-in-Exile.

apparently had no problem with the Czechoslovak proposal as far as the future of the German minority in Czechoslovakia. Its unequivocal vocal support of transfer of Sudeten Germans actually offered Stalin a welcome opportunity to move Beneš and his government deeper into the sphere of Soviet influence.

Beneš' Report to the Nation

When we read today, Beneš's *Report to the Nation* – the speech he delivered to the Czechoslovak Parliament on the occasion of the first National Day after the liberation from the Nazi yoke to inform the nation about his second "foreign action" that opened the path to its radiant postwar future[304] – we have before us clear evidence of the ultimate source of his profound political misjudgment.

On May 16 of 1945 he returned victoriously to Prague Castle as President of liberated Czechoslovakia. Was he aware at this moment of triumph, whether it was finding itself again at the historical crossroads, and whether the philosophy of history he inherited from Masaryk and further elaborated was not working? Did he realize that division of Europe into two antagonistic blocks rather than the Wilsonian "world safe for democracy" was the most likely outcome of the redistribution of power after the war? Was he ready to assess, as an *idealistic realist*, all the consequences of the new geopolitical constellation in the world – with the Soviet Union as the biggest military power on the Eurasian continent – for his "small country" at Europe's heart?

> *You all know how I approach the problem of our time. I refuse to treat the individual facts or situations which have occurred in our recent past separately and independently, but strive at their synthesis; I perceive them as components of a whole and look for their deeper philosophical meaning rooted in human history.*[305]

---

[304] Edvard Beneš: *"Zpráva národu"* [*The Report to the Nation*]. In: *Paměti III*, p. 585-601.
[305] Op.cit., p. 589

All the events that brought us to the current historical moment, he followed like a teacher whose role is to educate his pupils – starting from the crisis that led to the First World War and culminating in the results of the Second World War which has just ended – must be perceived as one great aggregate. Being *"connected with each other, interlocked, tied causally and mutually conditioned,"*[306] they constitute our era, he said, an era which began at the outset of the 20th century and would continue in the next years. What was going on in the world after the defeat of Nazi totalitarian evil, Beneš argued, was, indeed, a profound transformation of social and political structures with really profound consequences:

> *In world history and in the history of Europe this era will represent a very special, great and extremely revolutionary chapter. It will belong among the most turbulent historical moments and will be marked as the passage, turning point and time of creation – in the midst of deep crises, wars and immense human suffering – of a new phase of human society, or at least as attempts to create such a new society and its beginnings. Together with Masaryk, I emphasized after the First World War that we have to follow the path of European and really worldly politics; that we always have to strive to perceive us as Czechoslovaks in the broader context of the historical processes in the world, with regards to the deeper meaning of world history; that we always have to try to understand, where the world – not just this or that nation – is going to and is aiming at; that this should determine our own way forward and this way must always be directed by truth and ruled by the law…It is obvious and utterly comprehensible at the same time that as a relatively small state, we will seek the partnership with such state [i.e. the Soviet Union] and stick to such orientation that will result in more safety and more security for us.*[307]

Really? We know now what happened. Two and half years later, in February 1948 the Communist *coup d'état* took place that sealed the fate of Czechoslovakia for another more than forty years. Beneš resigned and died a couple of months later. With all due respect to him and all his

---

[306] Op.cit, p.590
[307] Ibid.

achievements – he will still rightly be remembered as one of the most accomplished Czech politicians of the 20th century – we cannot escape tough and maybe unpleasant questions that are still important for us today. What does it mean to be an *"idealistic realist"* in our Czech context? How are we to conceive our *"Czech question"* in *"worldly terms"* in our uncertain world today? What kind of philosophy of history, if any, are we recommended to subscribe to? What are our current *"national interests"* and how can we protect them?

Wasn't it actually Beneš's disproportionate, immoderate personal ambition to become a bridge builder between the East and the West, based on his philosophical beliefs – and not necessarily the decisions made in Teheran or Yalta, at the conferences of the world leaders – that brought us into the abyss after World War II? Wasn't it here, where our "road to serfdom," into the Babylonian captivity that lasted more than four decades, had in fact begun?

Exercise 11

Patočka between
Masaryk and Havel[308]

(An Attempt at Symphonic Composition Consisting of a Prelude, Two Movements and a Coda)

Prelude: Beneš's vision for postwar Czechoslovakia

When the second Czechoslovak Beneš returned to Prague in May 1945, his goal was not only to restore under new geopolitical circumstances the previously existing Czechoslovak state – a state created after World War I under the leadership of his great teacher and older friend Tomas Garrigue Masaryk. He intended to turn it into a stable, responsible, reliable, prosperous, democratic and socially sensitive bridge between East and West. His ambition was to formulate a new Czechoslovak foreign policy adequate to the new world order – relying, above all, on lasting friendship with the Soviet Union, the greatest winner of World War II, and on constructive cooperation with the like-minded democratic Western Allies.

The liberated nation under his leadership should have been inspired again and directed in all its actions by the same philosophy of history, the origins of which can be traced back to Masaryk's ideas formulated in the last decades of the 19th century, when the Czech lands were still a part of the Austro-Hungarian Empire. The *"Czech question"* should have been again understood *"in worldly terms."* Its solution should have been linked to progressive historical trends that were – despite

---

[308] Written as a follow-up of Exercise 10

possible temporary setbacks such as the Second World War – inevitably and irreversibly prevailing.

The result of the Second World War was the ultimate proof for Beneš that it was he and not Hitler who had won in life-and-dead confrontation that started in the Munich Crisis of 1938; that it was he and not Hitler who was capable of interpreting the signs of the time – despite his defeat in their duel in the Munich crisis – forcing him to resign his post in early October 1938 and leave the country; that it was he, and not Hitler, who was finally vindicated by the verdict pronounced at the *"Court of the World, History and Providence"*[309] – sending Hitler's Third Reich to its doom and promising to his democratic Czechoslovakia the shining prospects of great tomorrows.

In retrospect – after having experienced what that *"new phase of human society"* Beneš saw coming was all about – we know very well now that his perspective articulated in his *Report to the Nation* in October 1945, was just a great illusion. A little more than two years later, in February 1948, the Communist *coup d'état* took place and sealed the fate of Czechoslovakia for another forty-one years. It imposed a totalitarian form of government instead of democracy on its population and turned a once prosperous state that aspired to play an active, constructive and peaceful role in the world emerging from the horrors of the Second World War, into a stagnant Soviet satellite, willingly keeping its citizens in slavery and turning them by force and propaganda into the builders of socialism; a state serving obediently the global ambitions of the new hegemon on European soil, divided by the Cold War into the socialist camp under the Soviet leadership, and the liberal capitalist democracies of the West which got much the better lot in the second half of the 20th century than their Eastern ideological opponents – economically reconstructed with the help of *Marshall Plan*; protected by the "nuclear umbrella" of the United States; making the first steps in the direction of ever deeper economic and political integration.

Having been spectacularly deceived not only by politicians, both domestic and international, but by the divinities ruling world history, Beneš resigned on June 7, 1948, and only two months later passed away.

---

[309] Edvard Beneš: *Paměti III*, p. 601

With all due respect to his political skills and achievements and despite his tragic role in the events leading to our postwar enslavement, we have to ask ourselves, when observing the state of public affairs in our country, in Europe and in the world today, at the end of the second decade of the 21st century: Wasn't it actually Beneš's false beliefs – and not only our unfortunate geopolitical location at the "heart of Europe" – which brought us into the abyss? Wasn't it actually the progressive philosophy of history Masaryk and Beneš subscribed to and relied on uncritically in their political actions – and not just the existing global power constellation – where our road to our Babylonian captivity that lasted more than four decades, had in fact begun?

And furthermore: are we taking today this bitter historical lesson seriously enough – after having been offered the chance to be free again thanks to the Velvet Revolution that took place in the *"annus mirabilis"* 1989 when the Cold War ended, Soviet Communism collapsed and we could finally start our homeward journey and return to Europe? Wasn't Václav Havel – a leader of the liberated nation (shouldn't we call him, sticking to the prewar political hagiography, "President-Liberator?") – finding himself in a similar situation as his great predecessors and thus tempted to inherit and subscribe to the same progressive philosophy that failed them when exposed to critical reality tests? What actually was his basic philosophical message to Czechs and Slovaks when he came to Prague Castle on December 29, 1989, and throughout the next thirteen years of his first Czechoslovak and then Czech Presidency?[310]

And last: what kind of philosophy of history should we depart from in our current situation – when trying to understand what is going on around us and to formulate, as a body politic, the Czech "national interests" in the "post-Havelian" era – in an uncertain world we are a part of today, at the end of the second decade of the 21st century?

The objective of this paper is to look at least for some answers to all these politically touchy and entangled questions. Our guide will be a

---

[310] President Václav Havel's New Year Address pronounced on January 1, 1990
Czech text: https://archive.vaclavhavel-library.org/File/Show/157114
English text: https://archive.vaclavhavel-library.org/File/Show/157738

Czech philosopher whose life and work best can offer us at least a point of departure for this attempt: Jan Patočka.

First Movement: Patočka's Ten Stations through his BIOS FILOSOFIKOS[311]

Station One: Family Pictures

Patočka was born in 1907 in Turnov, a town in North Eastern Bohemia, in the family of a secondary school teacher, a well-educated *homme de lettres* and enthusiastic classical philologist. It was thanks to him that Patočka started learning at a very early age Ancient Greek, followed by the world of Greek art and culture. The humanistic tradition connected with the name and spirit of Tomas Garrigue Masaryk evidently belonged to the atmosphere of his family upbringing, and quite symptomatically: his father was an intellectual of the Masarykian type fully reliant on the power of independent human reason; his mother was a believer for her whole life, a Roman Catholic Christian, but, in Patočka's words, *"her main religious expression was work, a prayer of hands."*[312] When the Czechoslovak state came into existence in October 1918, Patočka was just over eleven years old, attending secondary school. Maybe he already sensed at that important historical moment for his nation what he would want to dedicate his life to and the best use of his extraordinary intellectual capabilities: philosophy.

---

[311] The basic resource of information, both for life and work of Jan Patočka, is Jan Patočka Archive in Prague (https://archiv.janPatočka.cz/). The English sources: Erazim Kohák: *Jan Patočka. Philosophy and Selected Writings*; Aviezer Tucker: *The Philosophy and Politics of Czech Dissidence. From Patočka to Havel*, University of Pittsburg Press, 2000; Ivan Chvatík and Erica Abrams (eds): *Jan Patočka and the Heritage of Phenomenology. Centenary Papers*. Dordrecht-Heidelberg-London-New York (Springer) 2011

[312] Jan Patočka: *K filosofovým šedesátinám. S Janem Patočkou o filosofii a filosofech* [*Under the occasion on the philosopher's sixtieth birthday* [*On Philosophers and Philosophy with Jan Patočka*] In : *Češi I,* p. 609

Station Two: The Student Years in Prague

In 1925, at the age of eighteen, Patočka started to study at Charles University. The postwar crisis was over. A new democratic political system stabilized. The visible signs of prosperity were everywhere. Masaryk's Czechoslovakia was in its best years. The problem Patočka ran into immediately from the beginning of his studies was that philosophy (attracting Patočka's interest much more than philology with a special focus on Romance and Slavonic Studies in which he was originally enrolled, following the advice of his father) was mostly taught there by professors influenced by and subscribing to positivism – a philosophical doctrine whose foundations were laid in the 19th century and that still dominated institutions of higher learning in Europe that had emerged from the cataclysm of the "Great War" and was, therefore, vulnerable to the progressivist optimism professed by most positivists. Masaryk's "realism" was influential here, as well – bringing into the philosophical discussion the practical problems in connection with the historical existence of the thriving democratic Czech society. Notwithstanding the monumental spiritual authority of "the President-Founder," his moralistic approach to politics was insufficient to open fundamental questions posed by contemporary philosophy, which Patočka was attracted by and tried to think through and articulate.

The 1920s was undoubtedly an opportune period, thanks to the Czechoslovak democracy that guaranteed freedom of thought and expression, for the dynamic evolution of a specifically Czech brand of philosophical thought, and Patočka was undoubtedly benefiting from it. There was, however, another aspect of academic life in prewar Czechoslovakia that must be considered, if we want to understand his own personal philosophical growth and development. Besides the Czech Charles University in Prague, there was also the Prague German University; with its professors and attractive, high-quality academic programs; open to all Czech students and serving as a natural bridge over waters of nationalism that had been, indeed, "troubled" so often in the past; enabling by its very existence a fruitful dialogue, instead of clashes and disputes, between those who were departing from either their Czech or German cultural *milieux* and might have had, therefore, different points of view, especially when it came to the assessment of and reflection on the current political situation.

There was more in it for a young philosophical apprentice, stubbornly seeking his own path into the world of great philosophers and their ideas that was now opening before him. The contacts Patočka established at the Prague German University during the first years of his studies, were, in fact, crucial for his own philosophical formation and offered him a much larger, more "worldly" perspective than was currently available at Charles. They enabled him, in the first place, as he himself later acknowledged, to liberate himself from the prevailing positivist spirit and get acquainted with a new spiritual orientation that started to gain ground in Germany: phenomenological philosophy.

Station Three: A Student Abroad

Patočka spent the academic years 1928/29 and 1932/33 abroad. In the first case, he went to Paris to the Sorbonne through a scholarship from the French Government. Not only the whole rich world of current French academia was offered to him during his studies there, but he didn't miss an event in Paris that turned out to be his life-changing experience. In February 1929 he attended two lectures Edmund Husserl gave at the Sorbonne in which he introduced the basic ideas of his "transcendental phenomenology" to the French academic public. Patočka later described how he felt about his first opportunity to see Husserl lecturing live – in an interview he gave almost four decades later, on the occasion of his sixtieth birthday:

> *I sensed in the air a compelling necessity to lay down anew the foundations and to look at a new direction to achieve historical depth. At the same time, I saw a real philosopher in front of me; someone who was not reading a paper about somebody or commenting on something, but just sitting in his study, as if alone, struggling with his problems, paying no attention to the world or the people around....*[313]

---

[313] Jan Patočka: *Vzpomínky na Husserla* [Remembering Husserl]. In : *Češi I*, p. 631

At this moment Patočka decided, definitely and irreversibly, to join Husserl's philosophical school and become a phenomenologist.

Patočka's second trip abroad followed immediately after his graduation at Charles University in the spring of 1931. He went to Germany on a scholarship from the Humboldt Foundation. He spent the winter semester 1932/1933 in Berlin and used the opportunity to get acquainted with the current state of German philosophical scholarship. Something else, however, was attracting his attention and occupying his mind besides the inspiring philosophical performances of his German professors. The virulent political environment that prevailed in the German capital then sent a frightening message regarding Europe's future. Here are Patočka's words from the same interview. He found himself surrounded in Berlin by

> *the atmosphere of that witches' cauldron, in which the end*
> *of Europe, and in conjunction with it the tragic turn in the*
> *lot of phenomenology and so many phenomenologists, was*
> *already in the process of preparation.*[314]

In this state of mind he left Berlin, where Adolf Hitler had just become German Chancellor, and in April he arrived in Freiburg where he registered himself with the Faculty of Philosophy in the seminar of Martin Heidegger, Husserl's most famous student, the acclaimed author of *Sein und Zeit*, but also a supporter of the Nazi movement, thanks to which he was also the newly appointed Rector of Freiburg University.

Besides participation in Heidegger's seminar Patočka had another point on his study plan at Freiburg; a point more important for him than anything else. With a letter of recommendation from the Humboldt Foundation, he hoped he would be able to get in touch with Husserl, who was retired by then, but still working on his phenomenological project presented in Paris, surrounded by a close circle of his younger co-workers and students.

Again, here is Patočka's description of his first face-to-face encounter with the man who was to become his principal philosophical teacher: He received an invitation to come to Husserl's home to discuss

---

[314] Ibid.

the terms of his apprenticeship. When he rang the bell, Husserl himself opened the door and said:

> *Finally! I had students from all over the world, but so far*
> *no fellow-countryman. ...If you are coming to me unspoiled*
> *by philosophical doctrines and without spiritual blinders, if*
> *you really want to learn to see, then you are warmly*
> *welcome here.*[315]

This was the beginning of the personal relationship between Patočka and Husserl which lasted until Husserl died in April 1938.

Station Four: Prague Philosophy Circle

After his return from Freiburg, Patočka again immersed himself in Prague's philosophical life. He published his first philosophical articles and reviews, mostly in the journal *The Czech Mind* (*Česká mysl*). In 1936 his first book was out and submitted for his successful habilitation: *"The Natural World as a Philosophical Problem,"*[316] a theme he took over from and discussed with Husserl during his stay in Freiburg.

Being back on his home turf, at first he felt rather isolated in his philosophical orientation. However, paradoxically, Hitler's rise to power in Germany quickly ended his isolation, thanks to the flow of emigrants who were escaping from the oppressive Nazi regime and finding in Czechoslovakia at least temporarily their refuge. If Czechoslovakia was perceived in the last years before World War II as a remaining "island of democracy" in Central Europe, surrounded by authoritarian states, philosophy also seemed to be flourishing on this blessed island where freedom still prevailed.

The first and most important new contact for Patočka was Emil Utitz, a new professor at the German Prague University.[317] Utitz, who had

---

[315] Ibid.

[316] Jan Patočka *Přirozený svět jako filosofický problém*. In: *Fenomenologické spisy I*, p. 127-261; Jan Patočka: *The Natural World as a Philosophical Problem*.

[317] Before he came to Prague, where he was born, Utitz, a former student of Brentano, was professor at the University in Halle. He belonged to a large and ever-growing circle of German philosophers influenced byHusserl. After the Nazis came to power in Germany he returned to his hometown and belonged to Patočka's closest cooperators at this time.

been forced to leave his post in Leipzig, came to Prague with a bold ambition: to turn the Czechoslovak capital into an international center for freedom-loving public intellectuals committed to resisting the totalitarian tendencies spreading currently like a plague in Europe and threatening not only freedom of thought and expression, but also, as it was to turn out soon, world peace.

The first thing Utitz suggested and was involved in, after arriving in Prague in January 1933, was the creation of the *"Cercle philosophique pour les recherches sur l'entendement humaine,"* the Prague Philosophy Circle. Patočka got on board immediately and became its Czech Secretary. This initiative was announced at the 8th International Philosophy Congress that took place later in Prague – chaired by Emanuel Rádl, originally a biologist known for his penetrating studies of the history of his science, but later an acclaimed public intellectual participating in his home country in all major public debates with philosophical underpinnings – and focused on the role of philosophy in defense of fundamental European values and democracy. Husserl didn't attend this gathering personally, but he sent a letter to its participants that was read by Patočka and apparently stirred among them a lively discussion.

Here are the fundamental questions raised, which occupied Patočka's mind ever since: Could Husserl's message he had the honor to deliver at the Prague Congress be powerful enough to bring the European nations to their spiritual renewal and reconciliation? Could his phenomenological point of view briefly articulated in his letter, further discussed in his two public lectures, given first in Vienna and then in Prague, and subsequently further elaborated in his last book[318] – arguing

---

The information about this period of Patočka's philosophical life can be found in Jan Patočka: *Vzpomínky na Husserla* [Remembering Husserl] (Cf. footnote 305); Jan Patočka: *Pražský filosofický kroužek* [*the Prague Philosophy Circle*].In : *Češi I*, p. 501-504; Jan Patočka: *K filosofovým šedesátinám. S Janem Patočkou o filosofii a filosofech* [*Under the occasion on the philosopher's sixtieth birthday* [*On Philosophers and Philosophy with Jan Patočka*] In : *Češi I*, p. 607-629.

[318] *Die Philosophie in der Krisis europäischen Menschheit.* (Husserl's public lecture in Vienna before the Kulturbund, May 7 and 10, 1935, read by Husserl in Prague before *Cercle philosophique de Prague pour les recherches sur l'entendement humain* in November 1935 under the title *Krisis der europäischen Wissenschaften und die Psychologie*).

that it is the sphere of subjectivity common to all human beings where the public debate about Europe's future should start – be turned into a platform for effective international action with the aim of protecting human freedom and saving European democracy against the emerging threats? Could Husserl's suggested return of European philosophy to the sphere of subjectivity and the life-world of human existence really prevent the fall of Europe into *"a barbarian hatred of spirit,"* so visibly present in the rising totalitarian movements?[319] Could Europe, with its origin in LOGOS and ratio discovered by the ancient Greeks and further cultivated throughout its subsequent history – a civilization irreversibly transformed over the course of the past three centuries, by the unprecedented achievements in modern sciences, but currently finding itself torn apart by the rising political conflicts – be reborn *"from the spirit of philosophy?"*[320]

At least in the short term, the answer to all these timely and increasingly pressing questions turned out to be, unfortunately, but unsurprisingly negative. The aggressiveness of Hitler's Third Reich simply could not be stopped by a sheer spiritual power of philosophy. Even Czechoslovakia, the only remaining island of democracy couldn't withstand the Führer's vitriolic attacks. First it was betrayed in September 1938 at Munich by its Western allies, and then destroyed entirely, in March of the next year when it became the German *Protektorat Böhmen und Mähren* and the pro-Nazi nationalist Slovak Republic.

When Czechoslovak democracy was dying, at least temporarily, and the new power holders were setting their imprint and imposing their restrictions on the free intellectual life of his country, Patočka and his German associates in the Prague Circle mobilized themselves for an unprecedented action, a clandestine operation whose central hero was Leo Van Breda, a Belgian Franciscan monk – *miles Christianus*, as Patočka

---

The English translation by Quentin Lauer as *Philosophy and the Crisis of European Man* (in: *Phenomenology and the Crisis of Philosophy*, Harper Torchbooks, New York, 1965, 149-192) or by David Carr as *The Vienna Lecture* (in: *The Crisis of European Sciences and Transcendental Phenomenology. An Introduction to Phenomenology.* Northwestern University Press, Evanston Illinois,1970), p. 269-299

[319] Edmund Husserl: *Philosophy and the Crisis of European Man* (in: *Phenomenology and the Crisis of Philosophy*, p. 192

[320] Ibid., p. 192

characterized him, *"for whom no cigarette was strong enough and no risk sufficiently terrifying."*[321] Its goal was to smuggle all Husserl's manuscripts brought to Prague by Utitz – tens of thousands of pages written in Husserl's special stenograph – to the Catholic University in Leuven, Belgium, where Husserl's Archives were just being created.

A similar action to rescue a philosopher's archive was repeated four decades later, when a small group of Patočka's students led by Ivan Chvatík, took all his manuscripts from his apartment the day after he died in the spring of 1977 and hid them in a secret place so that they couldn't fall into the hands of the Czechoslovak Communist secret police. This brave maneuver in the midst of "dark times" laid the foundations of the Jan Patočka Archive, a joint venture of Charles University and the Czech Academy of Sciences, which exists, as principal guardian of Patočka's spiritual legacy to this day, with Ivan Chvatík as its Director.

Intermezzo: Tracing Basic Elements of Patočka's Philosophy

Patočka's texts written during this period reveal the main elements of his evolving philosophy; all the philosophical problems that he further developed under changing historical circumstances.

First, one would stress his classical education and language qualification handed down by his father and later perfected during his studies. Patočka always worked with the original texts of both ancient and modern philosophy to articulate his own point of view. He always tried to establish direct communication with their authors and engage in a dialogue with them, in order to understand the meaning of their message and their philosophical will, without projecting his own ideas into his reading of their texts. In that respect he was actually very shy and careful in his philosophical beginnings and repeatedly warned others not to fall into this trap every young apprentice in philosophy is lured into – of trying to

---

[321] Jan Patočka: *K filosofovým šedesátinám. S Janem Patočkou o filosofii a filosofech* [On the occasion of the philosopher's sixtieth birthday [On Philosophers and Philosophy with Jan Patočka]. In: *Češi I*, p. 622

become an original thinker in his/her own right too quickly, but rather to be aware of and overcome it.[322]

Even those who are not personally attracted by his choice of philosophical school have to recognize that Patočka's early texts show him to be an excellent, skillful, precise reader of both classical ancient and modern philosophy, and thus a very special and highly qualified philosophical interpreter. But more than that: there is an inclination among some of experts on Patočka to present his unique skills to interpret others as the main feature of his philosophy.[323]

The second thing to be restated here is obvious. Patočka was clearly affiliated with and remained devoted to a well-defined philosophical school. As the last pupil of Edmund Husserl, he decided to follow his great teacher on the path opened by his transcendental phenomenology with its "Cartesian" point of departure, as it was presented in the "Paris lectures." Although well aware of all the tensions between the philosophical perspective of Husserl and Heidegger's philosophy of existence (to which he was also introduced into during his stay in Freiburg in 1933 and which evidently had also a lasting impact on his own philosophical thinking), he never abandoned fully Husserl's point of view. Till the end of his days he was ready to use Husserl's questions and his philosophical ethos to articulate his own philosophical problems and strive, carefully and methodically, for their solutions.

The third point in Patočka's early writings which he retained in all his later intellectual endeavors, is his extraordinarily strong personal commitment to philosophy; his definite and unshakeable belief that philosophy is not just an academic discipline among other humanities – to be studied as the history of philosophical ideas, and further developed at universities and other institutions of higher learning; that as a genuine "love of wisdom" it actually represents a fundamental basis and a principal guardian of our own humanity. In short, Patočka from his youth was essentially a philosopher in the Socratic mold. He took this role deadly

---

[322] Jan Patočka: *Mládí a filosofie* [*Youth and Philosophy*]. In: Jan Patočka: *Péče o duši I*, p. 122

[323] Erazim Kohák: *A Philosophical Biography*. In: *Philosophy and Selected Writings*, Edited and Translated by Erazim E. Kohák, University of Chicago Press, Chicago and London, 1989, p. 3-135;

seriously, with all the possible implications that such a stance could have for him. The *locus operandi* of his thinking, in short, was never limited by the boundaries of academia and academic philosophy, his home playing-field, but extended to the public space he shared with fellow-citizens.

And finally my fourth point: Patočka's genuine philosophical "socratism" opened before him a somewhat unusual philosophical topic, as he himself was well aware; a topic that interests us more than anything else in this essay: the Czech national philosophy and its role in modern Czech history; its impact on the present and the future of the Czechoslovak state – created with the help of Masaryk's ideas and later adapted to the changing international environment by his successor in Prague Castle Edvard Beneš; the "Czech question," conceived by both of them in *"worldly terms"* and stretched between its past and its future....

All these topics, present, at least *in nuce*, in Patočka's early writings, became constant themes of his later reflections; he kept returning to them, in one way or another, in all the future stages of his philosophical life. We will focus on this dimension of Patočka's philosophy in our next chapter.

Station Five: Philosophy as an Act of Resistance during the German Occupation

The result of the Munich Conference, followed by the resignation of President Beneš and exile, caused an overwhelming shock throughout Czech society. For two decades, its members had been used to living in the liberal atmosphere of Masaryk's state – with all its confusion, tension, political and social conflicts – and suddenly, they found themselves in the poisoned political climate of the "Second Republic." Those who even before it happened, had been hostile towards Masaryk's solutions of the "Czech question" and the conception of Czechoslovak politics and political life advanced in his name, might have felt vindicated and were ready to seize their chance. Public figures like writer Karel Čapek, to mention the most notorious example – the people who were directly connected with Masaryk's humanistic tradition and perceived as "his men" – became the immediately targets of vicious public attacks and defamation. A specifically Czech brand of petty nationalism started to spread like an infestation in the weeks and months after Munich, and, in fact, only the German occupation in March 1939 stopped this trend and exposed the whole nation – including all these small, horn-mad Czech fascists, or just "sour minds" that emerged in a short-lived "Second Republic"- to a much tougher question: How should one behave in this new situation? Be loyal to the Czechoslovak Republic that just perished, to the last breath, or find some acceptable *modus vivendi* in the new situation, with the new power structure in place – headed certainly not by the sitting president Hácha and the current government, but by the Reichsprotektor appointed by Hitler, who followed orders from Berlin?

Patočka was, like any other citizen of the Protectorate, not spared by this dilemma and made his choice. He didn't go abroad or join a clandestine resistance movement at home – like some other, undoubtedly more heroic individuals did, ready to sacrifice their lives. He just remained a Czech philosopher, deeply devoted to his nation, carefully selecting the specific "weapons" he could use for its defense; remaining faithful to his vocation in the upcoming confrontation, in which nothing less than national survival was at stake.

He kept lecturing at Charles University, until it was closed in November 1939. Then he taught at a Prague secondary school. And in the last year of the war, when he was sent as forced laborer to build the Vinohrady railroad tunnel, he did this job. He was married, with three children – his youngest son was born less than three months before the end of the war – and naturally, the protection of and care of his family was his major concern during the war years. What then did his personal, non-violent and "just" philosophical resistance to the existing totalitarian regime consist of?

The answer to this pointed question can be found in his wartime writings, published once as a part of irregular volumes or a series of studies, or in journals like *Česká mysl* or *Život* (Life), or in the cultural and critical review *Kritický měsíčník* (Criticism Monthly) published by his friend, the literary critic, Václav Černý. Despite tough control and censorship in the Protectorate, there were still small islands of free thought and free expression available for Czech public intellectuals in these difficult times, and Patočka regularly used this opportunity.

First he strived to digest not only the bitter Munich experience,[324] when Czechs rightly had felt themselves to be betrayed by their Western allies, but also the traumatic post-Munich situation when Czechs had been offered a not very pleasant opportunity "to know themselves" in the moment of national disaster. So what was the first step along the way to overcome this collective state of mind, recommended by Patočka in his writings?

To remain bold, self-conscious and self-reflective in the current dire situation and make use of it by raising again the question of Czech culture and education within European civilization; by trying to rediscover and reexamine critically once more the spiritual roots of the Czech nation in the context of its history, and by doing so to find for all possible future Czech collective endeavors a new energy and creativity, vitally necessary for the nation's survival and liberation.[325]

Faithful to this line, Patočka continued his program of phenomenological investigations of the fundamental structures of the Husserlian *Lebenswelt* ("natural world"), using the Czech romantic poet Karel Hynek Macha, as his point of departure.[326]

In his study *Two Senses of Reason and Nature in the German Enlightenment* from 1942, devoted to the philosophy of Herder,[327] he dared to start by stating bluntly something that had to fly directly into the face of the Nazis. In the opening paragraph of this study he openly articulated what was, according to him, philosophically disturbing in the current German ideology of National Socialism and should have been reflected on, thought through and thus illuminated in its substantive deficiency:

A century ago, this thought was devoted to idealism; since

---

[324] Jan Patočka: *Reflections on Defeat* In: *Living in Problemacity*, pp. 29-31

[325] Jan Patočka: *Česká vzdělanost v Evropě* [*Czech Culture in Europe*]. In: *Umění a čas*, pp. 27-52

[326] Jan Patočka: *Symbol zeme u K.H. Máchy* [*The Earth as a Symbol in K.H. Mácha*]. In: *Umění a čas* pp.104-124

[327] Jan Patočka: *Dvojí rozum a příroda v německém osvícenství. Umění a čas*, pp. 81-99; Jan Patočka: *Two Senses of Reason and Nature in the German Enlightenment: A Herderian Study.* In: Erazim Kohák: *Jan Patočka. Philosophy and Selected Writings*, pp.157-174

> *Nietzsche's time, it has become anchored at the opposite pole, in a naturalism with a strikingly irrationalistic emphasis, fusing in the national socialist world view, an irrationalism of goals with a rigid rationality of means.....*[328]

When one studies Patočka's war time texts, it is clear that they all were written without any ideological bias and, on the contrary, with a great akribia; that there is the same Socratic appeal in them like in the prewar texts; the same devotion to "return to the things themselves," and to turn them into a topic of unbiased philosophical investigation – with no concession to be made to the political regime currently in power.

When Hannah Arendt tried, after her experience with the Jerusalem trial of Adolf Eichmann,[329] to articulate her insights from this encounter with a monstrous, but banal evil of the German brand of totalitarianism, personified by the accused, she concluded that the most remarkable quality of this Nazi criminal, was his *"thoughtlessness;"* first his unwillingness and later inability *"to stop and think,"* in order not to become a mass murderer. And based on that encounter she argued that it is not necessarily only the ideological fanaticism of supporters of totalitarian regimes, but also this strange Eichmannian quality that has to be factored in, when one wants to understand the nature of these regimes and find the hidden source of their destructive power.

I think it was exactly this Eichmannian *"thoughtlessness"* and the enormous *"capacity for coordination"*[330] which people can discover in themselves when trapped by totalitarianism, which Patočka in his Czech *milieu* tried to resist. One can agree that his philosophical resistance simply cannot be compared to the actions of real national heroes and martyrs; to the courage displayed by the resistance fighters who were directly staking their lives and then often paid the highest price for their courage. At the same time, however, Patočka's war record proves that he was ready to demonstrate by his "actions" his personal commitment to the

---

[328] Op.cit., p. 157

[329] Hannah Arendt: *Eichmann in Jerusalem. A Report on the Banality of Evil.* First Published by the Viking Press, 1963.

[330] Hannah Arendt: *"What Remains? The Language Remains:" A Conversation with Günter Gaus)*, in: *Essays in Understanding 1930-1954*, pp.10-11

final message of his great teacher to his fellow-Europeans, pronounced in Prague in 1935: that a necessary part of the solution of the current crisis of our civilization – fallen temporarily into barbarity – is the *"heroism of reason"* of philosophers (Husserl), the readiness to live one's life *"in amplitude;"*[331] that what was at stake for the Czech nation during the German occupation (and what has remained at stake ever since, one can add), is not only the readiness of its members to stand up and defend its cause, if necessary with arms – thus putting their lives at risk and making their personal sacrifices – but also the capacity to renew the European philosophical spirit in its midst; its readiness, when the right moment comes, for a new beginning.

Station Six: At The Faculty of Arts of Charles University after the War

The liberation of Czechoslovakia in May 1945 was rightly perceived as the beginning of a new era – the end of all humiliation, all unspeakable miseries and sufferings endured in the past six years. Of course, there were different ideas in circulation among the Czechs, suggesting what to do and what not to do in this historical moment for which the nation waited so long.

The general consensus was that the perpetrators of all the crimes that had been committed during the German occupation – both Germans and Czechs – should be brought to justice – accused, tried, and if found guilty, punished for their deeds. There was also a general agreement that it was the unwillingness of the German minority on Czechoslovak territory to find a reasonable, i.e. fair and balanced solution to their "question" before the war – in spite of the good will and all the efforts of the prewar Czechoslovak Government and President Beneš – that played decisively into the hands of Hitler and led to the destruction of the Czechoslovak state in the years 1938/39. Consequently, it was this problem that had to be resolved first in the moment of Czechoslovakia's renewal.

---

[331] Jan Patočka: *Life in Balance, Life in Amplitude*. In: *Living in Problemtiacity*, pp. 32-42

For a sizable part of Czech society, just liberated from the horrors of war – particularly for many young people, susceptible to a new secular faith – the end of Nazi rule was perceived as a historical new beginning. To achieve this goal, Czechoslovakia would have joined other nations liberated by the heroic Red Army – and marched towards its Communist "radiant future."

President Beneš, who was generally perceived as "a national hero" after his return from exile and recognized by a large majority of the population as its uncontested leader, had obviously a quite different vision of the nation's future. Its most important element was his concept of legal continuity between the prewar and postwar Czechoslovakia. Therefore, the first step after the end of war, was the full *restitutio ad integrum* of the Czechoslovak "First Republic" as it had existed before Munich. The second step, according to Beneš was to set this fully restituted body politic – recognized as such internationally and built into an emerging new system of international relations – on the path of its evolutionary political reforms; transforming its originally "bourgeois" nature – rooted in the past with all its social injustices and political inequalities – into a strong, forward-looking, socially sensitive and economically prosperous democratic state, serving as the natural bridge between East and West.

As for the German question, Beneš was actually quite inconsistent in his vison. As mentioned above, the reconstitution of prewar Czechoslovakia in its borders – a legal position, advocated by him internationally from the beginning of his second "foreign action," according to which the Munich Agreement had to be considered "null and void" from the very beginning (as if it had never taken place) – didn't include the Czechoslovak citizens of German origin. Unable to consider some other, more conciliatory solution of the problem of future co-existence between Czechs and Germans in the new Czechoslovakia, Beneš unequivocally opted for a peaceful "transfer" of its German population – except for those able to prove their innocence, (which was virtually impossible in most cases) – back to their "homeland."

Patočka, I am sure, was attentively observing the brawling political life in the restored Czechoslovak democracy, but there are no signs to be found of his active participation in its sometimes friendly and moderate, sometimes heated and aggressive controversies concerning new choices for his liberated nation. He kept publishing his articles and reviews and articulating his philosophical views, as he did before and during the war, freely and without any internal constraints – without urgency about the challenges connected with the current "Czech question." He was fully focused on his own vocation, without any indication that the moment was near when Czech society would have been tested again; when its every member would have to make up his/her mind again and ask what the modern Czech nation as a collective of individuals united by its history and culture, wanted to be in the coming decades. He simply returned to Charles University and, as soon as it was reopened for students (it happened already in summer of 1945), he started to teach a class *A Concise Overview of the History of Philosophy.*

And here is how my father, who was among the students, described to me his experience with it.[332] His testimony is actually quite telling. When he made this choice, he didn't do it because he was already aware of Patočka's exceptional philosophical qualities, but because he liked the title. He just wanted to get some basic facts about the topic that was advertised, successfully pass the examination and move on in his studies. Something very different, however, was on offer in the packed lecture hall, when Patočka – thirty-eight years old – stood in front of his students for the first time and started to lecture.

Instead of facts to be remembered, written down for future examinations, the students were being introduced, step by step, to the world of genuine philosophy. In the six years in which Patočka was allowed to teach it, he managed to get from the presocratic thinkers only to Aristotle in his *"concise overview"* of the history of philosophy. What a disappointment for those who had been expecting just "facts!" Something else very important was happening, thanks to Patočka's very unusual form of teaching.

Within a year, my father found himself belonging to a circle of devout students who might not have been prepared yet to follow him into his philosophical depths, but started to accompany him on his way home

---

[332] Radim Palouš: *Dobrodružství pobytu vezdejšího* [The Adventure of Daily Living]. Karmelitánské nakladatelství Kostelní Vydří 2016, p. 73-75

after the classes and slowly learning during these night walks, their professor's main message: that philosophy – with its history going back to the ancient Greeks, yet still present in their current situation – is not, and never was, just an academic discipline to be learned during their study program and then practiced at universities or other institutions of higher learning; that it always was a vocation in the first place, endowed with a transformative power to change human lives. Instead of just lecturing on the history of philosophy, Patočka was laying the groundwork for his own philosophical school.

Station Seven: A Philosopher in the Shadow of Stalin's Statue

The "Victorious February" of 1948 brought a radical political change to the country and ruined Beneš' postwar political program, which he had conceived, in accordance with his philosophical views, *"in the broader context of the historical processes in the world"* and *"with regards to the deeper meaning of world history"* – as he boastfully announced in 1945.[333] The Communist Party headed by Klement Gottwald, supported by Stalin's Soviet Union, seized power, destroyed Czechoslovak "bourgeois democracy," and started to transform the Czechoslovak state – by violence or persuasion – according to its revolutionary blueprint. Not only were patriotic democrats imprisoned – turned overnight into "class enemies" – and some of them even executed for high treason or other offences against the state. Even ordinary citizens, who just were not able to coordinate themselves quickly enough with the new political order, met the same fate. It was only three years after Czech society had a chance in 1945 to open up and breathe freely after six years of terror, that it was again forcefully closed.

Immediately after the Communist *coup d'état* Patočka first tried to stand aside and continue his philosophical activities. For two more years he still taught his class at the College of Arts of Charles University. In the atmosphere of continuing Communist purges, however, it was only a matter of time that his turn would come. In 1950 – when he was occupied

---

[333] Edvard Beneš: *"Zpráva národu" [The Report to the Nation].* In: *Paměti III*, p. 590

with Aristotle – Patočka was notified by the Dean that as a non-Marxist, i.e. "bourgeois" philosopher, he was fired.

Because the closing of Czechoslovak society under the red banners of Communism was proceeding only gradually, he was immediately able to find a new job in the T.G. Masaryk Institute – where he worked as a researcher appointed to organize its archives, until this institute was closed in 1953 as a seat of "reactionary" Masarykianism and its archival materials were transferred to the Institute of History of the Czechoslovak Communist Party.

After the closure of the T.G. Masaryk Institute, Patočka managed to secure another job and discovered a new theme for his research. He was allowed to work as a researcher-specialist on Jan Amos Komensky (Comenius), the 17th-century Czech philosopher, pedagogue, theologian and last Bishop of the Unity of the Brethren. As a result of the defeat of the army of the Bohemian Estates at the Battle at White Mountain on November 8, 1620 – the Bohemian prelude for the devastating Thirty Years' War – Comenius had to go into exile, became known as a propagator of universal education and the author of a famous language textbook.[334] He had access to a number of Protestant rulers engaged in the conflict and unsuccessfully tried to lobby for the Czech cause at their courts.

Within four years of his work as "researcher-specialist" at the Academy of Sciences, Patočka managed to bring Czech Comenius studies to a much higher level, very different from the way Comenius had been studied in the Czech environment. He compared Comenius with René Descartes, the founder of modern European philosophy, and put his universal pansophist efforts to amend human matters in a larger "worldly" context. He also opened contacts for those involved in Comenius research at home with their contemporary German and French colleagues.

But there was another activity to which Patočka devoted time and energy during the Stalinist 1950s. He remained in an intensive personal communication with the circle of his former students at Charles University, eventually joined by several other like-minded people, who

---

[334] *Ianua linguarum reserata* (*The Door of Languages Unlocked*) published during the Thirty Years War and translated into most European languages.

had been too young to listen to his lectures in the late 1940s. He met them regularly in various private settings, engaging them in a contemporary Socratic dialogue – starting with various topics from the history of philosophy, later turning into a friendly, but sharp conversation focused on public matters. When one looks back at these activities, hidden from the public eye, it was clear that this was the spiritual foundations of the "parallel polis" – a tiny, but quite resistant body politic that was going to emerge in the Czechoslovak public sphere distorted by the ruling totalitarianism, decades later.

This was actually also the first time I saw Patočka "in action." One of these groups in Patočka's philosophical circle held their meetings from time to time at our home, in the apartment where I lived with my parents, grandparents and brother. I had no idea what brought all these people together, nor what the topic was of their sometimes relaxed, sometimes excited, passionate conversations. But I loved to watch them, drinking tea, eating small snacks, and talking and talking.

Station Eight: During the Thaw, on the Way to the Prague Spring

Soon after Stalin's death in 1953, the signs started to emerge that the era of "intensified class struggle" with both the external and internal enemies of the socialist order in the Soviet Empire, might come to an end one day. In reality, it took some time. The people in Czechoslovakia had to wait until 1960, when it was clear that the "building of socialism" reached its new – certainly less brutal and more relaxed – historical phase. A new constitution was adopted that year and, thanks to the general amnesty pronounced in connection with this fundamental legal change, most of the political prisoners of the Communist regime were released.

But into what kind of society were they being released? They had to reconcile themselves with the reality of its profound transformation that had taken place during their jail-time. Practically all intermediary bodies, previously existing between the citizens and the state, disappeared or were replaced by some surrogate, state-controlled entities or institutions. Czech society, once open, became effectively closed. The question was whether this state could be overcome and its traditional openness renewed.

There is no doubt that Patočka, who in the last years of the 1950s had started slowly to make his comeback in the official academic structures – because even his Marxist opponents recognized and respected the exceptional breath of his education and his unique philosophical qualities – observed the arrival of the Czech version of the "Golden Sixties" with some mental reservations, but also with a cautious optimism. He was certainly well aware of fundamental limitations of the existing political regime. The gradual changes, however – visible everywhere in Czech cultural life from the beginning of the 1960s – inspired hopes and his own activism. In spite of the persistent ideological rigidity of the Communist power holders and their political cadres, one could see an emerging and continuously growing space for independent, or at least semi-independent thought and activities; a space in which he would be able to freely examine his ideas and submit them for public testing and deliberation. No surprise, the winds of change were felt widely, including in Patočka's private philosophical circle. As a teenager I was following reunions of "Patočkians" in our home with an increasing interest and I registered a growing excitement in our visitors – seeing them energized and ready to take part in the new Czechoslovak intellectual life wherever and whenever it was possible.

And here is a story from the very beginning of the process of the "thaw" that started after 1960, that shouldn't be forgotten because it illustrates nicely who Patočka was and the nature of the relationship between him and his former students. Immediately after one of them, Jaroslav Kohout (1924-2013) – who spent, as a young social-democratic leader in 1948, ten years in Communist jails – returned home, Patočka invited him to go together to Krkonoše, the Giant Mountains, to spend a couple of days there in the fresh mountain air – to walk in the snow, to talk and think; to "metabolize" in common, as friends and with the help of philosophical conversation, what happened in the dark times and to discuss the possible Czechoslovak roads forward, towards the unpredictable, but at that time quite promising future.

Patočka's surge in the 1960s took place on two different, but interconnected fronts. In his home country he was finally allowed to return to the official sphere of academic philosophy. He had full employment in

the Philosophical Institute of the Czechoslovak Academy of Sciences –
first as a "specialist" in the "document department" – and later allowed,
even as a pronounced "non-Marxist" philosopher, to participate at its
regular seminars. In 1964, he published his second book *Aristoteles: jeho
předchůdci a dědicové* [*Aristotle, his Forerunners and his Heirs*][335] – a
well-researched study of the concept of movement in Aristotle – that
convincingly demonstrated his privileged position in the field of classical
Greek studies in the Czech environment. Based on this philosophical
accomplishment, he obtained the title "doctor of sciences," the highest
scientific degree given in academic institutions. In the same year he started
to lecture again – first as an external lecturer and then as a full professor –
at Charles University. For the first time he had an opportunity to teach
about Husserl's philosophy not just privately, in the small circles of his
friends, but in the regular academic setting, where he established contacts
with a new generation of students. He could participate at conferences,
publish articles in *Filosofický časopis* (The Journal of Philosophy) and in
other periodicals or as a part of various non-periodical publications – about
nearly all possible themes he selected. And as revealed in his
bibliography,[336] he did that quite frequently – contributing in his own way
to the "dialogue" the Marxist philosophers proposed to lead in these times
with their "ideological opponents."

The second front was international. Suddenly, he was allowed to
travel abroad in the 1960s. This enabled him to lecture at Western
European universities and renew old and establish new philosophical
contacts: those he made before the War – with Eugen Fink or Ludwig
Landgrebe, for instance – and those made first indirectly in the context of
his Comenius research – with several important German or French
specialists in the field of educational philosophy (for instance, Theodor
Ballauff, Klaus Schaler or Marcelle Denis). He was thus finally given an
opportunity to communicate in person with the people working at the

---

[335] Jan Patočka: *Aristoteles: jeho předchůdci a dědicové* [Aristotle: His Predecessor
and His Heirs].Nakladatelství československé akademie věd, 1964
[336] *Jan Patočka. A Bibliography.* In: Erazim Kohák: *Jan Patočka. Philosophy and
Selected Writings*, pp. 349-377; *Jan Patočka. Bibliografie 1928-1996*, OIKOUMENE
Praha, 1997Patočka's publications in 1960s,
http://www. ajp.cuni.cz/biblio.html

Husserl Archives in Leuven and to make use of these communications as an important new impulse and inspiration for his own phenomenological studies.

In 1965, Patočka delivered at Leuven a series of six lectures, in which he tried to answer for his Western colleagues the question of what was the *"Czech contribution to the ideal of modern science"*[337] – he intended to mediate his Czech experience, having its own specific genesis and evolution in modern European history, and the West's own, also historically conditioned perspective.

In the second half of the 1960s Patočka was influenced by the changing political climate in the country and started to appear increasingly in the public sphere. For instance, thanks to Ivan Vyskočil, who was a psychologist, writer, actor and playwright, he established intimate relations with the world of Prague's "small theaters," where he first met Václav Havel. He also became more active in his non-philosophical public statements: signing petitions, publishing articles in *Literární Noviny* (a literary weekly that was a recognized herald of all sorts of non-conformist views in the 1960s and was viewed by the orthodox Communists as a voice of political opposition), or in a new magazine *Tvář* (*The Face*) that was perceived by Party officials as even more "reactionary."

During 1968 Patočka was preparing a book of essays *Concerning the Meaning of Our Time*[338] – based on previous lectures and writing, with the aim of putting the political debates of the "Prague Spring" into the broader context of modern Czech history and Czech national identity. The fate of this project, which was scheduled to appear only in 1969, is telling. The invasion of the Warsaw Pact armies led by the Soviet Union ended by force the "process of regeneration" started in January 1968, and thus also ended the distribution of Patočka's collection of essays in bookstores. With the exception of a few tens of copies that were saved and distributed among friends, the entire edition was confiscated and destroyed.

---

[337] Jan Patočka: *Lovaňské přednášky. Příspěvek českých zemí k ideáu moderní vědy* [*Leuven Lectures. The Contribution of the Czech Land to the Ideal of Modern Science*]. In: *Češi II*, pp. 157-242

[338] Jan Patočka: *O smysl dneška* [*Concerning the Meaning of Our Time*]. In: *Češi I*, pp. 231-338

I still remember my encounter with Patočka on August 21, 1968 in the Philosophical Institute in downtown Prague. We were observing the situation on the streets from its balcony and heard gunshots nearby. The week of spontaneous popular protests against the occupation was about to begin and our hopes that, against all odds, our short-lived freedom could still be preserved and the impact of the Soviet presence reversed or at least tamed, were dying hard. But Patočka was right on this tragic day, when he observed: This would last at least twenty years! And, as it turned out, he was almost exactly right.

Station Nine: Back in the World Where Tomorrow Was Already Yesterday

The years after the unsuccessful attempt of the Prague Spring of 1968 are known as the "period of normalization." The prevailing mood among the Czechs was frustration, anger, distress and anxiety. Following the short-lived hopes and excitement caused by the near miraculous arrival of freedom into our closed society, we were not only back where we had been before the "regenerative process," but fared much worse in its aftermath.

Tens of thousands people emigrated. Those who stayed could only observe helplessly the restoration of the totalitarian regime. Having taken their *"lessons from the years of crisis,"*[339] the "normalizers" closed the society again and liquidated systematically every remnant of short-lived freedom.

All the party members who took part in the "counter-revolution," were removed from any position where they could exert influence on society. Political apartheid was exerted against them, and also applied to those who refused to repent and were not willing to conform to the orderly functioning of a closed totalitarian society. Extensive and detailed

---

[339] The Lessons of the Years of Crisis was a document of the Czechoslovak Communist Party adopted in 1969 as a blueprint for the policies of "normalization" after the counter-revolutionary attempt of the "Prague Spring" to undermine the very foundations of socialism failed and the "order" was restored (see Skilling H.G. (1976). *Czechoslovakia's Interrupted Revolution*, Center for Russian and East European Studies, University of Toronto)

measures were adopted in the media, schools, publishing houses, scientific and cultural institutions, in order to eliminate any free flow of information, any open public debate, so that in the future similar disruptions of the "socialist order" could never reoccur.

At the same time a kind of "social contract" – a relatively undisturbed private life and even some personal benefits for loyalty to the regime – was offered to the silent majority. Thanks to the existing power constellation – in Czechoslovakia and in Europe and in the world – there were no signs on the horizon that this situation could ever change. The strategy of the "normalizers," whose primary aim was to compel cooperation from the people by every means, and to use only the minimum force necessary to regain total control over their spontaneous, and thus by definition politically dangerous behavior, was apparently working. Brought back to life in the process of "screening," the main instrument of the policies of normalization, was the ugliest brand of Czech political realism, based on the capacity of members of a small and weak nation to conform to the situation in the world dominated by more powerful players: to resign temporarily their own freedom, truth, honor and dignity, but to survive.

Patočka's teaching position at Charles University was not – as at it had been the case twenty years ago, in 1948 – immediately affected. For the next five years – until he was retired for political reasons immediately after he reached the age of 65 – he could continue his lectures and seminars.

In his last academic year at Charles University I joined a quite colorful and multifarious group of his students. The title of his course was Plato's *Care for the Soul and the Just State*. The relation Patočka managed to evoke in the lecture hall – packed to the roof again – between the Platonic perspective on politics and the bleak political atmosphere of today, was abundantly clear. It was visible on the faces of the audience, especially the actions of note-takers and tape-recorder operators – saving and registering Patočka's lectures for the future. The second generation of students in Patočka' "private" school of philosophy founded after WWII was present. His twenty-years-old philosophical circle, was up and running, abounding in enthusiasm and full of renewed energy. The message could not be clearer: Patočka's retirement simply would not terminate his philosophical life. On the contrary, its most important phase – to complete his philosophical work on all its fronts – was still ahead. Its decisive steps – in the spirit of the old Latin adage saying that only *finis coronat opus* – had still to be made.

Now retired, Patočka halted his communication with official philosophical institutions – except for the few who remained loyal to Patočka to the end of his life and even attended his private seminars. In 1973 he even launched his own personal philosophical "counteroffensive" against them. Most likely inspired by his experience with the 8th International Philosophy Congress in Prague thirty-nine years earlier, he decided to travel privately to Varna to its 15th reunion and presented there – without the consent of the head of the Czechoslovak delegation and shouted down by its members – at least the main ideas of his prepared paper, before he was silenced by the chair of the meeting. The name of his contribution was telling: *"The Dangers of Technicization in Science in the Thought of Edmund Husserl and the Essence of Technology as a Danger in the Thought of Martin Heidegger"*[340] – his mature attempt to follow up the questions already raised in the 1930s by Husserl's exposition of the philosophical problem of European spiritual crisis in the 20th century, and Heidegger's reinterpretation of this Husserlian theme.

Throughout the whole period of normalization, Patočka tried to keep in touch with all his foreign philosophical colleagues – even though his passport was taken from him immediately after he returned from Varna, and he was not allowed to travel to the West again. His recently published exchange of letters with a young Polish phenomenologist, Krzystof Michalski, is quite telling in this regard.[341]

---

[340] *The Dangers of Technicization of Science according to E. Husserl and the Essence of Technology as Danger according to M. Heidegger. (Varna Lecture1973).* In: Erazim Kohák: *Jan Patočka. Philosophy and Selected Writings* , pp. 327-339 (German original presented at International Philosophical Congress, Varna, 197, but omitted from the Congress's *Acta*: *Die Gefahren der Technisierung in der Wissenschaft bei E. Husserl und das Wesen der Technik als Gefahr bei M. Heidegger*

[341] *Letters between Krzysztof Michalski and Jan Patočka (1973-1976).* In: *The New Yearbook for Phenomenology and Phenomenological Philosophy, Volume XIV, 2015, Religion, War and the Crisis of Modernity. A Special Issue Dedicated to the Philosophy of Jan Patočka*, pp. 223-270

Undoubtedly, however, the most important component of his philosophical life, and the main inspiration for his writing in this period, were his private, "underground" philosophical activities at home that started immediately after his retirement. Here is the opening to his cycle of lectures *Plato and Europe* for his private philosophical circle that met in the apartment of one of them in the fall of 1973:

> *Today people often get together to talk about abstract and eventually lofty things to escape for a moment the distress in which we all find ourselves, so that they may lift both their spirits and their minds. While I think that this is all very well, it is more like entertainment for old ladies. Philosophical reflection ought to have a different purpose, it should somehow help us in the distress in which we are; precisely in the situation in which we are placed, philosophy is to be a matter of inner conduct.*[342]

In sheer defiance of the corrupting and morally bankrupt state of affairs in Czechoslovakia at the beginning of the 1970s, the basic tone of Patočka's philosophical activities became more exhortative, and he put in the forefront the main mission of the philosopher in such a situation: to advise on how to resist the destructive effects of corrupt social and political order. What could still make a difference, despite the seemingly hopeless political situation, was our inalienable human capacity of reflection and insight!

And Patočka continued:

> *Our reality is always situational so that if it is reflected upon, it is already different by the fact that we have reflected. Of course, the question is whether by reflection, reality is improved. This is not stated in the least. But, in any case, a reflected-upon situation – in contrast to a naïve situation – is to certain extent a clarified one, or at least on the way to clarification.*

> *...A situation is entirely different, depending on whether people who are in a situation of distress give up or do not give up. In a hopeless situation it is still possible to behave*

---

[342] Jan Patočka: *Plato and Europe*, p. 1

in very different ways.[343]

In no historical situation is man allowed, Patočka noted, developing further the theme taken from Husserl, to resign his elementary task to think, to examine constantly his DOXAI and to keep transforming them into EPISTÉME. In no historical situation should man refuse to put his life under the test of reason and stop caring for the soul. In no historical situation can man escape the elementary consequences of his freedom and be absolved from the task to be "good" – from the duty to behave morally, to resist by all available means the decline and degeneration threatening always the very core of his human identity. And this truth should immediately be taken seriously here and now. It concerned also the members of currently normalized Czech society, who should not have kept their eyes closed and their ears shut – remaining "thoughtless" and cultivating only their "capacity for coordination" which Hannah Arendt pointed to when she encountered it personally and then analyzed the phenomenon of totalitarianism. What they were exhorted to do was to resist such a spiritual degradation, to wake up, start to think again and defend their own human integrity to change their minds…

Patočka's writings on this philosophical position in this period are illuminated by three major later works that one should look at: the lectures *Plato and Europe* given in 1973 and 1974 – just quoted above (published in samizdat after having been transcribed and edited by his pupils in the early 1980s); *Heretical Essays in the Philosophy of History* (written and published in samizdat in 1975); and the text *Europe and the Post-European Epoch* – found on the desk in his study after his death, that led the editors of the Collected Works to believe that Patočka didn't consider this text entirely finished, and was still working on it (translated into Czech from the German original and published as a book in 1992.)[344]

---

[343] Op.cit., p. 2

[344] Actually, two versions of this text written in German were found, translated into Czech by Věra Koubová - Jan Patočka: *Doba poevropská a její duchovní problémy* [Post-European Epoch and Its Spiritual Problems] and *Evropa a doba poevropská* [*Europe and the Post-European Epoch*]. In: *Péče o duši II*, p. 29-44, p. 80-148

Station Ten: The Spokesperson of Charter 77

When the main idea behind Charter 77 was discussed and its original declaration (defining it as "a loose, informal and open association of people of various shades of opinion, faiths and professions, united by the will to strive individually and collectively for the respecting of civic and human rights in our own country and throughout the world"[345]) was still in the process of its formation in the fall of 1976, Patočka was not among the original "conspirators." From the beginning of the 1970s, however, he was involved in the emerging independent public space being created step by step in the manifestations of individual resistance to the normalization pressures and in the isolated protests against oppressive acts of the regime, trying to deprive the Czech society of its moral strength.

Patočka's public statements in the case of the philosophical archive of Karel Kosík, seized by the Communist secret police in one of its raids, or his reaction to the trial of the Plastic People of the Universe, allegedly for indecent lyrics in their songs, are only two of the best known examples of Patočka's growing determination in the 1970s that as a philosopher he simply could not be silent, or sit on the sidelines; the time came, when he as a philosopher had no choice other than to turn his reflections on the current state of the world taking place in the privacy of his "interior domus" into a worldly, i.e. visible and audible public action.

The rest is history. When Václav Havel approached him in December of 1976 and offered him a role as one of the three Charter 77 spokespersons, Patočka accepted (Was he surprised by it? I don't think so.) without much hesitation – knowing very well, as a classicist well-oriented in Plato's dialogues and a philosopher in the Socratic mold in one person, that philosophy is not only a form of participation in public matters, but also, and maybe primarily, the philosopher's preparation for death.

I clearly remember my last encounter with him. It was at the end of February when he briefly stopped at the apartment of my parents – to report on what was happening around him in the past days. When he was

---

[345]Quoted from the English version of the Charter 77 Manifesto (http://www. cnn.com/SPECIALS/cold. war/episodes/19/documents/charter. 77/).

about to go home he asked me to accompany him on the way to the tram stop. In was about eleven o'clock in the evening, there was no sign that the agents of secret police were around, we walked through the dark streets of Prague's Little Quarter and talked about the situation in which we momentarily found ourselves. Then his tram number 22 arrived, he got in, waved at me from the inside, the signal for departure sounded and he was gone. I would never see him again.

A Closing Remark on Patočka's *via dolorosa*: A Synchronic or Diachronic Reading of Patočka's Philosophy?

At the end of this quick exposition of Patočka's journey through his philosophical life in ten stations, I will return to the question that struck me again and again when I was re-reading Patočka's texts in preparation for this paper, and inspired me to include an "intermezzo." I stated there that Patočka's reader can in his first texts identify *in nuce* all the main motifs he pursued ever since; all the philosophical problems he returned to again and again and tried to re-formulate in the course of his lifetime, characterized on the one hand by his own personal philosophical growth and evolution, and at the same time influenced by all the ups and downs of Czech history in the 20th century.

Eric Voegelin, Patočka's contemporary, once wrote when he wanted to characterize the peculiar, sometimes hardly understandable activities of philosophers: They should be seen primarily not as the authors of their philosophical "doctrines," but as human beings, living among their fellow-citizens in their cities, *"engaged in an act of resistance against the personal and social disorder of (their) age."*[346] Without any doubt, Patočka fits this definition in a more convincing manner than most of his philosophical contemporaries, including Voegelin himself. This essential feature of his philosophizing, however, is a great challenge for his interpreters, because it involves a serious conflict of interpretation: a tension any reader of his texts must feel between a synchronic or a diachronic reading them.

---

[346] Eric Voegelin: *Reason, Classical Experience*. In: *Published Essays 1966-1985*, p. 265

Synchronic reading of Patočka's texts requires departure from the historical context in which they were written and cluster them accordingly into their distinct historical periods. In contrast, *diachronic reading* means to connect the texts based on their content and read them in order to trace the topics of Patočka's philosophical examination over time, from its early beginnings to their definitive shape in his mature philosophy.

Whereas the second approach seems to be more appropriate for Patočka's phenomenological studies and the other big questions of mainstream "perennial" philosophy, the first approach fits his "marginal" philosophizing about the "Czech question," which should be seen, as Masaryk urged his fellow-citizens, in "worldly" terms. This will be my focus in the next part of this text.

We will need to think through carefully in this context two problems clearly present from the beginning to the end: his concept of transcendence, and in connection with that the way Patočka deals with a potential conflict between a historian studying the contemporary epoch and a philosopher engaged in it by the means of his/her internal "actions."

Second Movement in Four Parts: Patočka as a Philosophical Bridge-Builder between the Past and the Future

Part One: The Question of Czech National Identity

Let us start from Patočka's general view of his "modern" Czech nation. Who are the modern Czechs? What kind of nation do they now – as a human collective composed of people living on a certain territory, connected by a common historical lot, a shared language, culture – belong to? Who are they, as people sharing a public space formed over the course of its history? Not only storing in its memory the traces of all the past struggles and situations their ancestors were involved in, but also serving those living today, where are the Czech national interests being discussed with the nation's visions of its future?

One can say that, as any Czech public intellectual, Patočka had to live with the painful questions of his national identity all the time. Especially as a philosopher in the Socratic mold he could not escape these questions his whole life – as is clearly evidenced in a number of texts he wrote throughout his philosophical career – always motivated by his need to react, in his own philosophical way, to the political situation of the moment. It is quite significant, however, that it was only in the depressing atmosphere of "normalization" after the failed Prague Spring of 1968, when he felt obliged to give his own comprehensive answers to all these questions – in a series of private letters sent to his German female friend who was supposedly considering a move to Prague, in which Patočka tried to offer her a *"concise overview of the facts"* plus an *"attempt at an explanation"* of the Czech national character and its collective identity.[347]

Here is Patočka's main thesis. If we look at Czech history as a whole, from its beginnings in the formation of Christian Europe to the present, what stands out clearly, is a great discontinuity; a gap, separating its older, medieval phase (the traces of which can still be seen in the architecture of Prague and other historical cities and towns throughout the Czech lands) from its modern period the living Czechs are still a part of; a difference between their pre-modern ancestors and the current nation. What then has to be recognized without prejudice and romantic sentiments – if today's Czechs want to understand themselves and to assess realistically their collective capabilities as a distinct body politic – is the fact that the modern Czech nation originated by *"being re-born from below."* This is still active in it, as its "primordial genetic disposition;" what till today points to the main endemic political problem of the Czech nation: its "smallness."

The decisive factor influencing modern Czech politics and political culture – from their origins in the late eighteenth century, and up to their present forms and habits – is, according to Patočka, the composition and structure of Czech society. Being "re-born from below" means, that for historical reasons, the modern Czechs lacked at their birth as a political nation an aristocratic element (which was largely present and politically active in many other European societies also undergoing the complex processes of modernization in the 19th century, including Austrians, Hungarians or Poles, for instance). Who were among the dominant players decisively influencing the changing political environment and being the most outspoken in the on-going national debate

---

[347] Jan Patočka: *Co jsou Češi?*. In: *Češi II*, pp. 255-324

that burst out in the transition from the 18th to the 19th century in the Czech case? Individuals from the middle strata of society to be modernized, i.e. awakened, enlightened and educated: teachers, writers and poets, historians, journalists, priests, university professors and playwrights. Looking at how the Czech re-awakening began and contrasting what can be characterized as "Czech-style-modernization" with other, more glorious and more visible forms of the similar process, Patočka pronounced – in an unusually straightforward, unsparing and almost self-deprecatory manner – the following diagnosis:

> *The Czechs are a nation of liberated servants. They did not liberate themselves. They did not carry out any revolutionary act of liberation necessary to achieve such a goal. Rather, they were liberated by an act of an emperor, being themselves much less radical than their liberator – the emperor himself.* [348]

However, Patočka observed at the same time that it was exactly this "re-birth" of the Czechs "from below" that made them – as a modern political nation, formulating and pursuing its political program with the central aim of political emancipation and trying to find its place among other nationalities partaking, in their own unique way, in the universal history of mankind – specifically democratic. And he also recognized that in comparison with others, the Czech achievements in the process of modernization were actually quite impressive.

The main feature of Czech national behavior was patient steady progress in the building of a specifically Czech "civil society." Throughout the 19th century, this idea was captured by the term *drobečková politika*, which could be translated as "small aims, small gains," with the word "small" understood as a gradual and evolutionary development. In its last decades, the Czech lands were inhabited by a developed industrial society with a quite impressive educational system and an active associational life. Czech politicians traditionally had all sorts of complaints about the centralist policies of the government in Vienna, or the oppressive

---

[348] Op.cit. p. 303

strategies of the Austrian secret police, but among themselves they happily adjusted to their own kind of "democracy."

Such a democratic spirit, however, also had its weaknesses. Czech smallness, as far as its aims and gains (Patočka emphasized that "smallness" here describes not only the lack of resources and the disadvantage that results from small numbers, but also a kind of "quality," substantively influencing political behavior), has always been threatened by its own tendency towards closedness, opportunism, lack of self-confidence, as well as its permanent need for self-excuse and self-defense. Confronted by the outer world controlled by greater, more worldly powers, the spirit of "liberated servants" was not only wonderfully democratic, but often turned out to be too parochial, too small-minded, insufficient to perceive itself being measured on larger international/ geopolitical/universal or cosmopolitan scales; to address the root causes of all challenges to the Czech lands from the outside; troubling periodically Czech national political life that could never be isolated from world history with its major questions, crossroads and crises.

As soon as Patočka's private letters were published in Czech translation in 1992, a number of critical voices started to be heard. The first question was, whether these letters should have been used at all as the author's contribution to the public debate on the Czech national character and identity – when he himself had never intended to do so. And in this respect, it is, of course, the editors, and not Patočka himself, who should have eventually been blamed for their decision. But the criticism didn't stop here. It was, above all, several historians specializing in modern Czech history, who stepped in and started commenting on Patočka's uncomplimentary description of modern Czechs as a "nation of liberated servants." The strongest critic of Patočka from their ranks so far has been Eva Hahnová, in her recent book "Češi o Češích" (The Czechs about the Czechs) – published only two years ago – as her obvious contribution to all our anniversaries of 2018 – which aims to *"offer examples of perspectives in the current disputes concerning Czech history, with a special focus on the problem of derogatory stereotypes."*[349]

---

[349] Eva Hahnová: *Češi o Češích, [Czechs on Czechs].* Academia Praha 2018, p. 10

According to Hahnová, Patočka's contribution to the debate about *"who we are as modern Czechs"* offers only a cursory and also significantly biased perspective, especially when confronted with the historical facts and their more careful treatment and articulation in the works of qualified historians – the real experts on the given period of Czech history, equipped with sufficient knowledge of historical sources and using the standard methods of historical research. What Patočka tried to communicate with his intimate German friend, is just an entirely inappropriate generalization. It is just one example in a series of *"pictures"* with its place in the *"gallery of Czech lamentations,"*[350] but not in serious Czech historiography.

Patočka's perspective itself can be seen as a historical fact, in that it explains the state of mind of an important Czech philosopher who undoubtedly left his significant trace in Czech contemporary history. As far as its role in its proper reading and qualified interpretation, however, its use is rather dubious than inspirational. The fact that the current Czech discourse in this regard has been heavily influenced by Patočka's various philosophical heirs end epigones – including President Václav Havel – who seem to be subscribing to his understanding of the allegedly typical Czech mentality characterized by incurable mediocrity and provincialism – is just disturbing and unacceptable, according to Hahnová. It is rather a symptom of our chronic national disease of self-accusation and self-deprecation, and certainly not a first step on the way to its healing.

What should be done, according to her, instead of continually disseminating *ad nauseam* Patočka's subjective message from the period of normalization, is to work patiently on the real cultivation of the current Czech public discourse that is and always has been much more than a never-ending series of quarrels among members of a European nation uniquely composed of *"liberated servants;"* to try to improve our capability to reflect adequately and sharply enough on our collective past as other European nations – confident enough and mindful of their inherent value – are doing; to re-examine patiently our collective myths and keep replacing them with the relevant critical ideas that are the life-blood and

---

[350] Eva Hahnová: *V Galerii nářků* [*In the Gallery of Lamentations*]. In: op.cit. pp. 21-52

conditio sine qua non for the continuing existence of any national society having its roots in a genuinely European, i.e. free-minded spiritual tradition and aspiring to be also *in futuro,* an active and visible member of the family of universal mankind.

There is no place here to go into detail through the concrete points in which Hahnová attacks Patočka's efforts to present to his addressee – his *"Hertzbewohnerin"* (she who occupies his heart) – his philosophical analysis of Czech national identity. But first it is not clear to me why she had to violate the rules she herself associates with her profession of historian in her assault on Patočka: to examine and judge the historical facts not in isolation, but also in the perspective of their historical, i.e. "evolutionary" continuity. What would not have escaped her attention then, would be another "fact" she seemed to omit entirely: that Patočka was developing the themes touched on in these letters in the context of his overall, life-long philosophical projects and endeavors; that there are other important texts to be found in the whole corpus of his writings, the reading of which would have helped her, for sure, to come to a much more balanced judgement and to weaken her own, quite inaccurate, vague and philosophically untenable conclusions as far as Patočka's position in the debate on the "Czech question."

I am sure, that, based on the further reading of Patočka, Hahnová might be able to find a much better use for it, even within her own declared efforts to put the work of qualified historians in the service of the cultivation of Czech public discourse. As *pars pro toto*: her refusal to recognize the existing tension between the two mutually competing concepts of the Czech national revival Patočka was pointing to – one connected with that of Josef Jungman, putting the Czech language in the forefront as a main driver of this process; the other one, whose main proponent was Bernard Bolzano, who sought to ground it in the European enlightened rationalist tradition.[351] Wasn't here an opportunity for her – missed entirely – to think through and articulate more precisely the current *"Czech perceptions of Czechs"* with the help of Patočka's exposition of

---

[351] Jan Patočka: *Dilema v našem národním programu. Jungmann a Bolzano* [Our National Program and its Dilemmas. Jungmann and Bolzano]. In: *Češi II*, pp. 2 93-305

the relation between nation and state in the context of the Czech national revival in the 19th century? Between nation as an ethnic community – rooted in a common past and common language and protecting its national culture as its first priority – and nation as a body politic animated by the European concept of freedom – whose members don't share primarily their ethnicity, but are unified by a future-oriented project based on the shared universal humanist values, regardless whether they belong to the Czech or German speaking communities?

But I believe there is more at stake here than Hahnová's clearly misguided criticism of Patočka could demonstrate. Doesn't her defense of the "real" nature or character of the modern Czech nation against Patočka's alleged philosophical "defamations," demonstrate that there is a fundamental difference between the point of departure of a philosopher in the Socratic mold and an essentially disengaged position of a contemporary historian? That it is this difference that generates a conflict in their interpretations? Whereas philosophers are essentially actors whose reflections, always personal and rooted in their finite human "subjectivity," are driven by their will to get involved in the public affairs of their polis by the means of *"internal action"* – to repeat once more Patočka's words from his lecture from the early 1970s – historians by their nature are observers of historical events, always coming only *post festum;* never being themselves personally engaged in the situation being historically studied, but just sitting as umpires and pronouncing their judgments.

The thing is that Hahnová's criticism of Patočka seems to ignore the true point of departure in his private letters and what he perceived, when he was writing them, as his personal vocation of contemporary Czech philosopher: to keep alive in the environment of Czech society he was a member of – awakened in the course of the 19th century, turned into a body politic thanks to independence gained in 1918, but remaining tormented by world crises ever since – a possibility to escape against all odds the predicaments of its endemic "smallness;" a possibility to free itself from the depressing *status quo*; a possibility to preserve the *"movement of truth" and of the care for its "soul"* – its *"sensorium of transcendence"* as Eric Voegelin would put it – in its midst; a possibility to re-awaken among its members the sense of civic responsibility; a possibility to exhort them to step out from the protective shells of their privacy and start paying attention again to the public affairs of their country and acting "in concert."

Part Two: Masaryk's Answer to the Czech Question Perceived in "Worldly Terms"

Let's take a step forward by looking for examples of such behavior in the Czech environment that attracted Patočka's attention, when scrutinizing the modern Czech nation, composed, according to his words, of *"liberated servants."* There is a whole list of people he recognized and was highly appreciative of in this context – writers, poets, journalists, historians or philosophers – who tried, each of them in his/her own specific way during his/her lifetime, to bring at least some dose of "greatness" into the "small" Czech world; to open the windows and invite a fresh breeze into the somewhat airless Czech national environment. Only one of them, however, got his full attention as the most outstanding example of these efforts: Thomas Garrigue Masaryk, a university professor who was involved in all of the major political debates of his time; a man who exhorted Czechs to think about themselves, their politics, and their national identity in "worldly terms;" who spoke openly against the fabricated Czech mythologies and false self-illusions; who strongly defended the rights of women and struggled against anti-Semitism; who married an American and had strong personal, academic and political ties with the United States, and who, in the end, became the first president of the democratic Czechoslovak state.

When looking at Patočka's life and work, one can immediately see that Masaryk was not for him just a monumental political figure with a significant impact within the "marginal" Czech national environment – someone who is great at home, but simply doesn't bear comparison with great thinkers of the past and the present – but represented for him a lifelong philosophical problem; that this problem was not only related to the history of the "small" Czech nation, but also belonged, in Patočka's perspective, to the realm of "perennial" philosophy – and as such had to be examined in the context of the "dialogue of mankind" the great philosophers have been leading over the centuries. From his family environment, where he, thanks to his father, was introduced to the humanistic spirit of Masaryk's Czechoslovak republic and decided to devote his life to philosophy, through the Christmas celebration in 1934 in Freiburg when Husserl gave him as a Christmas present Masaryk's wooden reading board he himself had got from him many decades before during his studies in Leipzig (and thus made Patočka, according to his own words, *"the heir of a ‚great' tradition, something he never felt he deserved"*[352]), to one of his last texts devoted to Masaryk's concept of religion[353] (written only months before he became Charter 77 spokesperson and faced his Socratic trial and death), he was accompanied by this great personality of modern Czech history – both as his admirer, and, at the same time, as his philosophical critic.

On the one side, he emphasized one, indeed, quite unusual quality of Masaryk the thinker. There was no other significant European philosopher, according to Patočka, at least in his times, who managed like Masaryk, to transform his thoughts and words into effective "worldly actions." First as a university professor and a Czech politician in the times of the Austro-Hungarian Empire – always ready to stand up, loud and clear, for his cause and go, if necessary, in the defense of his ideas and values "against the current;"[354] then during the "Great War," when he decided to abandon definitely the traditional "austroslavism," that throughout the 19th century had shaped the mainstream of Czech national politics, and to start struggling, at first almost alone, for the nation's future independence; and then last, when he became the President-Founder of the democratic Czechoslovak state and acted – turning the old Platonic dream into living reality – like a real "philosopher-king" at Prague Castle.

---

[352] Jan Patočka: *Vzpomínky na Husserla* [Remembering Husserl]. In: *Češi I*, p. 639
[353] Jan Patočka: *Kolem Masarykovy filosofie náboženství* [*On Masaryk's Philosophy of Religion*]. In: *Češi I*, p . 366- 422; On Masaryk's Philosophy of Religion. Translated by Jiří Rothbauer. Revised by James Dodd, Christina Gschwandtner and Ludger Hagenhorn. In: The New Yearbook for Phenomenology and Phenomenological Philosophy, Volume XIV, 2015, Religion, War and the Crisis of Modernity. A Special Issue Dedicated to the Philosophy of Jan Patočka, pp. 95-135
[354] Gordon Skilling: *T.G. Masaryk. Against the Current, 1882-1914*, Macmillan, 1994

At the same time, Patočka studied carefully the unspoken presumptions and tried to articulate the philosophical points of departure of Masaryk's thought, and in this regard he was always ready with his critical comments and remarks. He found in Masaryk a representative of the dominant progressive positivism and argued convincingly from his own phenomenological perspective, taken from Husserl and later developed in communication with the thought of Heidegger and other students of his great teacher: the solution of the crisis of modern European civilization articulated by Masaryk and turned by him into a successful political action during the First World War was insufficient and untenable in the long-term perspective; Masaryk was incapable of plumbing the depth of the problem and remained, thanks to his positivism whose founding fathers (Comte, Mill, Spencer *et alii*) decided to reject – instead of giving a new meaning to – European metaphysics. A major unresolved philosophical problem was actually hidden in the very core of Masaryk's interpretation of the "raison d'être" of the "First Republic" he managed to successfully create: his progressivist concept of history – articulated, for instance, in his speech delivered to the Czechoslovak National Assembly before Christmas of 1918, right after he returned home from his exile; in his essay "New Europe" prepared for the participants at the Paris Peace Conference in 1919;[355] and in his book *The Making of a State* (in Czech *Světová revoluce* [The World Revolution]),[356] published in 1925 and written primarily for his Czechoslovak public as his detailed account of his "foreign action" in the war years 1914-1918 that irreversibly changed the world and opened the door for the processes mankind, the Czechs included, was to be confronted with in the coming century.

Patočka's succinct final pronouncement concerning his own evaluation of Masaryk's perspective perceiving the First World War as a decisive watershed between the international politics of the 19th and the 20th century that offered the possibility even to small Central European nations, can be found in the beginning of his sixth "heretical essay," one

---

[355] Tomas G. Masaryk: *New Europe*. In: *The Spirit of Thomas G. Masaryk 1850-1937*, pp. 205-217
[356] Tomas G. Masaryk: *Czechoslovakia and the World*. In: *The Spirit of Thomas G. Masaryk 1850-1937*, pp. 218-236

of his crucial texts from the last years of his life when he tried to articulate his own conception of philosophy of history:

> *The First World War provoked a whole range of explanations among us, reflecting the efforts of humans to comprehend this immense event, transcending any individual, carried out by humans and yet transcending humankind – a process in some sense cosmic. We sought to fit it into our categories, to come to terms with it as best we could – that is, basically, in terms of nineteenth century ideas.*[357]

Masaryk, according to Patočka, clearly belonged to the category of thinkers who tried to do just that, and it is the main reason why his interpretation of the First World War as a *"world revolution,"* in which democracy defeated theocracy, was just a speculation that didn't materialize in the international politics of the 20th century. Here is Patočka's argument why Masaryk's political construction that was intended to fit perfectly with the democratic times that were allegedly coming, was built not on the solid bedrock of progressive European history, but on a treacherous subsoil of what was really coming, that turned out to be quicksand, and for that reason was doomed – only twenty years later – to its demolition.

But already in 1946, right after the Second World War – when Masaryk's disciples and especially Edvard Beneš as their most visible face and spokesperson, still seemed to believe, that Masaryk's legacy was still alive and strong enough to endow him – in his capacity of Masaryk's legitimate heir – with the historical "mandate" to repair the national construction only temporarily destroyed by Nazi Germany, on the basis of its original blueprint – Patočka wrote this, clearly aware that the times were changing, thus making this blueprint outdated and raising a question again what alternative philosophy of history might better serve as its possible future foundation.

I will quote *in extenso*:

This whole [Masaryk's] interpretation [of the world

---

[357] Jan Patočka: *Heretical Essays in the Philosophy of History*, p. 119

situation resulting from the WW I] was on the one side almost obvious. It was clearly understandable. It was also influential because it gave Masaryk – a victorious authority – a great respect and popularity. But it had also its flip side that was dangerous for him in his capacity of philosopher of the First World War. Because time and events haven't stopped. They haven't got stabilized naturally in a state Masaryk considered as desirable and predictable. Yesterday's winner is now in a rather different position: The revolution has continued with much greater perseverance when compared to the First World War. And also, the new powers have appeared, taking part in it. Despite the fact that certain analogies can be found in the basic features of the two wars – first of all, that something like world unity was formed and came into being to opposed the convulsive system of authority, uniform violence and arbitrariness that was accepted by the rest of the world; despite the fact that Masaryk's analyses could help us to understand some details of our contemporary times; despite all of that, I am sure we all feel that the situation resulting from the WWII is different. We miss today the air of overall optimism breathing from the pages of Masaryk's "Making of a State". In this war, even more global than the previous one, entirely new actors got engaged: the Soviet Union, China, non-European and non-American states and nations. All that is why we need new analyses, more detailed and more thorough, to sufficiently assess the real meaning of this conflagration. The world of postwar democracy, so much welcomed by Masaryk as the decisive victory of the modern spirit, has succumbed in less than twenty years to the greatest crisis. Democracy which Masaryk so much hoped for and believed in, has turned out to be weak in the decisive moments. And it is not just a temporary weakness, but a constitutive one. It seems obvious that the reason for this weakness should be looked for in social fragmentation, in the unresolved social problem which represents a serious challenge for all bourgeois democracies. In this sense, Masaryk's philosophy of modern history – based on the analyses of the spiritual situation of modern man and perceiving political democracy as a road to democracy endowed with a significant social element, which should be its natural continuation – fails to grasp the meaning of the latest great events.[358]

Today's critics of Patočka can use this passage as a "proof" that even this great Czech philosopher of the 20th century succumbed to the pressures of the virulent and seductive atmosphere of the years immediately following the liberation of most of Czechoslovak territory by the Soviet Red Army and became, at least temporarily a "socialist." I am deeply convinced – and the proof for it can be found both in synchronical or diachronical reading of Patočka's other texts, in his behavior during this period and in the consequences, the Communist takeover had for him personally a few years later – that it was not the case. The thing is, actually, quite simple. Patočka's main point here was – as it had been before and was ever after – that we need to return from Masaryk's answers, no matter how nicely they might sound in our ears, to his original questions; to think them through again in our current situation and search, with their help, for our own way towards the future.

Part Three: Patočka's Judgment on Edvard Beneš

I will follow up with a short remark on Masaryk's successor, Czechoslovak second President Edvard Beneš. Patočka wrote a couple of articles before the war, analyzing philosophical presumptions of his approach to politics inspired by Masaryk, and trying to articulate what it means to be, as Beneš described himself, an *"idealist realist."* Even in 1948 he remained silent as far as Beneš's concrete policies and made just a couple of comments on Beneš's philosophical humanism. It was only in the 1970s when he finally decided to assess in retrospect his role as "President-Builder" in Czechoslovak history, in which he, according to Patočka, tragically failed – especially in the pivotal event of his political life, the Munich crisis of 1938. Instead of acting as Masaryk's true heir in Prague Castle and leading his nation in the difficult upcoming fight, he turned out to be a *"weak man, good as a secretary, but nothing more."*[359]

---

[358] Jan Patočka: *Masaryk včera a dnes* [Masaryk Yesterday and Today]. In: *Češi I*, p. 93-94 (translated by MP)
[359] Jan Patočka: *Co jsou Češi?*. In: *Češi II*, p. 322

And here is Patočka's final verdict:

And it was this man who happened to have in his hands the decision concerning the future moral profile of the Czech nation – he had to make a choice and he chose "smallness." Most likely definitively, because the small ones will be offered less and less an opportunity to act in the future world and thus to accomplish something great in the field of history. It is a tragedy of modern Czech identity that the efforts of modern Czechs, with their dogged persistence in the close fight, to succeed in the struggle for recognition that they stand equal to the great ones, were thwarted, maybe definitively – thanks to the failure of an average man and a weak politician, who was momentarily entrusted to make decisions on the nation's behalf.[360]

In her direct reaction to this passage from the Patočka's letters to his German friend, Eva Hahnová wrote that pressing such hollow charges against a man who as the leader of his nation was finding himself in a life-and-death confrontation with Adolf Hitler and Nazi Germany, does not only lack material substance, but is immoral. We certainly can leave this question open, but Beneš's own writings (first of all his own memoirs published in 2008[361]) and also well researched works of Hahnová's colleagues (Igor Lukeš's book, for instance, quoted extensively in this volume,[362] for instance), demonstrate more than clearly that Patočka had a point here. What is at stake here is not, for sure, just to blame Beneš for all the future miseries that fell upon his nation after his death, but to keep a possibility of catharsis in the Czech tragedy open for future generations.

Part Four: When a Playwright Is Turned into a Philosopher-King

In his review of Patočka's *Co jsou Češi? Was sind die Tschechen?* published in the Times Literary Supplement in 1993, Ernest Gellner, a

---

[360]Ibid.

[361] Edvard Beneš: *Paměti. Od Mnichova k nové válce a novému vítězství*, Orbis Praha 1947, Edvard Beneš: *Paměti I, II, III*

[362] Igor Lukeš: *On the Edge of the Cold War. American Diplomats and Spies in Postwar Prague*

British-Czech philosopher and social anthropologist, wrote: The pre-war Czechoslovakia founded by Masaryk inherited in a way his "professorial" qualities. But it happened, in the course of the complicated history of the 20th century, in which its inhabitants repeatedly lost their freedom, that *"professors" simply "run out."* So when finally a new opportunity came for their liberation, they had to be *"satisfied with a playwright."*[363] The life-story of Václav Havel, who was elevated – unexpectedly and all of a sudden – by the Velvet Revolution of 1989 to the position of Czech "philosopher-king," and especially his deep personal relationship with Patočka we will now focus on, demonstrates clearly, in my view, that this remark, most likely meant like a friendly nudge, contained actually a much deeper observation. How did these two – a philosopher with "professorial" qualities and playwright – meet? What did this encounter mean for them? What did they have in common? How did Patočka influence Havel's own approach to the "Czech question" and his political vision for the future, a vision he started to promote and implement, immediately after he was elected the head of state at the moment of its return from its previous position of Soviet satellite into the family of free European nations? What kind of philosophy of history can be found here, inspiring and directing all his practical efforts, before and after 1989? Did Václav Havel change, when he stopped being a dissident and became president and thus stepped into the shoes originally worn by Masaryk? Did he also succumb to the trap of being perceived as *"victorious authority,"* or did he manage to face up successfully to what Patočka named as *"its flip side?"*[364]

According to his own words, Havel got his hands on Patočka's first book *The Natural World as a Philosophical Problem*, brought to him by a friend who had access to the special collection of publications in the Prague University Library that were not normally accessible at that time to the general public, when he was sixteen years old; he read it through in one sitting – difficult for me to imagine – from beginning to end. As a teenager born into a "bourgeois" family, he felt little like a stranger in the

---

[363] Ernest Gellner: *Reborn from Below. The Forgotten Beginnings of the Czech National Revival.* in: *The Times Literary Supplement*, 14. 5. 1993, č. 4702, pp. 3-5
[364] Jan Patočka: *Masaryk včera a dnes* [Masaryk Yesterday and Today]. In: *Češi I*, p. 93

world where the "classless" society was just being built and socialist ideals were turned into reality by the methods of "enhanced class struggle." With this personal imprint and looking for his own way through life, he liked to discover the hidden layers of Czech cultural traditions still existing in the 1950s somewhere under the surface of the overwhelming societal transformations. His first reading of the somewhat arcane text of a Prague phenomenologist apparently confirmed to him that it was a right choice. Since then, Havel didn't miss any opportunity to get acquainted with any text of Patočka he happened to come across.

In the "Golden Sixties," when thanks to "the thaw," Czech society started slowly to rediscover its ideologically suppressed identity and return to the creative sources of its national spirit – with its complicated and often troubled history and permanent struggle with Czech "smallness" – Havel and Patočka met for the first time face to face, in the theatre *On the Balustrade*, where Havel got an opportunity not only to read Patočka, but to listen to him and observe in person his philosophical *"inner actions:"* impromptu lectures in the theater bar after the performances, for an audience usually composed of actors and other theater employees, including the stage personnel. A kind of silent dialogue between them was initiated on these occasions and Havel started to realize what actually brought his fascination with the dramatic art that just was becoming his life-long vocation together with Patočka's relation to philosophy: a theater play – a *"study of the human soul in the moment of dramatic action,"* to use Voegelin's analysis of ancient tragedy[365] – and Patočka's relentless philosophizing had common ground: they both had capacity to be socially effective and change, at least for a moment, the minds and hearts of those who were exposed to their miraculous influence.

The communication between Patočka and Havel continued – most likely involving a growing number of more actual, political themes – during the years of crisis 1968/1969, but it was only the period of normalization in the 1970s that brought them closer and closer together and their rapprochement culminated in their joint action when they both accepted, together with Jiří Hájek, the former minister for foreign affairs, the difficult role of spokespersons of Charter 77.

---

[365] Eric Voegelin: *Tragedy*. In: *The World of the Polis*, pp. 317-340

The first step on this road was that both articulated, each of them in his specific way, but in principle the same position, as far as the current political situation in the country was concerned. Whereas playwright Havel wrote his open letter to Dr. Husák, which quickly became a significant catalyst in the nascent independent public space that was to make its full appearance at the moment of publication of *the Charter Manifesto* at the beginning of January 1977, Patočka expressed his view on Husák's regime to his own usual audience, i.e. his "philosophical circle."

Here is how he characterized it – in full agreement with Havel's analysis (that was actually written only two years later!) – in his opening lecture of the above mentioned home-seminar "Plato and Europe." The political regime currently in place in Czechoslovakia represented, in his words, a sheer *"human machinery of decline and degeneration,"* the basic aim of which was *to "extinguish in advance the smallest glimmer of mobilizable social initiative...to deprive the society entirely, or almost entirely, of its moral strength,"* nonetheless allowing at the same time *"its external physical capacities...to grow;"* using as its basic method of governance

> *fear, disorientation, wiles of comfort, possibility to gain advantages in the environment of general scarcity, creating here an artificially interconnected complex of motivations.*[366]

It was exactly here, where Patočka's idea of philosophy and Havel's idea of theater met – offering all their spiritual energy and persuasive power they were endowed with thanks to their unique talents, to the service of a concrete human community finding itself in a difficult existential situation – and their mutual interference resulted in the end in their joint act of open civic resistance.

And finally, the last encounter between Havel and Patočka, described in Havel's short text written in the spring of 1977 in Ruzyně Prison, where Havel was held in detention, investigated for the alleged *"subversion of the republic in connection with foreign powers,"* used as

---

[366] Jan Patočka: *Doba poevropská a její duchovní problémy.* In: *Péče o duši II*, p. 100

the main source of information in this chapter.[367] It had taken place in the second week of January of that year, in the waiting room for the interrogated persons of the same state facility. The three fresh Charter 77 spokespersons – Patočka, Havel and Hájek – were sitting there, waiting for their turn, and were *"philosophizing."* Their conversation could have been interrupted in any moment by their interrogators, but

> *professor Patočka seemed to be utterly undisturbed by this fact: in an improvised seminary on the history of the idea of human immortality and human responsibility, he weighed words with the same care and prudence, as if they had had an unlimited amount of time for it.*[368]

Havel didn't feel himself at that moment – as he had felt many times in Patočka's presence in the past, like a student whose only role was just to listen his professor and eventually take notes of what was said by him. He realized that at that moment he became an equal partner in a real philosophical dialogue. Patočka was visibly animated by this fact, too, and invited Havel to come to see him at home in the near future, so that they could continue at their conversation. Havel gladly accepted his invitation and wished to pay Patočka his visit as soon as possible, in the best case in the evening of the same day. But this proposed visit never took place. Havel was detained after his interrogation that day and returned home only four and half months later. Patočka passed away in mid-March, having suffered a stroke in the hospital where he ended, exhausted after a series of whole day-long police interrogations.

After Patočka's death, their dialogue had obviously to take a different form, but it was never terminated, Patočka becoming only a silent partner in it. Released from prison in late May 1977 and before being imprisoned again two years later (this time spending more than four years in jail), Havel had an opportunity to read (and I am sure he really did), all Patočka's last texts devoted to his Charter 77 activities. As his response,

---

[367] Václav Havel: *Poslední rozhovor* [The Last Conversation]. In: *Jan Patočka. Osobnost a dílo.* Index, 1980, pp. 105-109 (a short text written in Ruzyně Prison, where Václav Havel was kept in detention on May 1, 1977)
[368] Op.cit.

he himself wrote his best known essay *Power of the Powerless,*[369] dedicated to Patočka's memory. And the silent dialogue between Havel and his philosophical teacher went on and on – Havel being in and out of jail – and its traces can be found in all his writings in the years to come.

The background for all Havel's contributions to it was the "parallel polis" of Charter 77 – a small, but open, dynamic human community composed of individuals from all walks of life – that refused together to be manipulated by the current holders of power. It was this dissidents' world, that was the natural basis for Havel's originally non-political politics, that was becoming more and more political by the end of the 1980, when his unexpected rise to power began, and his almost miraculous transformation from the most well-known Czechoslovak dissident, first to the leader of the Velvet Revolution and then, as its direct consequence, to the position of Czechoslovak and later Czech President took place.

Right after he moved his operation to Prague Castle, Havel started to deliver speeches on various occasions in which he tried to lay out his political program in his new capacity. In the conclusion of this passage I will quote from and comment on two of them: his first New Year Address to the Nation, and his address to the Joint Session of the US Congress that was held on February, 22, 1990, on the occasion of his first official visit to the United States.

The message sent out was clear: Masaryk's spirit, which had come to rule in Prague Castle in 1918 and then disappeared in the course of the "short" 20th century, – a period in world history that started with the First World War and ended with the collapse of Communism in Europe – was back again with the arrival of a new era. When listening to Václav Havel on January 1, 1990 – after the traditional celebrations of the night before, that were most likely especially intensive for political reasons all over the country that year – the Czechoslovak citizens could easily ask themselves the same rhetorical question raised by Masaryk in his first presidential address to the members of the revolutionary National Assembly, a day after his election:

---

[369] Václav Havel: *The Power of the Powerless.* In: *Open Letters, Selected Writings 1965-1990,* p§p. 125-214

> *Are we living in a fairy-tale? This is what the politicians of
> all nations are asking, and I ask myself the same question.
> And yet it is all real reality, the result of four years of
> struggle on the part of all the nations of the world. The
> world split into two camps, and in the terrible contest
> victory came to those who defended the ideals of justice –
> the idealists have won, spirit won over matter, right over
> violence, truth over deviousness.*[370]

What they heard from their new president had to sound very
similar in their ears. The Velvet Revolution brought two important lessons
that now, President Havel said, should have been put into the foundations
of new democratic Czechoslovak politics:

> *First of all, people are never just a product of the external
> world; they are also able to relate themselves to something
> superior, however systematically the external world tries
> to kill that ability in them. Secondly, the humanistic and
> democratic traditions, about which there had been so much
> idle talk, did after all slumber in the unconsciousness of our
> nations and ethnic minorities, and were inconspicuously
> passed from one generation to another, so that each of us
> could discover them at the right time and transform them
> into deeds.*[371]

And President Havel went on:

> *Masaryk based his politics on morality. Let us try, in a new
> time and in a new way, to restore this concept of politics.
> Let us teach ourselves and others that politics should be an
> expression of a desire to contribute to the happiness of the
> community rather than of a need to cheat or rape the
> community. Politics can be not simply the art of the
> possible, especially if this means the art of speculation,
> calculation, intrigue, secret deals and pragmatic*

---

[370] Tomáš G. Masaryk: *'Our People is Free and Independent'* (the address to the
members of the revolutionary National Assembly, pronounced on December 21,
1918). In. *The Spirit of Thomas G. Masaryk 1850-1937*, p. 191
[371] Václav Havel: *The New Year Address to the Nation (Prague, January 1, 1990*. In:
Towards a Civil Society. Speeches and Writings 1990-1994. Translated and edited by
Paul Wilson. Lidové noviny Publishing House, Prague, p. 16

maneuvering, but that it can also be the art of the impossible, that is, the art of improving ourselves and the world.

We are a small country, yet at one time we were the spiritual crossroads of Europe. Is there a reason why we could not again become one? .... Our main enemy today is our own bad traits: indifference to the common good, vanity, personal ambition, selfishness, and rivalry. The main struggle will have to be fought on this field....[372]

And in Washington on Capitol Hill, he presented again to the assembled senators and representatives who applauded and gave him standing ovations more than twenty times, his basic vision concerning the upcoming politics of transition:

The Communist type of totalitarian system has left both our nations Czechs and Slovaks – as it has all the nations of the Soviet Union, and the other countries the Soviet Union subjugated in its time – a legacy of countless dead, an infinite spectrum of human suffering, profound economic decline, and above all enormous human humiliation. It has brought us horrors that fortunately you have not known.

At the same time, however – unintentionally, of course – it has given us something positive: a special capacity to look, from time to time, somewhat further than someone who has not undergone this bitter experience. A person who cannot move and live a normal life because he is pinned under a boulder has more time to think about his hopes than someone who is not trapped in this way.

What I am trying to say is this: We must all learn many things from you, from how to educate our offspring, how to elect our representatives, all the way to how organize our economic life so that it will lead to prosperity and not poverty. But it does not have to be merely assistance from the well-educated, the powerful and the wealthy to someone who has nothing to offer in return.

We too can offer something to you: our experience and the

---

[372] Op. cit, p. 18

knowledge that has come out of it.[373]

One can hear here not only Masaryk's spirit and tradition revived, but also clearly the reverberations of Havel's silent dialogue with Patočka, their common conviction that the place where the world and history are being changed is not the enlightened scene of visible historical events where the historical forces clash and the competing interests of the powerful are balanced, but the inner sphere of individual human life – the human soul; that *"it is the stillest words,"* as Nietzsche famously put it in *Thus Spoke Zarathustra, "that bring on the storm;"* that it is *"thoughts that come on doves' feet,"* and not popular slogans of the day, that *"guides the world."*

It was natural for the citizens of the liberated Czechoslovak state to look for the inspiration for their way forward in its founding father Masaryk and connect its future with his legacy. The principal point of departure, however, of the current transition can't be found – and here is again the voice of Patočka as Masaryk's philosophical critic – in the ideas belonging to his progressivist philosophy of history. It must be looked for primarily in the experience of encounter with totalitarianism made only after Masaryk's death in the course of the 20th century, and in *"the knowledge that has come out of it."* The current task to bring democracy back, required, for Havel – Patočka's docile apprentice in this matter – not just the ability to adapt the existing liberal model of democratic government to the Czechoslovak condition with all its institutions and to "return to Europe." It also required the readiness of its citizens to reassume collectively the role of spiritual crossroads of Europe, the Czech lands once were and should be again – in the situation when the Europe's role as the main center of civilization was definitely over and all her nations were experiencing and needing to adjust their policies to the arrival of the "post-European" age.

To sum it up: If one is looking for the spiritual basis of Havel's concept of politics of transition from Communism – his emphasis on the indispensable role of civil society in it, on active policies, both domestic

---

[373] Václav Havel: *The Joint Session of the US Congress, Washington, D.C., February, 21, 1990.* In: op.cit., p. 42

and international, in the area of human rights, on civic education with the main goal to revive the spirit of responsibility for public matters in individual citizens and in raising general awareness that man qua man must cultivate his/her capability to "transcend" his/her finiteness and exist face-to-face with the Mystery of Being – it is neither a philosophically dressed-up version of progressivism, still present among liberal intellectuals of the West, nor utopianism of some other provenance fashionable in these days. It is Patočka's phenomenological philosophy of history that speaks out here. What is its message through Havel as its messenger? Thanks to him we can be better aware now that the success of a politician cannot be measured only by its concrete temporary political achievements, but by the impact of policies enhanced and implemented by him on the "soul" of his polis – a human collective that today takes the form of, but transcends at the same time, the level of nation-state. Thanks to him we can be better ourselves and try not to miss, in the context of our life activities taking place in our concrete place, in our *hic et nunc*, our own unique opportunity to hear Nietzsche's *"stillest words"* that are invisibly changing the world.

Coda: The Czech Question – in Worldly Terms – Today? In Search of a Philosophy of History at the Beginning of the 21st Century

The world in 2018 is certainly a very different place from what it was when Patočka – between Masaryk and Havel – tried to think through and formulate his philosophy of history. All three of them are dead and what remains are just their legacies. As we can see, the "Czech question" still needs to be perceived "in worldly terms" – with the same urgency with which it was originally posed – if we don't want to be absorbed and ultimately defeated by our "smallness." The philosophy of history that turned out to be more of a trap than a reliable guide for our past politicians – as Beneš's tragic example clearly demonstrated – simply cannot be thrown away as useless rubbish and replaced by the sheer pragmatism of short-sighted "national interests," that can be defended by the means of "transactions" with all others who are around to step into the political power games. One doesn't need to be Cassandra to predict that such a stance would lead us, given our position at the "heart of Europe" that cannot be changed, sooner or later into an untenable position with the result, as it happened in the past, of the loss of our freedom. What we should do, instead, is to think through again and again the works of Masaryk, Patočka and Havel as our Czech participation in the philosophical "dialogue of mankind;" to try to keep their legacies alive and give them meaning that would preserve our democracy for future generations.

Exercise 12

Charter 77- A Retrospective[374]
dedicated to the memory
of Liu Xiaobo[375]

The aim of this exercise is threefold. First, to think through again the origins of the historical movement that brought us from our totalitarian enslavement by the Soviet Empire to the present.

Second, to make use of our Charter 77 experience to understand better where we Czechs are now, at the beginning of the third decade of the 21st century – again a part of Europe composed of different, sometimes not entirely like-minded elements; the nations subscribing to the same fundamental values and principles of European civilization, but living within their specific historical experiences, cultures, traditions, and historical points of view.

Third, to articulate our Central European perspective in the context of the on-going dialogue on the future of liberty in the world not only among Europeans and their direct heirs, but also with the active participation of members of all civilizations belonging to today's post-European more and more globalized mankind.

Before I start, I have to issue a warning. When I am driven by circumstances to speak or write something about Charter 77 I always have feelings of a certain absurdity about my situation – assuming the role of a

---

[374] I presented its parts at several meetings of the Eric Voegelin Society, organized regularly at annual conventions of the American Political Science Association.

[375] A Chinese writer, literary critic, human rights activist, philosopher, Nobel Peace Prize laureate, who died in prison after having been sentenced to eleven years in prison, among other "crimes," his participation in "Charter_08," inspired by Czechoslovakia's Charta 77.

guide in a museum in which I function also as one of the objects on display. Can someone who himself personally participated in certain events become a reliable observer capable of unbiased critical analysis?

Having said that, however, I am well aware that I am not the only one who runs into such difficulties; such as a general "methodological problem" accompanying all the attempts to examine phenomena belonging to the field of contemporary history[376] – being too close not only to their participants, but also to their historians, and thus making it difficult even for them to dissociate the object of their study from their own attachment to it; to look at it from a safe distance and tell – truly and reliably, *sine ira et studio* – *"wie es eigentlich gewesen."*[377]

With this in mind, what I offer in this paper is not a comprehensive analysis of the history of Charter 77, but just a couple of personal remarks, historical reminiscences and general observations.

I

What was Charter 77? I will start by recalling the basic facts leading to its creation. In a nutshell: it was the collective reaction of a relatively small group of Czechoslovak citizens (the initial declaration of Charter 77 was signed by two hundred forty-two individuals and the total number of signatories who joined this "civic initiative" between 1977 and 1990, was less than two thousand) to the reality and policies of the totalitarian regime in power in Czechoslovakia since the Communist

---

[376] The term "contemporary history" used here comes from a classical book written in the 1960s by Geoffrey Barraclough (Geoffrey Barraclough: *An Introduction to Contemporary History*. First published by C.A.Watts in 1964. The quotations in this text are from the 9th edition by Penguin Books, 1976): Contemporary history according to Barraclough is not *"the history of the generation now living"* (p. 13). It *"follows...an almost contrary procedure to history of the traditional type"* (p. 17). Whereas the latter *"starts at a given point in the past....and works systematically forward, from the chosen starting point"* (p. 17), the point of departure of the former is the presence of a historian. It is only here that his search for the beginning of contemporary history in time and space can begin; its historian's first and maybe most important task: *"to establish its distinguishing features and its boundaries"* (p.12).

[377] The famous dictum of Leopold von Ranke (1795-1886), the founder of German historicism in the 19th century.

"Victorious February" of 1948 until its sudden collapse during the November "Velvet Revolution" of 1989.

The key turning point in the history of this regime was a failed attempt to liberalize it – or at least "to endow this regime with a human face" – during the Prague Spring of 1968. As Václav Havel pointed out in his essay *Stories and Totalitarianism*: there was a remarkable difference between the revolutionary ethos and terror of the Stalinist 1950s and the depressive, deadening atmosphere – *"dull inertia, pretext-ridden caution, bureaucratic anonymity, and mindless, stereotypical behavior"*[379] – of the 1970s and 1980s; the collective state of mind so typical of the era of "normalization" that spread throughout Czechoslovakian society like a plague after the defeat of the process of the socialist system's "rejuvenation" – a futile attempt to reform it, considered by the Soviet leaders in Moscow and their local cronies as a "counter-revolution."

In its original version, the defining feature of the totalitarian Communist regime in Czechoslovakia was a combination of idealistic hopes for a better world with the use of brute force and physical violence. The society that had been essentially "open" before World War II (and obviously the Nazi occupation 1939-1945 already strongly undermined this capacity!) was forcibly "closed" after the Communist constitutional coup d'état of February 1948. The building of a socialist "radiant future" foreseen in Marxist-Leninist ideology, was accompanied by the ruthless and oppressive policies of the Communist Party, which seized the monopoly of power and started mercilessly to eliminate all its enemies, whether real or just in the wild "revolutionary" imagination of its members.

But, of course, it was not only the immoderate lust for power of the new rulers combined with the blind conviction and commitment of the *"young enthusiasts of the new faith"*[381] for their historical mission, that sent Czechoslovakian democracy into the abyss. The Czechoslovakian Communists certainly had their share in it, but the real "historical force" behind their success was the Soviet Union, whose territorial and political

---

[379] Václav Havel: *Stories and Totalitarianism*. In: *Open Letters, Selected Writings 1965-1990*, p. 331
[381] Ibid.

gains had to be recognized in postwar Europe and whose emerging global influence was also reflected in the American policy of "containment."

In Havel's description, however, in spite of the fact that the 1950s can, indeed, be perceived in retrospect by the citizens of Czechoslovakia as a "nightmare," there was something in this period that surprisingly could be labelled as "positive!" Even though the closing of Czechoslovak society – the systematic destruction of all its institutions, structures, and intermediary bodies (in the sense of Tocqueville) – was carried out by brutal and ruthless means, this "revolutionary transformation" took place in an environment that was still non-totalitarian.

As evidenced by historical records, the societal customs and habits, including the lifestyles and self-presentations of the Communist leaders themselves – who enthusiastically assumed the role of "millenarian tyrants"[383] entrusted by history to destroy the bourgeois democracy of the past – still bore some traces of the old, prerevolutionary world. It was this "ancestral" aspect that gave the beginning phase of Czechoslovakian totalitarianism its specific "local color" and, if we are allowed to use this word in view of the enormous suffering and tragedy experienced by thousands of innocent people, its "flavor." What was not entirely missing in the 1950s and what immediately took on more perceptible, and socially more significant forms after the Stalinist "nightmare," was the hope for the future. When people began to feel and later to perceive the signs of a new day, the dimension of the human condition arose that was still able, despite all terrors, tragedies and deaths, to impart meaning to human life; the fundamental sense of historical

---

[383] I am referring here to the, "taxonomy" of tyrants that have emerged througoutthroughout the history of mankind in the recent book by Waller Newell (Waller R. Newell: *Tyrants: A History of Power, Injustice & Terror*. Cambridge University Press, 2016). Newell distinguished between three basic types of tyrants: the "garden variety" (who ruled over entire countries and societies as if it had been their property); "the tyrants-reformers" (the rulers with a vision to make the state they governed with an iron fist, powerful, prosperous and great again); and finally the "millenarian tyrants:" *These rulers are neither content to be mere garden-variety tyrants, gluttons, and exploiters, nor even to be reforming tyrants who make constructive improvements. They are driven by the impulse to impose a millenarian blueprint that will bring about a society of the future in which the individual will be submerged in the collective and all privilege and alienation will forever be eradicated.*" (p. 4)

continuity of time and the faith that the painful experience of the past and the irreversible losses could be healed, or at least saved from oblivion by the means of storytelling. It was this attitude that helped people to see the light at the end of the tunnel, even when there was no real reason to believe that the Communist regime had to collapse quickly, and when it turned out that the widespread speculations during the 1950s concerning the American planned intervention against the Communist "evil empire," were from the very beginning a sheer illusion.

This same state of mind nourished the gradual change in the social and political atmosphere of the 1960s. It made the vast majority of Czechs and Slovaks believe during the Prague Spring of 1968, even when they saw Soviet tanks in the streets of Prague and other cities in August of that year, that socialism – whatever this word meant for them – was reformable after all: Central Europeans were not doomed to remain forever – as Kundera wrote in 1984, reflecting on Czechoslovak experience of 1968 – the *"victims and outsiders"* of world history.[384]

The 1970s and 1980s saw the end of this hope, the unpleasant discovery that there was no saving bridge over the gap between the past and the future; that Central Europe was, indeed, finding herself at a dead-end of her contemporary history. The bipolar political architecture of the Cold War turned out to be a much stronger element in shaping her destiny than the desire of Central Europeans to actively participate, at least in some limited way, in its creation. The period of "normalization" in Czechoslovakia started not at the moment of the Soviet occupation, but when the huge majority of Czechs and Slovaks simply gave up and conformed to their historical lot – by either willingly cooperating with a rehashed ruling power, or retreating to the private sphere of their lives and succumbing to passivity. The spirit of resistance of 1968 was taken over in 1969 by the *"captive mind"* named and analyzed by another outstanding

---

[384] Kundera M., Tragedy of Central Europe, in: New York Review of Books, April 26, 1984: *"Central Europe, as a family of small nations, has its own vision of the world, a vision of deep mistrust of history . . . history, that goddess of Hegel and Marx, that incarnation of reason that judges us and arbitrates our fate, that is the history of conquerors. The peoples of Central Europe are not conquerors. They cannot be separated from European history. They cannot exist outside of it. But they represent the wrong side of history. They are its victims and outsiders."*

Central European, the Polish poet Czeslaw Milosz.[385] The regime that emerged under these circumstances served, as Václav Havel pointed out in 1986, *"as a textbook illustration of how an advanced or late totalitarian system works."*[387] It depends:

> *on manipulatory devices so refined, complex, and powerful that it no longer needs murderers and victims. Even less does it need fiery Utopia builders spreading discontent with dreams of a better future. The epithet "Real Socialism," which this era has coined to describe itself, points a finger at those for whom it has no room: the dreamers.*[388]

In other words: being exposed to the influence of an external imperial power, the Czechoslovak version of totalitarianism dramatically changed its style and external manifestations.

First, what was lost entirely was the original revolutionary character of totalitarian government. Although politically it uncompromisingly adhered to the dogma of the "leading role of the Communist Party," at the same time it dropped its original intention to transform the existing social and political order according to the Marxist-Leninist ideological blueprint. It *"set itself a single aim: self-preservation."*[390] Instead of using the straightforward draconian policies of its early days, instead of perpetrating acts of open violence against the defeated social classes (which were to be physically destroyed and eliminated) and building a new world according to its ideological blueprint, the "normalization" regime was created by unprincipled opportunists who simply desired to keep themselves in power by any means and were ready to make practically any turn as far as the system of their beliefs was concerned, to achieve this goal.

With the exception of a relatively small group of "counter-revolutionaries," who deserved exemplary punishment, all others were offered the possibility to preserve their own well-being and their relatively

---

[385] Milosz, C., The Captive Mind, Vintage Books, New York, 1981
[387] Václav Havel: *Stories and Totalitarianism.* In: *Open Letters, Selected Writings 1965-1990*, p. 331
[388] Op.cit., p. 332
[390] Op.cit., p. 331

safe and undisturbed existence. The ticket one had to buy to be admitted to ride in this train was quite cheap and the vast majority of people was easily persuaded. No class origin, no conviction, no commitment, not even difficult moral choices were required to get on board, just the formal agreement with the Soviet occupation and at least tacit consent with the basic goals of "normalization;" the readiness to give up all ideals and noble visions and to just play the game and be flexible enough to adapt oneself to the requirements of the new situation. All idealistic motivations and aspirations had to be rejected at this stage of the history of Communism, and what remained was a strange variety of petty and down-to-earth political realism.

The ruling power simply offered to the ruled a kind of bizarre "social contract" – based on the party document titled the *"Lessons of the Years of Crisis:"*[392]

1. Any effort to open up the socialist system and to reform its form of government was considered dangerous and would lead to destabilization, intolerable to the ruling forces of this world.

2. Only fools and martyrs could be so crazy as to act against this fundamental and invincible "law" of human history.

3. In the era of Real Socialism being built in Czechoslovakia, politics should be understood not as a sphere of human responsibility and agency, but just as a mechanistic, empty pseudoritual: The principal aim of current normalization policies was not to take care of human matters in the open field of human history, but to stay in line; to keep them in the state in which they already were and fiercely suppress anything that might signal the need for change.

4. It was perfectly acceptable that under given circumstances not everybody had ambition – or stomach – to become involved in public matters of the ritualized socialist state – that not only didn't "wither away," as the founders of Marxist-Leninist doctrine had been predicting, but

---

[392] *The Lessons of the Years of Crisis* ("Poučení z krizového období ve straně a společnosti po XIII. Sjezdu KSČ") was an infamous document adopted by the ruling Communist Party in 1970 which formulated the basic framework for the policies of so-called, "normalization" - – with the aim to punish all counterrevolutionaries, to make a large, "screening" of the Party membership and eradicate all the elements of freedom that appeared in Czechoslovak society thanks to the Prague Spring of 1968.)

became bigger than ever. In that case he/she was not to be rebuked, or even punished, but just to be advised to mind his/her own business and to stay away from "politics."

There is no doubt that such a "liberalization" of the traditional elements of totalitarianism – i.e., the reinterpretation of the above-mentioned "social contract" – made life much easier and more bearable for the enslaved citizens. At the same time, however, it obviously did not mean any increase of their freedom, but, on the contrary, their further enslavement. A society where an advanced or late totalitarian system came into being was not decimated any more by the revolutionary "reigns of terror and virtue," and some socialist governments even managed to offer to their populations a relatively acceptable standard of living. But it did not save its members from the destructive effects of what Havel called *"the radiation of totalitarianism."*[394]

There was no unmanipulated public space available for them, no ideologically undistorted language to address the relevant social issues and to formulate and discuss new political ideas.

There was no substantive communication between the organs of the state and its citizens regarding the public good and matters of common interest.

There were no events other than various anniversaries to make the news and to form stories; no social movements to be seen; no experiences to be transformed into political knowledge; no hope, at least for living generations, that the political situation could ever be changed.

What remained was a society, surviving under a kind of socialist welfare condition, but suffering a strange disease that Havel used to compare to asthma: one is still alive but permanently struggling for air to oxidize the blood, having permanent difficulties in breathing.

II

What could people do *"to resist nihilization?"*[396] How should they react to the existing political condition in Czechoslovakia – certainly

---

[394] Václav Havel: *Stories and Totalitarianism.* In: *Open Letters, Selected Writings 1965-1990*, p. 349
[396] Op.cit., p. 350

not bad enough to decimate its population and thus to outrage again *"the conscience of mankind,"* to use the language of the Preamble to the UN Universal Declaration of Human Rights,[397] but "only" penetrating to the depth of their personal lives and destroying their human identity? There was an option here, for sure, used by many: to leave. More than eighty thousand Czechs and Slovaks decided to emigrate, and find new homes in Western Europe, the United States, Canada, Australia, South Africa, or other foreign countries.

Václav Havel, however, – in contrast to Milan Kundera, for instance, who decided to emigrate to France – opted for another way to protect his human identity. Having decided to stay home, in April 1975 he wrote an open letter to the General Secretary of the Communist Party – and soon also President of the Republic – Dr. Gustáv Husák.[398] Here, as if inspired as a playwright by his great English predecessor who once clearly stated through one of his *dramatis personae*, what was the elementary *"purpose of playing"* –

> *to hold, as 'twere, the mirror up to nature; to show virtue her own feature, scorn her own image, and the very age and body of the time his form and pressure.*[399]

- Havel decided to do something unprecedented: to submit to the attention of the current Czechoslovak ruler a clear description of the state of public affairs in Czechoslovakia under his leadership. Here are the opening paragraphs of Havel's submission to Dr. Husák:

> *In our offices and factories work goes on, discipline prevails. The efforts of our citizens are yielding visible results in a slowly rising standard of living: people build houses, buy cars, have children, amuse themselves, live their lives.*

> *All this, of course, amounts to very little as a criterion for*

---

[397] http://www.un.org/en/udhrbook/pdf/udhr_booklet_en_web.pdf

[398] Gustáv Husák (1913-1991) was a Slovak politician, President of Czechoslovakia (1975-1989) and Secretary General of the Communist Party of Czechoslovakia (1969–1987)

[399] William Shakespeare: *Hamlet, (Act III, Scene II, 21-27)*. In: William Shakespeare. Complete Plays, Fall River Press, 202, p. 689

the success or failure of your policies. After every social upheaval, people invariably come back in the end to their daily labors, for the simple reason that they want to stay alive; they do so for their own sake, after all, not for the sake of this or that team of political leaders.

Not that going to work, doing the shopping, and living their own lives is all that people do. They do much more than that: they commit themselves to numerous output norms which they then fulfill and over-fulfill; they vote as one man and unanimously elect the candidates proposed to them; they are active in various political organizations; they attend meetings and demonstrations; they declare their support for everything they are supposed to. Nowhere can any sign of dissent be seen from anything that the government does

These facts, of course, are not to be made light of. One must ask seriously, at this point, whether all this does not confirm your success in achieving the tasks your team set itself – those of winning the public's support and consolidating the situation in the country. [400]

.....

I make so bold as to answer: No! To assert that, for all the outwardly persuasive facts, inwardly our society, far from being a consolidated one, is, on the contrary, plunging ever deeper into a crisis more dangerous, in some respects, than any we can recall in our recent history. [401]

.....

The basic question one must ask is this: Why are people in fact behaving in the way they do? Why do they do all these things that, taken together, form the impressive image of a totally united society giving total support to its government? For any unprejudiced observer, the answer is, I think, self-

---

[400] Václav Havel: *"Dear Dr. Husák"* In: *Open Letters, Selected Writings 1965-1990*, pp. 50-51
[401] Op.cit. p. 51

evident: They are driven to it by fear.[402]

And here is what Havel wrote in the conclusion of his letter – his blunt and audacious advice/warning to Dr. Husák:

> *So far, it is the worst in us which is being systematically activated and enlarged – egotism, hypocrisy, indifference, cowardice, fear, resignation, and the desire to escape every personal responsibility, regardless of the general consequences....So far you and your government have chosen the easy way out for yourselves, and the most dangerous road for society: the path of inner decay for the sake of outward appearances; of deadening life for the sake of increasing uniformity; of deepening the spiritual and moral crisis of our society, and ceaselessly degrading human dignity, for the puny sake of protecting your own power.*[403]

> *As a citizen of this country, I hereby request, openly and publicly, that you and the leading representatives of the present regime consider seriously the matters to which I have tried to draw your attention; that you assess in their light the degree of your historic responsibility, and act accordingly.*[404]

I am sure, Havel was certainly not surprised that Dr. Husák didn't react to his letter at all – the only thing Dr. Husák did for sure, was to pass it to the organs of State Security, because in his mind, such "subversive acts of civic disobedience" fell primarily under their discretion and responsibility.

This unusual communication between the dissenting playwright and his ruler, however, had another, but very significant effect. It was received by people with access to it, thanks to its open nature, as a wake-up call. Havel's letter to Dr. Husák hit a nerve in Czechoslovak society and mobilized at least some of its members. It was copied and disseminated among an ever growing number of people. They finally heard again a voice of someone who dared to say, loud and clear, their

---

[402] Op.cit. 52

[403] Op.cit. , p. 82-83

[404] Ibid.

own opinions, but what they themselves were carefully hiding in the depth of their hearts.

Of course, not every reader of Havel's letter was ready to join him in his ceaseless on-going efforts to break the deadening silence and speak the truth. His plain and simple argument, however, made in the midst of the spiritual crisis to which the Czechoslovak society succumbed in the 1970s, really shattered its "collective soul." The road leading twenty months later to the creation of Charter 77 opened. The trial of the Plastic People of the Universe – an iconic rock band of the emerging Czech underground movement, taking place in the summer of 1976[405] – became the last impulse to trigger the process of unification of many hidden currents surviving in the various spheres of Czechoslovak society – composed of people trying to resist Husák's normalization on their own terms and for their own reasons. During December 1976 the text of the original declaration of Charter 77 was being prepared by the group of "conspirators," including Havel, and the signatures under this document started to be assembled.

III

Let us remind ourselves now once more of the principal arguments and main messages of the Manifesto of Charter 77 dated January 1, 1977. It began with the following legal reasoning:

> *In the Czechoslovak Register of Laws No. 120 of October 13, 1976, texts were published of the International Covenant on Civil and Political Rights, and of the International Covenant on Economic, Social and Cultural Rights, which were signed on behalf of our Republic in 1968, reiterated at Helsinki in 1975 and came into force in our country on March 23, 1976. From that date our citizens have enjoyed the rights, and our state the duties, ensuing from them. The human rights and freedoms underwritten by these covenants constitute features of civilized life for which many progressive movements have striven throughout history and whose codification could greatly assist humane developments in our society. We accordingly welcome the*

---

[405] https://en.wikipedia.org/wiki/The_Plastic_People_of_the_Universe.

> *Czechoslovak Socialist Republic's accession to those agreements....*[406]

The text continued with a demonstrative list of grievances, addressing openly facts known to all citizens of Czechoslovakia, because they faced them in their daily lives. The rights and freedoms guaranteed by these covenants existed currently in Czechoslovakia on paper alone. It stated that the Czechoslovak Government was systematically violating them and thus had to be reminded of its international obligation to refrain immediately from such unlawful behavior.

This was, indeed, a harsh criticism of a government not used to hearing such from its own enslaved population. The worst in the eyes of its representatives, however, was still to come. The announcement following the list of grievances could be understood by the Czechoslovak authorities as an openly hostile declaration of war by a group of reactionary outcasts against the very foundations of the Czechoslovak "socialist" state:

> *...Responsibility for the maintenance of rights in our country naturally devolves in the first place on the political and state authorities. Yet not only on them: everyone bears his share of responsibility for the conditions that prevail and accordingly also for the observance of legally enshrined agreements, binding upon all individuals as well as upon governments.*

> *It is this sense of co-responsibility, our belief in the importance of its conscious public acceptance and the general need to give it new and more effective expression that led us to the idea of creating Charter 77, whose inception we today publicly announce....*

> *....Charter 77 is a loose, informal, open association of people with various shades of opinion, faiths and professions united by the will to strive individually and collectively for the respecting of civic and human rights in our own country and throughout the world -- rights*

---

[406] The Charter 77 Manifesto (http://www. cnn.com/SPECIALS/cold. war/episodes/ 19/documents/charter. 77/)

accorded to all men by the two mentioned international covenants, by the Final Act of the Helsinki Conference and by numerous other international documents opposing war, violence and social or spiritual oppression, and which are comprehensively laid down in the U.N. Universal Charter of Human Rights.

Charter 77 springs from a background of friendship and solidarity among people who share our concern for those ideals that have inspired, and continue to inspire, their lives and their work.

Charter 77 is not an organization; it has no rules, permanent bodies or formal membership.

It embraces everyone who agrees with its ideas and participates in its work. It does not form the basis for any oppositional political activity. Like many similar citizen initiatives in various countries, West and East, it seeks to promote the general public interest.

Charter 77 does not aim, then, to set out its own platform of political or social reform or change, but within its own field of impact to conduct a constructive dialogue with the political and state authorities, particularly by drawing attention to individual cases where human and civic rights are violated, to document such grievances and suggest remedies, to make proposals of a more general character calculated to reinforce such rights and machinery for protecting them...[407]

And the final words of the Charter 77 Manifesto:

..We believe that Charter 77 will help to enable all citizens of Czechoslovakia to work and live as free human beings.[408]

Who actually were signatories of Charter 77? At first two hundred forty-two and in the end nearly two thousand individuals added their signatures under the text which sounded almost like the Czechoslovak Declaration of Independence. What was their motivation for joining this

---

[407] Ibid.
[408] Ibid.

bold and quite ambitious, but very dangerous "civic initiative?" What was this group of people coming literally from all walks of life – Christians of various denominations, Jews, ex-Communists expelled from the party for their revolt in 1968, independent liberal intellectuals and young people from underground with no specific background, creed, goals or expectations – aiming at? Each of them had his/her specific personal reasons for signing, yet all of them were sending one and the same message to the Czechoslovak authorities: We cannot remain silent, with hypocrisy as an accepted norm in today's Czechoslovakia, where all basic human rights *"exist, regrettably, on paper alone"*[409] and many people have become *"victims of a virtual apartheid."*[410] We want to speak the truth again, no matter what, and we will!

In short: the arguments made by Václav Havel in his letter to Dr. Husák were right on target and – as the emergence of Charter 77 persuasively demonstrated – they worked.

The historical significance and true meaning of Charter 77 were actually demonstrated right away by the profoundly negative, almost hysterical reaction of the Communist regime: The propagandists in the state media launched immediately a massive smear campaign against it. The repressive apparatus of the state opened a criminal investigation to discover the main culprits of this "hostile and subversive activity" – allegedly inspired by Western reactionary circles and coordinated by the US intelligence services.

The instruction from the highest echelons of power in Czechoslovakia was swift and clear: the signatories of Charter 77 were to be selectively punished for their "anti-socialist" behavior – if not imprisoned right away, then interrogated by the organs of the Czechoslovak Secret Police, exposed to public condemnation and harassment, losing their jobs, passports, driver's licenses....

There is one aspect of this broad counter-offensive the Czechoslovak state launched against a small group of dissenters, that deserves our special attention: the way the Communist government dealt with the introductory legal arguments of the Charter 77 Manifesto, based

---

[409] Ibid.
[410] Ibid.

on the implementation in Czechoslovakia of two major international human rights covenants, and particularly on the fact that the unambiguous references to these covenants were reiterated repeatedly in the Final Act of the Helsinki Conference.[411]

Not just the regime propagandists and ideologues, but also the honorable professors of law from Charles University in Prague offered their expertise in the struggle against the reactionary elements who got together in Charter 77 with the aim to "disrupt and undermine the Czechoslovak socialist system of government" – departing in their reasoning not only from the ideological dogmas of Marxism-Leninism, but trying to tie their arguments even with the venerable normativist legal traditions of the pre-war "bourgeois republic;" traditions active at the moment of its creation, unambiguously subscribing to the principle of supremacy of constitutional law over international law.[412]

First of all, according to this legal philosophy, the international agreements signed by the Czechoslovak Government and ratified in a due constitutional process could not be seen as a legitimate source of rights for Czechoslovak citizens. Czechoslovak citizens thus could not lawfully appeal to these agreements when seeking redress for their grievances or

---

[411] https://history.state.gov/milestones/1969-1976/helsinki

[412] According to Zdenek Neubauer, a disciple of Frantisek Weyr and Karel Engliš, the founding fathers of Czech normative and teleological legal theory which had the decisive influence on the legal and political thought in pre-war Czechoslovakia, for the founding fathers of this state the supremacy of constitutional over international law in the Czechoslovak legal order was not a matter of choice, but the necessity corresponding to the current historical situation: *"In contrast to the state law, there was not a common subject of norm-creation in the international law and the probability of correspondence between the requirement of its norms and the reality of their execution even against the will of those who have obligation to obey them, was practically non-existent."* (Zdeněk Neubauer: *Státověda a teorie práva* [*Theory of State and Law*]. SLON, Sociologicke nakladatelstvi, Praha, 2006, p.82, transl. into English by MP). Consequently, when defining the place of international law within the legal order of the new state, the givers of Czechoslovak Constitution from 1920 decided to use the dualistic model: the domestic legal effects of international treaties could only arise by means of domestic legislation. The Czechoslovak courts of justice were obliged to apply international treaties in their adjudication only by means of application of the norms of domestic law (Cf. Jiří Malenovský: *Mezinarodni právo veřejné, jeho obecná část a poměr k vnitrostatnímu právu, zvláště k právu českému* [*International Law, Its General Part and Relationship to Constitutional Law. The Czech Case*]. Masarykova Univerzita and nakladatelství Doplněk, 2004, pp. 409-467).

just expressing their personal opinions about the state of Czechoslovak public affairs, as the Charter 77 Manifesto was suggesting. Their fundamental human rights were fully articulated and guaranteed, according to the law professors at Charles University, by the Czechoslovak Socialist Constitution. It was the socialist legal order based on it that was available, and wholly sufficient, for any complaint or constructive criticism Czechoslovak citizens might have had.

The signatories of Charter 77 – bypassing all the existing provisions and mechanisms the Czechoslovak socialist state was generously offering them (in the context of the "social contract" described above, one has to add!), and instead resorting to their subversive petition – were simply undermining the state. What they decided to do was openly to engage in reactionary, treasonous and thus punishable activities – either driven by their own malicious designs and intentions or, in a more charitable interpretation, seduced by others, not clearly aware of the consequences of their action.

And secondly, what did the same experts have to say at the level of public international law, above all in the context of the Helsinki Process launched by its Final Act?

International conventions on human rights to which Czechoslovakia was now a party, could never sideline or impair the existing Czechoslovak legal order and undermine the sovereignty of the Czechoslovak state. What all its international partners – and primarily the diplomats of all Western capitalist countries participating at the Helsinki Process – had to be reminded of was that Article 2(7) of the UN Charter, clearly recognized in and confirmed by the Final Act, implicitly rejected any intervention in the domestic affairs of UN member-states. The repressive actions taken by the organs of the Czechoslovak state against the group of *"losers and self-appointed politicians"*[414] who signed Charter 77, was an internal matter and no one else's business; no one from the outside world had a legitimate right to step in, and criticize it, or even support, in any way, their dirty, destructive and selfish political cause.

---

[414] The title of a famous article in *Rudé Právo*, the daily of the Czechoslovak Communist Party, published a couple of days after the Charter 77 Manifesto appeared in the Western press, that launched the official smear campaign against it.

Taking these legal positions into consideration, and also the fact that the Communist regime had all power to enforce them under its control – openly declaring its survival, in its own words, the defense of socialism against all enemies, as the number one goal of its policies – it was obvious what the greatest and almost unsurmountable challenge was for the Charter 77 signatories: How to conduct under the given circumstances *"a constructive dialogue with the political and state authorities"* proposed in their Manifesto? Given the totalitarian nature of the Communist regime, wasn't this a sheer fantasy, the ultimate proof that despite their personal "heroism" chartists were just utopian dreamers, entirely out of touch with political realities? But even worse than that: didn't their declaration of readiness to talks with the totalitarian Communist governments imply its legitimization?

IV

The central – in fact the only – institutional feature of Charter 77 granted Jiří Hájek, Václav Havel and Jan Patočka to act as Charter 77's spokespersons – *"endowed with full authority to represent it vis-a-vis state and other bodies, and the public at home and abroad."*[416] Their signatures were to *"attest to the authenticity of documents issued by the Charter."*[417]

Hájek and Havel well deserve great credit for their roles in Charter 77's beginnings, as well as for their contributions to this "civic initiative" during its whole existence. It was, however, the third of them, philosopher Jan Patočka, who turned out to have the decisive influence as far as Charter 77's spiritual grounding and public identity. Patočka's significance for the formation of Charter 77 was indispensable and his death only several weeks after its creation – caused by the harsh police treatment he was exposed to in his role – only sealed the fact that it was classical philosophy revived in our times that was at the very center of the Charter 77 story, and still remains the core of its legacy.

Originally, it was quite surprising that it was he of all other possible candidates who assumed this challenging role and stood in the

---

[416] The Charter 77 Manifesto (http://www. cnn.com/SPECIALS/cold. war/episodes/ 19/documents/charter. 77/)
[417] Ibid.

forefront of the "dissidents" revolt. Up to this time Patočka was enjoying, even among his Marxist opponents, a reputation as a profound theoretical thinker and a renowned academic scholar. He was highly thought of in the informed circles of the intelligentsia as a master in his field and a great teacher, endowed with exceptional capability to elucidate the history of philosophical ideas and to open for his students the gate leading to the wonderful (veritably wonder-awaking) world of Western philosophy. Forced to retire from his post at Charles University in 1972, he kept lecturing to small circles of his disciples in private seminars organized in private apartments – still primarily engaged in his own phenomenological investigations and other fundamental problems of contemporary philosophy.

If for most of his life Patočka was in the habit of approaching his topics *more philosophico*, from the perspective of a distanced observer of the world of human existence (*die Lebenswelt*, in the terminology of his principal teacher, the founding father of phenomenology Edmund Husserl), when accepting the role of Charter 77's spokesperson, he apparently radically changed course. He decided, metaphorically speaking, to step down from his philosophical "observatory," to enter the public realm of his polis, at the time undergoing a deep spiritual crisis, and set himself – with his specific philosophical reasoning – into action.

And what happened? Charter 77's signatories – most of them certainly not trained in philosophy and unable to orientate themselves in the subtle intricacies of contemporary philosophical discourse – found the "reasons" formulated by philosopher Patočka, understandable and they were ready to hear and respond positively to his appeal!

These reasons can still be found in six short texts Patočka wrote in the last weeks of his life, shortly before he died. When one reads them, it is clear that they were not written in an environment that would generally be considered as opportune for philosophizing. Quite the contrary, they came into existence in the midst of the most serious political struggle their author had ever engaged in, interrogated daily by the secret police and threatened by the State Prosecutor with charges of subversion and "antisocialist" activities.

At the same time, however, it was evident to the reader of these texts that in spite of their focus on actual matters connected with the extremely difficult first weeks of existence of Charter 77, its author was a philosopher – aware that his audience was not the usual academia, but the entire polis of all his fellow citizens, whom he had to address accordingly.

As Patočka repeatedly stated in his Charter 77 texts: publicly defending human rights, Charter 77 was not intended to interfere in politics *sensu stricto* – with politics conceived as a power struggle whose basic aim has always been and must always be to replace those who are momentarily in government by others with different policies. Charter 77's activities had to be limited to a non-political goal: by pointing to the individual violations of human rights and proposing a dialogue about it to the ruling power, to resist the devastating consequences of the late totalitarianism of the 1970s.

Charter 77 activities should have been based, according to Patočka, on what should not be given up by humans under any political circumstances – on the moral claim made on each of us striving to live in unity with him/herself; on the claim which not only turned all participants of the Charter 77 movement into political "dissidents" undermining the totalitarian Communist regime, but brought them at the same time from the world of sheer lies, deceptions, false pretentions and endless manipulations, back to the journey of search for the truth and the care for the soul; the claim which opened for them the door into the largely forgotten and abandoned realm of classical political philosophy.

In the text *Čím je, a čím není Charta 77 ?* [What Charter 77 Is and What It Is Not] Patočka decided to bring *"to everyone's clear awareness"* the *"truths of which we are all in some sense aware"*[418] – his own philosophical definition of human rights. According to conventional wisdom the concept of human rights elaborated in the international covenants the authors of the Charter 77 Manifesto were appealing to, is rooted in the European Enlightenment of the late 18th Century. Patočka's moral argument, however, his cautious references to *"the truths of which*

---

[418] Jan Patočka: *Čím je, a čím není Charta 77 ?* In : *Češi I*, p. 429. Translated as *The Obligation to Resist Injustice*. In: Erazim Kohák: *Jan Patočka. Philosophy and Selected Writings*, p. 341

we are all in some sense aware," sounded rather like a voice coming to the present from a distant past, bringing to life something that did not fit well in the contemporary discourse on human rights, but belonged to premodern and largely abandoned spiritual traditions.

His argument that respect for human rights represents the moral foundation of any human society – that it is our recognition of the sovereignty of moral sentiment which constitutes them – shifted the focus from the modern emancipated individual who simply possesses human rights as his/her "entitlements," to the ancient conflict between politics and philosophy. It turned the attention to the trial of Socrates, who seemed to have been the inspiration for Patočka's approach to political matters in general, and, for his own activities in the public realm, his great example and predecessor.

V

What is the legacy of Charter 77? The first thing that comes to mind is civil society being re-born after the fall of Communism in East Central Europe; the booming world of NGOs being created following the Charter 77 example in a new era, assembling engaged individuals ready to work "from below" for the sake of the "public interest" and for the protection of human rights. Without underestimating this evident inspiration of Charter 77, I will skip it here to focus on another thing which is, in my view, more illustrative and has greater consequences: the birth of the new Constitutional Order of Czechoslovakia, and later of the Czech Republic.

In the previous section of this text I have mentioned the legal arguments by which the Czech Government rejected the reasoning of Charter 77. Looking at the Czech Constitutional Order of today, it is evident that the way the distinguished law professors at Charles University argued forty years ago against both points made by the Charter 77 – the place of international human rights conventions in the current Czech Constitutional Order and the role of individual citizens in its dynamic evolution – has been rejected. But not only the Communist totalitarian deformation of law was discarded thanks to the Velvet Revolution; even the legal traditions of the pre-war democratic republic – subscribing to the primacy of constitutional law over international law – have been overcome thanks to the historical process Charter 77 was an indispensable part of.

Let us start from the question: what actually happened from the legal point of view in November 1989? And here is the answer: power was handed over by means of negotiations at a round table, but the continuity of law was upheld.

At the same time, isn't it undeniably correct to say that there is a clear dividing line between the "law" of the Communist era and the legality which came into existence after the Communist power had been dismantled? But how actually did it happen? How and when exactly was the new legal order, now valid in the Czech Republic, created?

What must be clarified here first is the concept that still plays an important role in Czech legal thought – a "legal revolution." According to normativist tradition, created after the First World War and still strongly present in the legal thought, the legal order is equal to a set of legal norms derived from one "focal point," from one supreme norm which is considered as the genuine source of law. One can clearly distinguish between the *continuity of law* – which persists as long as a certain focal norm (usually the constitution of a state) remains valid – and the *discontinuity of law* – which occurs when due to the "legal revolution," the old normative order is replaced by the new one.

> *"From the legal point of view, the revolution is a strictly negative concept. It means the denial of continuity between two sets of state norms, between pre-revolutionary and post-revolutionary legal orders, which as far as their content is concerned, are valid on the same state territory, for identical legal persons and in the same time. Because the old and the new legal orders are two mutually isolated sets of legal norms, what is not valid between them is the principle lex posterior derogat priori. The pre-revolutionary law is non-existent from the point of view of the post-revolutionary legal order and it is not necessary to abrogate it explicitly. On the contrary, what is necessary if the pre-revolutionary law is to be kept valid after the legal revolution, is its explicit reception by the*

post-revolutionary legal order." [419]

The articles establishing the leading role of the Communist Party in Czechoslovak society were thrown out of the socialist constitution right at the start of the post-November development. A fundamental normative change, however, a "legal revolution," took place much later, specifically not until January 1991, when the Federal Assembly passed the Constitutional Law 23/1991 Sb., by which *the Charter of Fundamental Rights and Freedoms* and international conventions on human rights and fundamental freedoms were made an integral part of the Czechoslovak Constitutional Order. This norm gave the Charter of Fundamental Rights and Freedoms a super-constitutional power and established that:

> *Constitutional acts, other statutes, and additional legal enactments must be in conformity with the Charter of Fundamental Rights and Freedoms, as must the interpretation and application thereof.*

> *The fundamental rights and freedoms included in the Charter of Fundamental Rights and Freedoms shall be under the protection of the Constitutional Court.*

> *International conventions on human rights and fundamental freedoms, ratified and promulgated by the Czech and Slovak Federal Republic, shall be generally binding on its territory and take precedence over statutes.*

> *Statutes and other legal enactments must be brought into conformity with the Charter of Fundamental Rights and Freedoms by 31 December 1991 at the latest. On that date any provision which is not in conformity with the Charter of Fundamental Rights and Freedoms shall lose force and effect.*

> *Laws and other legal norms shall be put in harmony with the Charter at the latest by December 31, 1991, and on this day those not in compliance with the*

---

[419] (Zdeněk Neubauer: *Kontinuita našeho ústavního práva [Continuity of Our Constitutional Law]*. In: Právník 1945, Vol. 9)

Charter become invalid.[420]

From the normative point of view, it is of key importance to realize that no Czechoslovak/Czech law ceased to exist immediately after November 1989! A clear dividing line between the "ancien regime" and the new, i.e. democratic one still had to be established. It happened at the moment of the acceptance of the Charter of Fundamental Rights and Freedoms, and by the recognition of the obligatory character of international human rights agreements. By this legislative act – the Czechoslovak Federal Assembly acting at this moment as a constituent assembly – a new legal order has come into being. A new "focal norm" has been given, establishing the elementary principles of its construction.

The first two principles belong to the traditional legal equipment of the European liberal state: the principle of inviolability of natural human rights and the principle of the supremacy of the law and the principle of inviolability of natural human rights.

What follows from the acceptance of the first? The positive concept of justice created by the state and by its normative activity must be presented in harmony with the rights and freedoms which have their origin in human nature – which independently work within the state and its current law and which have only to be respected and protected by it – based, in the language of the Preamble to the Charter of Fundamental Rights and Freedoms, *"on the bitter experience of the years when human rights and fundamental freedoms were suppressed in our country."*[422] The givers of the constitution decided to build the Czech legal order on the basis of natural right – distinguishing the fact that it was the state and its institutions who were the main perpetrators of wrongs and oppressions.

The principle of inviolability of natural human rights in the Constitution of the Czech Republic implies that these rights neither can nor may be touched by future constitutional development and must remain a permanent part of the legal order. It is not possible to set them aside by

---

[420] https://www.usoud.cz/fileadmin/user_upload/ustavni_soud_www/Pravni_uprava/AJ/23_1991_EN.pdf

[422] The Charter of Fundamental Rights and Freedoms https://www.usoud.cz/fileadmin/user_upload/ustavni_soud_www/Pravni_uprava/AJ/Listina_English_version.pdf

means of referendum, nor by a legal regulation of an arbitrary power. The Charter of Fundamental Rights and Freedoms protects them when the legal means for their effective application are paralyzed by the means of power:

> *Citizens have the right to place themselves in opposition to anyone who would set aside the order of human rights and basic freedoms established in the Charter, should the activity of the constitutional institutions and the effective use of legal means be disabled.*[423]

Human rights cannot be voluntarily surrendered nor yielded to someone else (they are vested and inalienable) and not even the fact that for some time they may not have been applied or been suppressed changes anything in their continuance (they are unlimited).

The sovereignty of the law, established both in the Constitution and in the Charter, is the second basic principle and is complementary to the first. Human rights and freedoms as a "superpositive" source of Czech law, cannot only be declared. In order to be fully effective, they must be translated into the concrete forms of laws and other legal regulations. They must be protected by the activity of courts of justice, and as necessary of other institutions established for the purpose of their protection. Even here the intention of the givers of the Constitution of the Czech Republic should be understood as a basic rejection of the legal practice of the past, when it was not the law which ruled but the Communist Party; when the Party's ideology and political directives stood above the current positive law.

But today's Czech Constitution introduced one more principle whereby the newly-created legal order clearly distinguishes itself not only from the "socialist law" of the Communist regime, but also from the democratic legal order of the pre-war Czechoslovak Republic: the recognition of the obligations of international agreements concerning human rights and their superiority in law.

Whereas during the founding of Czechoslovakia in 1918 constitutional law unquestionably stood above international law, at the time of the renewal of Czech statehood at the end of the 20th century we are witnessing an essential change. International law is granted the

---

[423] Op.cit. Article 23

opportunity to function within internal law, to penetrate the space not long ago regarded as the domain of state sovereignty.

What is relevant here is not only the *"bitter experience of the past"* under totalitarianism, but the need to give the Czech legal order a clear orientation for the future. A state which intends to be based on the democratic values of Western civilization and which intends to survive all the dramatic changes which not only Europe but the whole international system is experiencing after the fall of Communism, must internationalize its law, must strengthen its position by integrating itself into international structures. Its "national" or "state" interest must be perceived as a part of an open global community of free nations, which recognizes the inviolability of natural human rights and the sovereignty of the law.

But even that is not enough. As it is generally recognized by today's law professors at Charles University and other institutions of higher learning – and more importantly, as it has been repeatedly adjudicated by the Czech Constitutional Court – the combination of all three constitutional principles characterized above, however, has one additional significant implication. Their declaration is one thing; their introduction into life and their concrete implementation is quite another. Legal order is not a static system; it is above all a process in which the law "lives;" in which it constantly changes through legislative activity and through practices of the court, but also through the fact that it shapes and directs the life of the whole of society.

It has, however, the following consequence: the legal order which builds on the inviolability of natural human rights, the sovereignty of the law and the recognition of direct validity of international agreements concerning human rights cannot come into existence solely with the help of the changes enacted in the system of the current "written" law. In order to suit the requirements of the new "focal" norm a process must above all be initiated and kept in operation, in the framework of which it must become usual to bring the rule of the law into harmony with its principles; a process which is not only – or even primarily – about the letter of the law, but about the relationship between the state – that is, public power – and the individual citizen.

The thing is that the legal instruments for the protection of human rights in the Czech Republic's Constitutional Order doesn't belong to private law, but to public law. Their primary aim is to empower the individual who is not only entitled to use his/her rights in accordance with his/her free will, but also has the right to demand a certain standard of behavior from the state. These instruments should penetrate all various legal corpuses the Czech Constitutional Order consists of, creating an obligation on the part of the state, but binding also on the legislator.

The state is not and cannot be the first and the only actor in the matter of human rights, although it would certainly be erroneous to undervalue its role and be unaware of the importance of its activity; it has to be the individual citizen for whom these rights are part of his life, who has the fundamental right *"to seek"* and *"to promote the general public interest;"* who has at his disposal his own common sense and a natural feeling for right and justice...

So let me conclude this brief *tour d'horizon* through the world of the current Czech Legal Order by raising a direct question: Aren't the duties imposed on those who are actively involved in the process of law in the Czech Republic today, exactly what the Charter 77 Manifesto demanded, when a small group of foolish naive "idealists" – who according to all political "realists" of this world were doomed to wreck their rickety boat on the high and treacherous seas of politics, both internal and international – set itself forty years ago on its adventurous journey?

Can we conclude that the spirit of Charter 77 is still somehow present – in spite of the termination of Charter 77's existence – in the Czech Republic? Maybe not in the minds of its average citizens, but at least when it comes to the Czech Constitutional Order – in spite of all its current weaknesses, failures in confrontation with all the current challenges that deserve to be named openly and criticized – being shaped and permanently transformed, not only by the activities of all institutions entrusted to its legislation, execution and adjudication, but by virtue of the daily existence of all citizens? Aren't they called now to keep this spirit of Charter 77 alive, and care not only about themselves, but also about the *"general public interest,"* regardless of the changed circumstances?

VI

In the last section of this treatise focused on Charter 77's legacies I return to Jan Patočka's philosophical contributions built into Charter 77's foundations. His Socratic turn resulting in his acceptance of the role of Charter 77 spokesperson at the very end of his life, was certainly something unique in the context of the history of philosophy in the 20th century – an imminent act of courage to be perceived and thought through also in the context of the grand philosophical dialogue, taking place today not only among Europeans, but all global mankind.

There are certainly significant philosophical schools today that can be considered from this Patočkian perspective as like-minded, and their adherents accordingly perceived as natural partners for being engaged with him in such a dialogue – Arendtians and Voegelinians, for sure, represent two of the most distinguished of them.

For instance, as far as I can tell, the most recent book by David Walsh – *Politics of the Person as the Politics of Being*[424] – articulates with great clarity and comprehensiveness a number of thoughts that are close to Patočka's understanding of what always was, and what still is, the primordial task of real philosophy in the human world. With the basic ideas elaborated in this book in mind, I will conclude this treatise by pointing to a central philosophical question of Charter77 which represents, in my view, the most important element of its legacy: the question of transcendence that certainly still deserves to be taken care of, thought through and further elaborated not only by neo-Thomist Catholic thinkers (to avoid misunderstanding, I don't think David Walsh belongs to this category) – who can facilitate this task for them by finding the point of departure of their political thought in their personal religious beliefs – but by the contemporary "classical," i.e. Socratic philosophers.

In an interview for German television made in the early 1960s, Hannah Arendt – who had evidently a great impact on Patočka's thought in the last years of his life – articulated what must be recognized, according to her, as one of the central problems of contemporary political thought: it

---

[424] David Walsh: *Politics of the Person as the Politics of Being*, University of Notre Dame Press, Notre Dame, Indiana, 2016

is *"a vital tension between man as a thinking being, and man as an acting being."*[425]

The short texts Patočka wrote in his capacity as Charter 77 spokesperson could certainly serve us as an important guide to understand the depth and significance of this observation. I have decided – consistently with the basic ideas of Walsh's "personalism" – to articulate the tension between the human capacity to think and to act in my own personal way. As a point of departure I will use the text I wrote for Václav Havel, after he was released from jail in 1983, and asked all Czech independent philosophers to explain to him what they were doing:

My aim in this text (*Philosophy as Personal Experience and the Others,* p. 31-42 of this volume) was to describe two movements of transcendence I experienced daily being one of the citizens of Charter 77's "parallel polis:"

On the one hand, there were my internal reasons for all the activities I was involved in in this context: the movement of "inward" transcendence that was bringing me from the outside world of external appearances to the *"interior domus"* of my thinking.

As an inhabitant of the public space I shared with other dissidents, I had an opportunity to realize again and again that thinking presupposes, exactly as Hannah Arendt described it, *"to stop and think;"* to cease to be involved with others – to pass through the *"Gate of Day and Night,"* described in the ancient poem of Parmenides – and to dive into the depth of the noetic sphere that opens to the human being within his/her own soul.

But what is happening in the solitude of my "internal abode" when I am thinking? In contrast to Havel or Benda, for instance, I had only random opportunities to experience the solitary confinement of my prison cell, but when I got there occasionally I could check up, too, under these dire circumstances, on old Plato's elementary observations:

Thinking is conditioned by the human capacity of insight into the realm of eternal ideas. At the same time, however, it is – always departing from our fluctuating opinions – an activity literally penetrating our whole finite bodily human existence.

---

[425] Hannah Arendt: *"What remains? The language remains:" A conversation with Gunther Gaus.* In: *Essays in understanding 1930–1954,* p. 2

Thinking doesn't mean to free oneself from one's body and to come to a standstill in the sphere of pure spirit. Thinking is a movement we are engaged in our concrete situation; a movement beginning within our bodily existence in the world, directed by the Truth of Being that can be only searched, loved, cared for, but never had.

Thinking is not just a solitary spiritual intuition enabling humans – the rational beings "having logos" – to know the things around them and learn about their causes. Its principal primary challenge and task is to assist a concrete human being to live in unity with him/herself; to help him/her to be; to distinguish in his/her concrete situation what is and what is not; what is good and what is bad under the given circumstances.

Thanks to the finite human nature, thinking can never be "monologic." It is originally, as Plato taught, a soundless dialogue taking place inside of one's soul. It is a way toward the truth, with the meditating "I" led by a kind of invisible partner on human life's journey; a partner before whose face and in whose questions all the internal life of the "I" takes place; a partner who is always already there when the "I" wakes up and starts to be conscious of itself.

And here are the questions that were always haunting me when I happened to be in the police cell and tried to console myself with the help of "philosophy:" who actually is this partner? Is it the DAIMONION of Socrates? Is it the God, I believe in? Who knows!

Then there was the second, opposite movement of transcendence to be distinguished from the first that I intensively experienced as a signatory of Charter 77: the movement directed from the singularity of the thinking, meditating "I" to the world where "the others" were assembled and where our various actions were taking place.

Signing Charter 77 marked for me a very specific, somewhat bizarre, but very real entry into plurality. It meant a really strong existential encounter with those who were also finding themselves on board our small, rickety and thus permanently endangered boat that could sink at any moment; people to whom I was bound, whether I liked them or not, whether they were my good friends or weird and sometimes even crazy individuals, by an unbreakable bond of solidarity and mutual understanding.

I had my concrete, and thus unique opportunity to realize what were the fundamental features of the world that opened and was available for my actions – individual or performed in concert with others; what kind of personal, i.e. moral implications such *vita activa* had for my existence in it.

But not only that, I could also generalize from it. It was not just my particular, unique experience, but a "theater" in which I was finding myself, in the same way as anybody else who has lived, lives and will live in this world.

A conclusion? Whereas the thinking "I" in isolation basically means "two in one," the acting "I" that has entered the world – *theatrum mundi* – has become "one alongside others," a unique, independent participant therein. A human cannot furnish him/herself with a personality, but on the contrary receives it from the others whom he/she steps forth. One's personal being means "being perceived," it means being for others, not only for oneself.

I have also learned how strongly our being in the common world (our *In-der-Welt-Sein*, in the terminology of Heidegger) is connected with our capacity of speech; how compelling our human nature (as ZÓON LOGON ECHON) might have been for me during these challenging times.

It is through speech a person enters the shared world and operates in its "marketplace." It is "his"/"her" truth or a message to be communicated to others, and offered to them for discussion and consultation about shared things or events of common concern.

And the last thing connected with the movement of transcendence directed to the outside world – our *vita activa* – I have learned about, and actually sharply realized, thanks to our human rights initiative. The demarcation and successful defense of the common place for human agency is a *conditio sine qua non* of acting – and it is also the fundamental meaning of human laws we were trying to lead a dialogue about with the Czechoslovak Government, but discovered instead public space of our "parallel polis."

Acting as such is a manifestation of human freedom, however, and thus is not, and never can be, fully under the rule of human laws. It is originally guided by mutual love among humans and their God-given capability to forgive. For to forgive means, as Arendt put it, to give preference not to the "what" of an occurrence but to the "who," to the guilty person. It liberates that person from the consequences of his/her deeds. It means to value the other "I"s more highly than the fact of what they did.

So here is – as a kind of conclusion of this treatise – the summary of my experience with Charter 77, a "civic initiative" that would not have been what it was without the spiritual influence of Jan Patočka; a lesson that should not be forgotten or forfeited after the original historical reason for which it was made passed away long time ago:

It is capacity of Socratic dialogue, the Socratic "care for the soul," that connects our inner experience of thinking and our human activity of acting in the external world in the presence of all others who are around us, who share this world with us.

And it is these two primordial movements of human existence enabling us to keep transcending our immanence during our finite life – inseparable and complementary – that represent our ultimate weapon at the moment when our freedom is threatened and we might feel paralyzed by totalitarian radiation.

Exercise 13

A Philosopher and His History[426]

*The waking have one common world, but each of the
sleeping turns aside each into a world of his own.*[427]

Prologue

Let me begin with an anamnesis. When I tried to organize my
thoughts for the upcoming conference that was summoned to kick off this
project – spending long hours on the plane heading from New York via
Toronto to Hong Kong – I recalled what happened to me during my first
trip to this region in the early 1990s:

Being blacklisted by the Communist government until 1989, I had
to live for decades in Czechoslovakia as if in a big cage, reconciled to the
reality of a complete ban on travel abroad. After the Velvet Revolution all
the restrictions disappeared overnight and all of a sudden the world opened
up before me. I started to travel extensively abroad – privately, as a former
dissident turned public intellectual/academic at the invitation of organizers
of various seminars, conferences or other events dealing with the post-
Communist transitions, or in my official capacity of Deputy Minister for

---

[426] Based on a paper, I presented at a conference titled "Revolutions: Finished and
Unfinished, from Primal to Final" at the University of Hong Kong in March of 2010
and published in a slightly abbreviated version in Thesis Eleven journal (Martin
Palouš: *A philosopher and his history: Jan Patočka's reflections on the end of Europe
and the arrival of the post-European epoch*. Thesis Eleven, Vol 116, Issue 1, 2013)
[427] *HÉRAKLEITOS FÉSI TOIS EGRÉGOROSIN HENA KAI KOINON KOSMON
EINAI, TÓN DE KOIMÓMENÓN HEKASTON EIS IDION APOSTREFESTHAI*
(Herakleitos B89, Diels, Herman, *Die Fragmente der Vorsokratiker, Griechisch und
Deutsch, Erster Band*, Berlin, Weidmannsche Buchhandlung, 1906, p. 75, The
English translation is from John Burnet's *Early Greek Philosophy*, London, 1920,
quot. from *www.randyhoyt.net/projects/heraclitus*)

Foreign Affairs. To satisfy my long-suppressed yearnings for foreign countries, I have to admit, I was ready to go almost anytime and anywhere.

My travel schedule in the week when I was about to visit South East Asia for the first time, was almost insane. On Monday and Tuesday, I was touring several cities in Europe – first Berlin and then Strasbourg and Brussels. On Wednesday I traveled to the United States: from Prague, via Amsterdam and Detroit to attend a conference in New Orleans. On Friday, I was on my way back to Prague, arriving there on Saturday morning. In the evening of the same day, however, I was in the air again, accompanying the Czechoslovak Prime Minister on his almost two-week official trip to Thailand, Indonesia and Malaysia. We flew from Prague to Karachi, just to refuel our plane and to have an early breakfast on Sunday morning with some representatives of the local government. From there we headed to Bangkok for another round of welcome ceremonies with national anthems, lots of handshakes, lengthy speeches and even longer meetings between delegations.

The result of this Gargantuan appetite for travelling combined with so many opportunities was that my circadian rhythm was in total disarray. It was long after midnight, when I finally got to a luxurious hotel suite after the endless state dinner. I was exhausted and almost out of my mind, devastated by the fact that next day early in the morning I had to be prepared with my suitcase again to continue this hectic journey. In a state of desperation I arranged the wake-up call for 6:00 a.m., threw myself into a spacious, king-size bed and immediately fell asleep. After a while – I had no idea how long I slept – my body woke me up signaling its need for evacuation. But to meet its requirement was not that simple, because I was finding myself in a peculiar situation, lying in complete darkness, unable to reach a switch to turn the light on, trying unsuccessfully to remember where I was and how I got there. But it was worse than that: I was not only lacking any positive information to help me with spatial orientation. Feeling only the presence of my body in the middle of nowhere, and conscious of time passing, I did not even know who I was! Thank God, it seemed just a fleeting moment before reality returned and my place in it restored. I found myself in the hotel room in Bangkok, managed to turn the light on – it was only 3 a.m. – met my bodily needs and fell asleep again. Three hours later I got up at the alarm clock signal, packed and joined the other members of the Prime Minister's delegation in the hotel lobby waiting to jump into the cars and roar off to the airport....

Observing the vast, uninhabited territories we were flying over, I was looking through my still unfinished paper to be presented at the Hong Kong meeting. My intention was also to invite my teacher, Czech philosopher Jan Patočka, to this conversation and to expound in this context his ideas about the end of Europe in the 20th century and the arrival of the post-European epoch. But thanks to the memory of what happened to me in the part of the world I was just heading to, twenty years earlier, I started to be haunted by disturbing, almost patricidal thoughts and questions (to paraphrase Plato's *Sophist*). In his exposé of the current constellation and on-going transformation of world politics, Patočka explicitly decided to depart from Husserl's arguments elaborated in his lectures delivered in 1935, first in Vienna and later in Prague that became the basis of Husserl's last great work, *The Crisis of European Sciences and Transcendental Phenomenology*.[428] Wasn't the weird *cogitatio* I was stricken by in Bangkok – a flash of thought of being just a body floating in time and space – clearly at odds with Patočka's Cartesian point of departure? What actually was the ontological significance of this experience? What were its implications from the point of view of philosophical anthropology? Didn't Patočka get it wrong, after all? Isn't it this perplexed state of mind, the temporary loss of identity (the Aristotelian ignorance – AGNOIA – that all humans, who *"by nature desire to know,"*[429] need to keep constantly escaping from in their noetic lives[430]), which should be our point of departure in our search for meaning? Isn't it exactly the point where our inquiry into the *translatio imperii* (handing over of empire) in the passage from the 20th to the 21st century, should also begin?

---

[428] Husserl, Edmund, *The Crisis of European Sciences and Transcendental Phenomenology* (1954) publ. Northwestern University Press, Evanston, 1970.
[429] Aristotle, *Metaphysics*, 980a1
[430] Op.cit., 982,b20

Part One: Four Preliminary Remarks Concerning Patočka's Philosophy

As indicated in the Prologue, the intention of this paper is to invite Jan Patočka to the conversation on the complex relationships between power and spirit in today's world, to expound in this context his ideas about the end of Europe in the 20th century and the arrival of the post-European epoch. Before turning my attention to the concrete texts in which he tried to formulate these ideas, however, I must first make four general remarks.

Remark one: the return of philosophy to Socrates

As evidenced sufficiently by his bibliography, Patočka's *locus operandi* was never limited by the boundaries of academia and academic philosophy, his home playing-field, but always included the public space he shared with fellow-citizens. Not only at the very end of his life when he became one of the spokespersons of Charter 77, but from his youth, Patočka tended to react *more philosophico* to the promptings from the public sphere, to tackle philosophical problems as they were presenting themselves in their broader context.[431] He always aspired to turn the results of his academic investigations into questions directed to each and every member of the general public; questions to be examined in the dialogue between philosophers and non-philosophers. He always was ready to "test" his ideas against the opinions circulating in various public *fora* and examine critically with their help various thoughts produced by the collective mind of the body politic of which he was part. He never hesitated to challenge contemporary sophists and ideologues. He tried repeatedly to formulate as precisely as possible the aim, content and method of his philosophical investigations, strongly convinced that

---

[431] *"Philosophy's most important task is never to speculate in abstracto,"* he wrote already in 1936, at age twenty-nine, but rather *"to criticize life in all its components and manifestations;" "to express what society has hitherto wanted without being aware of it, to put into words its unvoiced tendencies, but also to show what is behind them, to clarify their essence, their genesis, their intricacies and problems, and to attempt then to resolve them."* (Jan Patočka: *Kapitoly ze současné filosofie* [*Chapters from Contemporary Philosophy*]. In: Jan Patočka: *Péče o duši I*, p.92

accuracy of expression, meticulousness of language (AKRIBEIA)[432] is an indispensable, or even the most important virtue of a philosopher. However, he never turned the results of these investigations into a definitive, and thus closed philosophical system.[433]

In other words: In order to understand Patočka's philosophical life work as a whole – its fundamental aspiration and tendencies, its scope and achievements – we must consider the strongest motive of his philosophizing: to challenge the sclerosis of mind threatening not only his own political community, but all good European societies during his lifetime; *"to be engaged,"* to use the formulation of Eric Voegelin, *"in an act of resistance against the personal and social disorder of (his) age; "*[434] to think and act with respect to the current crisis of European civilization as a classical, i.e. Socratic philosopher speaking from the depth of the ancient origins of philosophical thought; for whom the essence of philosophizing was not to formulate metaphysical doctrines but to "care for the soul."

Remark two: Patočka and Masaryk, the question of Czech national philosophy

There is one important aspect of Patočka's lifelong Socratism: his preoccupation with Czech national philosophy. The term itself might arouse suspicion: does it not evoke, when taken at face-value, the ghost of nationalism? The answer obviously is, if only with regard to what I have said in the preceding remark, no. Undoubtedly, Patočka was not a nationalist and he never intended to use his philosophical ideas as a weapon in the service of nationalistic ideology. On the contrary, Patočka tried again and again to evoke in the Czech milieu the spirit of open philosophical dialogue. Here he was clearly following the example of Masaryk and inspired by his Czech national program, the essence of which was to conceive the "Czech question" in "worldly terms." As his great

---

[432] Aristotle, Nicomachean Ethics, 1094b24

[433] Cf. Martin Palouš: *Filosofovat se Sokratem* [*Philosophizing with Socrates*]. In: Filosofický časopis, year XXXVIII, 1990, issue 1-2, pp. 45-58

[434] Voegelin, E: *Reason, Classical Experience.* In: *Published Essays 1966-1985*, p. 265

predecessor, he also regularly admonished his fellow-Czechs for their parochialism and provincial mindset and repeatedly emphasized the need of Czech national society to open itself to the external world; to face philosophical problems of universal humanity; to examine critically its own views and opinions, and to resist *more philosophico* its endemic smallness.

Patočka's overall relationship to Masaryk, a philosopher who became the first president of the modern Czechoslovak state, would certainly deserve a thorough and detailed analysis. This text, however, only allows me to make a rudimentary remark in this regard. On the one hand, as a phenomenologist Patočka criticized Masaryk's positivism. He argued repeatedly that no matter how genuinely and religiously motivated Masaryk's resistance to the decadent tendencies of modern European civilization might have been, the school of thought Masaryk was affiliated with – the positivistic philosophy of history, the basic principles of which were laid down by Auguste Comte – simply could not open the way forward from the current crisis of European civilization. His clash with the philosophical underpinnings of Masaryk's national program culminated in his outline of the interpretation of history of the 20th century and rejected flatly Masaryk's analysis of the causes and consequences of the First World War in the beginning of his sixth "heretical essay."[435]

On the other hand, it should never be forgotten that in spite of this criticism, Patočka had the highest respect for Masaryk the philosopher. Throughout his life he was literally fascinated by Masaryk's practical attitude towards theoretical philosophical ideas. He never missed an opportunity to emphasize the importance of Masaryk's stubborn belief that what matters is not only how they emerge in the life of the mind (BIOS THEÓRETIKOS, *vita contemplativa*) of philosophers, but how they can be "used" by men of action and what their concrete effects are in the human world. In this sense, Patočka always considered Masaryk as a genuine contemporary Czech philosopher whose originality consisted simply in his ability to connect his theoretical reflections with his public engagement; who was always ready to test his philosophical ideas against

---

[435] Jan Patočka: *Heretical Essays in the Philosophy of History*, p. 119

the political realities in which he participated; and when he got into conflict with public opinion, to go against the current!

Remark three: the last apprentice of Edmund Husserl

Usually, the point of departure for interpretation of Patočka's philosophy is his relationship with Edmund Husserl. Patočka's own description of the two first encounters with the man who inspired him to pursue for the rest of his life the path of phenomenology, is quite telling:

In 1929, Patočka was a visiting student at the Sorbonne in Paris. Husserl came there at the end of February to give two lectures of introduction to his *"transcendental phenomenology."*[436] Patočka, who already considered him to be "his" philosopher, could not miss this opportunity. He said about his experience of being in the audience:

> *I sensed the air of compelling necessity to lay down anew the foundations and to look at a new direction to achieve historical depth. At the same time, I saw a philosopher in front of me, someone who was not reading a paper about somebody or commenting on something, but just sitting in his work-room, as if alone, struggling with his problems, paying no attention to the world or the people around....*[437]

Three years later Patočka finally had an opportunity to meet Husserl face to face. After spending the winter semester 1932/1933 in Berlin – where he had experienced, according to his own words, *"the atmosphere of that witches' cauldron, in which the end of Europe, and in*

---

[436] On February 23 and 24 of 1929 Husserl delivered two lectures in Paris at the invitation of the Institut d'Études germaniques and the Société francaise (see also Husserliana I Cartesianische Meditationen und Parisier Vorträge, ed. by S. Strasser, The Hague, Netherlands: Martinus Nijhoff, 1973. The English Trans. The Paris Lectures, trans. by P. Koestenbaum, 2nd ed. The Hague, Netherlands: Martinus Nijhoff, 1976, see also: Husserl's Syllabus for the Paris Lectures an "Introduction to Transcendental Phenomenology." Trans. by Herbert Spiegelberg. Journal of the British Society for Phenomenology. (1976): 18-23. "Husserl's Syllabus for the Paris Lectures an "Introduction to Transcendental Phenomenology." Translated by Herbert Spiegelberg. McCormick, Peter and Elliston, Frederick A. eds. Husserl: Shorter Works. Notre Dame, Indiana: University of Notre Dame Press, 1981, 78-81.
[437] Jan Patočka: *Vzpomínky na Husserla* [Remembering Husserl]. In : Jan Patočka : *Češi I*, p. 631

conjunction with it the tragic turn in the lot of phenomenology and so many phenomenologists, was already in the process of preparation"[438] – he came for the summer semester of 1933 to Freiburg. As a holder of a Humboldt Foundation scholarship he had a letter of recommendation from the Foundation which he hoped would help him to get into the close circle of Husserl's students. He received an invitation to come to Husserl's home to discuss the terms of his apprenticeship. When he rang the bell, Husserl himself opened the door and said:

> *"Finally! I had students from all over the world, but so far no fellow-countryman. ...If you are coming to me unspoiled by philosophical doctrines and without spiritual blinders, if you really want to learn to see, then you are warmly welcome here.* "[439]

Here we have the beginning of the personal relationship between Patočka and Husserl which lasted for the next five years (until Husserl died in April 1938) – a relationship that decisively influenced his future philosophical life. Is what we clearly observe here – the emerging bond between an old master and his young disciple seeking initiation into the master's salutary teachings – commensurate with the spirit of philosophy? Or, on the contrary, is it something we should be particularly disturbed about? Is it the moment in which philosophical schools with their distinct traditions and methods of research are coming into existence, or is it rather something that actually points to the weakest, the most problematic – one would be inclined to say, the most tragic – spot, the proverbial Achilles heel of both Husserl's and later also Patočka's own philosophizing? Should it be defended or should it be further reflected upon and overcome by Patočka on his own path inspired by Husserl's phenomenology? Is it also the greatest challenge and the principal task for Patočka's current disciples and other friendly interpreters of his philosophy?

The reverence a young phenomenologist felt for his old teacher – Husserl, after all, was willing to train him in all he would need to master, in order to pursue successfully his own phenomenological research in his

---

[438] Ibid.
[439] ibid.

area – is not at all surprising. As the historical record shows, since the beginning of the 20th century, the phenomenological movement inspired by Husserl[440] started to dominate universities particularly in Germany[441] and brought a new vigor and hope not only to philosophy, but to many other disciplines, especially in the fields of humanities and normative sciences.[442] As Patočka described the prime of phenomenology after the publication of Husserl's *Logical Investigations* in 1901 in his postscript to the Czech translation of *Cartesian Meditations*:

> *A philosophical atmosphere arose, that had not been here for a long time; the atmosphere of new confidence in philosophy as an autonomous, rigorously scientific discipline, entirely independent of specialized sciences, disposing, as they do, of its own bulk of knowledge – generally recognized and extendible by the continuous fruitful research – as it is in mathematics or physics.*[443]

The fallacy in the expectations accompanying the emergence of Husserl's new concept of "philosophy as a rigorous science" is more than obvious. First of all, as it became clear at the beginning of the 1930s, even Husserl himself did not meet them. His Paris lectures – where a Czech student Jan Patočka was in attendance, and admired him *"sitting alone,"* not paying much attention to his audience, but *"struggling with his problems"* – actually demonstrated quite clearly the fundamental difficulties of his seemingly apodictic and self-evident beginning. It also turned out that the rigorous phenomenological research pursued by his loyal disciples, was certainly not just adding new pieces to the edifice built under the watch of its main architect, but was rather sending them out, step by step, on their own philosophical paths. All of them, including Patočka, were brought to the point when they had to decide about their way forward, and to start questioning the hitherto uncontested Husserlian point of departure.

---

440 Jan Patočka: Postscript to the Czech edition of Husserl's Cartesian Meditations, (Edmund Husserl: *Karteziánské meditace*, Svoboda, Praha, 1968, p. 161-190)
441 op.cit. p. 166
442 ibid.
443 Ibid.

Even more worrisome when Patočka started his apprenticeship with Husserl, was what was brewing in the Berlin's *witches' cauldron*, as he aptly described the political situation of the Weimar Republic as Adolf Hitler was on his way to seizing power. The rise of totalitarianism of the German, Italian or Russian brand raised serious questions about Husserl's belief that the main battlefield in the crisis of European civilization in the 20th century would be science and philosophy; that the reconciliation of all those who found themselves for different historical reasons to be mutual enemies could be eventually achieved[444] – because the *"European 'world' was born from ideas of reason,"*[445] to quote the final paragraph of a lecture Husserl delivered on May 7, 1935 in Vienna – by means of the *"rebirth of Europe from the spirit of philosophy."*[446]

When it became clear that phenomenology had to be understood as an open-ended journey of philosophers rather than a "rigorous science," where should their philosophical questioning actually begin? When it turned out that philosophers were simply unable to ward off a catastrophe in Europe with their rigorous scientific knowledge, would it be philosophy of history informed by phenomenology, taking up not only its "collective" insights concerning the history of mankind, but also the particular experiences of phenomenologists themselves with it – rather than a-historic Husserlian transcendentalism – where philosophers should start their resistance and search for some new points of departure?

Remark four: the way from transcendental phenomenology to the philosophy of history

This brings me to my last and shortest general remark concerning Patočka's philosophical work as a whole. The philosophy of history is clearly an essential or even the most significant part of it. It is, without any doubt, its ultimate achievement and its culmination. Its point of departure,

---

[444] Jan Patočka: *Vzpomínky na Husserla* [Remembering Husserl]. In: Jan Patočka : *Češi I*, p. 632

[445]Edmund Husserl: *The Crisis of European Man*. In: Edmund Husserl: *Phenomenology and the Crisis of Philosophy*. Translated by Quentin Lauer, Harper Torchbooks, 1965, p. 191

[446] Ibid. p. 192

as we are going to see in the following section of this text, is on the one hand clearly based on Patočka's critical reception of Husserl's concept of the crisis of European mankind. At the same time, however, it is characterized by two other elements distinctive of his thought which were mentioned previously. It always should be kept in mind that it is a classical Socratic philosopher who is speaking; a philosopher whose "program" in the end is not to express his thoughts in the form of propositional knowledge, no matter how much importance he ascribes to the "exactness" of his own concepts, expressions and propositions, but the philosophical "care for the soul." And, it should never be forgotten that Patočka approaches the theme of universal human history from his own position; that he is a Czech philosopher, involved in the Socratic manner primarily with his own Czech national community; a thinker who sees the world through the lenses of specific experiences of his own nation; for whom the big question of the future of European mankind and of its legacy at the end of its golden modern age is inseparably connected with a "small" one: the question of Czech national existence, the question of the future of the "small" Czech nation in the changing world and its freedom.

Part Two: Patočka's "Europe and the Post-European Epoch"[447]

The text I am going to focus on was written sometime between 1970 and 1977 – it is a late work of Patočka. Besides the much more known *Heretical Essays* and the lecture series *Plato and Europe* from the same period, it contains one of the most important articulations of Patočka's philosophy of history. The fact that it was found on top of other papers lying on his desk after he passed away on March 13, 1977, led the editors of the Collected Works to believe that in spite of the fact that no significant changes were recently made, Patočka did not consider it entirely finished and was still working on it.

---

[447] *Jan Patočka: Evropa a doba poevropská. In: Jan Patočka: Péče o duši II*, pp. 80-148

The audacious hypothesis

The text opens with the following announcement:

"What is proposed here will be most likely found by historians a-historical. Philosophers, on the contrary, will consider this proposition as a tributary to the accidental historical events. Both of them will criticize its overmuch constructivism. Its author, however, is ready to accept this risk. His aim is to propound problems, which are concealed behind the things we can see in our immediate surroundings – thanks to the fact that our momentary anxiety has made us shortsighted; to do away with what is closest to us and to let appear what is most distant from us. The realization of this aim, however, requires construction or rather destruction. Destruction is, after all, also a kind of construction.

This essay departs from a hypothesis which is deliberately audacious. To let the whole process of European history revolve around one single principle, or rather around only one implication of this principle, is a nonstarter lacking any credibility in the eyes of both historians and philosophers – irrespective of the fact that this implication is apparently huge and decisive. Nonetheless, such a bold decision can be adopted more easily in the present times, thanks to a great thinker, who has already discovered the way on which something like a principle of European spirituality, distinct from all other spiritualities, can be found: Edmund Husserl, who in his book Crisis of European Sciences assumed the task of the renewal of rationality. To be sure, the notion that Europe is logos and ratio; that it is in Europe where the idea of universality – the only idea capable of turning the world into one world – emerged, has been known since long ago... "[448]

There are two things that must be thought through carefully when one reads the opening paragraphs of Patočka's essay. On the one hand, it is his Husserlian hypothesis itself: what makes Europe from the very beginning of her history a spiritual unity distinct from all other cultures

---

[448] Op.cit., p. 80

and civilizations, is her *"logos and ratio,"* originally discovered by Greek philosophy. But what we also should not leave unnoticed is Patočka's characterization of his hypothesis as *"deliberately audacious."* Why does Patočka actually need to say that? Would it be the same if he said "deliberately provocative?" Does he merely refer to a conflict pending between him and other historians or philosophers? Does he just provoke them by indicating that their histories and philosophies probably are among those things that must be destructed and removed if our capacity to see the fundamental problems of our epoch is to be restored?

Or does the characterization of his hypothesis as *"deliberately audacious"* indicate more than that? Is it his intention to bring us from the surface of things to the region of deeper phenomena which will arise before our eyes only after we manage to overcome our momentary anxiety and sharpen our weakened spiritual sight? Can it happen that what we will discover then will be the connection between *"logos and ratio"* inquired into by European philosophers and their *audacity*?

The point of departure: Husserl's concept of the crisis of European man

A year before his last major book on the current European crisis was published in 1936 Husserl delivered two similar lectures, first in Vienna and later in Prague (before the *Cercle philosophique de Prague pour les recherches sur l'entendement humain,* in which Patočka served as one of its two secretaries).[449] The basic message of these lectures can be summarized as follows:

---

[449] *Die Philosophie in der Krisis europäischen Menschheit.* (Public Lecture in Vienna before the Kulturbund, May 7 and 10, 1935). The English translation by Quentin Lauer *Philosophy and the Crisis of European Man* (in: *Phenomenology and the Crisis of Philosophy,* Harper Torchbooks, New York, 1965, 149-192) or by David Carr *as The Vienna Lecture* (in: *The Crisis of European Sciences and Transcendental Phenomenology. An Introduction to Phenomenology.* Northwestern University Press, Evanston Illinois,1970, 269-299). The same lecture was read by Husserl again under the title *Krisis der europäischen Wissenschaften und die Psychologie.* before the *Cercle philosophique de Prague pour les recherches sur l'entendement humain* in Prague in November 1935

In spite of all progress achieved during the modernization of the last three centuries, European civilization finds itself in the 20th century in a deep crisis. The reason, according to Husserl, is that *"European nations are sick,"*[450] and *"Europe itself is…in critical condition;"*[451] that the core element of European identity is omitted by Europeans. Europe, Husserl reminds us, *"is now no longer a number of different nations bordering each other, influencing each other only by commercial competition and wars."*[452] Europe has never been fully determined *"geographically, as it appears on the map, as though European man were to be in this way confined to the circle of those who live together in this territory."*[453]

Since the very beginning of European history *"the title Europe designates the unity of a spiritual life and a creative activity."*[454] Being European has always meant joining other Europeans *"in spirit…in the unity of one spiritual image….exhibiting the philosophical idea immanent in the history of Europe."*[455] Europe, states Husserl, can only survive on the current historical crossroads if today's Europeans will manage to rediscover that what they inhabit is not a piece of land, but a civilization, having its spiritual roots and being endowed with *"its immanent teleology;"*[456] requiring throughout its history animation by a *"a new spirit stemming from philosophy and the sciences based on it, a spirit of free criticism providing norms for infinite tasks,… creating new, infinite ideals."*[457]

What characterizes Europe more than anything else in the current phase of its history, and what is the most important outgrowth of its innate entelechy, is modern science and technology. As a decisive social force in modern society, it has undoubtedly tremendous potential to empower men technically and to improve the material condition of human life. Its

---

[450] Edmund Husserl: *The Crisis of European Man.* In: *Phenomenology and the Crisis of Philosophy.* Translated by Quentin Lauer, Harper Torchbooks, 1965, p. 150
[451] Ibid.
[452] Op. cit., p. 177
[453] Op.cit., p. 155
[454] Ibid.
[455] Op. cit. 156
[456] Ibid.
[457] Op. cit., 177

"efficacious" knowledge, which is increasingly capable of changing the human world according to human plans and wishes, however, is failing to serve *les maîtres et possesseurs de la nature*, when asked to become a reliable guide to protect and enhance the rational sense of their life. The reason is that its cherished rationality has fallen into the trap of *"naturalism and objectivism,"* and as such cannot be perceived as a signpost of Europe's progress, but rather *"on a level with the rationality of the Egyptian pyramids!"*[458]

This crisis, then, Husserl concludes, *"can end in only one of two ways: in the ruin of a Europe alienated from its rational sense of life, fallen into a barbarian hatred of spirit or,"* as I already quoted above, *"in the rebirth of Europe from the spirit of philosophy."*[459] What can help Europeans achieve such a renaissance? Husserl's answer is not surprising. It is his transcendental phenomenology, the aim of which is to bring the lost *"spiritual image of Europe"* back to the attention of Europeans. It sets for itself the following fundamental tasks: to recover *"through a heroism of reason"* the broken thread of communication between the realm of scientific objectivity and the primordial sphere of human matters given to us in our immediate subjective experience; to rehabilitate the philosophers' *"theoretical attitude,"* and to oppose it to the *"natural attitude"* human beings adopt towards their fellow-men and things they are surrounded by in their life-world; to attempt a philosophy of history that would enable us to rediscover the forgotten TELOS, the inner motive of European civilization: the idea of human life based upon insight.

Patočka's adoption of Husserl's motive

The previous chapter explains why Patočka could anticipate certain criticism and misunderstanding. Does not Husserl's concept of the crisis of European man he chose as his point of departure represent the clearest example of Eurocentrism of the past that simply cannot grasp fully both the spiritual and political challenges of our times? What about the schema of world history implied in it – putting the discovery of THEÓRIA

---

[458] Op. cit., 186
[459] Op. cit., 192

by the Greek philosophers at its beginning and Husserl's own discovery of transcendental subjectivity as a new apodictic origin of philosophy at its end? Did Husserl really believe that he discovered history's ultimate TELOS? Wasn't Patočka's proposal somewhat *démodé*, if we consider that postmodern winds were already blowing in nearly all European philosophical salons at that time? In short: To want to build a contemporary philosophy of history in the 1970s on Husserlian foundations? Wasn't it an enterprise doomed in advance and likely to fail?

I can offer two preliminary reactions to all these objections and doubts. First, even if it were true that Patočka, one of the contemporary Socratic philosophers, accepted entirely Husserl's Eurocentric interpretation of the history of mankind, his own Eurocentrism in this particular text still would need to be qualified. Having expressed many times before the highest admiration for his teacher, he stated a little later: *"Husserl's work, which was written to avert the final catastrophe of the European world,"*[460] should serve a somewhat different purpose in our current historical situation:

> *it still might be able to assist in the elucidation of the situation of mankind after this catastrophe already happened, and even to shed some light on the first short lap on our way into the emerging post-European world.*[461]

And the second point: regardless of whether the above-mentioned schema of world history – with the discovery of a new apodictic beginning of philosophy chosen as its decisive turning point and with the discoverer himself elevated to the position of founding father and highest priest of a new sect of self-appointed *"functionaries of mankind"* – can be imputed to Husserl or not, Patočka certainly had somewhat different ambitions. Husserl's identification of European spirituality with *"logos and ratio"* must be, according to Patočka, related to and primarily perceived through the lens of the real groundbreaking discovery Husserl made much earlier

---

[460] Jan Patočka: *Evropa a doba poevropská a její duchovní problémy.* In: *Péče o duši II*, p. 83
[461] Ibid.

in Logical Inquiries, concerning *"the elementary bond of opinion and insight."*[462]

Turning his attention to this philosophical problem, Husserl, in fact,

> *recurs to the Platonic distinctions, examines the oldest switches, where decisions were made on the paths of reason for whole millennia and formulates the problems of reason in such a concrete way, that they can become the key to the questioning situated in the open field of history.*[463]

What Husserl managed to achieve by getting hold of this key was

> *to demonstrate for the first time in the history of the mind the elementary bond connecting EPISTÉMÉ to DOXA. The products of EPISTÉMÉ – thinking containing the active element of reflection – become parts of the life-world; they reshape and transform this world, both on the level of its individual things, and that of its elementary structures. As such, however, they can never surpass it entirely and make it unnecessary. Their relationship to the life-world is fundamental. Only through this relationship, though, and thanks to it they can always make sense and be at all comprehensible.*[464]

And here is the real question which, I believe, has attracted Patočka's interest: Isn't it just *"the elementary mechanism of opinion and insight"* – this *"miraculous, so far unexplored and unseen through, mysterious triviality,"* the principal cause of wonder of the classical Greek philosophers, rediscovered in present times by Husserl, and contained in his teleological idea animating, according to him, Europe from the very beginning of its history – where we should start to overcome our momentary anxiety? Doesn't this define the starting point of the new historical journey from the European past to the unknown post-European future? Isn't it what must be explored first, if we want – in our dark times,

---

[462] Op.cit., p. 80
[463] Op. cit., p. 81
[464] Ibid.

to paraphrase Hannah Arendt – to claim our right, or at least to hope, for some illumination?[465]

Philosophy as an act of resistance

Husserl's observation that EPISTÉMÉ is founded on DOXA and not vice versa – the seeming triviality of his ascertainment that in order to adopt the *"theoretical attitude"* towards the phenomena brought to our attention in the world in which we live, we have first to leave the primordial *"natural attitude"* towards them through the movement of our thought – has, or at least can have, as Patočka was well aware, significant implications. What is the DOXA we are advised by phenomenologists to depart from? How is it changed after the phenomenological "epoché" has liberated us from the shackles of our natural attitude towards reality and has put us for a passing moment in the role of *"the disinterested spectator of the world that is demythologized before his eyes?"*[466]

DOXA, as we all know, means "opinion." It designates the immediate contents of our own unreflected and unexamined noetic life. It covers everything that the cultural environment we are a part of, has taught us. It denotes what we have inherited from our ancestors as our beliefs we share with all (significant) others. It is what we have received as "pieces of knowledge" or "skills" in the process of education at home, at schools, or just were imprinted in us thanks to the fact that we live in a certain society with its practices and habits. We can be confident, on the one hand, that all our DOXAI never miss reality entirely and always contain some elements of truth.[467] On the other hand, we should be aware that they also

---

[465] *"That even in the darkest of times we have the right to expect some illumination, and that such illumination may well come less from theories and concepts than from the uncertain, flickering, and often weak light that some men and women, in their lives and their works, will kindle under almost all circumstances and shed over the time span that was given them on earth – this conviction is the inarticulate background against which these profiles were drawn."* (Hannah Arendt: *Preface.* In: Hannah Arendt: *Men in Dark Times*, p. ix)

[466] Edmund Husserl: *The Crisis of European Man.* In: *Phenomenology and the Crisis of Philosophy.* Translated by Quentin Lauer, Harper Torchbooks, 1965, p. 182

[467] Aristotle, Metaphysics, Book II 993a30-993b7: *"The investigation of the truth is in one way hard, in another easy. An indication of this is found in the fact that no one is able to attain the truth adequately, while, on the other hand, we do not collectively*

harbor idiosyncrasies, illusions, misperceptions and even lies; that they can deceive us, instead of correctly advising us; to blind us instead of letting us see; to bemuse us instead of steering us towards wisdom.

What is then the matter with truth in our human situation? Our DOXAI – as Socrates discovered and all Greek classical philosophers were very well aware – can never be complete, unchanging and self-consistent. They must always be further examined, controlled, tested against reality and corrected in the light of experience. They should always be susceptible to further transformations in the process of noesis – described by Plato in his famous Seventh Letter as a sequence of steps leading first from DOXA to DOXA ALÉTHÉS, and from there through EPISTÉMÉ to NOUS[468] – we take part in as rational animals, living beings having LOGOS, endowed with capacity of reflection and insight.

The real moment of truth for human DOXAI, their most serious test, comes obviously with our actions, which they inspire and initiate. Is TI AGATHON – *"some good,"* every human endeavor *"is thought to aim at,"* to use the famous first sentence from the Nicomachean Ethics of Aristotle,[469] the real good or is it not? Are our words and deeds by which we make our presence in the world – and also appear before others, who can listen to us, observe us in the course of our action and pronounce their judgment about it – capable of passing the test of reason true to the standards of EPISTÉMÉ? Can they be accepted when perceived *sub specie aeternitatis*, or, at least, judged with the help of socially recognized values? Are they meaningful or meaningless? Do they follow some relevant target or are they rather confused and erratic? Are they moral or immoral, legitimate or illegitimate, law-abiding or unlawful? Do they keep

---

fail, but every one says something true about the nature of things, and while individually we contribute little or nothing to the truth, by the union of all a considerable amount is amassed. Therefore, since the truth seems to be like the proverbial door, which no one can fail to hit, in this respect it must be easy, but the fact that we can have a whole truth and not the particular part we aim at shows the difficulty of it."

[468] Plato, the Seventh Letter, 342a6-343c6

[469] *"Every art and every inquiry, and similarly every action and pursuit, is thought to aim at some good;"* (Aristotle: *The Nicomachean Ethics*, 1094a1-3. Translated by W. D. Ross.

http://classics.mit.edu/Aristotle/nicomachaen.html

us on the right road in our passage through life, or are they, on the contrary, sending us in a wrong direction, something that should be changed if we want to escape at the moment of our death our "final," i.e. irreversible, damnation?

It is in the area of these and similar questions where Patočka – a Czech Socratic philosopher at the end of the European era – steps in. And his point of departure in the noetic process from DOXA to EPISTÉMÉ is – and it cannot be otherwise! – a concrete historical situation he himself is a part of. This is what he said in the introduction of the first lecture from the series *Plato and Europe* to a close group of his disciples in a private apartment in the fall of 1973, after he was forced, for the second time in his life, to leave his chair in the Department of Philosophy at Prague's Charles University:

> *Today people often get together to talk about abstract and eventually lofty things to escape for a moment the distress in which we all find ourselves, so that they may lift both their spirits and their minds. While I think that this is all very well, it is more like entertainment for old ladies. Philosophical reflection ought to have a different purpose, it should somehow help us in the distress in which we are; precisely in the situation in which we are placed, philosophy is to be matter of inner conduct.*[470]

What was actually happening in Czechoslovakia in the fall of 1973 when these sentences were delivered? How did Patočka and his students perceive the surrounding world at that time? What were their DOXAI, their actual opinions of it? What were their expectations? What about their preliminary thoughts, by which they tried to transform these DOXAI in the process of noesis into at least a kind of EPISTÉMÉ – a knowledge the exactness of which didn't necessarily need to be measured by the established standards of humanistic sciences or philosophy, but just to respond to their basic natural desire to know (OREXIS TOU EIDENAI), to paraphrase Aristotle again, and thus shield them from the otherwise potentially devastating existential impact of their momentary situation?

---

[470] Jan Patočka: *Plato and Europe*, p. 1

A quick historical reminiscence: the years that followed the unsuccessful attempt of the Prague Spring of 1968 to reform the totalitarian Communist regime and endow socialism with a "human face,"[471] when Patočka was giving the lecture series *Plato and Europe* and writing about the end of Europe and the arrival of the post-European age, are known in contemporary Czech history as the "period of normalization." The then prevailing mood among Czechs and Slovaks was frustration, anger, distress and anxiety. After a couple of months of 1968, full of hopes and excitement caused by the almost miraculous arrival of freedom in our closed society, they were not only back where they had been before the "regenerative process," due to the invasion of the armies of the Warsaw Pact led by the Soviet Union on August 21, but actually fared much worse in its aftermath. Tens of thousands, who rejected the idea that they would be doomed to spend the rest of their lives in Communist enslavement, emigrated. Those who stayed could only observe helplessly the restoration of the totalitarian regime in the country. Having taken their *"lessons from the years of crisis,"* the "normalizers," backed and supervised by their Soviet masters, started to close the society again and liquidate systematically every single remnant of short-lived freedom. All those among the party members who took active part in the "counterrevolution," were purged and removed from any position where they could exert any influence on society. Political apartheid was not only exerted against them, but also applied to those who refused to repent and were not willing to conform to the rules and habits essential for the orderly and smooth functioning of a closed totalitarian society. Extensive and detailed measures were adopted in the media, at schools, publishing houses, scientific and cultural institutions, etc., in order to eliminate any free flow of information or any open public debate, so that in the future similar disruptions of "socialist order" could never happen again. At the same time a kind of "social contract" – a relatively undisturbed private life and even some personal benefits in exchange for loyalty to the regime –

---

[471] There are many publications about the failed attempt to reform Communism in Czechoslovakia in 1968. My own personal account of this period of our contemporary history *Revolutions and Revolutionaries (Three Czech Encounters with Freedom)* is a part of this volume as Exercise 1

was offered to the silent majority of the resigned and subdued population. Thanks to the existing power constellation – in Czechoslovakia and in Europe and in the world – there were no signs on the horizon that this situation could ever change.

Everyone could observe in the beginning of the 1970s an *"advanced or late totalitarian regime,"*[472] emerging step by step and penetrating all aspects of life of the social body, brutally awakening its members from their 1968 dream. And the strategy of the "normalizers," whose primary aim was to compel cooperation from the people by every means, and to use only the minimum force necessary to regain total control over their spontaneous, and thus by definition politically dangerous behavior, was apparently working. What was brought back to life in the process of "screening," which was the main instrument of the policies of normalization, was the ugliest brand of typical Czech political realism, well known from the past, based on the capacity of members of a small and weak nation to conform themselves to the situation in the world dominated by bigger and more powerful players: to renounce temporarily their own freedom, truth, honor and dignity, but to survive.

When this attitude prevailed it was not at all surprising that it became relatively easy for the power holders, as Patočka observed, *"to extinguish in advance the smallest glimmer of mobilizable social initiative....to deprive the society entirely, or almost entirely, of its moral strength,"* nonetheless allowing at the same time *"its external physical capacities...to grow."* The form of government established in the process bluntly characterized by Patočka as *"human machinery of decline and degeneration,"* didn't need the iron fist to have its way. What could be seen in action here was rather *"fear, disorientation, wiles of comfort, possibility to gain advantages in the environment of general scarcity creating here an artificially interconnected complex of motivations."*[473]

In sheer defiance of the corrupting and morally bankrupt state of affairs in Czechoslovakia in the beginning of the 1970s, the basic tone of Patočka's philosophical activities during this period was, in spite of their

---

[472] Václav Havel: *Stories and Totalitarianism.* In: *Open Letters, Selected Writings 1965-1990*, edited by Paul Wilson, Alfred A. Knopf, New York, p. 331
[473] Jan Patočka: *Doba poevropská a její duchovní problémy.* In: *Péče o duši II*, p. 100

highly abstract and theoretical foundations and motivation, resolute, exhortative and audacious. Even in the bleak and stressful situation in which Czechs found themselves in the period of normalization, Patočka did not miss an opportunity to remind them *more Socratico* what the main mission was of a philosopher in such a situation: to come with his advice on how to resist the destructive effects of corrupted social and political order. What still could make a difference, according to Patočka despite the fact that all hopes connected with the "regenerative process" of the Prague Spring 1968 were irretrievably lost, was philosophical thought conceived as our *"internal action"* based on our capacity of reflection and insight! Patočka clearly stated in his lecture quoted above:

> *Our reality is always situational so that if it reflected upon, it is already different by the fact that we have reflected. Of course, the question is whether by reflection, reality is improved. This is not stated in the least. But, in any case, a reflected-upon situation – in contrast to a naïve situation – is to certain extent a clarified one, or at least on the way to clarification.*
>
> *...A situation is entirely different, depending on whether people who are in a situation of distress give up or do not give up. In a hopeless situation it is still possible to behave in very different ways.*[474]

The Czechs might have lost all hopes that they could ever be liberated from their current Babylonian captivity in the Soviet empire, but the advice given to them by a classical Socratic philosopher in their midst had to remain always the same: Do not give up, say no to this machinery, and insist under any circumstances on your right to live in harmony with your insight!

In no historical situation is man allowed to resign his elementary task, to think, to examine constantly his DOXAI and to keep transforming them into EPISTÉMÉ. In no historical situation should man refuse to put his life under the test of reason and care for the soul, to gain at least spiritual orientation in his situation. In no historical situation can man escape the elementary consequences of his freedom and be absolved from

---

[474] Jan Patočka: *Plato and Europe*, p. 2

the task to be "good," from the duty to behave morally, to resist by all available means the decline and degeneration threatening always the very core of his human identity.

The suggestion Patočka came up with in the bleak atmosphere of the early 1970s was not at all surprising, at least for those who knew how he had reacted to the social and political crises in the past: *consolatio philosophiae*, the turn to philosophy in an attempt to formulate general, universally valid questions which would help us to gain a basic orientation to our situation, because it is here we should start our search for solutions to our particular problems. So what did emerge before the eyes of those who were seized by his appeals? Who followed in the 1970s the demolition works of his *"audacious hypothesis,"* according to which Europe is a civilization that has come into existence the moment the ancient Greeks discovered its ruling principle – the idea of human life controlled and enlightened by reason – and this discovery began the whole process of human history?

To let Patočka's philosophical perspective enter the public discourse he shared with his fellow-citizens – shortsighted by the current political odds – meant first of all to enlarge dramatically the horizon of the world observed; to broaden radically the narrow-minded and originally very limited scope of this discourse; to bring into it the elements of generality and transcendence. If its original point of departure was a particular historical situation that could be compared to the situation of the crew of a ship which had just been wrecked, the question to start from, according to Patočka, was the human condition as such: we can understand our own possibilities in our concrete situation *hic et nunc* only when we first become aware of the limitations we have to accept because of our human nature. And here we have to realize: *"Man is a being committed to an adventure, which, in a certain sense, cannot end well."*[475] As finite beings, on our way through life from birth to death, *"we are a ship that necessarily will be shipwrecked."*[476]

The confrontation with our own finiteness turned our attention to the realm of classical philosophy. Patočka, however, had a still more

---

[475] Ibid.
[476] Ibid.

challenging announcement to make in this context: the finiteness of human existence does not concern only individual human beings. Historical formations – including Europe as a civilization – are also finite entities, proceeding from their birth through the prime of their lives to their death. The most important aspect of the historical situation in which we now find ourselves is that the European age is over, that Europe's central position in human history has ended!

What we are experiencing in the world around us is the beginning of a new epoch in the history of mankind. Thanks to the destructive wars of the 20th century, Europe has ceased to play the hegemonic role. Her political and economic rule over the world, her supremacy based on the rationality of European civilization, especially on her modern science and technology, which guaranteed for centuries Europe's monopoly of power, its complacent and self-serving belief that *"it compassed all of mankind, that it is mankind and that all else is worthy of neglect,"*[477] all of that is now definitively over. *The rebirth of Europe* Husserl still hoped for in the late 1930s was, according to Patočka, observing the historical situation in the early 1970s, simply not going to happen. What could a contemporary Socratic philosopher do under the current historical circumstances? Patočka's response was, as I have already indicated above, clear and straightforward: to confront his *audacious hypothesis,* the origin of which he owed to Edmund Husserl, with the reality of the end of Europe and to start to examine with its help the emerging "post-European world;" to prospect at least the first stretch of the road on which mankind – no longer European – has set off, and to try to elucidate its spiritual problems, old and new.

The contemporary history of Geoffrey Barraclough

An important inspiration for Patočka's exploratory ventures into the post-European world came from the British historian Geoffrey Barraclough (1908 – 1984), the author of the then influential book *"An*

---

[477] *Plato and Europe*, p. 9

Introduction to Contemporary History" which was originally published in 1964[478] and was apparently read by Patočka sometime in the early 1970s.

First of all, what is contemporary history? *"The problems involved not only in the writing but also in the conception of contemporary history,"* wrote Barraclough in the introductory chapter,

> *have given rise, ever since 1918, to a long, contentious, and ultimately wearisome controversy. The very notion of contemporary history, it has been maintained, is a contradiction in terms. Before we can adopt a historical point of view we must stand at a certain distance from the happenings we are investigating. It is hard at all times to 'disengage' ourselves and look at the past dispassionately and with the critical eye of the historian. Is it possible at all in the case of events which bear so closely upon our own lives? It must be said immediately that I have no intention of entering into a discussion of these methodological questions.*[479]

Despite this rather lamentable declaration, however, a number of important points were made. Where does contemporary history actually begin? Barraclough pointed out that in spite of the trivial fact that it concerns primarily the most recent historical events, contemporary history cannot be delimited only by a period studied:

> *"Contemporary" is a very elastic term and to say – as is often done – that contemporary history is the history of the generation now living is an unsatisfactory definition for the simple reason that generations overlap. Furthermore, if contemporary history is regarded in this way, we are left with ever-changing boundaries and an ever-changing content, with a subject-matter that is in constant flux.*[480]

---

[478] Geoffrey Barraclough: *An Introduction to Contemporary History*. First published by C.A.Watts in 1964. The quotations in this text are from the 9th edition by Penguin Books, 1976

[479] Op.cit., pp. 14-15

[480] Op.cit., pp. 13-14

According to Barraclough, "contemporary history follows…an almost contrary procedure"[481] to "history of the traditional type."[482] Whereas the latter "starts at a given point in the past….and works systematically forward, from the chosen starting point,"[483] the point of departure of the former is the presence of a historian. It is only here that his search for the beginning of contemporary history in time and space can begin and where his first and perhaps most important task comes – "to establish its distinguishing features and its boundaries."[484]

However, it must be said immediately: Barraclough is quite cautious to think instantly about some fixed specific dates, places or events in this context. He wants first to bring to our attention and make us think through a general phenomenon bearing upon today's situation of man in the world and having the decisive influence on our perception of contemporary history. It is "the sense of living in a new period"[485] as a prevailing mood of our historical consciousness; the sense of living in a world in which the element of change seems to be much stronger than the element of permanence; the sense of living in a time which is, as Hamlet put it, "out of joint;" the sense of living in a period of transition, at a turning point of human history.

The simplest truth of our life-world is that its presence differs dramatically from what we knew and still remember as "the world of yesterday."[486] Isn't it just this difference – felt, experienced, subjectively lived through by individual men and women finding themselves in their concrete, and thus always unique, situations – that actually represents the very gist of contemporary history? What makes it different from "history of the traditional type," history following the ideal coined by the school of German historicism founded by Leopold von Ranke, the ambition of

---

[481] Op.cit, p. 17

[482] Ibid.

[483] Ibid.

[484] Ibid.

[485] Op.cit. p. 13

[486] I am borrowing this term from Stephan Zweig who used as the title for his autobiography (Stephan Zweig: *The World of Yesterday: An Autobiography*, Cassel, London, 1943.)

which is nothing other than keeping the exact record of the happenings of the past, to show the subject of its study only "wie es eigentlich gewesen?"

A seemingly textbook triviality, that history always has a double meaning (on the one hand it is what happened to men and women at a certain time at a certain place, and on the other hand it is an account of these historical happenings produced by a historian), obtains a new meaning and becomes a real problem here! If the difference between modern and contemporary (or post-modern) is to be justified by a historical analysis, the historian's role by definition must be different from the role of a traditional historian. Contemporary history – the features and boundaries of which he is first tasked to establish – needs to be his history, a history he cannot distance himself from in order to obtain necessary impartiality. He has to be willing and able to accept his role in it as its historian. In the words of Barraclough: only as long as

> *we keep our eyes alert for what is new and different...(and)...have the real gulf between the two periods fixed in our minds can we start building bridges across it.*[487]

Aren't we moving in this reasoning in a circle? At the same time, isn't it something we should rather accept than try to avoid? Isn't it true after all, that Ranke's *"idea of history as an objective and scientific study of the past 'for its own sake,'"*[488] is also an idea conditioned historically? Isn't this idea also just *"a product of the identifiable circumstances of a particular time"*[489] – European modernism which had grown to its prime in the 19th century? Isn't it true after all that, as Barraclough realized, quoting from R.W. Seton-Watson – that in spite of all the indisputable achievements and contributions of Ranke's scientism for the adequate precision and objectivity of our knowledge of historical processes, *"from the time of Thucydides onwards, much of the greatest history has been contemporary history?"*[490] Should *"the sense of living in a new period,"* which brings contemporary history into being and which turns its

---

[487] Geoffrey Barraclough, op.cit., p. 13
[488] Op.cit., p. 15
[489] Ibid.
[490] Ibid.

historians into bridge builders between the world of the past, sinking into oblivion, and the new, arriving and thus still unknown world of the future, be used as an impulse to build yet one more bridge, between contemporary history and classical philosophy? Wouldn't it be here, in their renewed communication and dialogue, that all the methodological questions Barraclough decided to leave behind – the question of periodization of history; the question of continuity or discontinuity of historical processes; the question of historical causality and explanation; the question of the historian's necessary distance from historical happenings; the question of historical truth, etc. – can and should be unfolded, examined and eventually answered?

Barraclough unfortunately remains utterly indifferent to such calls and proceeds immediately to a *tour d'horizon* of the landscape of contemporary history, which for him means the period between 1890, when Bismarck resigned his post of Chancellor of the German Empire, and 1961, when J.F. Kennedy became President of the United States. This period should be perceived, according to him, as a watershed, a great divide between the old and the new, an era of transition, when people live, finding themselves in the gap between the past and the future, in need of the bridge-building activities of contemporary historians. On the one side, there is still the Eurocentric modern world our ancestors had still been living in during the 19th century; on the other side, our world today – the beginnings of which were announcing themselves, according to Barraclough, already in the last decades of the 19th century – where not only Europe, but all the continents have started to play an increasingly significant role in the formation of its order, where non-Europeans have become equal partners with Europeans shaping a new civilization.

For sure, there is no single cause of this historical process, and this process by its very nature does not have a single historical explanation. There is no simple historical force, materialistic or idealistic, behind it, but rather multiple factors are at work, mutually influencing and eventually reinforcing each other, taking effect in their interaction.

The individual chapters of the Barraclough's book then offer their sketchy studies:

1. The on-going industrial revolution which has changed in the course of time and still is changing man's life-world;

2. The "dwarfing" of Europe – the reality of the progressing decline of Europe's population;

3. The loss of Europe's power in the world and the replacement of the European balance of power by a new form, i.e. non-Eurocentric world politics;

4. The transformation of political organization within states, the rise of mass democracy and party politics;

5. The emergence of Asian and African nations on the world scene and their revolt against European hegemony;

6. The impact of the Bolshevik revolution and the creation of the Soviet Union;

7. The reflection of the new spiritual situation of the contemporary world in art and literature.

And finally, the conclusion of Barraclough's analysis:

> *The European age... is over, and with it the predominance of the old European scale of values... The civilization of the future, whose genesis I have tried in the preceding pages to trace, is taking shape as a world civilization in which all the continents will play their part.*[491]

To sum it up: there is no doubt that as a historian Barraclough did a fine job. He certainly put his finger on something essential when he turned our attention to *"the sense of living in a new period."* He managed to collect a sufficient critical mass of relevant historical facts to support his point concerning the difference between modern and contemporary history. His concrete suggestions as far as *"its distinct features and boundaries"* – which indeed, *"begins when the problems which are actual in the world today first take visible shape"*[492] – seem to make a lot of sense from his current perspective (his book was written in the very beginning of the 1960s). Nonetheless, Patočka simply could not identify himself with Barraclough's analysis of the end of Europe and the arrival of the post-

---

[491] Op.cit.,. p. 268
[492] Op.cit., p. 20

European age, and the reasons for his criticism did not consist in his disagreement with its results, but concerned its philosophical presumptions.

The care for the soul in the post-European epoch

Patočka in principle endorsed Barraclough's conclusion that the dominant feature of contemporary history as observed in the 1960s is the transition of power (*translatio imperii*) from Europe to her non-European successors. At the same time, however, he clearly indicated, regardless of how inspired he was by Barraclough's book, that his text was not its corroboration but a *"critical follow-up;"*[493] that his philosophical approach to the problem of the post-European epoch was not to be linked, but contraposed to Barraclough's contemporary history. The question to be clarified then is: where is the line dividing these two?

Unlike Barraclough, who was fully focused on phenomena discernible in the world of politics today that would enable him to study changing power constellations, Patočka intended to explore first of all its fundamental spiritual aspects; to approach the arrival of the post-European epoch not as a matter of current "realpolitik" – as the transition from the European balance of power to a new form, i.e. non-Eurocentric world politics – but primarily as a philosophical problem. From this perspective he had to say, however, that Barraclough's attempt to clarify what is at stake in the world today did not offer a way out of the current crisis, but a blind alley:

> *His 'contemporary history'...is an approach which is perfectly pertinent for political analyses of this or that situation. It takes a stand in the middle of events and attempts to make from there a kind of sortie in different directions. This is, however, exactly the reason why this method is unable to illuminate and define the present in its essential relation to the past. The fact that the contemporary situation is post-European, that it is deeply affected by the negative element of the prefix "post," hinders its real use*

---

[493] Jan Patočka: *Evropa a doba poevropská a její duchovní problémy*. In: *Péče o duši II*, p. 85

by Barraclough. And further, "post-Europe" presupposes the idea about Europe's past, about what it was. The depth of this divide can be fully measured only when we try to grasp the contours of Europe as a whole. All of that can hardly be revealed if we stick to this method.[494]

Following are three disclaimers of Patočka:

1. Barraclough presupposes one single mankind in the sense of mankind already Europeanized;

2. Barraclough accepts uncritically, without reflection, the European periodicity of history as if it were something that belongs to history as such. He does not consider the possibility – and most probably the necessity – of the existence of the pre-European historical epoch, the European epoch (further divided into antiquity, Middle Ages and Modern Times) and the post-European epoch;

3. Barraclough is unable to delineate in a convincing manner the contemporary situation, because he does not take into consideration its starting point in the inner sense.[495]

Is Patočka entirely fair to Barraclough when making these points? Isn't he himself missing something important here? Isn't it actually a basic problem and major weakness of the philosophy of history at which he is aiming at, inspired by Husserl, that he rejects the assistance and cooperation of a contemporary historian? I will get to these questions only in the subsequent chapter of this text. Now I will focus on Patočka's own philosophical analysis.

First of all, there are three things to be distinguished, according to him, when speaking about Europe and her civilization in the moment of Europe's end and arrival of the post-European epoch, *"in order to achieve the maximum of clarity:"*[496]

1. The European principle, the principle of rational reflection, according to which all human activities,

---

[494] Op.cit, p. 96
[495] Op.cit., p. 97
[496] Op.cit., p. 83

including the activities of thinking, must be based upon insight;

2. Europe as a single historical reality, political, social and spiritual, including the ways in which this reality came into existence, the institutions created in the course of European history and also the forces working in the direction of unity even after Europe disintegrated into a group of sovereign particular organisms;

3. The European heritage, which consists of things which all heirs of Europe accept from her and what they avouch to be as a matter of course, their common possession: science, technique, the rational organization of economy and society.[497]

As far as the European principle of "logos and ratio" is concerned – whose future status might be uncertain in the long-term perspective, which, however, should at least *"shed some light on the first short lap on our journey into the emerging post-European world"* – one should always bear in mind: it doesn't put a detached "theorist" on the pedestal of European humanity, but it is essentially a Socratic principle! The fundamental presupposition to bring this principle into action is the commitment and determination of concrete men and women living in their *"poleis (cities)"* in an open historical situation to resist the personal and social disorders of their age; to strive for unity with themselves under this condition, regardless of all the uncertainties, risks, temptations and distractions of social and political life, and thus to "care for the soul."

It presupposes their clear awareness that the insight – the examined life, according to Socrates, the only way of human life worth of living – should be based upon, cannot be made from the safe distance of solitary observers of human matters, but only in their midst, within the confines of a given and historically constituted public space. It requires their recognition that this public space is inhabited not only by a few philosophers (pretending to the role of *"functionaries of mankind"*), but by the plurality of "ordinary" citizens, by a concrete social and/or political body, having on the one hand its historically developed sense for

---

[497] Op.cit., p. 84

transcendence and universality of "principles" and "values," but at the same time characterized by all its peculiarities (religion, traditions, customs, rules and practices, etc.).

If the primordial task of phenomenology is to rehabilitate the *"theoretical attitude"* of classical philosophers as opposed to the *"natural attitude"* of humans toward their *"life-world,"* this rehabilitation cannot be conceived by separating the former from the latter; as an attempt to escape from a concrete historically conditioned situation to the *domus interior* of our thought. On the contrary, the insight which is at stake here can be achieved only as a result of the direct encounter or confrontation of philosophers with their political communities. It isn't available in the form of "divine wisdom" (SOFIA TOU THEOU), but only as a kind of "human wisdom" (HÉ ANTHRÓPINÉ SOFIA),[498] the manifestation of their Socratic audacity. It is, for sure, enabled by their "private" exposures to philosophical ideas – by all *"intimations of transcendence"* (to use the wording of an important contemporary political philosopher, David Walsh[499]) they may have received – but it is what can be shared with all significant others, or at least with those who happen to be around. In this sense, it is not only their passive reflection (or speculation) of what is; it is not just a quiet meditation concerning pure being, penetrating from the surface of our human matters we are busy with in our daily existence within our life-world, into the depth of metaphysics; it is their "internal action" in the world inhabited by the plurality of others; it is their philosophical deed.

Then briefly as far as the next two points: Europe as a single historical reality and Europe as a legacy, as a heritage in the common possession of those who are emerging on the world stage in the post-European age – as something inherited by them as a matter of course, or as if, to use the Arendtian expression, *"without testament."*[500] As a single historical reality, Europe lends herself undoubtedly as a rich and complex object for historical and/or socio-political inquiry and analysis. As a

---

[498] Plato, *Apology*, 23a6

[499] Cf. David Walsh, *The Growth of the Liberal Soul,* University of Missouri Press, Columbia and London, 1997

[500] Cf. Hannah Arendt, *Preface: The Gap between Past and Future, Between Past and Future.* In: *Eight Exercises in Political Thought*, p. 3-15

heritage, Europe certainly still is and will be around in the contemporary world – in the form of products of modern European science and technology, or as the rational organization of economy and society, which also have become indispensable parts of our life-world thanks to the progress achieved by European humankind in the process of modernization.

However, what about this distinction itself, the distinction between what Europe was and what Europe still is in the post-European world, being inherited, accepted and understood by Europe's current heirs? Aren't we confronted here with something that lies at the very heart of the philosophical problem of the incipient post-European epoch? Because, who are actually Europe's "heirs"? What is the challenge they face in the moment they have received Europe's past achievements and can claim that all of that is *"their common possession?"* Here is where Patočka's philosophical reflection does begin. Much as Barraclough rightly identified the changing geopolitical constellation in the world and newly emerging patterns of distribution of power in the post-European age, according to Patočka, he still seems to be viewing this through the European lens. What we observe today is considered by Barraclough as the result of one history of one mankind that progresses in a linear motion. He wrongly believes, Patočka says, that one humankind is a historical fact and forgets easily that humankind and Europe are not one and the same thing; that there is no humankind yet, but multiple humankinds that still wait to be united, transformed into one global and genuinely post-European civilization.

> *The heirs of Europe are very heterogeneous. Some are legitimate descendants of Europe, emancipated offspring of her body that have grown in the distant areas of the world to planetary magnitude. They are the formations in which Europe is still active to a large extent and also vice versa: they have also exerted their influence – not only political, but also spiritual – on Europe. The others are essentially pre-Europeans, characterized by different degrees of pre-Europeanism. During the European age they stood aside, or they were just manipulated objects and never subjects in the sense of active players in history, proceeding thanks to*

Europe's initiative.[501]

The core of Patočka's criticism of Barraclough lies in the inability of his contemporary history to formulate and think through with sufficient clarity and precision the real in-depth problem of the contemporary phase of world history, namely the grand reawakening of pre-Europeans accompanying the arrival of the post-European age, the fact that makes the gap between the past and the future much deeper, more fundamental and thus more revolutionary than Barraclough could ever think:

> *The moral superiority, the awareness of insurmountable strength, which had spoken once in the orders of Chinese emperors, even in the moments of their most profound humiliation, turns in the times when those who up to now ruled the world, have lost their power, into a new bond for enormous consensus. What claims its rights here is the energy kept intact by isolation, untouched by barbarian rule, strengthened by humiliation, steeled thanks to its entry into the world processes during the revolution which lasted for long decades, the energy zeroing in an unknown direction; mankind speaks here, all of a sudden, from the abyss of times, which were pre-European; unconquered Egypt which persisted in isolation and waited for its moment to come back and reveal itself in its full strength. Post-European mankind speaks here from the pre-European depth, and if the language used is the one of all contemporary revolutionaries – Marxist terminology – it is only conducive to the fallacy Europe so easily succumbs to...*[502]

And Patočka's consequential questions:

> *What entitles us to expound the latest phase of the history of East Asia from the European perspective and view the phenomena such as the Chinese revolutions in 1912 and 1949, as the Europeanisation of China as matter of course, instead of at least considering – mindful of Europe's own evolution through various catastrophes to an ever more*

---

[501] Jan Patočka: *Evropa a doba poevropská a její duchovní problémy*. In: *Péče o duši II*, p. 84
[502] Op.cit., p. 94

complex new formation of the same principle – that what we might be confronted with here is, on the contrary, Sinicization of certain European cultural elements?[503]

Is Chinese Marxism a continuation of the Marxian way thinking, applied to the Chinese material, or it is rather the continuation of Chinese universalism which uses the conceptual equipment of Marx as a welcome means of how to articulate its own historical mission?[504]

This observation, however, leads Patočka to a single unambiguous conclusion which is evidently based upon Husserl's diagnosis and also his proposed remedy of the European crisis. It is certainly not Marxism or any other modern European ideology that should guide us in our efforts to understand our current situation in the world. Nor is it a postmodern relativism with its somewhat ridiculous attempts to get rid of all European metaphysics. On the contrary, if we want to prevent in the future what Husserl was warning about in the 1930s – *"the fall into a barbarian hatred of spirit"* – it is the return to the core European principle of logos and ratio, the revival of European classical philosophy, that can help us to understand our current dilemmas and illuminate our current cross-roads. As much as the situation changed between then and now, states Patočka – and the emergence of totalitarianism which brought unimaginable and unprecedented suffering to hundreds of millions of people gave us a horrible lesson, indeed, – there are basically still two alternatives, foreseen by Husserl, as far as the future of Europe's legacy in the post-European world:

Europe has put forward two ways the earth can be opened: the outward way of conquest and domination of the world, which brought about the eclipse of Europe as a single historical formation; the inward way of opening the earth in a sense of unlocking of the world, the transformation of the life-world of human existence as such. This is the course we should find, after all outside catastrophes and inner

---

[503] Op.cit., p. 96
[504] Op.cit., p. 96

confusions, and stay on it to the very end.[505]

Coming to this conclusion, Patočka, however, leaves definitively the field of contemporary history, and descends to the philosophical depth of his own point of departure. Opting unambiguously for the second way of opening the earth and unlocking of the world, instead of its conquest and domination, he allows both *"legitimate descendants of Europe"* and also the other heirs of European power who emerged in the post-European epoch, as if arriving from the pre-European age, to be busy with their own actual political problems and agendas. He invites his companions to take the path of classical philosophy, and guides them – as he did many times before – from the origins of philosophy in myth through the pre-Socratics, Democritus, Socrates, Plato and Aristotle and develops again the ever recurring theme of his thought: "the care for the soul".….

Contemporary classical philosophers versus contemporary historians

And now finally, I want to return to the questions raised in the previous chapter. Did Patočka use fully his encounter with Barraclough for the sake of his own cause? Wasn't his critical interpretation of Barraclough, basically rejecting his concept of contemporary history rather a missed opportunity?

Let us start with the restatement of what might be, or as I believe should be, a matter of implicit agreement between a contemporary classical philosopher and a contemporary historian. First, it is the prevailing mood in contemporary societies: *"the sense of living in a new period;"* the feeling that we all live in a world finding itself in a deep crisis, a world different from the *"world of yesterday,"* a world undergoing, whether we like it or not, a profound and irreversible transformation. Second, not only a contemporary historian, but a contemporary classical philosopher, too, needs to establish *"distinguishing features and boundaries"* for his analysis; to identify the events of the past, thanks to which *"the problems which are actual in the world today first take visible shape;"* to point not only to the pragmatic happenings affecting the

---

[505] Op.cit, p. 94

existing power constellations, but also, and maybe in the first place, to the events in the sphere of the mind – to the decisive *"spiritual outbursts"*[506] that took place in the course of human history – in order to clarify our contemporary situation.

It must be stated immediately, however, that it is exactly here, where their connections end. Barraclough decided, as we know, to pick the year 1890 as his *terminus a quo* – adding the last decades before the outburst of the First World War to the period to be marked out as "contemporary." Choosing on the other side 1961 as his *terminus ad quem*, he clearly delimited the subject matter of contemporary history – the period of Europe's end – separating it from the previous historical epochs, namely from the Modern era, which catapulted Europe into the role of uncontested global leader, disposed to discover and conquer other continents of the world, to "civilize" them by imposing on them the Eurocentric world order, and ruling over them without any restraints for centuries.

In contrast to that, Patočka as a contemporary classical philosopher decided to return – in order to penetrate to the starting point of our contemporary situation in the "inner sense" – to a much deeper and more distant past. In order to recall in the contemporary situation the elementary truth that Europe as a civilization has been always animated by a certain principle – Europe as "logos and ratio" – he had to move back not only horizontally, but also vertically: to the very beginning of the process set into motion in the city states of ancient Greece, where not only Western politics, but also Western philosophy was born; the process which sent Europe on her historical journey, leading from ancient times through the Middle Ages and Modernity to its end in the present times – thanks to the tragic events which happened during the 20th century.

At first sight it appears, and Patočka himself seems to be confirming this point of view, that the overlap between approaches of contemporary historians and contemporary classical philosophers is actually very small. Barraclough stays on the surface of political matters,

---

[506] I am borrowing the term from Eric Voegelin (Eric Voegelin: *Autobiographical Reflections.* In: *Autobiographical Reflections Revised Edition with a Voegelin Glossary and Cumulative I*ndex, p. 492-493

but lacks the necessary philosophical depth. Patočka looks towards the deeper spiritual strata of contemporary European political reality, but leaves the ephemeral politics of the day with its power struggles and sometimes painful concrete existential questions behind. His *consolatio philosophiae*, offered primarily to his Czechoslovak fellow-citizens whose country was at that moment stricken by the totalitarian plague and had to struggle with the morally corrupting effects of the on-going normalization, sounds, when read now more than thirty-five years later, rather like an invitation to a contemporary Platonic Academy and certainly not as an appeal to wake up the spirit of resistance in the *polis* that fell into a deep crisis and start the Socratic struggle against the general morass, decayed morals and the resulting social and political decline. Nonetheless, is there anything wrong with this assessment? Wouldn't such a conclusion be in clear contradiction to what has been said above, starting with the four general remarks about Patočka's philosophy?

In order to respond to these questions with sufficient precision and clarity and at the same time to reassess the relationship between contemporary classical philosophy and contemporary history which was laid out by Patočka himself in his criticism of Barraclough, one would need to unfold the whole field of Patočka's philosophy of history in a more comprehensive manner. We need to use as points of reference Patočka's other writing relevant to this topic. Such ambition would certainly exceed the possibilities of this text and would require the scope of a monograph. That's why I will limit myself at its very end just to one key point made by Patočka in the most famous and also the most controversial chapter of his *Heretical Essays in the Philosophy of History*, in the sixth one, called *Wars of the Twentieth Century and the Twentieth Century as War*.[507] Here, in my opinion, Patočka got closer to the sphere of contemporary history and to the questions posed by Barraclough than he thought.

Having started the project at the moment of transition from "prehistory" to European "history" and examining carefully its origins, after he analyzed in the previous (fifth) essay the nature of modern "technological civilization" – with its special relationship to Force that seemed to replace the relationship to Being dominant in the preceding

---

[507] Patočka, J, *Heretical Essays in the Philosophy of History*, p. 119-137

Christian era of European humanity – Patočka finally arrived at that event which marked the end of Europe and served as a gate for humankind to enter the post-European world. This is what he wrote in the first paragraph of the sixth essay, identifying the heart of the problem of the relationship between contemporary history and contemporary classical philosophy. This text also demonstrates effectively what was, and still is, the most significant endemic weakness of the political program with which Czechs and Slovaks entered the 20th century – under the leadership of Masaryk (the first president of their democracy created as the result of the "world revolution" of WWI):

> *The First World War provoked a whole range of explanations among us, reflecting the efforts of humans to comprehend this immense event, transcending any individual, carried out by humans and yet transcending humankind – a process in some sense cosmic. We sought to fit it into our categories, to come to terms with it as best we could – that is, basically, in terms of nineteenth century ideas.*[508]

What WWI really was necessarily escaped the attention of most of its interpreters thanks to a fact which was practically unavoidable: they were endowed with ideas coming from the past. The real meaning of this "cosmic event" – an event that was powerful enough to change not only the power constellations in this or that part of the world but the whole world – started to come out only in the light of future experiences of humankind during the 20th century. What really happened has become known gradually, only thanks to those contemporary historians capable of acting as builders of a bridge erected over the gap which opened between the past and the future, and also with the help of the ideas of contemporary classical philosophers. The thing is that only the process of understanding itself, with both contemporary historians and contemporary classical philosophers participating, can offer a clue to what is at stake in the stage of human history opened by WWI; to answer the question of what has remained after the dust settled in the European battlefields, of European hegemony, and can be offered to all Europe's heirs as her legacy.

---

[508] Op.cit. p. 119

When one reads this text now, there is no doubt that Patočka, attempting in the Sixth Heretical Essay to give his own account of WWI, indeed, managed to sketch this great drama of modern humanity with an exceptional existential urgency and all the persuasive power of his philosophical ideas. But what should not escape our attention and what is of essential importance to the argument, is the fact that Patočka didn't pay attention at all as usual historians certainly would have in this case – to the causes and results of it, but invites the reader to turn his attention to something else – to the phenomenon of the *"front experience"* – and states clearly what his main purpose is: to allow this experience to acquire the form *"which would make it a factor in history."*[509] What emerged from this experience, according to Patočka, was the most important aspect of the European heritage left to Europe's heirs – *"the solidarity of the shaken."*

Patočka's philosophical diagnosis of our contemporary situation in the 20th century is as follows: The world in the age of the end of Europe is and will be formed by "Force" unleashed thanks to the European "logos and ratio" – turned, thanks to the scientific revolutions of modernity, into science and technology. Force itself, offered by Europe to the emerging global humanity as its legacy, however, can become deadly and open the door to the invasion of a thus far unknown and unprecedented evil to our life-world, the evil that took the form of totalitarianism with all the unspeakable crimes committed in the name of ideas and ideological political projects against humanity. The only "weapon" that can be offered by a philosopher engaged in the act of resistance against this danger cannot be his idea only, but the *"solidarity of the shaken."*

> *The solidarity of the shaken is the solidarity of those who understand. Understanding, though, must in the present circumstances involve not only the basic level, that of slavery and of freedom with respect to life, but needs also to entail an understanding of the significance of science and technology, of that Force we are releasing. All the forces on whose basis alone humans can live in our time are potentially in the hands of those who so understand. The*

---

[509] Op.cit. p. 134

solidarity of the shaken can say "no" to the measures of mobilization which make the state of war permanent. It will not offer positive programs but will speak, like Socrates' daimonion, in warnings and prohibitions. It can and must create a spiritual authority, become a spiritual power that could drive the warring world to some restraint, rendering some acts and measures impossible.[510]

The interpretation of WWI with the help of ideas coming from the 19th century was commonplace not only among historians and scholars. It was also built into the foundations of the independent democratic Czechoslovak state. Its founding father and first president, the retired university professor Tomas Garrigue Masaryk, subscribing to his positivistic creed concerning the history of humankind, and endowed with his set of political ideas strongly believed that what happened in Europe and in the world in the years 1914-1918 was a *"world revolution."* Because it was essentially a progressive event, he saw in it a sufficient guarantee of our future free existence: *"The history of Europe since the 18th century,"* he wrote in a seminal essay whose main ideas were submitted to the attention of the Paris Peace Conference in 1919 and that precisely reflected the dominant and unambiguously optimistic spirit prevailing in Czechoslovak society at the time,

proves that given their democratic freedom, small peoples can gain independence. The world war was the climax of the movement begun by the French Revolution, a movement that liberated one oppressed nation after another. And now, there is a chance for a democratic Europe and for freedom and independence of all her nations.[511]

The fallacy of all these expectations, when we take into account the historical experience of Czechs, Slovaks and other Central European peoples in the 20th century, is more than obvious. And also, going back to the atmosphere of the early 1970s when Patočka was sharing his philosophical "consolatory" thoughts and ideas with his stressed Czech

---

[510] Op.cit., p. 135

[511] Masaryk, T.G., *The Making of a State.* In: *The Spirit of Thomas G. Masaryk 1850-1937*, p. 219

compatriots, we already know what was Patočka's own and final response to the current crisis; what was his personal concrete way of acceptance that the most important part of the European heritage in the post-European age is, as he phrased it, the *"solidarity of the shaken."*

Patočka finished his last philosophical seminars and lectures in December 1976 thirty-three years ago and became the spokesperson for Charter 77. He died shortly after – having been exposed to all sorts of harassment from the Communist government and a series of prolonged police interrogations. What is, then, his final philosophical message, the last word to our on-going debate about *translatio imperii*, about the end of Europe and the arrival of the post-European age? Most likely it is something that can't be contained and thus found in philosophical texts and that transcends the very activity we under normal circumstances call philosophy:

> *The solidarity of the shaken is built up in persecution and uncertainty: that is its front line, quiet, without fanfare or sensation even where this aspect of the ruling Force seeks to seize it. It does not fear being unpopular, but rather seeks it and calls out quietly, wordlessly. Humankind will not attain peace by devoting and surrendering itself to the criteria of everydayness and of its promises. All who betray this solidarity must realize that they are sustaining war and are the parasites on the sidelines who live off the blood of others. The sacrifices of the front line of the shaken powerfully support this awareness.*[512]

Epilogue

Patočka died more than thirty three year ago. If a contemporary classical philosopher were seeking the inspiration from a contemporary historian today – in a similar way as he was inspired by Barraclough in the first half of the 1970s – he would have to admit at the beginning of his "critical follow-up" of contemporary history written in 2010, that the world has changed dramatically in the meantime.

---

[512] Patočka, J, *Heretical Essays in the Philosophy of History*, p. 135

The spirit of the 1960s and 1970s, present clearly in both Barraclough's book and Patočka's philosophical reaction to it, is gone. The short 20th century – "the age of extremes," as Eric Hobsbawm characterized it[513] – ended already in 1991, after Communism collapsed in Europe in the wave of revolutions that passed throughout her Eastern part and the Soviet Union fell apart. The bipolar political system that came into being in the "old continent" as a result of the Second World War, disappeared. The new geopolitical situation emerged which can be perceived as a kind of happy end to the East Central European "tragedy."[514] The nations of this part of the world, doomed to live for more than four decades separated by the "iron curtain" from the free world of the West, were suddenly offered a tremendous opportunity to turn their dreams into reality and to "return to Europe," to which they have always belonged, at least according to their own convictions and beliefs; to open again their temporarily closed societies; to rebuild (or build anew) democratic political regimes and market economies; to become members of the same regional institutions and bodies as their Western European partners; and to start forming with them a new, this time single and unified political architecture.

From the Central European point of view, the world certainly looked rosy in the days when I was visiting South East Asia for the first time in my life, and on top of that, in an "official capacity" – something that was utterly unimaginable in the world that came to pass in 1989. The delegation of Czechoslovak Prime-Minister, Marian Čalfa, of which I was a member, visiting three states of South East Asia in 1991, was actually exactly on this kind of mission: to spread the news about the victory of democracy in the country at the "heart of Europe" over totalitarianism throughout the whole "Ekumene;"[515] to let everybody know about the new democratic countries emerging from their Communist past, returning to

---

[513] Eric Hobsbawm: *The Age Of Extremes, A History of the World 1914-1991*
[514] Milan Kundera: *The Tragedy of Central Europe*
[515] I am borrowing this term from Eric Voegelin: *"Ekumene (ecumene, oikumene). The "world" conceived as a realm that might potentially be organized through power. In antiquity, the Greek or the Roman world, a universal community."* (Eric Voegelin: *Autobiographical Reflections.* In: *Autobiographical Reflections Revised Edition with a Voegelin Glossary and Cumulative Index*, p. 157)

the arms of Western civilization, ready to be engaged in constructive cooperation with all their old and new partners, European and non-European....

History, however, was then preparing another lesson: nothing was over yet. If one could believe then that what we were experiencing, thanks to the new wave of European revolutions, was indeed its "end"[516] – the final victory of liberal ideas over all thinkable alternatives in the political realm – the years which followed helped us quickly to get rid of this illusion. A rather simplistic (and Eurocentric!) vision that the post-Communist transitions could be perceived as the central event of our times – that we were assigned the key role in this last act of the drama of mankind – turned out to be rather short-sighted and in need of substantial corrections.

The period of reunifications in Europe was soon replaced by the period of fragmentations. If the journalists' slogan "from Yalta to Malta," born in the revolutionary heyday, opened the debate that actually triggered the process that ended in the dismantling of the foundations of the existing bipolar European security system, it became more and more obvious that the destabilization of European political architecture goes much deeper; that the movement of change just started is much more radical and is going to have much bigger consequences than anyone could have thought – taking place in three concentric circles.

The post-Communist transitions (the "first circle"), undoubtedly an important and, indeed, history-making event, have had undoubtedly significant regional consequences (the "second circle"). On the one hand, the desire of East and Central Europeans to "return" as quickly as possible to "Europe" – or to be more correct, to become part of the process of European integration that started without their participation after the Second World War – forced those who were already there to accept the idea of another enlargement process; to open again the institutions the Western part of the European political architecture consisted of in the pre-revolutionary era, and launch willy-nilly a new round of reform.

---

[516] Francis Fukuyama: *The End of History and the Last Man.* Harper Collins, 1992); Timothy Burns and Littlefield Adams (eds.): *After History? Francis Fukuyama and his Critics.* Quality Paperbacks, 1994

There was, however, another serious consequence of the outburst of freedom in the region affected after World War II by the evils of Soviet Communism. Regardless of how keen the liberated nations had been to accelerate as much as possible the process of the restoration of their "natural" place within European civilization, all of them were first returned to their own national histories. They were finding themselves exposed again to all the unresolved questions concerning their identities and self-perceptions – kept as if in a kind of frozen state in the past decades. The ghosts of nationalism were unleashed in the whole region and turned out to be the biggest challenge, the first and most important test for the new East Central European – rediscovered or built from scratch – democracies.

The movement of contemporary history, however, did not stop here. Already when the post-Communist countries were taking their first steps on their homeward journey from their "Babylonian captivity" in the Soviet "evil empire," the signals started to come practically from all over the world that the emerging new order was going to be very different, indeed, from the one that had shaped the "world of yesterday." Not only the political architecture of the "old continent," is being rebuilt now, but the other continents as well have been affected profoundly by the on-going transformation (the "third circle"). Already during the 1990s, conflicts of a new type – "clashes of civilizations" in the terminology of Samuel Huntington[517] – new wars and new security threats started to emerge and have changed, step by step, the international atmosphere, the whole playing field and the mindset of both practitioners and theoreticians of international affairs. With the dramatic decrease of tensions between East and West after the end of the Cold War, the "orthogonal" dimension of global affairs was quickly gaining in importance, and started to overshadow the ideologically defined conflicts of the past: the relationships between the developed North and the developing South.

By far the strongest message that humankind is now finding itself on the threshold of a new historical era was undoubtedly sent by the barbarous attack of Al-Qaida on US soil on September 11, 2001. If 11/9

---

[517] Samuel P. Huntington: *The Clash of Civilizations and the Remaking of World Order*. Simon and Schuster, New York, 1996.

of 1989 when the Berlin Wall fell, could have been perceived as the beginning of the end of an era, a revolutionary turning point in contemporary European history, one can rightly say that 9/11 of 2001 has brought us definitely to the 21st century; changing irreversibly our perception of historical time, introducing into it the strong and, indeed, unforgettable sense of the difference between the world before it happened and the world after. And after this tragic event happened – and what happens once, can't be undone! – the process of world history has gone into a full swing again, with increasing speed – the profound and so far open-ended reconfiguration of the international system as a whole becoming the dominant and unescapable aspect of our contemporary political reality.

There is, for sure, a host of facts or happenings between 2001 and 2010 that should be at the center of attention of today's contemporary historians and considered accordingly by contemporary classical philosophers; illustrating, practically on a daily basis, that we aren't living any more in the European, but rather in the post-European age, again with a strong "sense of living in a new period;" in a world with an open historical horizon, a world whose post-modern inhabitants simply lack what their modern ancestors had and what characterized the "spirit of the time" for long centuries: the unshakeable confidence in the victorious project of Europe as *logos and ratio* and in the idea of its permanent progress.

This is, however, exactly what both Barraclough and Patočka were clearly aware of and reflected upon in their writings, and to which I have tried to bring to attention in this text. The fact that both passed away long before the revolutions of 1989, and thus couldn't foresee and comment on this development, doesn't diminish at all the value of their analyses. To sum up once again the gist of my text: In spite of sinking into the past, Patočka's concept of the "end of Europe" – a "critical follow-up" of Barraclough's version of contemporary history – lends itself as a possible point of departure for a largely absent (and that is why badly needed) philosophical reflection on the world we are living in today. Speaking up "in an act of resistance against the personal and social disorder" in which he himself was engaged in his home country during the 1970s, Patočka as a contemporary classical philosopher coming from the Socratic tradition joins the conversation concerning the complex relationships between power and spirit in today's world – as our task was defined by the organizers of the Hong Kong conference.

As I said in the beginning: I set off on a journey to Hong Kong from New York, where I live temporarily as the Permanent Representative of the Czech Republic to the United Nations, indeed a place where these relationships are being shaped and thus can be observed almost as if *in statu nascendi*. Especially with my everyday experience as a diplomat working there for a small Central European state in mind, I want to return in the conclusion of my text to the question I raised at its very beginning: didn't Patočka get it wrong with his Cartesian point of departure? Isn't it rather the confusions and open questions of the world today, and our correspondingly perplexed state of mind – and not any ideology, scientific knowledge or religious creed, where our inquiry into the *translatio imperii* (handing over of empire) in the passage from the 20th to the 21st century, should begin today?

I originally thought I had the answer but the more I was progressing with my text the more I realized that there is a kind of Socratic irony in action here. Regardless of what exactly their argument might be, both the critics of Patočka and those who would be willing to stand up in his defense would be obliged in an attempt at finding an answer to start to think. They both would have to rediscover for themselves in their particular and unique historical situation the essential Socratic question concerning TO ANTHRÓPINON AGATHON, the human good. They both would have to stand up against the danger of their own thoughtlessness, and to keep escaping their own ignorance. They both would have to become part of the "solidarity of the shaken" and join with their predecessors, who had in the past the philosophical audacity to resist confusions threatening the essentially "open" human soul.[518] They both

---

[518] The first and still the deepest articulation of what this openness means can be found in Heraclitus: PSYCHÉS PEIRATA IÓN OUK AN EXEUROIO PASAN EPIPOREUOMENOS HODON HOUTÓ BATHYN LOGON ECHEI (B 45) in Diels, Herman, *Die Fragmente der Vorsokratiker, Griechisch und Deutsch, Erster Band*, Berlin, Weidmannsche Buchhandlug, 1906, p. 68; (Traveling on every path, you will

would have to perform their own act of resistance: to seek their own place in the on-going and never-ending dialogue that crosses the boundaries of the centuries – the genuine "dialogue of mankind."

not find the boundaries of the soul by going – so deep is its measure. – English translation in: Burnet, John, *Early Greek Philosophy*, London, 1920).

Exercise 14

Totalitarianism and Authoritarianism[519]

Introduction

Totalitarianism and authoritarianism are relatively new political terms that have appeared only in the 20th century. In short, it can be said that they denote contemporary autocratic political regimes; i.e., the form of government where the ruler is endowed with and exerts absolute power. Such political regimes, however, have existed from the very beginning of human history. Therefore, the first question a student of totalitarianism and authoritarianism may like to have answered touches upon these terms themselves. How are they related to other, older concepts that were used previously and actually are still being used as a name or "label" for autocracies, such as tyranny, dictatorship, despotism, or absolutism? The answer to this question can be obtained when we look at the history of political discourse in the 20th century. Before we do that, however, let us try to clarify the generic problem underlying our theme: what are autocratic and nonautocratic forms of government?

---

[519] This text was written for *Encyclopedia of Violence, Peace, & Conflict*, 3 vols. Oxford: Elsevier, 1st Edition 1999, 2nd Edition 2008 (Martin Palouš: *Totalitarianism and Authoritarianism*. In: Lester Kurtz (Editor-in-Chief): *Encyclopedia of Violence, Peace, & Conflict*, 2nd Edition, 2008, Vol. [3], p. 2129-2142). Its version presented here is a combination of the text published in the 2nd Edition of *Encyclopedia* and its updated version to be published in the 3rd Edition, under preparation right now.

Autocratic and Nonautocratic Political Regimes

The distinction between autocratic and nonautocratic governments seems to be as old as the very concept of Western politics, which emerged with the birth of the city-states (poleis) in ancient Greece (8th-6th centuries B.C.) Until then existing states-empires often stretching over huge masses of land-might have reached quite an impressive level of technical development and sophistication. Nevertheless as far as their form of government was concerned, they were administered like great households. The imperial rulers assumed the role of guarantors of order, imposing their rule from above, and acted as mediators between immortal gods and mortal men. They exercised complete administrative, managerial, judicial, military, and fiscal authority and were free to accept or to repudiate any laws and norms governing the society of their subjects at any time. No matter how different the style and results of their administration of human affairs might have been, they all were "despots." There was no "politics" under their domination. The "hydraulic" societies of the Old World, "political systems depending on the maintenance of large-scale irrigation systems for their survival," to use the terminology of Karl Wittfogel, could be poor or rich, underdeveloped, or, on the contrary, have a highly sophisticated and differentiated structure. They nevertheless lacked that dimension of human life for which the necessary condition is the existence of public space and which cannot materialize in the company of slaves but only among one's peers: freedom.

The Aegean region inhabited by the Hellenic tribes was located on the outskirts of the world organized from the capitals of mighty ancient empires. The state power was weak and decentralized and the region was highly unstable, finding itself in permanent flux and reconfiguration. Whereas the traditional "imperialistic" approach to the problem of instability and disorder would have been conquest followed by centralization of power, the Greek solution was radically different. It was achieved gradually in a process that extended over centuries and which is known as "synoeicismos." Those who administered their affairs at home, i.e., within their own "private" households (oikiai), as autocratic despots, established the polis – a common space to deal with common matters. The rule (arche), instead of being in possession of one, was put, as Herodotus reports several occasions, into the midst of the people (es meson toi demoi). As opposed to "barbarian" autocratic rule, there was no human ruler in the Greek polis endowed with the supreme authority. Not the divine will of Emperor or Pharaoh, but the law, nomos, was accepted as the genuine source of order in the human world.

This change had a revolutionary implication: Whereas prepolitical societies are structured hierarchically – Egyptian pyramids were, indeed, the materialization of this social form – the constitution of a political community ruled by law presupposes a principally horizontal organization. Isonomia, the equality of citizens before the law, required the radical limitation of ruling power and introduced an entirely new concept of governance. Citizens should have felt free of the risk of being killed, imprisoned, enslaved, or otherwise harmed in their daily lives by the actual ruler. The elementary intention of the "rule of law" was to give them freedom and to protect them against willful tyrants and usurpers, inclined to overstep their human lot and to seek illegitimately their own personal aggrandizement. Conflicts and disputes in the polis could not be resolved by intervention of absolute power from above, but strictly within the margins of political justice. Binding decisions in all disputed matters could be taken only by the proper judiciary organ of the polis in a "due process of law." Freedom and equality of citizens in the sphere of justice meant that they had the right to submit accusations against each other and when sued they were entitled to a fair and public trial. Elected jurors who sat in judgement of their fellow citizens, swore to listen impartially to both sides and vote strictly on the issue at hand.

There is no doubt that the ancient and modern rules of law can be compared only with great caution. The ancient society and state differ substantively from their modern equivalents. Not including the fundamental difference between the Greek "pagan" understanding of human identity and the Christian idea of humanity, it is true, for instance, that in protecting the "common good" the polis enforced "public interests" by means which modern Europeans would certainly label as evident violations of individual rights. This fact, however (the historical records establish the evidence that the restrictions of the personal freedoms of citizens also did not happen often in many matters in the ancient Athenian democracy), is simply irrelevant for our current analysis. The point is that the political use of power, when the ruler acts as a "guardian of law," and the seizure of power, when he promotes his self-interests and uses his tyrannical will, were perceived by the Greeks – as they are by us – as two entirely different things. Despite the realistic observations of historians that these rulers did not always live up to their own promises and often disregarded moderation and self-control, the love of freedom and the contempt for tyrants represented undoubtedly the fundamental values underlying the Greek mentality. As we know from Herodotus, it was this distinction between the autocratic and nonautocratic forms of government, between sheer life and "good" life, in the words of Aristotle, between the slavish life of a society pursuing the goal of its self-preservation, sheltered by the superhuman activities of its divine ruler and organized as a kind of household, and the life that can be led only in the plurality of free human agents assembled in public space, acting and thinking in its light that brought the Greeks into revolt against the Persian king. And it is the same distinction, representing the core political idea of Western civilization, we want to comprehend and study when examining the contemporary phenomena of totalitarianism and authoritarianism.

The Totalitarian Search for a New Concept of the State

Totalitarianism represents a specific form of autocracy that has come into existence in the twentieth century. When this term appeared in the European political discourse for the first time in the 1920s, it was used both by its propagators and by its protagonists. It was Benito Mussolini and the theoreticians of Italian fascism (Giovanni Gentile)[520] who coined the term *totalitario* to describe a new type of state whose task was to lead Italy out of the postwar crisis. Also Antonio Gramsci, the most prominent

---

[520] The works of this Sicilian philosopher who tried to find an activist response to the postwar crisis is Italy and played a prominent role in the fascist government of Benito Mussolini are still a topic of the on-going contemporary debate (Giovanni Gentile: *Genesis and Structure of Society*. Translated by H. S. Harris. University of Illinois Press, Urbana, 1960; A. Gregor (ed.): *Origins and Doctrine of Fascism: With Selections from Other Works by Giovanni Gentile*, Transaction Publishers, 2004

Italian Marxist, presented the Communist Party as the vanguard of a "totalitarian movement."[521]

In Germany, the word *totale* was introduced into the political vocabulary by the nineteenth-century Prussian military strategist Carl von Clausewitz, who dealt with the concept of "total war." *Der Totale Krieg*, by Erich Ludendorff[522] and *Die Totale Mobilmachung,* by Ernst Jünger,[523] published in the 1930s, departed from the German interpretation of World War I and reflected an attitude that was deeply rooted in the German mind – one that viewed war not only as the use of force in the relations between states competing in the international arena, but as an eminent act of culture, a "spiritual necessity." The "turn to the total state" was seen by Karl Schmitt, the most prominent legal scholar at the time, as a necessary step in strengthening the feeble governance in the Weimar Republic which came into existence after the loss of the war.[524] Schmitt's critique of liberalism is especially important. Schmitt was not a political radical; on the contrary, he was a conservative. What he was afraid of was the decline of Western civilization he could observe during his lifetime, and especially the disorder spreading like plague within his own national society.

---

[521] Gramsci's ideas seem to also still resonate as a topic of current discussions among the left wing intellectuals, his prison notebooks being reedited, translated, reprinted and commented on. (Antonio Gramsci: (2018). *Selections From The Prison Notebooks ,* Paperback; Adamson, W. (2014). *Hegemony and Revolution: Antonio Gramsci's Political and Cultural Theory,* Paperback, 2018
(Gramsci's writing also available at people.duke.edu/~dainotto/Texts/Gramsci Reader.pdf)
What is symptomatic here, is a tendency to absolve Gramsci from totalitarian tendencies in his thought – by translating his word *totalitario* into English not as totalitarian, but "all-encompassing" (Cf. Sotiris, P. (2020). *A Philosophy for Communism: Rethinking Althusser,* Paperback
(https://books.google.com/books?id=3XvnDwAAQBAJ&pg=PA324&lpg=PA324& dq=Gramsci+totalitario&source=bl&ots=u5Zciul0yF&sig=ACfU3U316qHuZBXll1 OadnvrHxG-N4f4nQ&hl=en&sa=X&ved=2ahUKEwi6l- Tni_rpAhU5kHIEHUPRBi0Q6AEwAHoECAkQAQ#v=onepage&q=Gramsci%20to talitario&f=false)
[522] Erich Ludendorff: *Der totale Krieg*, München, Ludendorffs Verlag, g.m.b.h., 1935
[523] Ernst Jünger: *Die totale Mobilmachung*, in: *Krieg und Krieger.* Hg. von Ernst Jünger, Junker und Dünnhaupt, Berlin 1930, p. 9–30.
[524] See, for instance Carl Schmitt: *The Crisis of Parliamentary Democracy.* Translated by E. Kennedy. MIT Press, 1988; Carl Schmitt: *The Concept of the Political.* Translated by George Schwab, The University of Chicago Press, Chicago, 2008.

Schmitt's remedy for the political crisis of the Weimar Republic was to revive the use of strong unifying authority through an authoritarian rather than Nazi (national socialist) state.

The slogan of Mussolini, *"All within the state, none outside the state, none against the state,"* demonstrates clearly what totalitarians disliked in liberalism. It was "too little state" and too much privatization of life in liberal "bourgeois" society and its essentially negative concept of freedom as freedom "from" politics. It was its conformism, mediocrity, and easiness. It was its alienation from the public sphere which, they believed, ought to be again animated by the ancient Roman or traditional Germanic spirit. It was the fact that under the conditions of "mass society" emerging as a final result of the process of modernization, the form of government that was almost automatically associated with the general idea of progress – liberal democracy – was sinking into a deep crisis.

The Intellectual Resistance of the 1930s and 1940s

What was true nature of regimes emerging in Italy, Germany, and the Soviet Union as a response to the European spiritual crisis, became clear pretty soon. Totalitarianism, materialized in the actions of bureaucratic machineries of Nazi, Fascist, or Bolshevik states, made a large number of European public intellectuals state enemies and forced them to test their ideas against harsh reality. The stream of emigrants, especially from Germany, appeared first in many European cities and then later in the United States. Prominent philosophers, scientists, and journalists opened a kind of intellectual front against Nazism, Fascism, and Bolshevism and began their struggle for freedom by theorizing about totalitarianism and authoritarianism, mostly from either a liberal or Marxist point of view. Karl Manheim, Ludwig von Mises, Friedrich Hayek, Herbert Marcuse, Mark Horkheimer, Franz Neumann, Sigmund Neumann, Victor Serge, Emil Lederer, Raymond Aron, Franz Borkenau, Ernst Fraenkel, Herman Rauschnigg, Rudolf Hilferding, Eric Voegelin, Karl Popper, and many others, including Leon Trotsky, tried to cope with totalitarian phenomena in their writings and to formulate the principles of intellectual resistance. Marcuse's *The Struggle Against Liberalism in the*

Totalitarian View of the State,[525] or Sigmund Neumann's *Permanent Revolution: Totalitarianism in the Age of International Civil War*[526] are definitely classics in this field.

Of course, there were not only theoreticians, but also many free-minded writers among them – for instance, Arthur Koestler,[527] George Orwell[528] or Albert Camus,[529] to name just the most prominent ones. However, as artists they were not just taking political positions in their struggle against the deadly threat to Western civilization. As Geoffrey Isaac observed, "a new literary form" was invented on this occasion.

> *One development of the last ten years has been the appearance of the "political book," a sort of enlarged pamphlet combining history with political criticism*[530]

---

[525] Herbert Marcuse: *The Struggle Against Liberalism in the Totalitarian View of the State Negations: Essays* in: *Critical Theory*; with translations from the German by Jeremy J. Shapiro (London: Penguin, 1968.

[526] Sigmund Neumann: *Permanent Revolution: Totalitarianism in the Age of International Civil War*, London, Dunmow, Pall Mall Press, 1965

[527] Arthur Koestler (1905 –1983) was a British writer of Jewish/Hungarian origin. Between 1931 and 1938 he was a member of the Communist Party of Germany. Having had his insider's experience with totalitarianism he wrote *Darkness at Noon*, the novel that opened the eyes of many in the West and gained him world acclaim.

[528] George Orwell (pen name of Eric Arthur Blair, 1903-1950) was a British writer. Born in India and working for a couple of years as an imperial police officer in Burma, he had an opportunity to experience British colonialism in action. Back in his homeland, he became an inquisitive and sharp observer of the social and political condition of European societies in the 1920s and the 1930s. Considering himself a democratic socialist he took part in the Spanish Civil War on the Republican side and articulated his experience in his Homage to Catalonia (1938). Later he became a harsh critic of totalitarianism and published two books that have made him famous till today: the allegorical novella Animal Farm (1945) and the dystopian novel Nineteen Eighty-Four (1949).

[529] Albert Camus (1913 – 1960) was a French philosopher, author, and journalist of Algerian descent, the winner of the Nobel Prize in Literature in 1957. He took part in the French Resistance, serving as editor-in-chief of its underground newspaper *Combat*. After the war he became one of the most recognized French left-wing intellectuals who at the same time opposed Soviet-style totalitarianism. The most important novels of Camus articulating his anti-totalitarian stance are: *The Stranger* (1942), *The Plague* (1947) ,*The Fall* (1956).

[530] Jeffrey C. Isaac: *Arendt, Camus and Modern Rebellion*. Yale University Press, New Haven & London, 1992, p. 42

In short, totalitarianism was not just condemned by these writers, but served them also as a new and shocking source of their inspiration. The totalitarian world was phantasmagoric, it was a living nightmare, but still it *"could not be written off as unrealizable."*[531] It *"seemed literally to defy comprehension; it was confusing not only to its protagonists but to its victims and potential victims as well."*[532]

A disturbing question, indeed – raised and developed later by Hannah Arendt – was coming back again and again: What is the nature of this monstrosity? How can anything like it come into existence in the human world? Who are those who were able to come up with the idea of the "Final Solution?" What state of the human mind can bring into existence and keep in operation a bureaucratically organized and technologically advanced system of death factories?

Theorizing Totalitarianism during the Cold War

The "classic" period in the history of totalitarianism started with the conference held by the American Academy of Arts and Sciences in Boston in March of 1953. Organized by Carl J. Friedrich, who later published a seminal work in the research of the totalitarian phenomenon with Zbigniew Brzezinski *Totalitarian Dictatorships and Autocracy,*[533] and opened by a lecture of George Kennan, the conference made the first step toward a comprehensive definition of totalitarianism based on the presupposition that *"totalitarian regimes constitute a relatively novel species in the long history of autocratic government."*[534]

The political situation in the world was obviously different at that moment from the times when European intellectuals had been offered the first opportunity to reflect on their experience with the totalitarian regimes. World War II ended in Europe by the unconditional surrender of Nazi Germany on 8 May 1945. Only a few years later, however, the victorious

---

[531] op. cit. p. 43

[532] Ibid. p. 44

[533] Zbigniew Brzezinski and Carl Friedrich: *Totalitarian Dictatorship and Autocracy.* Frederick A. Praeger, New York, 1967

[534] Carl Friedrich (ed..): *Totalitarianism. Proceedings of a conference held at the American Academy of Sciences, March 1953,* Harvard University Press, 1954

coalition broke up and Europe was again torn apart by a new "ideological" conflict between the liberal West and the Communist East. The "old" continent lost its supremacy in world affairs and was divided into two "antagonistic" camps led by two uncontested nuclear superpowers after the war, the United States and the Soviet Union.

The Western perspective was clear enough: one form of totalitarianism was defeated, but the second one became much stronger than ever before. The Fulton speech of Churchill in March 1946[535] and the Long Telegram of George Kennan from Moscow to the State Department in the same year, followed by the famous "X" article *The Sources of Soviet Conduct* published in Foreign Affairs in the summer of 1947,[536] and by the declaration of a new foreign political doctrine by President Truman in the same year,[537] represented unmistakable signs that the times were, indeed, changing. Within a few years, the Cold War was in full swing. This has to be borne in mind when looking at all attempts, especially those in the 1950s, at a new conceptualization of twentieth-century autocracy.

First of all it was argued by Friedrich and Brzezinski that

> *totalitarian dictatorship is historically unique and sui generis...that fascist and Communist totalitarian dictatorships are basically alike, or at any rate more nearly like each other than like any other system of government, including earlier forms of autocracy.*[538]

Totalitarian dictatorship according to them could be characterized by six basic traits:

> *1. an official ideology, consisting of an official body of doctrine covering all vital aspects of man's existence, to which everyone living in that society is supposed to adhere, at least passively; this ideology is characteristically focused and projected toward a perfect final state of mankind, that is, it contains a chiliastic claim, based upon a radical rejection of the existing society and conquest of the world*

---

[535]   https://winstonchurchill.org/resources/speeches/1946-1963-elder-statesman/the-sinews-of-peace/
[536] X: *The Sources of Soviet Conduct, Foreign Affairs*, 25 (4): 566–582
[537] https://history.state.gov/milestones/1945-1952/truman-doctrine
[538] Zbigniew Brzezinski and Carl Friedrich: *Totalitarian Dictatorship and Autocracy*

for the new one;

2. a single mass party led typically by one man, the "dictator," and consisting of a relatively small percentage of the total population (up to 10%) of men and women – a hard core of them passionately and unquestioningly dedicated to the ideology and prepared to assist in every way in promoting its general acceptance – such a party being hierarchically, oligarchically organized and typically either superior to, or completely intertwined with the bureaucratic government organization;

3. a system of terroristic police control, supporting but also supervising the party for its leaders, and characteristically directed not only against demonstrable "enemies" of the regime, but against arbitrarily selected classes of the population; the terror of the secret police systematically exploiting modern science, and especially scientific psychology;

4. a technically conditioned near-complete monopoly of control, in the hands of the party and its subservient cadres, of all means of effective mass communication, such as the press, radio, and motion pictures;

5. a similarly technologically conditioned near-complete monopoly of control (in the same hands) of all means of effective armed combat; and

6. a central control and direction of the entire economy through the bureaucratic coordination of its formerly independent corporate entities, typically including most other associations and group activities.[539]

This definition can still serve as a point of departure for any research of totalitarian phenomena. Nevertheless, it must be noted that the expectations of those whose aim was to use the term totalitarianism in various fields of value-free scientific research remained unfulfilled. The problem was methodological: As the proceedings of the above-mentioned Boston conference demonstrate, what characterized this gathering of

---

[539] Ibid.

prominent personalities was an atmosphere of mobilization. The Cold War context set the tone of the totalitarianism debate and created around it, *"the mood of political crisis and ideological urgency."*[540]

Totalitarianism, which now took the shape of Soviet Communism, was perceived not so much as an "academic" problem – as one would expect from a conference organized by American Academy of Arts and Sciences – but rather represented a serious challenge to Western freedom. Its clarification became, in Friedrich's words, *"the central problem of our time."*[541] Or as George Kennan put it in the first sentences of his opening lecture:

> *We have come together to discuss a phenomenon of our time that has brought the deepest possible misery to untold millions of our contemporaries…(which) has demeaned humanity in its own sight, attacked man's confidence in himself, made him realize that he can be his own most terrible and dangerous enemy, more bestial that the beasts, more cruel than nature.*[542]

Did George Kennan speak here as a scholar, or rather as an official herald of American postwar realism in international affairs? What was more important for him, the shock, supported by the well-proven empirical evidence that totalitarian dictatorships are materialized evil, transforming the human world into hell? Or the fact that such regimes were regarded by the State Department as enemies of the United States?

The idea that the Soviet Empire should be "contained" offered a clear direction to US foreign policy in the age of the atomic bomb. It should not be overlooked, however, that as far as the nature of totalitarianism itself is concerned, this perspective happened to be the root cause of many serious confusions.

The largest among them concerns the distinction between totalitarianism and authoritarianism that gained currency in the political

---

[540] Carl Friedrich (ed.): *Totalitarianism. Proceedings of a conference held at the American Academy of Sciences, March 1953.* Introduction by Carl Friedrich, Harvard University Press, 1954
[541] Op. cit.
[542] Ibid.

vocabulary of the Cold War period, misleading not only those who studied contemporary autocratic forms of government academically, but also those who had to use these concepts in practice. It was undoubtedly true that there were very remarkable differences between the military dictatorships in Latin America or Southeast Asia (which were labeled as authoritarian) and the totalitarian form of government in power not only in Moscow, but all-over the Soviet Empire. Nevertheless, the fact that the former were friends and the latter foes of the United States could be accepted as sufficient reason only by those who were used to looking at the realm of international politics through the lens of American "national interests;" who most probably rightly argued that the United States should not hesitate to protect freedom by intervening militarily in the American "zone of influence" and to head off the Communist world revolution by all available means. However, as far as the debate on totalitarianism is concerned, this perspective was simply too narrow and too determined by the existing geopolitical situation.

Retreat from Totalitarianism: The Attempts to Deconstruct the Concept in the 1960s

The process of gradual change in the Soviet Union and in the other socialist countries in eastern Europe, which started in the middle of the 1950s and culminated at the end of the 1960s, still bears a name that explains how strongly the Communist variety of totalitarianism was connected with the chief dictator: de-Stalinization. Joseph Stalin died in 1953. Nikita Khrushchev delivered his famous secret speech, denouncing the "cult of personality" of the previous adored leader and disclosing the horrible crimes of Stalin's regime, in 1956 to the 20th CPSU Congress. No matter whether Khrushchev's proclaimed goal to return from Stalinism to true Leninism was meant sincerely and regardless of the principle question whether any reform of Communism was only a vain effort and an attempt to "square the circle," the political situation in Europe at the end of the 1960s was remarkably different from the previous decade.

Thanks to Khrushchev and other reformers, Communism lost its cruel, numb, but at the same time unfathomable face and acquired at least some human qualities. The whole world was observing with a kind of relief and with hope that what was going on in the socialist camp under the label of de-Stalinization was showing unmistakable signs of being capable of at least some positive developments. For sure, there were crises within the system (the Hungarian Revolution of 1956) or crises between superpowers (the Cuban missile crisis of 1962, which brought the world closer to nuclear conflict than ever before). Nevertheless, all these problems were overcome in the end, free from the pure totalitarianism known in the Stalin era. In spite of various setbacks, the reformist spirit seemed to be prevailing, even gaining, step by step, new ground. The ideological confrontation between East and West was being reformulated. If at the outset of the Cold War East-West relations were characterized by an uncompromising Manichean struggle between life-and-death enemies, the relaxed 1960s gave birth to a much more benign concept of "peaceful coexistence of the countries with different social systems."

The "thaw" in the Eastern bloc contributed positively to the stabilization of the international situation. The Cold War was not over, but no one could doubt that it entered a new, qualitatively different phase. The tension declined and in retrospect, the 1950s could be easily perceived as a "nightmare." The scene cleared up and in daylight, everything that had come into existence in the darkness began to reveal its ghostly nature. This shift was also found in political terminology and it is not at all surprising that under the new circumstances, the classic definition of totalitarianism came under fire – in the United States from those who intended to clarify the content and validity of the term "totalitarianism" from the point of view of behavioral social and political sciences. What behaviorists disliked, when they tried to find its place in the context of their research, was that they heard in it – as Michael Curtis put it – too many *emotive overtones.* [544] According to these critics, the term "totalitarianism" should be tested as an analytical toot to be used in the process of causal explanations and for that purpose it had to be, above all, depoliticized. The "counter-ideological uses of totalitarianism" could not guarantee that this

---

[544] Michael Curtis: *Retreat from Totalitarianism*, in: Carl Friedrich, Michael Curtis, Benjamin Barber (eds.): *Totalitarianism in Perspective: Three Views.* Praeger Publishers, New York, Washington, London 1969, p. 53

term was justified from the point of view of value-free, neutral, and objective science; that there is at all such a social and political reality.

A scientific term, it was argued, can be useful only if it is sufficiently general to be applied to a number of cases. As a matter of fact, all available definitions of totalitarianism-sometimes reflecting the reality of Hitler's regime in Germany, sometimes corresponding to the Stalinist period of Soviet Communism – were strangely at odds with this requirement. Those who suggested that societies formed by these regimes should be studied as examples of a new social "species," of a new type of society characterized by a number of distinctive traits, simply did not respect well-established scientific methodology. Such an approach to social phenomena involved too much categorization, too much essentialism, and an excessive concern with the uniqueness of extremist criminal regimes which in their pure form existed only for a very limited period of time (the Nazi regime in Germany became truly totalitarian only after 1939 and Stalin's regime in the Soviet Union corresponded to the above suggested definition in the period of the "great purges" in the second half of the 1930s and again after World War II until Stalin's death in 1953). The conclusion was clear: the concept of totalitarianism was of very limited analytical or heuristic value. The best thing would be to "retreat from it," to not use it at all and let it disappear from the political lexicon.

The second type of criticism came from those who were convinced that what was at stake in the ongoing totalitarianism debate concerned, above all, the realm of prescriptive political ideas. The most important example here was the German case. For in Germany, for obvious reasons, it was more difficult than anywhere else, or rather impossible, to separate social and political sciences from politics and to keep the scientific discourse neutral and value-free in the Weberian sense. Throughout the postwar period, the German debate concerning the nature of contemporary autocratic regimes took place in the context of denazification. Germans, burdened with their own totalitarian past, simply could not identify themselves with the American point of view. No doubt, it was the American Marshall Plan of postwar reconstruction of Europe that helped to overcome the gap which the war opened between Germany and all other Europeans. No doubt, it was the pro-American foreign policy of the first chancellor of the post-Nazi German state Konrad Adenauer that helped to build a bridge from the totalitarian past toward a "democratic" future and enabled Germany to rise from the ashes and to overcome the postwar marasmus and disorder. Nevertheless, as the heated polemics that burst out at the beginning of the 1960s triggered by the scandalous discoveries of the Nazi pasts of many prominent German politicians clearly demonstrated, neither American money invested in future European stability nor Adenauer's awareness of the importance of close transatlantic cooperation could solve the central problems of the newly democratic and newly liberal German political community: how to achieve a real reconciliation; how to restore the shattered spiritual balance; and how to heal the German mind, which seemed still disturbed by what had happened during the war despite all indisputable signs of economic growth and political recovery.

While the dominant feature of the American perception of totalitarianism was that it was Communism that had to be contained now and kept out of the free world, the German focus was clearly on the home front. The arguments that appeared first in the 1960s, however, indicate that real soul-searching was extremely difficult in the existing climate of ideas. The thaw in the East did not so much provoke questions concerning the future of the divided European continent, but inspired the left-wing Western European intelligentsia to take up sometimes very militant anti-American attitudes and to condemn, as had happened many times before, the antihuman traits of world capitalism.

The renaissance of the left in the 1960s brought another resolute attack against those who used the term "totalitarianism." It was criticized as an instrument of the Cold War, serving, above all, the interests of American hegemonic policy. Especially in Germany, it could be unmasked as part and parcel of a self-righteous strategy of those who wanted to divert attention away from their own disgraceful Nazi past and make a new career in the democratic regime. If the principal argument of Friedrich and Brzezinski was that *"totalitarian regimes constitute a relatively novel species,"* the left-wing opponents of the term were suggesting its deconstruction, that is, the return to the traditional, ideological antagonism and to the terms "Fascism" and "Communism."

Whereas the reforms in the East demonstrated dynamism and the still-unexploited potential of the socialist movement, right-wing extremism had to be condemned by all "progressive" people in the world – not so much on moral grounds but because history itself was following the path of progress. With this move, however, the debate on contemporary autocracies came, as Karl Bracher, who opposed the left-wing criticism of totalitarianism, pointed out, full circle.[545]

The arguments that were based on the differences between Fascist and Communist political ideas and socioeconomic concepts – rather than on similarities between the "forms of government" and social realities produced by Communist and Fascist political praxis – were unpleasantly reminiscent of the critique of Western liberalism in the 1920s and 1930s.

Bracher's opposition to the left-wing deconstruction of the term "totalitarianism" is worth mentioning. To dump this term *is historically wrong, because this move simply fails to consider the long history of the totalitarianism debate started in 1922 and 1933.* The criticism of the Cold War uses of the term – which had its champions still in the 1970s and 1980s, for instance, Jean Kirckpatrick[546] – might be justified. What was not acceptable for Bracher – and what makes this strategy to "solve" the problem more than dubious from any reasonable point of view – was the ideological bias of those who presented it. What seemed to be completely forgotten by the left-wing critics was the original meaning of the term: that what is at stake here is the struggle of European civilization in the twentieth century for its freedom; that it is vital in this struggle to be able to distinguish, under the conditions of the contemporary world, between dictatorship and democracy.

Bracher agreed with Friedrich and Brzezinski and other supporters of the classic definition that the structural similarities are more important than the ideological differences between left-wing and right-wing totalitarian governments. On the other hand, he was neither on the side of those who were actively engaged in Cold War international politics and

---

[545] Karl D. Bracher: Totalitarismus und Faschismus. Eine Wissenschaftliche und Politische Begriffkontroverse (Kolloqioum im Institut für Zeitgeschichte am 24. November 1978, Munchen, Wien-Oldenbourg, 1980

[546] Jean Kirkpatrick: *Dictatorships and Double Standards*, Harper, New York, 1980

were striving to "contain" the archenemy, nor did he subscribe to any value-free, neutral scientific methodology. As a German, he was quite aware of the political dimension of the totalitarian problem. On the other hand – and again as a German, we may add – he was also aware that to understand totalitarianism requires a different type of knowledge. What must be looked for in the totalitarian debate is a knowledge that "knows" how to cope with the generic problem of autocratic versus nonautocratic forms of government in our times and that is able to see the general dilemma our civilization was confronted with, from the very beginning, in the concrete social and political, that is, historical context we are part of. However, it is this context that has to be properly reflected in the first place. The totalitarianism debate itself represented a serious problem for Bracher, a problem that by its nature, as we will see in the final section of this article, opens the door not only to the core problem of European politics, but also of European philosophy. What matters is not only the term itself, but – to repeat once more Bracher's argument – how it was used under the given concrete circumstances and what set in motion its own history.

From Revolutionary Terror to the Asthma of Normalization: Totalitarianism Lived and Analyzed by Václav Havel

The political developments of the "golden sixties" when the concept of totalitarianism practically disappeared from the political vocabulary reached their peak in the revolutionary year 1968. The student protest movements sweeping throughout the West, and the Prague Spring – an unprecedented attempt within the socialist camp to open the closed Communist system and to endow it with a "human face" – were monuments of the spirit of the times, but at the same time marked the end of an era.

The prevailing climate of ideas in the 1970s was different. The students of the French, German, or American universities stopped making revolution and returned to their classrooms. The reformist spirit of the 1960s was replaced by a more traditional version of international politics – conceived as an interplay of security and "national" interests, first of all, of the two leading superpowers whose competition for influence and control over world affairs was moderated by their shared concern for avoiding nuclear conflict and for keeping global balance and stability.

What on the Western side of the Iron Curtain could be registered as just a shift of paradigm, was perceived by the liberal inhabitants of the East as a catastrophe. Almost one hundred thousand people fled from Czechoslovakia after the Soviet led invasion on 21 August 1968, convinced that there was no future for them in that part of the world. The icy blow of "Realpolitik," the fact that the Soviet step was in fact approved by Washington as an operation within the confines of the Soviet "zone of influence," gave to the new emigrants a lesson that was later best articulated by Milan Kundera, a Czech writer, living from 1975 in exile in France, as a Central European "tragedy." Central Europe, wrote Kundera,

> *is a family of small nations (which) has its own vision of the world, a vision based on a deep distrust of history. History, that goddess of Hegel and Marx, that incarnation of reason that judges and arbitrates our fate, is the history of conquerors. The peoples of Central Europe are not conquerors. They cannot be separated from European history; they cannot exist outside of it; but they represent the wrong side of history; they are its victims and outsiders.*[547]

With due respect to Kundera and all others who solved this Central European problem in their individual lives by escaping to the West, it was not in the circles of emigrés, but among those who stayed at home – and this is definitely different from the situation in the 1930s and 1940s – that important arguments emerged which significantly enriched the ongoing totalitarian debate.

There are many individuals in all countries behind the Iron Curtain that should be mentioned in this context. Only one of them will be mentioned here: a Czech playwright and later the president of the newly liberated, post-Communist state, Václav Havel.

Havel's reflections on totalitarianism noted the remarkable difference between the *"revolutionary ethos and terror"* of the Stalinist

---

[547] Kundera, M: *The tragedy of Central Europe, The New York Review of Books.* April 26, 1984,

1950s and the depressive, deadening atmosphere – *"dull inertia, pretext-ridden caution, bureaucratic anonymity, and mindless, stereotypical behavior"*[548] – so typical of the era of "normalization" that spread throughout Czechoslovakian society after the defeat of the "counterrevolution" in 1968.

In its original version, the defining feature of a totalitarian regime was the combination of idealistic hopes for a better world with the use of brute force and physical violence:

> *In the fifties there were enormous concentration camps in Czechoslovakia filled with tens of thousands of innocent people. At the same time, building sites were swarming with tens of thousands of young enthusiasts of the new faith singing songs of socialist construction. There were tortures and executions, dramatic flights across borders, conspiracies, and at the same time, panegyrics were being written to the chief dictator.*[549]

The society that was essentially liberal and "open" before the Second World War was forcibly "closed" after the Communist constitutional *coup d'état* in February 1948. The building of socialism was accompanied by the ruthless and oppressive policies of the Communist Party which seized the monopoly of power and quickly formed a totalitarian political regime. It must be noted, however, that it was not only the immoderate lust for power of the new rulers combined with the blind conviction and commitment of the *"enthusiasts of the new faith"* that sent Czechoslovakian democracy into the abyss. The Czechoslovakian Communists certainly had their share in it, but the real "historical force" behind their success was the Soviet Union, whose territorial and political gains had to be recognized in postwar Europe and whose emerging global influence was reflected in the American policy of "containment."

As Havel noticed, what did not disappear entirely in the 1950s and what immediately took on more visible and socially more significant forms after the worst excesses of Stalinism were gone, was the hope for a

---

[548] Václav Havel: *Stories and Totalitarianism.* In: *Open Letters, Selected Writings 1965-1990,* p. 331
[549] Ibid.

better future. When people began first to feel and then later to perceive the signs of a dawning new day, there appeared the dimension of the human condition that is able, despite all terrors, tragedies, and deaths to impart meaning to human life: the faith that even the painful experiences with Communism could be healed and that society could somehow return to the state in which it had existed in its pre-totalitarian past. It was this attitude that was helping people to see the light at the end of the tunnel, even when there was no real reason to believe that the Communist regime had to collapse quickly and when it turned out that the broadly spread speculations concerning possible American military interventions against Communism was a sheer illusion. And it was this state of mind that nourished the gradual change in the social atmosphere of the 1960s; that made the vast majority of Czechs and Slovaks believe, during the Prague Spring of 1968 and even still when they saw Soviet tanks in the streets in August of that year, that socialism – whatever this word meant – could be reformed after all; that Central Europeans were not doomed to remain forever – as Kundera said in 1984 – the "victims and outsiders" of European history.

The 1970s meant the end of this hope. The bipolar political architecture of the Cold War turned out to be a much stronger element in shaping her destiny than the desire of the Central Europeans to actively participate in its creation. The period of "normalization" in Czechoslovakia started not at the moment of Soviet occupation, but when the huge majority of Czechs and Slovaks simply gave up and conformed to their historical lot – by either willingly cooperating with a "rehashed" ruling power or retreating to the private spheres of their lives and succumbing to passivity. The spirit of resistance of 1968 was taken over in 1969 by the "captive mind," named and analyzed by another outstanding Central European, the Polish poet Czeslaw Milosz.[550] The

---

[550] Czesław Miłosz (1911 - 2004) was a Polish-American poet, prose writer, translator, and diplomat. In 1980 he won the Nobel Prize in Literature. Miłosz survived the German occupation of Warsaw during World War II and became a cultural attaché for the Polish government during the postwar period. When the Communist authorities threatened his safety, he defected to France and ultimately chose exile in the United States, where he became a professor at the University of California, Berkeley. His poetry—particularly about his wartime experience – and his appraisal of Stalinism in

regime that emerged under the domination of this "captive mind" in Czechoslovakia could serve, as Václav Havel pointed out in 1986, *"as a textbook illustration of how an advanced or late totalitarian system works:"*[551]

> *(It) depends on manipulatory devices so refined, complex, and powerful that it no longer needs murderers and victims. Even less does it need fiery Utopia builders spreading discontent with dreams of a better future. The epithet "Real Socialism," which this era has coined to describe itself, points a finger at those for whom it has no room: the dreamers.*[552]

The totalitarian form of government in Czechoslovakia dramatically changed its style and external manifestations. It *"set itself a single aim: self-preservation."*[553] Instead of using the straightforward ruthless policies of its early days, the "normalization" regime was created by unprincipled opportunists whose only desire was to keep themselves in power. Except for a small group of counterrevolutionaries, Czechs and Slovaks were offered a possibility to preserve their own well-being and their relatively safe and undisturbed existence. The ticket one had to buy to get on board was cheap, and the vast majority was easily persuaded. No class origin, no conviction, no commitment, not even difficult moral choices were required; just the formal agreement with the Soviet occupation and tacit consent with the basic goals of "normalization;" the readiness to give up all ideals and be flexible enough to adapt oneself to the requirements of the new situation.

The ruling power simply offered to the ruled a bizarre "social contract:" a relatively undisturbed private life and even some personal benefits in exchange for loyalty to the regime, willingness to accept its concept of politics, and understanding what the nature and role of public space is in "socialist" society.

---

a prose book, *The Captive Mind,* brought him renown as a leading *émigré* artist and intellectual. (https://en.wikipedia.org/wiki/ Czesław_Miłosz)

[551] Václav Havel: *Stories and Totalitarianism.* In: *Open Letters, Selected Writings 1965-1990,* p. 331

[552] Op.cit, p. 332

[553] Op.cit. p. 331

The "lessons of the years of crisis"[554] were formulated in the language of the old revolutionary slogans, but its purpose and messaging were entirely different:

1. Any effort to open the socialist system and to reform its form of government was considered dangerous and leading to destabilization, intolerable to the ruling forces of this world.

2. Only fools and martyrs could act against this fundamental and invincible "law" of human history.

3. In the era of Real Socialism, politics should be understood not as a sphere of human responsibility and agency, but as a kind of ritual. Its principal aim was to protect society from any change – to keep it in the state in which it already was.

4. It was perfectly acceptable that, under the given circumstances, not everybody had the ambition, or the stomach, to become a "politician." In that case he was only advised to mind his own business and to stay away from politics.

There is no doubt that this "reinterpretation" of Communist ideals made life more bearable for the enslaved peoples. A society where such an "advanced" totalitarian system came into being was not any more decimated by the revolutionary "reigns of terror and virtue." But it did not mean – and that is the principal message of Václav Havel – that the inhabitants of the world of "Real Socialism" were safe from the destructive effects of "totalitarian radiation:"

> *It is not true that Czechoslovakia is free of warfare and murder. The war and killing assume a different form: they have been shifted from the daylight of observable public events, to the twilight of unobservable inner destruction. It would seem that the absolute, "classical" death of which one reads in stories (and which for all the terrors it holds is still mysteriously able to impart meaning to human life) has*

---

[554] The Lessons of the Years of Crisis was a document of Czechoslovak Communist Party adopted in 1969 as a blueprint for the policies of "normalization" after the counter-revolutionary attempt of the "Prague Spring" to undermine the very foundations of socialism failed and "order" was restored (see H.G. Skilling, *Czechoslovakia's Interrupted Revolution,* Center for Russian and East European Studies, University of Toronto, 1976)

been replaced here by another kind of death: the slow, secretive, bloodless, never-quite-absolute, yet horrifyingly ever-present death of non-action, non-story, non-life and non-time; the collectively deadening, or more precisely, anaesthetizing, process of social and historical nihilization. This nihilization annuls death as such, and thus annuls life as such: the life of an individual becomes the dull and uniform functioning of a component in a large machine, and his death is merely something that puts him out of commission.[555]

Havel's observations point to the very essence of totalitarian enslavement – to its destructive effect on human existence as such, on the capacity of each individual human being to think and act and to accept primordial responsibility for its life. It illustrates the closed totalitarian mind in action, endless conformism, and hopeless thoughtlessness of its protagonists. At the same time, it articulates the reasoning behind the dissident revolt against this system that spread all around Central Europe in the late 1970s and 1980s. It testifies to human confrontation with "nothingness" and social amnesia, but also to the essential uncertainty and vulnerability that accompanied the whole dissidents' enterprise. Again, in the words of Václav Havel:

I am attempting to say that the struggle of the story and of history to resist nihilization is in itself a story, and belongs to history. It is our special metastory.

We do not know how to talk about it because the traditional forms of storytelling fail us here. We do not yet know the laws that govern our metastory. We do not even know yet exactly who or what is the main villain of the story (it is definitely not a few individuals in the power center: they too are victims of something larger, just as we are).

It is clear: we must tell the story of our asthma, not despite the fact that people are dying from it, but because they are not.

---

[555] Václav Havel: *Stories and Totalitarianism.* In: *Open Letters, Selected Writings 1965-1990*, pp.329,330

One small detail remains: we have to learn how to do it.[556]

Did they learn it in the end? The miraculous year 1989 with its wave of East Central European revolutions brought a clear response.

The Chinese variety of totalitarianism for the 21st century

The basic facts must be stated first. China is an ancient civilization, with its specific historical experiences going back thousands of years, with its long historical memory, highly developed culture and many significant achievements. All of that always has to be taken into account in any efforts to understand the actions of the currently existing Chinese nation-state, the type of "social contract" between its government and its people, and also the way this state, today a global superpower, operates internationally. That is why it is necessary to consult real experts here, sinologists who are familiar with Mandarin and other Sinitic languages, Chinese history, Chinese culture, Chinese mentality; who have sufficient knowledge to penetrate into the Chinese collective soul and understand Chinese customs, religion, basic patterns of thought and social and/or political behavior. The reason is clear: there is no doubt, that a Chinese variant of totalitarianism represents a much larger and deeper phenomenon than just an extension beyond Europe's borders of certain "gnostic"[557] revolutionary currents of modern political thought that emerged sometime around the middle of the 19th century thanks to Karl Marx and Friedrich Engels. What we can see in action here, provoked by originally European political ideas, is a great Chinese re-awakening whose consequences for the future history of humankind are still unknown and cannot be fully assessed or predicted.

First of all, what we have to take into consideration, if we want to understand the origins of Chinese totalitarianism is a larger context of Chinese modernization in the 20th century that started in the decades before the First World War when the Eurocentric and self-confident world of

---

[556] Op. cit., p 350

[557] In the sense of term Gnosticism used in the "new political science" of Eric Voegelin, Charles Embry and Glenn Hughes (eds.): *The Voegelin Reader*, University of Missouri Press, 2017

previous centuries was about to die, together with many Europeans, in the fronts of the Great War 1914-1918; when a new era of humankind was already announcing itself in all sorts of signs of the time – first barely reflected, because coming on "doves' feet," to use the Nietzsche's words, but, as it was to be demonstrated pretty soon, bringing on the "storm."

In the case of China, the arrival of the 20th century first brought an end to a form of government in power there for many centuries.[558] On January 1, 1912, the imperial rule was terminated, and the Republic of China proclaimed. Sun Yat-sen, a scholar and statesman inspired by European ideas – for his whole adult life committed to launching a Chinese modernization project (who spent decades outside of China, in the United States, in Europe, in Japan, Hawaii, in British Hong Kong), organizing relentlessly all available political forces able and willing to join him in his efforts to set his homeland on the path of "progress" –was elected its first provisional president. His Nationalist Party (Kuomintang) became the leading political power in China and set for itself an ambitious goal: to lift the Chinese nation from its backwardness, underdevelopment, and poverty and transform it into a prosperous, healthy and self-confident member of the family of modern enlightened nations. But as it turned out, the Kuomintang's power was too weak, not only to start implementing Sun Yat-sen's political program, but even to keep the country united. Internal strife and rivalries broke out in the new Republic and China fell apart into several territories controlled by mighty local warlords.

In 1924, Sun Yat-sen's successor at the head of Kuomintang, Chiang Kai-shek, entered into a short-lived coalition with the new Chinese Communist Party (CCP). This partnership, however, resulted quickly in a fierce civil war between them that lasted, with the exception of a "truce" between them, during the eight years of Japanese occupation for more than twenty years, with the Kuomintang, having its stronghold in the Southern China and CCP in the Northwest.

Meanwhile, the traditional rival of China in East Asia, the Empire of Japan, also engaged in a project of modernization, was gradually turned

---

[558] A concise introduction to Chinese history can be found in Jeffrey N. Wasserstrom: *China in the 21st Century. What Everyone Needs to Know*, Oxford University Press, 2nd Edition, 2013

by its political leaders after the First World War into a more and more aggressive, chauvinistic, and militarized state. In 1931, its army, in evident disrespect for the Wilsonian principles of the New World Order agreed at Paris Peace Conference, decided to occupy China's northern province of Manchuria, taking advantage of China's current weakness and instability.

Since 1937, Japan, future military ally of Nazi Germany in the Second World War, controlled much of China. The Kuomintang and the CCP started to cooperate again to organize the resistance movement. After the Japanese defeat in the war in 1945, however, they resumed their armed conflict and the Communists prevailed in it, being able to mobile the "masses" to support their basic political goals: not only to seize total control over the Chinese people, but to start a worldwide campaign for the final victory of their revolution.

On October 1, 1949, on Tiananmen Square in Beijing, their leader, Mao Zedong, announced the creation of the People's Republic of China (PRC) and its program of socialist revolution. His rival, the head of the Kuomintang, Generalissimo Chiang Kai-shek, was pushed with his army off the mainland to his last bastion, where the Republic of China (ROC) has managed to survive: the island of Taiwan.

As a result of that, the CCP has been holding power in mainland China for more than seven decades. Its leading role is considered – in a very similar manner as the previous rule of Emperors was conceived as something that had its basis in the "Mandate of Heaven" – as an undisputable and sacrosanct foundation of unity for the Chinese people and a principal guarantor of territorial integrity for the Chinese state. And symptomatically, as if inherited from the imperial tradition, its leaders also have been and still are enjoying, when in power, an almost superhuman status.

On the one hand, Chinese history under Communist rule is marked by several important turns: Mao Zedong's "Great Leap Forward" in the late 1950s and the "Cultural Revolution" in the 1960s and 1970s;[559] Deng

---

[559] The most recent analysis of transition from the great helmsman Mao Zedong's original version of Chinese Revolution to its present version with Xi Jingping at the helm, can be found in: Julia Lowell: *Maoism. A Global History*, Alfred A. Knopf, New York, 2019

Xiaoping's "Open Door" policy that introduced a necessary flexibility and significant elements of liberalization and market economy in the 1980s and 1990s into the thus far very rigid Chinese economic model; the political and economic model coined and realized now, in the beginning of the third decade of the 21st century, by today's Chinese supreme leader Xi Jinping.

At the same time, however, there is a common denominator here, too. But it is not so much the rigid ideology of "scientific socialism" defined according to the teachings of Marx and Lenin, the language in which the Chinese state's doctrine has always been and still is articulated. The Chinese form of Communist government has another distinct feature, based on the Chinese historical experience: a strong concern for the stability of the Chinese state; a concern that today's Communist rulers inherited from their predecessors ruling in "the Middle Kingdom" of the past – always on guard against all sorts of separatists trying to break it into fragments, always suppressing all subversive elements, ready to exploit any praise of its weakness and destroy its order. And it is exactly the amalgamation of this concern for the state's unity with an ideology, the goal of which is to transform not only China, but the world in the name of Communist "radiant futures" by all available means, that creates a unique Chinese variety of totalitarianism, a new species among autocratic forms of government that emerged in the 20th century.

The ideology that the Chinese state subscribes to today, seems to be less ideological in terms of its adherence to the doctrine of "scientific socialism," and much more pragmatic as far as its practical uses and implementation. Instead of being dogmatic and stable, emphasizing the purity of its Marxist-Leninist creed, as it did in Mao Zedong's times, it has been in the decades after his death constantly developed and reinterpreted in the never ending efforts of CCP ideologues, now with Xi Jinping at their head, so that it can serve its main purpose: to keep the Chinese population obedient and under strict top-down control and to secure the China's hegemonic ambitions and revolutionize for this purpose the rest of the world.

This doctrine, which aims to lead the Chinese people from the current successful phase of socialist construction to an even better future, has actually brought about, thanks to Xi Jinping's leadership, a remarkable change in its history, more than seventy years old now. The so-called "proletarian internationalism" of Mao Zedong has been gradually replaced with today's self-confident and assertive Chinese nationalism, full of pride of what has already been achieved thanks to the wisdom and foresight of the CCP, but also having the tendency to revive in the current leader Xi Jinping's "cult of personality" the image of a wise and mighty Emperor, mandated to rule by "Heaven" – and in this context also allowing the Chinese people to rediscover its own great historical past in the old, no longer reactionary, but on the contrary, now venerable and respected Confucian traditions.

The main message of Chinese state ideology, however, is clear and simple despite its intrinsic fluidity and somewhat arcane formulations stemming from the huge body of Chinese historical experience and cultural traditions. It is its unambiguous denial of the Western liberal tradition – such as respect for inalienable and thus universal human rights, the rule of law, the separation of powers, the recognition of the importance of intermediary bodies of civil society, the civic participation in political processes, and the free competition of political parties – in short, of all the values and fundamental principles Western democracy (government *"of the people, by the people, for the people"* that in the famous phrase of Abraham Lincoln *"shall not perish from the earth"*) is built upon.

When one starts examining the realities of the Chinese state under the "leading role" of the CCP, all distinct features of totalitarianism promoted originally by Chairman Mao's revolution declared on Tiananmen Square in 1949 are still present there today, in even more robust form than ever before:

1) Power totally monopolized in the hands of top party leaders with a dictator at the helm, and, in the hands of all entrusted functionaries on the party ladder, who are in charge of and decide about practically everything;

2) No freedom of expression, no freedom of religion, no respect for privacy or other fundamental human rights;

3) Omnipresent State Secret Police, using huge networks of confidants and informers to collect information, ready to act

against anyone who shows the slightest sign of disagreement with the current party line;

4) Disappearances and long-term imprisonments of all dissenters and potential opponents;

5) Concentration camps, strongly reminiscent of practices of Nazi Germany and Stalin's Soviet Union, designed to reeducate their inmates by brainwashing and hard labor;

6) Omnipresent state propaganda, the system of state education fully subordinated to the needs of state ideology, the strict censorship of all media, the total control of social networks, the restrictive measures imposed on the use of the internet;

7) An economy totally controlled by the state and its huge enterprises and banking sector.

At the same time, however, there are indisputable facts here, too, that can't be ignored and overlooked. As far as its latest achievements, both domestic and international, the Chinese model of governance has turned out to be a great success in the past decade. The numbers and data speak for themselves in a way that simply cannot be denied:

Thanks to a really historically unique and unprecedented economic growth Chinese society has changed dramatically, beyond all imagination. From the status of a developing country, China has been transformed into the second largest economy in the world, on its way to overtake the current world leader, the United States. Chinese people are experiencing, under Xi Jinping's leadership, significant improvement of their standard of living. Large numbers of them are being lifted from poverty and underdevelopment into their current more comfortable position as members of the middle class, a fast growing, ever stronger, and thus also more and more self-confident, segment of Chinese society that seems to be, indeed, fulfilling the primary goal of Xi Jinping's policies, well "stabilized."

Under Xi Jinping's leadership China strengthened not only domestically, but also internationally. China has become an economic and military superpower, equipped with all weapon systems and technologies necessary for operations on a global scale. It can afford to be more and more assertive in the international realm by showing its muscles, but, at the same time, present itself as a "benevolent" and essentially non-aggressive player. Here is Xi Jinping's message to the world, pronounced at *the Belt and Road Forum* that met in October 2017 to discuss the Chinese prime global economic, and by definition also political, project launched in 2013 in Beijing:

> *"We should foster a new type of international relations featuring 'win-win cooperation', and we should forge a partnership of dialogue with no confrontation, and a partnership of friendship rather than alliance. All countries should respect each other's sovereignty, dignity and territorial integrity; respect each other's development path and its social systems, and respect each other's core interests and major concerns... What we hope to create is a big family of harmonious coexistence."*[560]

So, what is actually wrong with the Chinese totalitarianism, with respect to Xi Jinping's vision of its place in the future world outlined here? Shouldn't the advocates of the Western type of liberal democracy rather respect the Chinese specific *"development path and its social system,"* Xi Jinping was advocating here and seems to be ready to push forward with stubborn determination in the years to come? Does it make any sense, to keep trying instead, in vain, to force upon the Chinese effective and highly successful system of governance their own fundamental values, naming and shaming the Chinese regime as totalitarian? Isn't the best advice of our common sense combined with the realistic assessment of the current distribution of world power, both political, military and economic, to accept this fact, and co-ordinate with it their own, so China-centered politics?

Hannah Arendt's Difficulties of Understanding and the Future of Totalitarianism in the Era of Globalization

The last word is usually given to someone who is capable of summing up the previous discussions and bringing contradictory positions into proper perspective. Hannah Arendt was definitely not a harmonizer. She developed her own way of thinking about the political crisis of

---

[560] http://www.xinhuanet.com/english/2017-05/14/c_136282982.htm

European civilization in the 20th century. Especially the way she approached the Jewish tragedy of World War II when she agreed to go to Israel in 1962 as a journalist to cover the trial of Nazi war criminal Adolf Eichmann and publish her report on the "banality of evil," openly went against the mainstream understanding of the totalitarian phenomenon and was controversial, at the very least. It is, however, commensurate with the nature of the subject under investigation to conclude with the most challenging, the most provocative author in the field.

Hannah Arendt was a German Jew. Her first exposure to "totalitarian radiation" took place when Hitler seized power and ended the Weimar Republic in 1933. She fled from Germany in the same year, but before she left – first to work in France in an organization that facilitated Jewish emigration to Palestine and later to start a new life and a distinguished academic career in America – she had a chance to observe the emerging totalitarian regime in the first months of its existence, that is, literally *in statu nascendi*.

She commented on her experiences of 1933 more than 30 years later in an interview she gave on German public television in 1964. What was shocking for her when the new regime emerged, was not the radicalism of its political program and, above all, its openly anti-Semitic policies, but the strange social change that occurred almost instantly. Anti-Semitism as such was not anything new. As were all Jews in Germany, Arendt was used to its occasional manifestations. The radicalism of the Nazis in this respect was indeed a gloomy, ominous sign for the future. Nevertheless, it was not at all surprising: *"We didn't need Hitler's assumption of power to know that the Nazis were our enemies!"*[561]

Much more depressing than the political changes resulting from the nature of Hitler's Nazi regime was what Arendt characterized as a "personal problem" – to see *"not what our enemies did but what our friends did."* They simply *"co-ordinated or got in line."*[562]

> *In the wave of Gleichschaltung (co-ordination), which was*
> *relatively voluntary – in any case, not yet under the pressure*

---

[561] Hannah Arendt: *"What remains? The language remains:"* A conversation with *Günter Gaus*. In: *Essays in understanding 1930–1954*
[562] Op.cit. , pp. 10-11

*of terror – it was as if an empty space formed around one....
I will never forget that.*[563]

Isn't it exactly this "unforgettable" trait characterizing the majority of the German intelligentsia in the 1930s that should be identified and factored in as an important, but too often forgotten, element in the history of German totalitarianism? Isn't it here that the research of the nature of totalitarian regimes should start? Isn't it true that the capacity for coordination was not limited only to the German intellectuals after Hitler seized power in Germany, and occurred in many other forms and in many other situations in Europe in the twentieth century? The position Hannah Arendt departed from in her inquiries into the nature of totalitarianism could then be formulated as follows:

1. The emergence of totalitarianism in the 20th century was not the result of an attack against Europe led by barbarous villains who came from the outside and struck like a bolt from the blue.

2. It was enabled or at least facilitated by the striking inability of modern European societies to find individually or collectively, in the framework of the international system they created, an adequate response at the moment when the barbarians appeared.

3. The rise and hitherto only temporary success of totalitarian movements is a historical turning point. Both Hitler's and Stalin's regimes were in the end defeated, but something irreversible and epoch-making happened through their attempts at global domination. After Auschwitz, the world simply cannot be the same as before: *"The subterranean stream of Western history has finally come to the surface and usurped the dignity of our tradition."*[564]

Totalitarianism represents the most radical denial of human freedom, unknown and unprecedented in human history. How it could ever have happened that all these atrocious crimes against humanity were committed in the heart of 'civilized' Europe? That something like that was possible in the milieu of modern, enlightened, and progressive European society whose most common reaction to all these horrors was neglect of the victims and the attitude of "coordination?"

---

[563] Ibid
[564] Hannah Arendt: *The Origins of Totalitarianism*, p.ix.

What comes under fire at the moment of confrontation with the totalitarian threat are not only the institutions of the modern nation-state but also the basic ideas and fundamental values underlying the modem European concept of politics. Neither social sciences, describing and analyzing social reality from the neutral, value-free point of view (equating totalitarianism *"with some well-known evil of the past, such as aggression, tyranny, conspiracy"*),[565] nor the perspective of traditional liberal politics (committed to the protection of the free Western world and fighting against its external totalitarian enemies) can help us find an adequate response to the most fundamental political problem we have faced in the twentieth century. According to Hannah Arendt, the main difficulty with totalitarianism lies in our inability to understand it; *"to reconcile ourselves to a world in which such things are possible at all;"*[566] to regain the capacity to act at the moment when totalitarian tendencies emerge in the midst of turmoil and political crises; to keep public space open even if the plurality of existing options are fading away under the given social and political circumstances and the seemingly invincible Laws of Nature or Laws of History are requiring our unconditional surrender and "coordination."

According to its own anamnesis, modernity liberated man from the shackles by which his Promethean human nature had been bound to the Earth. It was the era of reason and science; the era of technological advances, industrialization, and urbanization; the era of fast development in all spheres of human life and the visible improvement of people's living conditions; the era that introduced the concept of religious tolerance; the era of social and political emancipation reaching all layers of the European population; the era when democracy, the rule by the many – which had appeared for the first time in ancient city-states – was rediscovered and adapted to the new conditions as a political form corresponding better than any other form of government to the progressive trends within European society; the era of constitutionalism, the rule of law, and liberal politics, based on common sense and enlightened self-interest, subscribing to the

---

[565] Hannah Arendt: *Understanding and politics.* In *Essays in understanding 1930– 1954*, p. 309

[566] Op.cit., p. 308

concept of limited government and declaring respect for the inalienable, that is, natural rights of man; the era when equal sovereign states replaced the medieval Christian Empire in Europe and gradually invented all new forms and procedures of international law and politics; the era when the world – literally discovered by Europeans – was really "Eurocentric," that is, Europe indisputably played a leading role in world affairs.

The actual political experience of the twentieth century, however, puts the whole modern period into a radically new perspective. Totalitarian governments have been created by political movements that have come into existence in the non-totalitarian world (surely *they have not been imported from the Moon,"* remarks Arendt ironically).[567] If we want to understand this event that according to Arendt is the central event of our times and the main symptom of the crisis of European civilization, it is Europe's modernization project that has to be questioned and thoroughly reconsidered in the first place. Totalitarianism must be studied in the proper historical perspective and its "crystallizing elements" traced back to their origins in previous centuries.

Besides the rise of totalitarian movements themselves in the 1920s – whose sharp criticism of Western "decadent liberalism" was accompanied by their *"avowed cynical realism"* and by *"their conspicuous disdain of the whole texture of reality"*[568] – there are two other nineteenth-century elements of totalitarianism that Arendt suggests we must consider: anti-Semitism, which became a kind of secular ideology, widespread in the emancipated European national societies; and imperialism, the element of *"expansion for expansion's sake,"* the limitless pursuit of power, which *"grew out of colonialism and was caused by the incongruity of the nation-state system with the economic and industrial developments in the last third of the nineteenth century."*[569]

> *In this sense, it must be possible to face and understand the outrageous fact that so small (and in world politics, so unimportant) a phenomenon as the Jewish question and antisemitism could become the catalytic agent for first, the*

---

[567] Op.cit., p. 310
[568] Hannah Arendt: *The Origins of Totalitarianism,* p. viii.
[569] Op.cit., p. xvii.

> *Nazi movement, then a world war, and finally the establishment of death factories. Or, the grotesque disparity between cause and effect which introduced the era of imperialism, when economic difficulties led, in a few decades, to a profound transformation of political conditions all over the world.*[570]

However, going back before the final crystallizing catastrophe took place in the 1930s, when Hitler seized power in Germany, does not mean for Arendt to get involved in anything like a scientific historiography: *"I did not write a history of totalitarianism but an analysis in terms of history,"* she replied to Eric Voegelin's critical review of her seminal book.[571] The aim of her study was not to offer a causal explanation of historical phenomena, but to let the event of the emergence of totalitarianism *"illuminate its own past;"* by enfolding the "story" in historical time to obtain better comprehension, thus allowing history to come into being.[572]

> *Comprehension does not mean denying the outrageous, deducing the unprecedented from precedents, or explaining phenomena by such analogies and generalities that the impact of reality and the shock of experience are no longer felt. It means, rather, examining and bearing consciously the burden which our century has placed on us – neither denying its existence nor submitting meekly to its weight. Comprehension, in short, means the unpremeditated, attentive facing up to, and resisting of, reality – whatever it may be.*[573]

"The process of understanding is clearly and perhaps primarily, also a process of self-understanding,"[574] says Arendt, connecting her studies on antisemitism, imperialism, and totalitarianism with the debate

---

[570] Op.cit., p.viii.

[571] Hannah Arendt: *A replay to Eric Voegelin.* In: *Essays in Understanding 1930–1954,* p. 403

[572] Hannah Arendt: *Understanding and politics.* In: *Essays in understanding 1930–1954,* p. 319

[573] Hannah Arendt: *The Origins of Totalitarianism,* p. viii.

[574] Hannah Arendt: *Understanding and politics.* In: *Essays in Understanding 1930–1954,* p. 310

concerning contemporary European politics. The twentieth century "has become indeed, as Lenin predicted," Arendt stated in the opening sentence of her study *On Violence, "a century of wars and revolutions, hence a century of that violence which is currently believed to be their common denominator."*[575] It has become a century when European civilization, instead of leading the world to its better future, has found itself in mortal danger, threatened by the totalitarian attempt at global conquest and total domination. It has become a century that has undermined and radically problematized the very foundations of European modernity.

> *Never has our future been more unpredictable, never have we depended so much on political forces that cannot be trusted to follow the rules of common sense and self-interest-forces that look like sheer insanity, if judged by the standards of other centuries. It is as though mankind had divided itself between those who believe in human omnipotence (who think that everything is possible if one knows how to organize masses for it) and those for whom powerlessness has become the major experience of their lives.*[576]

To understand the nature of totalitarianism presupposes the realization above all that in spite of their opposite attitudes as far as the necessary outcome of historical processes is concerned, *"Progress and Doom are two sides of the same medal."*[577] The task is not to stick to the one or the other and to become either a reckless optimist or a reckless prophet of despair, but to emancipate our thought from the superstition that all events in the human world are in the end dictated by "historical necessity."

What Arendt had been looking for with her writing was a comprehension of the human situation that would help people regain insight into what they – and not the blind forces of nature or history – are doing. To comprehend the totalitarian attempt at global conquest and total domination does not mean only to study certain sets of empirical

---

[575] Hannah Arendt: *On violence,* p. 3
[576] Hannah Arendt: *The Origins of Totalitarianism,* p. vii
[577] Ibid

observable facts – political and social systems, the methods of enforcement of state power, spontaneously grown worldviews and popular beliefs, the official state ideologies, and so on and so forth – but above all to be ready to receive from God the greatest gift a man could desire: the *"understanding heart King Solomon was praying for:" "the divine gift of action, of being a beginning and therefore being able to make a beginning."*[578]

What can save us from the spell or curse our century of totalitarianism imposed on us is not an intervention from outside or from above, but our own faculty of imagination

> *which alone enables us to see things in their proper perspective, to be strong enough to put that which is too close at a certain distance so that we can see and understand it without bias and prejudice, to be generous enough to bridge abysses of remoteness until we can see and understand everything that is too far away from us as though it were our own affair .... Without this kind of imagination, which actually is understanding, we would never be able to take our bearings in the world. We are contemporaries only so far our understanding reaches. If we want to be at home on this earth, even at the price of being at home in this century; we must try to take part in the interminable dialogue with the essence of totalitarianism.*[579]

Conclusion

Four varieties of attempt at totalitarian domination have been touched upon here. Three of them, Italian Fascism, German Nazism, and Soviet Communism are gone and will not return. The truth is that there are still places in the world, like Cuba or North Korea, where the ghosts of the past are still strongly embedded in their present political reality and block effectively any change, turning these countries, at least for the time being, into bizarre open-air museums of the 20th century's Communism.

---

[578] Hannah Arendt: *Understanding and politics*. In: *Essays in Understanding 1930–1954*, p. 322
[579] Op.cit., p. 323

It is also true that the Russian Federation is still struggling with the political legacies that it has inherited from the Soviet Union, and as a leading revisionist power, coping with the problem of loss of position on the global scene the Soviet Union had before 1989, it remains authoritarian.

We can still observe attempts at "revolutionary" transformations, products such as the project of "Bolivarian socialism for the 21st century" of Hugo Chavez and his successor Nicolas Maduro in Venezuela, that bear clear marks of being inspired not only by Marxist-Leninist variant of totalitarianism of the 20th century, but with a distinct "magical realist" flavor once brought by Castroism and Che-Guevarism to the realm of world politics.

The fourth variety of this species materialized in today's People's Republic of China, is, however, an entirely different case. It proves that totalitarianism is not just a matter of the past and thus a topic for historians; that a totalitarian form of government, combined with its aspirations at global domination, still has its great and very deadly potential for the future. This warning has been well-demonstrated in the coronavirus pandemics that burst out in the moment when the third edition of this Encyclopedia was prepared, and these lines were written. One can only hope that the current Chinese leader Xi Jinping will take the lessons from this crisis that originated in his country; that he will re-examine the basic principles of the form of government he is at the head of, in its light. And these lessons are:

1. There is no escape in the moment of global crisis from the triangle science-economics-politics and from conflicts of interpretations discussed and being corrected between those who day after day participate in these triangular communications.

2. It is not an ideology, but scientific rationality that must take the lead here as the only generator of effective solutions and strategies, both in short, medium and long term-perspectives, both on the domestic plane and internationally. And scientific rationality can exist and flourish only within open societies that do not avoid unpleasant inquisitive questions and respect fundamental human rights and freedoms – such as freedom of thought and freedom of expression.

3. The ultimate, the most powerful weapon and indispensable weapon against COVID-19, without which the global "war against the invisible enemy" cannot be won – and there will be more similar viruses to come in the future, threatening the very existence of mankind – is democracy – in its multiple forms based on specific cultural and/or religious traditions, respecting each other, but recognizing the same basic standards enabling all the nation-states on planet Earth to keep resolving their differences in the great dialogue of mankind.

Totalitarianism remains with us as the greatest threat and the greatest temptation for those who are, and eventually will be, endowed into the current world – in China, and wherever else – with power. The future is unknown and largely unpredictable – not dictated by the laws of history, as Soviet Communists claimed; not driven by the Darwinian biological teaching of the survival of the fittest turned by German Nazis to their murderous ideology of the ruling Nordic Race; not given as a "Mandate of the Heaven" as it was the case of Chinese Emperors – a legacy now inherited by the Chinese totalitarian rulers; even not determined by the laws of nature studied and discovered by the natural sciences, as some environmentalists seem to believe today, in their otherwise important, understandable and well-justified struggle against the "climate change."

The only hope we can have – confronted with all the uncertainties that create now the horizon of our daily lives, a horizon from which there is no escape – is that there always will be, at least some space for our own actions in the human world, now more interconnected than ever before; that we will not be forced just to "co-ordinate" our behavior with the changing external circumstances – as the most of the inhabitants of the Soviet Union used to do in its almost seventy five years long history; as a large majority of Germans did from 1933, when Hitler took power until the end of Second World War; as Cubans and North Koreans still do today, with few exceptions, under the rule of their obsolete, antiquated regimes and "magical realists" at their head; and, of course, as the inhabitants of the rising great power of the 21st century, citizens of People's Republic of China do, again with few exceptions, living now relatively well within their "well-stabilized," future-oriented, highly technological and thus more and more confident and assertive "reawakened" society.

The reality we cannot escape from is simple. We are not any more just citizens of our nation-states, signed into "social contracts" with our governments and protected from outside disturbances by their authority and the borders of our states. We may be Americans, or any other nationality, "first," enjoying our standards of living, cultural traditions, and being afraid about the future of our own, now threatened and more and more insecure national democracies. At the same time, and more importantly, however, we cannot omit the basic fact that we are human beings in the first place – living beings endowed with reason, as the old classical political philosophers used to say – belonging today to the emerging planetary mankind. As such we all have now our personal, but at the same time universal responsibility to resist the totalitarian threat, to keep our societies open, to preserve our democracies against their totalitarian enemies, to guard the openness of our natural world that has acquired planetary dimensions in the 21st century. Because what is at stake today is what it always has been at stake throughout human history: to maintain in it that element of freedom which still is the very essence of our humanity.

Afterword

Orlando Gutierrez Boronat
"The Universal Journey Within"

First impression

This book is, perhaps in proper Weberian fashion of true science, both the diary of an inner spiritual journey and a philosophical observation of how this journey, which constitutes not just the truth experience of Martin Palouš, but also of his country at a given moment, plays out in real historical time.

In the tradition of authentic philosophy, Palouš is both observer, analyst and participant: part of a group of democratic revolutionaries who stood up against Soviet power, eventually brought about a successful freedom revolution in their own country, and then affirmed this renewal of democratic and republican ideas in the international diplomatic world and through active solidarity with those still under the totalitarian grip.

The testament of the universality of these affirmations and the consequent constructive actions are evidenced by the fact that they trigger in someone like me, who although from a different culture and a different geographic region has come to experience the results of the onslaught of totalitarianism, a series of thoughts about the universal ontological nature of totalitarianism.

One does not "review," a book of essays such as these, one shares the thinking that it inspires, and the certainties towards which its truth experience help to point the way.

Thought and Storm

Neither history nor the realm of thought are constituted by "What Ifs," they are composed of real individuals, in historical time, whose personality function is generated at specific moments in the cultural and social development of their specific people. These individuals are simultaneously and personally also open, not just to given historical and cultural roles which they may or may not assume, but also to a *transcendent realm*, meaning that it has a life and rhythm all of its own which goes beyond the biological. Our species is oriented towards a *truth-beyond-circumstance* which structures its very ability to understand reality.

The connection between the political and social reality which man inhabits, within which he spends his life, and his sensibility towards a broader horizon where his being is not limited by death, can be thought to exist either *within,* which is to say in an unseen substantive continuum of what is real, or *without,* outside of man, in the overwhelming but also exhaustible world of nature.

The movement towards the crux, the matrix of his being, can therefore come in one of two ways: from the outside in, in a measurable process, or from the inside out, in a process that we have not yet learned how to fully gauge but the parts and phases of which tradition has identified.

The outside in perspective on the journey of man's conscience was described by Marxism as *"man thinks as he lives."* Ernesto "Che" Guevara once famously said that he didn't care if people weren't Communists inside, as long as they acted as Communism wanted them to act, because if they acted as Communists, they were Communists.

The great movements which have generated the liberating power of religion, philosophy, jurisprudence, republicanism, and democracy have been movements from the inside out, where the sovereignty of the uniqueness of the human experience overcomes the shackles placed on man's spirit by the petrification of the forms-in-becoming.

This petrification of the activity of consciousness through the separation between contemplation and action that is often brought about by the prolonged enthronement of any given caste, creates a pseudo essence or pseudo substance, an image rather than a symbol, to which ideational gravity is attributed since its process at this stage, appears more closely to resemble the rhythms of what is material and sensorial, and therefore more easily comprehensible.

Palouš quotes Eric Voegelin's observations on precisely this:

> *Anybody with an informed and reflective mind who lives in the twentieth century since the end of the First World War, as I did, finds himself hemmed in, if not oppressed, from all sides by a flood of ideological language – meaning thereby the language symbols that pretend to be concepts, but in fact are unanalyzed topoi or topics. Moreover, anybody who is exposed to this dominant climate of opinion has to cope with the problem that language is a social phenomenon. He cannot deal with the users of ideological language as partners in a discussion, but he has to make them the object of investigation. There is no community of language with the representatives of the dominant ideologies. Hence, the community of language that he himself wants to use in order to criticize the users of ideological language must first be discovered and, if necessary, established.[580]*

And he goes on to note that the dynamic of philosophical discourse, in order not to suffer from petrification, necessitates constant affirmation, refutation and renewal of the central arguments in the philosophical continuum:

> *An elementary fact in the history of thought is the emergence of philosophical schools around prominent thinkers. The disciples of a Master strived to preserve his work for the future, to carry through his basic intention and to continue in the implementation of the task pursued, but unattained by him in his lifetime. Nevertheless, there is another elementary fact in the history of thought. Such schools did not last usually more than one generation. After some time, the most talented disciples started seeing through the limitations of the standpoint from which their teacher approached philosophical problems and realized*

---

[580] Eric Voegelin: *Autobiographical Reflections.* In: *Autobiographical Reflections. Revised Edition with a Voegelin Glossary and Cumulative Index,* 2006, p. 118

> *the unattainability of the tasks he had set for himself. At a certain moment in time, they came to the conclusion that it was not possible to continue on the road marked out by him; that they were finding themselves at a new crossroads where they had to take new decisions, to unveil the open questions and issues behind all the answers the Master's philosophical "teaching" contained. By paradox, this moment of destruction of the teacher's legacy, however, does not necessarily mean its absolute end, its retreat from the human world and its fall into oblivion. On the contrary, it is exactly here where we can find the key to his potential immortality.*[581]

Further on, Palouš recognizes how Voegelin himself, in a sign of philosophical integrity, warned against transforming the "thought experience" of any one philosopher into a closed system:

> *Voegelin is undoubtedly one of those contemporary thinkers who – probably against their will and in spite of their own warning that philosophy will not allow itself to be closed into any systematic philosophical teaching – did create a kind of philosophical school.*[582]

Reality does not emerge from the petrification of circumstance, it is attained through the active and vital process of abstraction. And abstraction, which is an indispensable component for man's life on Earth and his relationship with nature, cannot take place without transcendence. This is the life process at its apex of ascendance towards episteme, or full knowing, or knowing-in-certainty.

The great dilemma that lies with the transformative results of the inner spiritual journey and the external but necessary forms of temporal administration is that more often than not, a conflict develops between the two different ranges of vision which they synthesize.

---

[581] Martin Palouš: *Common Sense and the Rule of Law: Returning Voegelin to Central Europe.* In: Embry C. R. and Cooper B. (eds.): Philosophy, Literature, and Politics. Essays Honoring Ellis Sandoz: Columbia and London. University of Missouri Press, 2005, p.258-259
[582] Op.cit., p. 259

The truly noteworthy pillar of American political thought is that in the concrete political act of the founding of the American Republic, the source of the *vita activa* in political and social terms was clearly established as the *vita contemplativa*. The non-interference by state power in the *vita contemplativa* was sacralized as the essence of the entire political system. Palouš describes this philosophical uniqueness of the American republic like this:

> *This figurative description of the process within which human knowledge is acquired, grows and is altered in the course of time, clearly implies an utterly different, much more positive attitude of "pragmatist" toward "common sense," than was the position of monism. At the same time, pragmatism has an incomparably higher appreciation for the singular facts given in the immediate experience of individual human beings, living in the presence of the known past, but open towards the unknown future.* [583]

The realm of the *vita contemplativa* was regarded as the place where the union with the mystical legacy of the Creator God takes place. The Creation is where God has bestowed upon man a moral framework upon which his existence in freedom can be based. This existence in freedom is continuous with the public and private domains in the republic (life, liberty and the pursuit of happiness…) in a real, "pragmatic," in other words, "problem-solving" manner.

Palouš comments:

> *The hypothesis of the universe's "oneness," the hypothesis of one world consisting of things seen by an omniscient knower "as forming one single systematic fact," the hypothesis of the actual world being present to the senses of a human spectator always within the finite horizon of his mortality, but "complete eternally," has important implications. Its discovery and conscious acceptance signal a genuine revolution in the historical process of human self-understanding.* [584]

---

[583] Op.cit., p. 272,
[584] Op.cit., p.270,

The radical center of this political entity becomes then, not the ethno-state of the original polis, or the divine tradition of the Roman republic, but rather the direct, constant ever-in-the-present bond between the individual conscience and the moral intelligence at the core of all existence. The universal judge of character which Adam Smith described as "the Invisible Observer," and references to which we find going back to Pythagoras and Socrates himself, in the dialogue with his *daimon,* the inner divine perspective which is always engaged with him in what Martin Palouš poetically describes as "a soundless dialogue."

One of the key contributions to the world of the Czech Revolution specifically, but also of the other Central European transformations in 1989, is that the fluidity between this inner sphere of necessary freedom of thought and what we understand as the public realm, where historical action signifies specific subjects with specific results in active policy, was liberated from the confines of petrified Marxism.

The historicism denounced by Raymond Aron delegated the public sphere to the determinist machinations of material laws. This petrified Marxism has clung on tenaciously. I believe that the concrete political and cultural fact of the Central European revolutions has become a powerful challenge to the hold of this perspective over Western academia, and a rebuke to the replacement in the classroom of informed open thinking by slogans disguised as concepts.

Thus, action remains always also a contemplative function, and the expansion or contraction of the democratic charter becomes not a technical, deterministically automatic matter, but rather a permanent recourse to the "common sense," the philosophical nature in man's identity. The vitality of American existence lies in that it is a nation of individuals and not of trapped masses.

A Spiritual View of Reality

A spiritual view of reality is endowed with a panoramic, expanding horizon. A cosmos of unlimited potential has been placed at the feet of a transcendent moral law.

A materialist view of human life is, ultimately and relentlessly focused on finality, on the inescapable certainty of entropy. Thus, all forms and contents of human action are fixed in time, since the material portions of the Earth's sustenance available are limited by the very nature of existence.

In one regard, totalitarianism offers the mediating, balancing role of an all-powerful state in order to confront the power of nature in the name of man. By doing so, the state will transform the Earth's scarcity into something more amenable to existence.

At the very least, it will better distribute scarcity, so all component parts of society have an equality of access and results. That, at least, is the promise. This sacralization of poverty as the only just way to sociably balance man's relationship with nature has been a key component of, for example, the Latin American totalitarian movement founded and led by Fidel Castro.

The state of war, Ernesto "Che" Guevara affirmed, makes people better. Totalitarian doctrine before the epochal transformations of Chinese Communism had a basic common denominator: either race or class allegiance was the only real political certainty in man's continuous war against nature.

Solzhenitsyn comes to mind:

After the Western ideal of unlimited freedom, after the Marxist concept of freedom as the acceptance of the yoke of necessity – here is the true Christian definition of freedom. Freedom is self-restriction! Restriction of the self for the sake of others.

Once understood and added, this principle diverts us – as individuals, in all forms of human association, societies and nations – from outward to inward development, thereby giving us greater spiritual depth.[585]

---

[585] Aleksandr I. Solzhenitsyn: *Repentance and Self-Limitation in the Life of Nations.* In: Aleksandr I. Solzhenitsyn. With Mikhail Agurky, A.B., Evgeny Baraganov, Vladimir Borisov, F. Korsakov, and Igor Shavarevich: *From under the rubble.* Translated by A.M. Brock, Milada Haigh Marita Saplets, Hilary Sternberg, and Harry Willets under the direction of Michael Scammell. With an Introduction by Max Hayward. Regnery Gateway, Washington, D.C., 1975
https://archive.org/details/SolzhenitsynAleksandrIsaevichFromUnderTheRubble

In his sojourn to America Solzhenitsyn discovered that ideology had begun to infest the American psyche. The founding of the American republic had begun to be reinterpreted, through ideology, in a way noxious to its ends.

> *Ideology dismisses the individual's true stature as an expression of divinity and attempts to squeeze the individual into its utopian vision.*[586]

And riding ideology came totalitarianism:

> *Ideology- that is what gives evil doing its long-sought justification and gives the evildoer the necessary steadfastness and determination. That is the social theory which helps to make his acts seem good instead of bad in his own and others eyes, so that he won't hear reproaches and curses but will receive praise and honors...*[587]

Totalitarianism cannot be understood simply as a malaise affecting a country where it took hold through its implementation by a first generation revolutionary regime. The actions of the West that have made such "implementations" possible are simply too numerous and essential for the consolidation in power of totalitarian states to be discarded as anything other than a different expression of the same ideational phenomenon generating totalitarianism.

Palouš himself reminds us that Voegelin referred to totalitarianism as the: "cadaveric poison of Western civilization." In other words, different symptoms of the same disease affecting culturally diverse social organisms in different manner, at different stages.

Given this state of ideological infection of the West, encountered at different historical moments by Voegelin, Solzhenitsyn, Havel and, as evidenced in this collection of essays by Palouš, the type of movement which resulted in the liberation of Central Europe from totalitarianism could not be properly understood by the West, save for a few enlightened sectors still within its fold, precisely because the movement itself was too Western. More about this further ahead.

---

[586] Ibid.
[587] Ibid.

It is not whether the Central European Revolutions did or did not bring forth "new" ideas, it is that they restored vitality to the inward movement of humanity and hence brought to the world something far more healing than a new ideology: a *new understanding.*

Human Rights

In this collection of essays, Palouš addresses what is a critically inevitable ontological issue in today's world: the metaphysical consequences of the doctrine of human rights. It would seem that in our world today, the constructive evolution of politics leads precisely both to human rights doctrine and an expansion of its understanding, of the axiological foundations of its universal tenets.

However, philosophical interpretations of natural science are heading in a different direction: towards the affirmation of a vision of reality that consists of a basically chaotic universe where islands of order have accidentally come into being in a disconnected manner.

It is amazing to find so many cases in the academia of social sciences in the West, and particularly in the United States, where in the literature of the social sciences, in lectures and in classroom activity, so many academics act as if totalitarianism had never existed or continued to exist, as if the great demonic force of the twentieth century were capitalism and the horror of the Gulag and the Cultural Revolution simply footnotes to this. As if this historical experience of totalitarianism, the fact of its happening, did not shed greater light on the understanding of the liberties and rights which have been passed on to the world by Classical civilization.

Perhaps that is why for so many in leadership positions in the West how to act, how to decide, in the face of totalitarianism becomes a constant perplexing enigma. There are too many in establishment academia that in every generation decide to "forget" what totalitarianism is, and what we have found it to be: the presence of malevolence in the historical realm. This malignancy constitutes the counterpart to and the rejection of, divinity as the source of human rights.

In this sense, writes Palouš:

> *If one is looking for the spiritual basis of Havel's concept of politics of transition from Communism – his emphasis on the indispensable role of civil society in it, on active policies, both domestic and international, in the area of human rights, on civic education with the main goal to revive the spirit of responsibility for public matters in individual citizens and in raising general awareness that man qua man must cultivate his/her capability to "transcend" his/her finiteness and exist face-to-face with the Mystery of Being – it is neither a philosophically dressed-up version of progressivism, still present among liberal intellectuals of the West, nor utopianism of some other provenance fashionable in these days. It is Patočka's phenomenological philosophy of history that speaks out here. What is its message through Havel as its messenger? Thanks to him we can be better aware now that the success of a politician cannot be measured only by its concrete temporary political achievements, but by the impact of policies enhanced and implemented by him on the "soul" of his polis – a human collective that today takes the form of, but transcends at the same time, the level of nation-state.*[588]

Palouš further believes that it is critical in this debate to address the core meaning of the concepts which constitute human rights precisely because they may, unlike the derivative social sciences, offer a prudent instrument that may be used, from the realm of the social, to attain a better view of the cosmic horizon within man:

> *Is it not true that without careful clarification of how these terms are constituted on the existential level, all answers to the question "what kind of God does human rights require?" could lead us astray and leave us lost in all sorts of metaphysical fallacies and perplexities?*[589]

---

[588] Exercise 12: Patočka between Masaryk and Havel
[589] Martin Palouš: *What Kind of God Does Human Rights Require?* In: Bucar, E.M. and Barnett B. (eds.): *Does Human Rights Need God?*, William Erdman's Publishing Company, Grand Rapids. Michigan and Cambridge, U.K., 2005, p.245

This book of essays by Martin Palouš is a symbol of this new understanding, of the re-visiting of truth in a world supposedly beyond truth, beyond good and evil, some would even postulate, beyond history.

> *The conflict between vita activa and vita contemplativa, the never-ending quest for the meaning of finite human life, does not take place in a vacuum, but always is a matter of concrete human beings finding themselves in concrete places and in concrete times. The context we have to pay attention to when reflecting on the relation between man and God is the open field of human history. Here we are touching upon an essential and important problem. The human openness towards transcendence and eternity introduces the element of movement into the human world.*[590]

Because it challenges the routine constituent perceptions of our modernity it is an uncomfortable book, as philosophical books should be. This is not a device where petrified ideas are groped, it is not a Communist Party training manual, or a collection of slogans and talking points. Thus, it is intense and refreshing, perhaps healing.

Symbol

By symbol, I don't mean an expression of empty modern-day advertisement, but rather something far more important.

In tradition, a symbol is a truth experience constituted as a human work of expression, of knowledge, which activates that same truth experience in the seeker. Symbols are alive, energized in the present, interacting with the process of human consciousness. Symbol should be differentiated from image, which is to say a representation, or an artifact, that conveys a message.

Human rights as a doctrine are a symbol of man's self-discovery through the ages. 'Human rights' symbolize the universal condition of the experience of humanity. Its source is fundamentally divine. From the necessity of human rights, a universal moral intelligence, a supreme

---

[590] Op.cit., p. 246

intelligence, is recognized not as a remote engine of creation, but as an active, vital and indispensable ordering principle of human affairs.

It becomes incumbent, faced by the unrelenting presence of totalitarianism, to understand human rights doctrine as an instrument through which to explore the nature of divine action in human affairs. If then, human rights doctrine exemplifies the role in the temporal sphere of ideas of non-human origin, of ideas of a divine nature, then we must logically assert that the opposite must also be true: that those doctrines which have systematically and scientifically negated human dignity are anti-life, anti-God, anti-Christ. What Solzhenitsyn came face to face with was the non-human origin of a doctrinal malevolence directed at the destruction of the truth experience in history and of its human vessel.

Eric Voegelin also courageously identified this as 'Satanic intelligence,' which, aware of the system of logic and justice laid in the cosmos before man, turns against it in defiance. Yes, totalitarianism, in its diverse expressions, make up a modern-day religion, one based on evil.

It is precisely this which modern, secular, atheistic civilization has found so hard to countenance, as Hannah Arendt so ably described. The truth experience of totalitarianism and the struggle to resist it, laid bare the centrality of the struggle between good and evil in the human drama. In a modern world which has sought to build a society 'beyond good and evil,' the totalitarian enigma is a constant reminder of the eternal vectors of man's journey towards the source of knowing.

What the Central European revolutions did was to be the restoration of the axiomatic principle to political affairs: that which Havel described as "the Metaphysical Certainty."

Palouš evokes it as thus:

> On the one hand, there is our being in the world which we share – engaged in three fundamental human activities: "labor, work, and action" iii – with the plurality of others. On the other hand, there are the noetic activities of man, taking place in the "soul," in the interior domus of his/her "self," i.e., in that inner space, where each of us can temporarily withdraw from the common world of appearances. iv As humans – belonging to the species zóon logon echón, animal rationale, according to the Aristotelian

taxonomy v – we are able to interrupt temporarily all activities we have been busy with and to "think," i.e., to see our own situation in the world as if from a distance.vi In the fleeting moment of contemplation we are able to discover the abyss lurking behind and beyond ta phainomena, the appearances of things around us, things given to us in our experience. The fundamental, and always awful, i.e., awe and wonder evoking, difference between Being and Nothingness (between "is" and "is not") not only reveals the nature of things experienced, but also makes us aware of our own finite existence in time, of our life that will pass away in the moment of our death and still cannot be lived well, without being directed by the nous or reason; without being informed by knowledge that is permanently tested against the horizon of the divine eternity.[591]

The 'Stillest Words:' Parallel polis and the solidarity of the shaken

Rebuilding politics in the aftermath of totalitarianism became the great task of the extraordinary Czech leader Václav Havel. He drank from a deep source: the humanist tradition of Czech intellectuals and the teachings of Jan Patočka.

Taking as a departure point the naturalness of the philosophical activity in the human soul, the constant questioning of reality and its constitutive components by the human mind, constitute the original public space. Man's dialogue with his consciousness, with his inner voice, represents the inner matrix of the public.

Dissidents trapped behind the Iron Curtain demonstrated what sociologists like Gene Sharp were discovering about other oppressed societies: that even under the worst conditions of repression, society symbolizes this inner primary action of philosophical authenticity, through spaces of public discourse that may be clandestine or open. These spaces, wherever they literally sprout, constitute the alternative city, the public

---

[591] Martin Palouš: *What Kind of God Does Human Rights Require?* In: Bucar, E.M. and Barnett B. (eds.): *Does Human Rights Need God?*, William Erdman's Publishing Company, Grand Rapids. Michigan and Cambridge, U.K., 2005, p. 244-245 , In this volume Exercise 6

square, that remains alive as a reflection of a sovereign inner dynamic that no state, not even one as powerful as a totalitarian state, could suppress.

As an example of this, Palouš recounts what has become an iconic moment in the history of thought in the 20th century:

> *And finally, the last encounter between Havel and Patočka, described in Havel's short text written in the spring of 1977 in Ruzyně Prison, where Havel was held in detention, investigated for the alleged "subversion of the republic in connection with foreign powers," used as the main source of information in this chapter.*[592] *It had taken place in the second week of January of that year, in the waiting room for the interrogated persons of the same state facility. The three fresh Charter 77 spokespersons – Patočka, Havel and Hájek – were sitting there, waiting for their turn, and were "philosophizing." Their conversation could have been interrupted in any moment by their interrogators, but "professor Patočka seemed to be utterly undisturbed by this fact: in an improvised seminary on the history of the idea of human immortality and human responsibility, he weighted words with the same care and prudence, as if they had had an unlimited amount of time for it." Havel didn't feel himself at that moment – as he had felt many times in Patočka's presence in the past, like a student whose only role was just to listen his professor and eventually take notes of what was said by him. He realized that at that moment he became an equal partner in a real philosophical dialogue. Patočka was visibly animated by this fact, too, and invited Havel to come to see him at home in the near future, so that they could continue at their conversation. Havel gladly accepted his invitation and wished to pay Patočka his visit as soon as possible, in the best case in the evening of the same day. But this proposed visit never took place. Havel was detained after his interrogation that day and returned home only four and half months later. Patočka passed away in mid-March, having suffered a stroke in the hospital where he ended, exhausted after a series of whole*

---

[592] Václav Havel: *Poslední rozhovor* [The Last Conversation]. In: *Jan Patočka. Osobnost a dílo*. Index, 1980, p. 105-109 (a short text written in Ruzyně Prison, where Václav Havel was kept in detention on May 1, 1977)

day-long police interrogations.[593]

This "philosophizing moment" in the face of repression (arrest and interrogation by the secret police), demonstrates what the Czech dissidents, and then Czech dissidents-turned-statesmen or turned-politicians, or turned-diplomats, have brought oppressed and persecuted people everywhere.

But it also constitutes a truth-event in the objective development of the human mind, in the continuum of human thought which keeps us aware of the immanent transcendence of our species, of its co-habitation in reality with an observing moral intelligence.

The ontological reality of common affirmative action of the human spirit in the face of persecution and repression transcends limitations of language and geography, it constitutes a new common ground where an authentic global community can be established. Perhaps, 'a republic of the soul,' a permanent parallel polis, city of God, where man's true voice is never adulterated or broken.

---

[593] *Exercise 11: Patočka Between Masaryk and Havel*

About Authors
and Bibliography

Ambassador Martin Palouš (born 1950 in Prague, Czechoslovakia, now the Czech Republic) is a Czech dissident-philosopher and public intellectual. He studied Natural Science, Philosophy and International Law. In 1974 he received a Doctorate of Natural Sciences (RNDr) and in 2001 he earned Higher Doctorate in Political Science/Philosophy (Associate Professorship), both at Charles University in Prague. In 2007 he received a PhD in Public International Law at Masaryk University in Brno. Since January of 2011, Martin Palouš is Senior Fellow and Director of the Václav Havel Program for Human Rights and Diplomacy at the Green School of International and Public Affairs at Florida International University. He is also President of the Václav Havel Library Foundation and President of the International Platform for Human Rights in Cuba. He belonged to the original signatories of Charter 77, served as its spokesperson in 1986 and participated at the creation of Civic Forum during the Velvet Revolution (November 1989). After the fall of Communism he was a member of Parliament (1990), Deputy Minister for Foreign Affairs (1990-1992, 1998-2001), Ambassador of the Czech Republic to the United States (2001-2005) and Permanent Representative of the Czech Republic to the United Nations (2006-2011).

Dr. Orlando Gutierrez-Boronat (born 1965 in Havana, Cuba) is an award-winning Cuban-American author, spokesperson for the Cuban Democratic Directorate, invited lecturer at Georgetown University, and community leader. His family settled in the United States from Cuba in 1971 seeking freedom. In 1990, he co-founded the Cuban American NGO, Directorio Democratico Cubano, seeking human rights and democratic change in Cuba. Dr. Gutierrez-Boronat holds a PhD in the Philosophy of International Studies from the University of Miami, alongside graduate and undergraduate degrees in Political Science and Communications from Florida International University.

Selected Bibliography of Martin Palouš

Jan Patočka versus Václav Benda. In: Gordon H. Skilling and Paul Wilson(ed.): *Civic Freedom in Central Europe/Voices from Czechoslovakia,* Macmillan

Academic and Professional, 1991; published also as *Parallel Polis after Twelve Years* in: *Uncaptive Minds*, 1988

Philosophy as Personal Experience and the Others. In: Marketa Goetz-Stankiewitz (ed.): *Good-bye, Samizdat/Twenty Years of Czechoslovak Underground Writing*, Northwestern University Press, Evanston, Illinois, 1992

Gérer le fait national: le cas tchécoslovaque. In: Politique Internationale, 1992

Post-totalitarian Political Experience and European Philosophy. In: Public Affairs Quarterly, vol.7,no. 2, April 1993

Farewell to Czechoslovakia. In: HCA Newsletter, n.6, Winter 1993

Farewell to Czechoslovakia (in Japanese). In: World Weekly 2/9 1993

Weaving a Security Net: Central Europe and the Structures of International Peace and Security. In: Jeffrey Laurenti (ed.): *Searching for Moorings – East Central Europe in the International System*, United Nations Association of the United States of America, 1994

Without Memory and Consciousness. In: Lustration Laws In Eastern and Central Europe, Helsinki Citizens' Assembly Publication Series 9, 1994

The Czechoslovak Divorce: "Velvet" Settlement, or Muted Coexistence? In: Craufurd D. Goodwin and Michael Nacht (eds.): *Beyond Government: Extending the Public Policy Debate in Emerging Democracies*, Westview Press, Boulder-San Francisco-Oxford, 1995

Questions of Czech Citizenship .in: André Liebich and Daniel Warner with Jasna Dragovic (eds.): *Citizenship East and West*, Kegan Paul International, London and New York, 1995

Five Years Later: Re-Reading of the Prague Appeal. In: The hCa Quarterly, n. 13, spring 1995

The Nature of the security debate five years on. In: The hCa Quarterly, n. 13, spring 1995

The Current Security Thought in Central Europe .In: Nacao e Defesa, Instituto da Defesa Nacional – Portugal, No.77-Janeiro-Marco de 1996

Return to Europe or Crisis of Civilization? In: Nacao e Defesa, No.78-Abril-Junho de 1996

Democracy and Dynamics of Globalization. Introduction. In: Democracy is a Discussion. Civic Engagement in Emerging Democracies, published by Connecticut College, 1996

Charter 1977 in 1996 – a closed chapter or a living heritage? Translated by Nancy Bishop, CTS-96-16

Beyond the Liberal Paradigm. In: Reflections on the State of Europe from the Perspective of Civil Society, hCa Quarterly, Summer 1996, No. 17. Czech Republic on the Threshold of NATO. In: The New Presence, Prague, August 1997

The United States and Europe: A Question for the Twenty-First Century. Helsinki Monitor, Volume 8 (1997),No. 3

Helsinki Citizens' Assembly. Mit der Ideen von 1989 in das 21. Jahrhundert? In: Christine M. Merkel (ed.): *Friedenspolitik der Zivilgesellschaft, Zugänge – Erfolge – Ziele,* Agenda Verlag, Münster, 1998

International Law and the Construction, Liberation, and Final Deconstruction of Czechoslovakia. In: Cecilia Lynch and Michael Loriaux (eds.): *Law and Moral Action in World Politics,* University of Minnesota Press, 1999

Democracy in the Czech Republic (with Zdenek Kavan). In: Mary Kaldor and Ivan Vejvoda (eds.): *Democratization in Central and Eastern Europe,* Pinter London, 1999

Totalitarianism and Authoritarianism. In: Lester Kurtz (ed.): *Encyclopedia of Violence, Peace and Conflict,* Volume 3, Academic Press, 1999

Beyond Liberal Paradigm. In: Magorka Golubovic and George F. McLean (eds.): *Models of Identities in Post-Communist Societies,* Yugoslav Philosophical Studies I, The Council for Research in Values & Philosophy, 1999

Between Idealism and Realism: Reflections on the Political Landscape of Post-Communism. In: Sorin Antohi and Vladimir Tismaneanu (eds.): *Between Past and Future: The Revolutions of 1989 and Their Aftermath,* Central University Press, Budapest, 2000

The Perspective of a Small State. In: ACE – Analysis, Current Events, published by Asian Studies & East European Studies, Baylor University for the Association for the Study of Nationalities, Vol. 14, No. 1, February 2002

What Does Democracy Mean Today? In: Idebate (A publication of IDEA, International Debate Association), October 2002, vol. 3, issue 1

Common Sense and the Rule of Law: Returning Voegelin to Central Europe. In: Embry C. R. and Cooper B. (eds.): *Philosophy, Literature, and Politics. Essays Honoring Ellis Sandoz.* University of Missouri Press, Columbia and London. 2005

What Kind of God Does Human Rights Require? In: Bucar, E.M. and Barnett B. (eds.): *Does Human Rights Need God?,* Wm. B. Erdman Publishing Company, Grand Rapids, Michigan and Cambridge, U.K., 2005

Totalitarianism and Authoritarianism. In: Lester Kurtz (Editor-in-Chief): *Encyclopedia of Violence, Peace, & Conflict,* 2nd Ed., 3 vols. Oxford: Elsevier, 2008

Le message socratique de Jan Patočka pour le XXIe siècle. Relire les textes de Patočka sur la Chartre 77 trente ans après. In: Sonia Dayan-Herzbrun, Nicole Gabriel at Valérie Lowit (eds.): *Tumultes – Au coeur de l'Europe quand un monde s'est écroulé*, Éditions Kime, Paris, numero 32-33, novembre 2009

Jan Patočka's Socratic Message for the 21ˢᵗ Century. In: Ivan Chvatik and Erica Abrams (eds.): *Jan Patočka and the Heritage of Phenomenology*, Series: Contributions to Phenomenology, Volume 61, Springer Dordrecht Heidelberg London New York, 2010

Revolutions and Revolutionaries, Lessons of the Years of Crises. In: Vladimir Tismaneanu (ed.): *Promises of 1968. Crisis, Illusion, Utopia*, Central European University Press Budapest-New York, 2011

To Invite or Not to Invite? Václav Havel's Hamletesque Question. In: Václav Havel, Martin Palouš: *Invite or Not Invite? Human Rights 25 Years After.* Václav Havel Library, 2014

Where are we? The State of Negotiation of a New Treaty Between The European Union and Cuba, Annual Proceedings of The Association for the Study of the Cuban Economy, vol. 24, 2014

Václav Havel. Statuary Hall, United States Capitol. November 19, 2014 (with Marta Smolíková), Václav Havel Library, 2014

Cuba in 2015: A Perspective from Central Europe, Identidades, Year 3, Number 8, June 2016

Václav Havel's Legacy and the Future of Cuba, Annual Proceedings of The Association for the Study of the Cuban Economy, vol. 27, 2017

Several Thoughts on Newell's Tyrants, Perspectives on Political Science, Vol. 46, 2017 – Issue 4

Contested Ground. The Campaign to Enhance the Status of the European Union in the UN General Assembly (with Katie Laatikainen), Globus Research Papers, ARENA, Centre for European Studies, University of Oslo, July 2018

A Philosopher and His History. Jan Patočka's Reflections on The End of Europe and the Arrival of the Post-European Epoch. Thesis Eleven, vol. 116, 1 or in: *The Solidarity of the Shaken: Jan Patočka's Legacy in the Modern World.* Edited by Martin Palouš. Academica Press Washington-London, 2019

Foreword and Postscript: Memory and Narrative within the Community of Human Beings (with Glenn Hughes and Henrik Syse). In: *The Presence of the Past: Essays on Memory, Conflict and Reconciliation.* Edited by Martin Palouš and Glenn

Hughes, St. James's Studies in World Affairs, Academica Press, Washington-London, 2019.

The Chinese Question in the Times of Coronavirus in: Modelo, publ. of CESCOS, Year I, document 6, 2020

Knowledge We Have Gained. In: Slovo, Czech and Slovak Museum & Library, Spring 2020

www.ingramcontent.com/pod-product-compliance
Lightning Source LLC
Chambersburg PA
CBHW070647250726
48662CB00001B/5